NINE CENTURIES OF SPANISH LITERATURE

NUEVE SIGLOS DE LITERATURA ESPAÑOLA

A Dual-Language Anthology

EDITED BY

Seymour Resnick

AND

Jeanne Pasmantier

DOVER PUBLICATIONS, INC.

NEW YORK

For MASON, KATHY, *and* JOHNNY

BIBLIOGRAPHICAL NOTE

This Dover edition, first published in 1994, is a slightly abridged and corrected republication of *Highlights of Spanish Literature*, originally published by Frederick Ungar Publishing Co., New York, in 1963.

LIBRARY OF CONGRESS
CATALOGING-IN-PUBLICATION DATA

Nueve siglos de literatura española = Nine centuries of Spanish literature : a dual-language anthology / edited by Seymour Resnick and Jeanne Pasmantier.
    p.   cm.
Corr. ed. of: Highlights of Spanish literature. 1963.
Includes bibliographical references (p.   ) and index.
ISBN-13: 978-0-486-28271-8
ISBN-10: 0-486-28271-6 (pbk.)
    1. Spanish literature.   2. Spanish literature—Translations into English.   I. Resnick, Seymour.   II. Pasmantier, Jeanne.   III. Highlights of Spanish literature.   IV. Title: Nine centuries of Spanish literature.
PQ6172.R46   1994
860.8—dc20   94-16769
                                                                              CIP

Manufactured in the United States by Courier Corporation
28271606   2014
www.doverpublications.com

ACKNOWLEDGMENTS

The editors and the publishers are grateful for the cooperation of those individuals and publishers who granted permission to use their copyrighted material. Every effort has been made to trace and to acknowledge properly all copyright owners. If any acknowledgment has been inadvertently omitted, the publishers will be pleased to make the necessary correction in the next printing.

Burns & Oates, Ltd. For the translations by E. Allison Peers of poems by San Juan de la Cruz, from *Poems of Saint John of the Cross*.

The Clarendon Press. For the following selections from *Spanish Poems and Poetry* by Ida Farnell: Luis de León, 'Ode to Salinas'; Campoamor, 'If Only I Could Write!'; Machado, 'Fields of Soria'. For the ballad 'The Prisoner' from *European Balladry* by W. J. Entwistle.

The Dolphin Book Co. Ltd. For 'Green' and 'I Would That All My Verses' by Juan Ramón Jiménez from his *Fifty Spanish Poems* with English translations by J. B. Trend.

Harcourt, Brace & World, Inc. For the 'Sonata of Spring' from *The Pleasant Memories of the Marquis of Bradomin* by Ramón del Valle-Inclán, copyright 1924 by Harcourt, Brace & World, Inc. and reprinted with their permission.

Hispanic Society of America. For their courtesy in granting permission to use several selections from *Translations from Hispanic Poets:* 'Axa, Fatima, and Marien'; 'Grace and Beauty Has the Maid'; and 'Pirate's Song'.

Harvill Press Ltd. and Pantheon Books. For a translation by Roy Campbell of 'Verses Written after an Ecstasy of High Exaltation' from *Poems of St. John of the Cross*.

Holt, Rinehart & Winston, Inc. for 'Count Arnaldos' and last stanza of Santillana, 'Serranilla VI' from *The Heritage of Spain* by Nicholas B. Adams. Copyright © 1959 by Holt, Rinehart and Winston, Inc. For Bécquer's 'Rima II' from *Main Currents of Spanish Literature* by J. M. D. Ford. Copyright 1919, copyright renewed 1947 by Holt, Rinehart and Winston, Inc. All reprinted by permission of Holt, Rinehart and Winston, Inc.

The Johns Hopkins Press. For 'Rider's Song' from *Contemporary Spanish Poetry*, translated by Eleanor Turnbull.

Elisha K. Kane. For quotations from his translation of *The Book of Good Love*.

Alfred A. Knopf, Inc. For selections reprinted from *The Tree of Knowledge* by Pío Baroja and from *Mist* by Miguel de Unamuno, each copyright 1928, 1956 by Alfred A. Knopf, Inc. For the selection reprinted from *The Cabin* by V. Blasco Ibáñez, copyright 1919, 1947 by Alfred A. Knopf, Inc. All by permission of Alfred A. Knopf, Inc.

Penguin Books Ltd. For the translation by J. M. Cohen of selections from Cervantes' 'Don Quixote', copyright 1950 by Penguin Books Ltd.

Routledge & Kegan Paul Ltd. For the selection from Chapter 3 of 'Paul, the Spanish Sharper'.

Charles Scribner's Sons. For the selection from 'The Bonds of Interest' reprinted with the permission of Charles Scribner's Sons, from *Plays*, First Series, by Jacinto Benavente, translated by John Garrett Underhill. Copyright 1917 John Garrett Underhill; renewal copyright 1945. For the selection from 'The Sheep Well' reprinted with the permission of Charles Scribner's Sons from *Four Plays by Lope de Vega*, translated by John Garrett Underhill. Copyright 1936 John Garrett Underhill.

Sheed and Ward, Inc., New York, and Sheed and Ward, Ltd., London. For 'I Die Because I Do Not Die' from *The Complete Works of Saint Teresa of Jesus, Volume III*, translated and edited by E. Allison Peers, from the critical edition of P. Silverio de Santa Teresa, D.C., published in three volumes by Sheed and Ward, Inc., New York.

University of California Press. For the selection 'The Poem of the Cid' from *The Lay of the Cid*, translated by Rose and Bacon.

PREFACE

To help make accessible to English-speaking readers the rich and varied literature of Spain, the present editors prepared a comprehensive *Anthology of Spanish Literature in English Translation*, published in 1958 by Frederick Ungar Publishing Co. Ideally, translations should be accompanied by the original works, but limitations of space prevented inclusion of the Spanish in our previous anthology. In this new volume, therefore, we have now chosen those selections—comprising a little more than one-third of the earlier anthology—which we consider indispensable as an introduction to Spanish literature, with the Spanish originals and the English translations on facing pages.

This bilingual edition should be of special value to readers who have previously studied Spanish and can enjoy the masterpieces of Spanish literature as they were written. For those whose grasp of Spanish does not yet allow a facile reading of the original alone, the facing translations help overcome linguistic difficulties. In addition, students of the art of translation will be able easily to compare the original with the English rendering. The great majority of the translations included here are faithful in word and feeling to the original works. An occasional translation, however, is relatively free—such as Harry Kemp's 'transmutation' of Tirso de Molina's *Burlador de Sevilla*—yet it captures the spirit and artistic intent of the Spanish selection. Among the translators represented in this volume are such well-known British and American authors as Lord Byron, Robert Southey, Henry Wadsworth Longfellow, William Cullen Bryant and John Masefield. Spanish literature has had a special appeal to some of our finest writers, and we are indebted to them for many excellent translations.

The Spanish language has not changed as much as has English during the past eight centuries. Since the language of the medieval period can be read today without too much difficulty, we have used Spanish editions which have modernized little more than the orthography of these early selections. An exception is our first selection, the *Poem of the Cid*, which we present in a modern poetic version.

Highlights of Spanish Literature is designed to serve as a text in a survey of Spanish literature course in college or in the fourth year of high-school Spanish. It may also be used to advantage in world literature classes where some of the students may not know Spanish.

Spanish-American literature has not been included here since it merits an extensive treatment of its own. We have, however, provided a short bibliography of Spanish-American literature for the English-speaking reader.

The introduction offers a basic outline of Spanish poetry, prose and drama, and the selections themselves are preceded by brief introductory remarks about the authors. For a more detailed background the reader is advised to consult one of the histories of literature listed in the Bibliography.

As a linguistic aid, we suggest a number of passages for memorization in Spanish. Educated Spaniards can recite perfectly most of the following selections; the English-speaking reader may derive great benefit as well as pleasure from learning some of them 'by heart':

Santillana	*Serranilla de la Finojosa*	44
Manrique	*Coplas* (stanzas 1, 3, 4)	50
Escrivá	*Ven, muerte (stanza 1)*	66
Ballads	*El prisionero*	70
Gil Vicente	*Muy graciosa es la doncella*	112
Garcilaso	*Soneto X*	124
Cetina	*Madrigal*	126
Fray Luis de León	*Vida retirada* (stanza 1)	144
	Al salir de la cárcel	152
Santa Teresa	*Nada te turbe*	154
Cervantes	*Don Quijote* (paragraphs 1 and 2)	174
Quevedo	*Poderoso caballero* (refrain)	230
Góngora	*Ande yo caliente* (refrain)	232
	La más bella niña (stanza 1)	236
Calderón	Ten lines beginning with—	
	Cuentan de un sabio . . .	272
	Six lines beginning with—	
	¿Qué es la vida? . . .	292
Iriarte	*El burro flautista*	300
Espronceda	*Canción del pirata* (refrain)	324
Bécquer	*Rimas*, especially numbers	
	XXI and XXXVIII	344

We are grateful to Marion E. Tupper of Great Neck South Senior High School, Great Neck, New York, for valuable advice and criticism, and to Lillian Resnick for many helpful suggestions throughout the preparation of this edition.

S.R.
J.P.

CONTENTS

Renaissance

The Golden Age

INTRODUCTION

Poetry

As is generally the case in the development of a national literature, epic poetry was the first genre to make its appearance in Spain. The *Poema del Cid* (*ca.* 1140) is the foremost of the early epics, most of which have not come down to us. This poetry of the people, known as *mester de juglaría*, was related originally by wandering minstrels. By the thirteenth century certain Spanish poets, writing in a set verse form, had begun to cultivate the type of poetry called *mester de clerecía*, often based on religious themes and frequently in imitation of Latin and French models. Gonzalo de Berceo is the best representative of this school. Of significance also are the four hundred religious poems, in varying metres, composed by Alfonso X. The latter were written in Galician-Portuguese, the language then considered more appropriate to lyric poetry than Castilian.

Spanish lyric poetry seems to begin with the thirteenth-century love poem *Razón de Amor* ('Song of Love'). Expansion of metres and themes continued in the fourteenth century, culminating in one of the greatest works of Spanish literature, the *Libro de Buen Amor* ('Book of Good Love') by the Archpriest of Hita, which brilliantly encompasses narrative, religious, amatory and satirical verse. Satire also marks López de Ayala's *Rimado de Palacio* ('Palace Rhymes') of the latter part of the fourteenth century.

Lyric poetry flourished in the court of Juan II during the first half of the fifteenth century. The *cancioneros* (collections of poems) of this period are filled mainly with love and topical poetry. Outstanding poets were Santillana, with his *serranillas* (mountain songs) and sonnets, and Juan de Mena, author of a long allegorical poem. Later in the century, Jorge Manrique's inspired stanzas on the death of his father overshadowed all other poetic works.

At the same time that this learned and often artificial verse was in vogue, there was developing a truly popular poetry which is one of the glories of Spanish literature—the *romances* (ballads), transmitted orally at first, later recorded and often imitated.

Through the influence of the renaissance in the sixteenth century, Spanish poetry underwent a major change. Garcilaso de la Vega, one of the most delicate of all Spanish poets, introduced certain

Italian metres which have been employed ever since. The *Siglo de Oro* (Golden Age, *ca.* 1550–1650) produced the greatest Spanish authors in all fields. Lyric poetry engaged the talents of the prolific Lope de Vega, the versatile Quevedo, and the enigmatic Góngora, to mention only three of a host of outstanding poets. In this period too, Spanish mysticism reached its highest peak, with the ethereal poems of Fray Luis de León, Santa Teresa de Jesús, San Juan de la Cruz and others. It must also be mentioned that the great dramas of this age were all in verse; Calderón and many other dramatists wrote lyric poetry of surpassing beauty.

The period of decadence which followed the Golden Age did not entirely stifle Spain's poetic genius. Its two leading writers of fables, Iriarte and Samaniego, lived during the second half of the eighteenth century. Meléndez Valdés wrote the best neo-classic poetry of the period, and Ramón de la Cruz composed his numerous *sainetes* (humorous skits) in verse. At the turn of the century, the moving heroic poems of Quintana and Gallego appeared.

The death of the tyrant Fernando VII in 1833 allowed hitherto-banished Spanish intellectuals to return to their homeland. They had, while in exile, come under the influence of British and French romanticism, and they brought its spirit to both the drama and poetry of Spain. The Duque de Rivas, Espronceda and Zorrilla were the three principal poets of Spanish romanticism. During the second half of the 1800s, the outstanding poets of Spain were the semi-philosophical Campoamor, the social-conscious Núñez de Arce, and the melancholy, love-sick Bécquer.

During the twentieth century, modernism, initiated by the Nicaraguan Rubén Darío, was adopted by many Spanish poets. Others developed styles of their own. Outstanding among the twentieth-century poets are Antonio and Manuel Machado, Juan Ramón Jiménez, and Pedro Salinas. Among other noteworthy poets of the contemporary period we may mention Jorge Guillén, Gerardo Diego, Rafael Alberti, Emilio Prados, Vicente Aleixandre, Luis Cernuda and Manuel Altolaguirre.

Prose

In the thirteenth century, King Alfonso X, called the Wise, helped standardize the Castilian language as a result of the voluminous prose works compiled at his direction. His nephew, Juan Manuel, was Spain's first great fiction writer with his fifty tales of *El Conde Lucanor*. In the fourteenth and fifteenth centuries, alert

observers recorded the noteworthy events of their day in chronicles important for their literary as well as historical value. Among the most interesting are the chronicles by López de Ayala and Hernando del Pulgar.

The best prose of the early 1400s is found in *El Corbacho* ('The Scourge'), by the Archpriest of Talavera, a satirical and realistic diatribe against women. During this century, however, books of chivalry, narrating fantastic adventures of ideal knights, became the most popular reading matter. The prototype of chivalric novels, *Amadís de Gaula*, appeared in 1508, although written about one hundred years earlier. Cervantes originally intended his *Don Quixote* (1605 and 1615) as a parody of the chivalric novel, designed both to ridicule and do away with this genre once and for all. He succeeded in creating not only the world's most celebrated novel but also its most perfect book of chivalry.

One of the greatest works in Spanish literature, important for its influence as well as its intrinsic worth, was published in 1499 : the dialogue novel, *La Celestina*. Several other prose genres appeared at the end of the fifteenth and during the sixteenth century. Two—the sentimental novel and the pastoral novel—trace their roots to Italy. The principal sentimental novel was Diego de San Pedro's *Cárcel de Amor* ('Castle of Love') (1492). The first Spanish pastoral novel was Jorge de Montemayor's *Diana* (1559), and other novels of pastoral setting were written by Cervantes (*La Galatea*, 1585) and Lope de Vega (*Arcadia*, 1598). A third type of work found favour, though to a lesser degree, during this period : the *novela morisca* or Moorish novel. The Moorish theme appears most strikingly in the anonymous short story *El Abencerraje* (1565), and in the slightly fictionalized historical account, *Guerras Civiles de Granada* ('Civil Wars of Granada') (1595 and 1604), by Ginés Pérez de Hita.

A literary genre of native Spanish origin also developed in the sixteenth century—the picaresque novel. *Lazarillo de Tormes* (1554) is the first and one of the best of these roguish autobiographies. Other notable picaresque novels are Mateo Alemán's *Guzmán de Alfarache* (1599 and 1604), Quevedo's *La Vida del Buscón* (1608) and Vicente Espinel's *Marcos de Obregón* (1618).

In addition, the prose of the Golden Age includes the elegant, euphuistic essays of Antonio de Guevara, the mystic writings of Fray Luis de Granada, Fray Luis de León, Santa Teresa and others, and the historical works of Hurtado de Mendoza and Father Mariana. At the end of the period we have the brilliant commentaries of the philosopher Baltasar Gracián.

The eighteenth century, while weak in original creations, did produce a number of scholarly works, notably Feijóo's encyclopedia. Father Isla's satiric portrayal of a pompous preacher, *Fray Gerundio de Campazas*, is considered the best novel of the century. Cadalso's *Cartas Marruecas* ('Moroccan Letters') are also noteworthy for their interesting descriptions and criticism of Spain.

The 1830s saw the revival of Spanish prose, first in the form of *artículos de costumbres* (essays on foibles of the day) by Larra and Mesonero Romanos. This was also the period of numerous historical novels in imitation of Walter Scott. In the middle of the century, Fernán Caballero began to write her realistic novels of regional background, which proved to be forerunners of the excellent realistic novels of the late nineteenth century. Pereda, Alarcón, Valera, Galdós, Pardo Bazán, Alas and Valdés are outstanding among the many novelists of the late 1800s.

Vicente Blasco Ibáñez, Pío Baroja, Ramón del Valle-Inclán and Ramón Pérez de Ayala are all leading novelists of the twentieth century. The essay, too, was extensively cultivated by the young authors of the early 1900s, called the Generation of '98. Miguel de Unamuno, philosopher, educator, novelist and poet, 'Azorín,' literary critic and careful stylist, and José Ortega y Gasset, philosopher and teacher, are among the most noteworthy essayists of the twentieth century.

Drama

The earliest manifestation of the drama in medieval Spain was of a religious nature. The only recorded work of this period which has come down to us is a 150-line fragment of the thirteenth century, *Auto de los Reyes Magos* ('Play of the Three Magi'). Juan del Encina, whose first *églogas* (eclogues) appeared in 1496, is credited with secularizing the Spanish drama. He was followed in the early sixteenth century by Torres Naharro, the Portuguese writer Gil Vicente, and Lope de Rueda, whose short humorous skits called *pasos* attained enormous popular success.

The Golden Age ushered in the greatest period of the national drama. The incomparably prolific Lope de Vega with his two thousand plays practically by himself established the national Spanish drama. Tirso de Molina's *Burlador de Sevilla* ('The Scoffer of Seville') created the striking characterization of Don Juan, often imitated in European literature. Mexican-born Juan Ruiz de Alarcón was the most moral and technically correct

dramatist of the period. Pedro Calderón de la Barca, the culmination of the Golden Age drama, is best known abroad for his philosophic *La vida es sueño* ('Life is a Dream'). Lope, Tirso, Alarcón and Calderón are only four among many first-rate dramatists who flourished in the seventeenth century.

The *entremés*, developed from Rueda's *pasos*, was cultivated by Cervantes, among others, in the early seventeenth century. In the eighteenth century, Ramón de la Cruz continued this genre in his *sainetes*. Except for the latter, the eighteenth-century theatre consisted mainly of neo-classic imitations of French plays or of Golden Age dramas. Moratín's *El sí de las niñas* ('When a Girl Says "Yes" ') is considered the best work of the neo-classic school.

The brief period of the romantic triumph in Spain witnessed many successful plays. Among these were Martínez de la Rosa's *La conjuración de Venecia* ('The Conspiracy of Venice') (1834), Larra's *Macías* (1834), the Duque de Rivas' overwhelming *Don Alvaro* (1835), Garcí Gutiérrez's *El trovador* ('The Troubadour') (1836), Hartzenbusch's *Los amantes de Teruel* ('The Lovers of Teruel') (1837) and Zorrilla's *Don Juan Tenorio* (1844).

During the mid-nineteenth century, Bretón de los Herreros poured out hundreds of light comedies in the style of Moratín. The finest dramatist of this period was Tamayo y Baus, author of *Un drama nuevo* ('A New Drama'). In the last quarter of the century, Echegaray's neo-romantic melodramas dominated the Spanish theatre.

During the early twentieth century, the great novelist Galdós composed many excellent plays, usually dealing with social problems. The most renowned dramatist of this period is the prolific Jacinto Benavente, whose masterpiece is *Los intereses creados* ('The Bonds of Interest'). Noteworthy also are the Quintero brothers, who collaborated on numerous comedies with an Andalusian background, Eduardo Marquina, who cultivated the historical drama, and Gregorio Martínez Sierra, author of a number of delicate and charming plays.

Jacinto Grau and Eduardo Casona are also among the best playwrights of this century.

THE POEM OF THE CID

[*c.* 1140]

Spain's national hero in the history of its wars with the Moors is Rodrigo Díaz de Vivar (1040?–1099). A nobleman of the court of Alfonso VI of Castile, he was given the sobriquet El Cid (the lord, master) because of his numerous victories and his intrepid courage. After the Cid's death, tales of his exploits—somewhat fictionalized and idealized—circulated among the people, and he became the subject of ballads, chronicles, and the great epic of early Spanish literature, the Poema del Cid *(also called* Cantar de Mío Cid*). Composed about 1140, it has been preserved in a copy made in 1307 by one Pedro Abad. Its 3,730 verses relate some of the adventures of the Cid in his maturity, and it is divided into three major sections or cantos. The first (from which the selections presented here are taken) deals with the exile of the Cid from Castile after falling into the King's disfavour. In the second canto, King Alfonso is reconciled with the Cid and arranges the marriage of the Cid's two daughters to the Infantes (Princes) of Carrion. The final division describes the shameful behaviour of the Infantes towards their wives and the Cid's revenge upon them.*

The Poema del Cid *does not contain fantastic or superhuman adventures, so common to the early epics of other nations. Rather it is notable for its realism and humanity—the stirring story of a flesh-and-blood hero.*

Our Spanish selection is taken from the modern poetic version by the Spanish poet and critic Pedro Salinas (1892-1951).

POEMA DEL CID

ADIÓS DEL CID A VIVAR

Los ojos de Mío Cid mucho llanto van llorando;
Hacia atrás vuelve la vista y se quedaba mirándolos.
Vió cómo estaban las puertas abiertas y sin candados,
Vacías quedan las perchas ni con pieles ni con mantos,
Sin halcones de cazar y sin azores mudados.
Y habló, como siempre habla, tan justo y tan mesurado:
'¡Bendito seas, Dios mío, Padre que estás en lo alto!
Contra mí tramaron esto mis enemigos malvados.'

Ya aguijan a los caballos, ya les soltaron las riendas.
Cuando salen de Vivar ven la corneja a la diestra,
Pero al ir a entrar en Burgos la llevaban a su izquierda.
Movió Mío Cid los hombros y sacudió la cabeza:
'¡Animo, Álvar Fáñez, ánimo, de nuestra tierra nos echan,
Pero cargados de honra hemos de volver a ella!'

Ya por la ciudad de Burgos el Cid Ruy Díaz entró.
Sesenta pendones lleva detrás el Campeador.
Todos salían a verle, niño, mujer y varón,
A las ventanas de Burgos mucha gente se asomó.
¡Cuántos ojos que lloraban de grande que era el dolor!
Y de los labios de todos sale la misma razón:
'¡Qué buen vasallo sería si tuviese buen señor!'

De grado le albergarían, pero ninguno lo osaba,
Que a Ruy Díaz de Vivar le tiene el rey mucha saña.
La noche pasada a Burgos llevaron una real carta
Con severas prevenciones y fuertemente sellada
Mandando que a Mío Cid nadie le diese posada,
Que si alguno se la da sepa lo que le esperaba:
Sus haberes perdería, más los ojos de la cara,
Y además se perdería salvación de cuerpo y alma.

Gran dolor tienen en Burgos todas las gentes cristianas.
De Mío Cid se escondían: no pueden decirle nada.

THE POEM OF THE CID

THE BANISHMENT OF THE CID

He turned and looked upon them, and he wept very sore
As he saw the yawning gateway and the hasps wrenched off the
  door,
And the pegs whereon no mantle nor coat of vair there hung.
There perched no moulting goshawk, and there no falcon swung.
My lord the Cid sighed deeply such grief was in his heart
And he spake well and wisely: 'Oh Thou, in Heaven that art
Our Father and our Master, now I give thanks to Thee.
Of their wickedness my foemen have done this thing to me.'

Then they shook out the bridle rein further to ride afar.
They had the crow on their right hand as they issued from Bivar;
And as they entered Burgos upon their left it sped.
And the Cid shrugged his shoulders, and the Cid shook his head:
'Good tidings Alvar Fañez! We are banished from our weal,
But on a day with honour shall we come unto Castile.'

Roy Diaz entered Burgos with sixty pennons strong,
And forth to look upon him did the men and women throng.
And with their wives the townsmen at the windows stood hard by,
And they wept in lamentation, their grief was risen so high.
As with one mouth, together they spake with one accord:
'God, what a noble vassal, an he had a worthy lord.'

Fain had they made him welcome, but none dared do the thing
For fear of Don Alfonso, and the fury of the King.
His mandate unto Burgos came ere the evening fell.
With utmost care they brought it, and it was sealèd well:
'That no man to Roy Diaz give shelter now, take heed.
And if one give him shelter, let him know in very deed
He shall lose his whole possession, nay! the eyes within his head
Nor shall his soul and body be found in better stead.'

Great sorrow had the Christians, and from his face they hid.
Was none dared aught to utter unto my lord the Cid.

Se dirige Mío Cid adonde siempre paraba;
Cuando a la puerta llegó se la encuentra bien cerrada.
Por miedo del rey Alfonso acordaron los de casa
Que como el Cid no la rompa no se la abrirán por nada.
La gente de Mío Cid a grandes voces llamaba,
Los de dentro no querían contestar una palabra.
Mío Cid picó el caballo, a la puerta se acercaba,
El pie sacó del estribo, y con él gran golpe daba,
Pero no se abrió la puerta, que estaba muy bien cerrada.
La niña de nueve años muy cerca del Cid se para:

'Campeador que en bendita hora ceñiste la espada,
El rey lo ha vedado anoche a Burgos llegó su carta,
Con severas prevenciones y fuertemente sellada.
No nos atrevemos, Cid, a darte asilo por nada,
Porque si no perderíamos los haberes y las casas,
Perderíamos también los ojos de nuestras caras.
Cid, en el mal de nosotros vos no vais ganando nada.
Seguid y que os proteja Dios con sus virtudes santas.'

Esto le dijo la niña y se volvió hacia su casa.
Bien claro ha visto Ruy Díaz que del rey no espere gracia.
De allí se aparta, por Burgos a buen paso atravesaba,
A Santa María llega, del caballo descabalga,
Las rodillas hinca en tierra y de corazón rogaba.
Cuando acabó su oración el Cid otra vez cabalga,
De las murallas salió, el río Arlanzón cruzaba.
Junto a Burgos, esa villa, en el arenal posaba,
Las tiendas mandó plantar y del caballo se baja.
Mío Cid el de Vivar que en buen hora ciñó espada
En un arenal posó, que nadie le abre su casa.
Pero en torno suyo hay guerreros que le acompañan.
Así acampó Mío Cid cual si anduviera en montaña.
Prohibido tiene el rey que en Burgos le vendan nada
De todas aquellas cosas que le sirvan de vianda.
No se atreven a venderle ni la ración más menguada.

EL CID SE DESPIDE DE SU ESPOSA

Aprisa cantan los gallos y quebrar quiere el albor
Del día, cuando a San Pedro llega el buen Campeador.
Estaba el abad Don Sancho, muy buen cristiano de Dios,

Then the Campeador departed unto his lodging straight.
But when he was come thither, they had locked and barred the
    gate.
In their fear of King Alfonso had they done even so.
And the Cid forced not his entrance, neither for weal nor woe
Durst they open it unto him. Loudly his men did call.
Nothing thereto in answer said the folk within the hall.
My lord the Cid spurred onward, to the doorway did he go.
He drew his foot from the stirrup, he smote the door one blow.
Yet the door would not open, for they had barred it fast.
But a maiden of nine summers came unto him at last :

'Campeador in happy hour thou girdest on the sword.
'Tis the King's will. Yestereven came the mandate of our lord.
With utmost care they brought it, and it was sealed with care :
None to ope to you or greet you for any cause shall dare.
And if we do, we forfeit houses and lands instead.
Nay we shall lose morever, the eyes within the head.
And, Cid, with our misfortune, naught whatever dost thou gain.
But may God with all His power support thee in thy pain.'

So spake the child and turned away. Unto her home went she.
That he lacked the King's favour now well the Cid might see.
He left the door; forth onward he spurred through Burgos town.
When he had reached Saint Mary's, then he got swiftly down.
He fell upon his knee and prayed with a true heart indeed :
And when the prayer was over, he mounted on the steed.
Forth from the gate and over the Arlanzon he went.
There in the sand by Burgos, the Cid let pitch his tent.
Roy Diaz who in happy hour had girded on the brand,
Since none at home would greet him, encamped there on the sand
With a good squadron, camping as if within the wood.
They will not let him in Burgos buy any kind of food.
Provender for a single day they dared not to him sell.

THE CID'S FAREWELL TO HIS WIFE

And it was night to morning, and the cocks full oft they crew,
When at last my lord the Campeador unto San Pedro came.
God's Christian was the Abbot. Don Sancho was his name;

Rezando ya los maitines apenas amaneció.
Y estaba Doña Jimena con cinco damas de pro
Rogando a San Pedro apóstol y a Cristo Nuestro Señor:
'Tú, que eres guía de todos, guíame al Campeador.'

A la puerta llaman; todos saben que el Cid ha llegado.
¡Dios, qué alegre que se ha puesto ese buen abad Don Sancho!
Con luces y con candelas los monjes salen al patio.

'Gracias a Dios, Mío Cid, le dijo el abad Don Sancho,
Puesto que os tengo aquí, por mí seréis hospedado.'
Esto le contesta entonces Mío Cid el bienhadado:

'Contento de vos estoy y agradecido, Don Sancho,
Prepararé la comida mía y la de mis vasallos.
Hoy que salgo de esta tierra os daré cincuenta marcos,
Si Dios·me concede vida os he de dar otro tanto.
No quiero que el monasterio por mí sufra ningún gasto.
Para mi esposa Jimena os entrego aquí cien marcos;
A ella, a sus hijas y damas podréis servir este año.
Dos hijas niñas os dejo, tomadlas a vuestro amparo.
A vos os las encomiendo en mi ausencia, abad Don Sancho,
En ellas y en mi mujer ponedme todo cuidado.
Si ese dinero se acaba o si os faltare algo
Dadles lo que necesiten, abad, así os lo mando.
Por un marco que gastéis, al convento daré cuatro.'
Así se lo prometió el abad de muy buen grado.
Ved aquí a Doña Jimena, con sus hijas va llegando,
A cada una de las niñas la lleva una dama en brazos.
Doña Jimena ante el Cid las dos rodillas ha hincado.
Llanto tenía en los ojos, quísole besar las manos.

Le dice: 'Gracias os pido, Mío Cid el bienhadado.
Por calumnias de malsines del reino vais desterrado.

'¡Merced os pido, buen Cid, noble barba tan crecida!
Aquí ante vos me tenéis, Mío Cid, y a vuestras hijas,
De muy poca edad las dos y todavía tan niñas.
Conmigo vienen también las damas que nos servían.
Bien veo, Campeador, que preparáis vuestra ida;
Tenemos que separarnos estando los dos en vida.
¡Decidnos lo que hay que hacer, oh Cid, por Santa María!'

And he was saying matins at the breaking of the day.
With her five good dames in waiting Ximena there did pray.
They prayed unto Saint Peter and God they did implore :
'O thou who guidest all mankind, succour the Campeador.'

One knocked at the doorway, and they heard the tidings then.
God wot the Abbot Sancho was the happiest of men.
With the lights and with the candles to the court they ran
    forthright,
And him who in good hour was born they welcomed in delight.

'My lord Cid,' quoth the Abbot, 'Now God be praised of grace!
Do thou accept my welcome, since I see thee in this place.'
And the Cid who in good hour was born, thereunto answered he :

'My thanks to thee, don Sancho, I am content with thee.
For myself and for my vassals provision will I make.
Since I depart to exile, these fifty marks now take.
If I may live my life-span, they shall be doubled you.
To the Abbey not a groatsworth of damage will I do.
For my lady do I give you an hundred marks again.
Herself, her dames and daughters for this year do you maintain.
I leave two daughters with you, but little girls they be.
In thine arms keep them kindly. I commend them here to thee.
Don Sancho do thou guard them, and of my wife take care.
If thou wantest yet and lackest for anything whate'er,
Look well to their provision, thee I conjure once more,
And for one mark that thou spendest the Abbey shall have four.'
And with glad heart the Abbot his full assent made plain.
And lo! the Dame Ximena came with her daughters twain.
Each had her dame-in-waiting who the little maiden bore.
And Dame Ximena bent the knee before the Campeador.
And fain she was to kiss his hand, and, oh, she wept forlorn!

'A boon! A boon! my Campeador. In a good hour wast thou
    born.
And because of wicked slanderers art thou banished from the land.

'Oh Campeador fair-bearded a favour at thy hand!
Behold I kneel before thee, and thy daughters are here with me,
That have seen of days not many, for children yet they be,
And these who are my ladies to serve my need that know.
Now well do I behold it, thou art about to go.
Now from thee our lives a season must sunder and remove,
But unto us give succour for sweet Saint Mary's love.'

Las dos manos inclinó el de la barba crecida,
A sus dos niñitas coge, en sus brazos las subía,
Al corazón se las llega, de tanto que las quería.
Llanto le asoma a los ojos y muy fuerte que suspira.
'Es verdad, Doña Jimena, esposa honrada y bendita,
Tanto cariño os tengo como tengo al alma mía.
Tenemos que separarnos, ya lo veis, los dos en vida;
A vos os toca quedaros, a mí me toca la ida.
¡Quiera Dios y con El quiera la Santa Virgen María
Que con estas manos pueda aún casar a nuestras hijas
Y que me quede ventura y algunos días de vida
Para poderos servir, mujer honrada y bendita!'

EL CID Y EL CONDE DE BARCELONA

Así ganó esta batalla, a gran honra de sus barbas.
Cogió al conde Don Ramón y a su tienda le llevaba,
A hombres de su confianza los mandó que le guardaran.
Le deja allí, y de la tienda el Campeador se marcha;
Por todas partes los suyos a juntársele llegaban.
Muy contento que está el Cid, muy grandes son las ganancias.
A Mío Cid Don Rodrigo gran comida le preparan;
Pero el conde Don Ramón no hacía caso de nada,
Los manjares le traían, delante se los plantaban,
Él no los quiere comer y todos los desdeñaba.

'No he de comer un bocado por todo el oro de España,
Antes perderé mi cuerpo y condenaré mi alma,
Ya que tales malcalzados me vencieron en batalla.'

Mío Cid Campeador bien oiréis lo que ahora dijo:
'Comed, conde, de este pan, bebed, conde, de este vino,
De cautiverio saldréis si hacéis lo que yo os digo,
Si no, en todos nuestros días no veréis ningún ser vivo.'

'Comed, comed, Don Rodrigo, tranquilo podéis estar,
Pero yo no comeré, el hambre me matará.'

Hasta pasados tres días no se vuelve el conde atrás.
Mientras ellos se reparten lo que hubieron de ganar
No logran que coma el conde ni una migaja de pan.

The Cid, the nobly bearded, reached down unto the twain,
And in his arms his daughters has lifted up again,
And to his heart he pressed them, so great his love was grown,
And his tears fell fast and bitter, and sorely did he moan :
'Ximena as mine own spirit I loved thee, gentle wife;
But o'er well dost thou behold it, we must sunder in our life.
I must flee and thou behind me here in the land must stay.
Please God and sweet Saint Mary that yet upon a day
I shall give my girls in marriage with mine own hand rich and well,
And thereafter in good fortune be suffered yet to dwell,
May they grant me, wife, much honoured, to serve thee then
　　once more.'

THE CID AND THE COUNT OF BARCELONA

By the victory there much honour unto his beard he did.
And then the Count to his own tent was taken by the Cid.
He bade his squires guard him. From the tent he hastened then.
From every side together about him came his men.
The Cid was glad, so mighty were the spoils of that defeat.
For the lord Cid don Rodrigo they prepared great stock of meat.
But namely the Count don Remond, thereby he set no store.
To him they brought the viands, and placed them him before.
He would not eat, and at them all he mocked with might and
　　main :

'I will not eat a mouthful for all the wealth in Spain;
Rather will I lose my body and forsake my soul forby,
Since beaten in the battle by such tattered louts was I.'

My lord the Cid Roy Diaz you shall hearken what he said :
'Drink of the wine I prithee, Count, eat also of the bread.
If this thou dost, no longer shalt thou be a captive then;
If not, then shalt thou never see Christendom again.'

'Do thou eat, don Rodrigo, and prepare to slumber sweet.
For myself I will let perish, and nothing will I eat.'

And in no way were they able to prevail till the third day,
Nor make him eat a mouthful while they portioned the great prey.

Dijo entonces Mío Cid: 'Conde, habéis de comer algo,
Que si no queréis comer nunca más veréis cristianos,
Mas si coméis a mi gusto, como os tengo mandado,
A vos, conde Don Ramón, y a dos de estos fijosdalgo
De prisión os soltaré y saldréis de entre mis manos.

Al oírlo Don Ramón mucho que se fué alegrando.
'Si vos, Don Rodrigo, hacéis eso que me habéis hablado,
Por el resto de mi vida quedaré maravillado.'
'Pues comed, conde, comed, y cuando hayáis acabado
A vos y a dos caballeros la libertad he de daros.
Mas, de lo que habéis perdido y yo ganado en el campo
Sabed, conde, que no pienso devolveros ni un ochavo,
Que mucha falta nos hace y andamos necesitados.
Cogiendo de vos y de otros hemos de irnos ayudando,
Y nos durará esta vida lo que quiera el Padre Santo,
Que eso le toca al que el rey fuera de su reino ha echado.'

Alégrase el conde y pide el agua para las manos,
Ya se la ponen delante, diéronsela sin retraso.
Con esos dos caballeros por Mío Cid designados,
Comiendo iba el conde y come Don Ramón de muy buen grado.
Sentado está junto a él Mío Cid el bienhadado:

'Conde, si no coméis bien como os tengo mandado,
Aún os quedaréis conmigo, no habremos de separarnos.'
Dijo el conde: 'Comeré, Mío Cid, de muy buen grado.'
Él y los los caballeros a comer se apresuraron;
Contento se pone el Cid, que allí los está mirando,
De ver que el conde Ramón trabajo daba a las manos.

'Cid, si así lo permitís, ya quisiéramos marcharnos,
A prisa cabalgaremos si nos dan nuestros caballos;
Desde el día que fuí conde no comí tan de buen grado,
El sabor de esta comida de mí no será olvidado.'

Tres palafrenes le dieron, los tres muy bien ensillados,
Danles buenas vestiduras, ricas pieles, ricos mantos.
Entre los dos caballeros el conde se ha colocado.
Hasta el fin del campamento con ellos va el Castellano:

'Ya os vais, conde Ramón, franco os vais, pues sois franco,
Agradecido os quedo por lo que me habéis dejado.

'Ho! Count, do thou eat somewhat,' even so my lord Cid spoke,
'If thou dost not eat, thou shalt not look again on Christian folk;
If in such guise thou eatest that my will is satisfied,
Thyself, Count, and, moreover, two noblemen beside
Will I make free of your persons and set at liberty.'

And when the Count had heard it exceeding glad was he.
'Cid, if thou shalt perform it, this promise thou dost give,
Thereat I much shall marvel as long as I shall live.'
'Eat then, oh Count; when fairly thy dinner thou hast ta'en
I will then set at liberty thee and the other twain.
But what in open battle thou didst lose and I did earn,
Know that not one poor farthing's worth to thee will I return,
For I need it for these henchmen who hapless follow me.
They shall be paid with what I win from others as from thee.
With the Holy Father's favour we shall live after this wise,
Like banished men who have not any grace in the King's eyes.'

Glad was the Count. For water he asked his hands to lave.
And that they brought before him, and quickly to him gave.
The Count of Barcelona began to eat his fill
With the men the Cid had given him, and God! with what a will!
He who in happy hour was born unto the Count sate near :

'Ha! Count, if now thou dinest not with excellent good cheer,
And to my satisfaction, here we shall still delay,
And we twain in no manner shall go forth hence away.'
Then said the Count : 'Right gladly and according to my mind!'
With his two knights at that season in mighty haste he dined.
My lord the Cid was well content that all his eating eyed,
For the Count don Remond his hands exceeding nimbly plied.

'If thou art pleased, my lord the Cid, in guise to go are we.
Bid them bring to us our horses; we will mount speedily.
Since I was first Count, never have I dined with will so glad,
Nor shall it be forgotten what joy therein I had.'

They gave to them three palfreys. Each had a noble selle.
Good robes of fur they gave them, and mantles fair as well.
Count don Remond rode onward with a knight on either side.
To the camp's end the Castilian along with them did ride.

'Ha! Count, forth thou departest to freedom fair and frank;
For what thou hast left with me I have thee now to thank.

Si acaso os da la idea, conde, de querer vengarlo
Y me venís a buscar, mandadme antes un recado:
O me llevaré lo vuestro o vos de lo mío algo.'

'Quedáos tranquilo, Cid, de ese peligro estáis salvo;
Eso por pago lo dejo por lo que queda de año.
Y de venir a buscaros, ni siquiera hay que pensarlo.'

El conde picó el caballo y ya comenzaba a andar,
Volviendo va la cabeza para mirar hacia atrás.
Miedo tiene porque cree que el Cid se arrepentirá;
Por todo el oro del mundo Mío Cid no haría·tal,
Deslealtades así no las hizo el Cid jamás.
El conde ya se ha marchado, da la vuelta el de Vivar,
Juntóse con sus mesnadas y muy alegre que está
Por el botín que de aquella batalla les quedará:
Tan ricos son que no pueden ni su riqueza contar.

GONZALO DE BERCEO
[1180?–1250?]

*The first Spanish author known to us by name is Gonzalo de Berceo, who
lived during the first half of the thirteenth century. A lay brother attached to
the Benedictine monastery of San Millán de la Cogolla, Berceo is one of
the most important representatives of the 'learned' school of poetry called
mester de clerecía; except for one brief passage, he does not deviate from*

de los MILAGROS DE NUESTRA SEÑORA

Yo maestro Gonçalvo de Verçeo nomnado
Iendo en romería caeçí en un prado
Verde e bien sençido, de flores bien poblado,
Logar cobdiçiaduero pora omne cansado.

Daban olor sovejo las flores bien olientes,
Refrescavan en omne las caras e las mientes,
Manavan cada canto fuentes claras corrientes,
En verano bien frías, en ivierno calientes.

If desire to avenge it is present to thy mind,
Send unto me beforehand when thou comest me to find.
Either that thou wilt leave thy goods or part of mine wilt seize.'
'Ha! my lord Cid, thou art secure, be wholly at thine ease.
Enough have I paid to thee till all this year be gone.
As for coming out to find thee, I will not think thereon.'
The Count of Barcelona spurred forth. Good speed he made.
Turning his head he looked at them, for he was much afraid
Lest my lord the Cid repent him; the which the gallant Cid
Would not have done for all the world. Base deed he never did.
The Count is gone. He of Bivar has turned him back again;
He began to be right merry, and he mingled with his train.
Most great and wondrous was the spoil that they had won in war,
So rich were his companions that they knew not what they bore.

R. SELDEN ROSE and LEONARD BACON

the school's characteristic cuaderna vía (*stanzas of four fourteen-syllable lines with a single rhyme*). *His works, all of a religious nature, consist of ten rather lengthy poems totalling about ten thousand lines. Of these, the best known is the* Milagros de Nuestra Señora, *which relates twenty-five stories, in each of which a miracle is performed through the intercession of the Virgin Mary.*

From THE MIRACLES OF OUR LADY

I, Gonzalo de Berceo, in the gentle summertide,
Wending upon a pilgrimage, came to a meadow's side;
All green was it and beautiful, with flowers far and wide,—
A pleasant spot, I ween, wherein the traveller might abide.

Flowers with the sweetest odours filled all the sunny air,
And not alone refreshed the sense, but stole the mind from care;
On every side a fountain gushed, whose waters pure and fair,
Ice-cold beneath the summer sun, but warm in winter were.

Avie hi grand abondo de buenas arboledas,
Milgranos e figueras, peros e manzanedas,
E muchas otras fructas de diversas monedas;
Mas non avie ningunas podridas ni azedas.

La verdura del prado, la olor de las flores,
Las sombras de los árbores de temprados sabores
Refrescáronme todo, e perdí los sudores;
Podrie vevir el omne con aquellos olores.

Nunqua trobé en sieglo logar tan deleitoso,
Nin sombra tan temprada, ni olor tan sabroso
Descargué mi ropiella por iazer más viçioso,
Póseme a la sombra de un árbor fermoso.

Yaziendo a la sombra perdí todos cuidados,
Odí sonos de aves dulces e modulados:
Nunqua udieron omnes órganos más temprados,
Nin que formar pudiessen sones más acordados.

ALFONSO X
[1221?–1284]

The cultural and literary life of thirteenth-century Castile centred in Toledo, in the court of King Alfonso X, called The Wise. Alfonso ascended to the throne in 1252, and his reign, unfortunate from a political point of view, lasted until his death in 1284. He achieved glory, however, in the field of letters, both as patron and participant. A man of unusual intelligence and catholic interests, Alfonso gathered about him the outstanding scholars of his day, Christian, Arab and Jewish. With their collaboration, he set about the task of compiling an encyclopaedic series of works embracing all human and scientific knowledge. Included are studies on such a variety of topics as law, astronomy, hunting, precious stones and chess.

LAS SIETE PARTIDAS

PARTIDA SEGUNDA, TÍTULO I, LEY X

Qué Quiere Decir Tirano, et Como Usa de su Poder en el Regno Despues que es Apoderado Dél.

Tirano tanto quiere decir como señor cruel, que es apoderado en algun regno o tierra por fuerza o por engaño o por traicion: et estos

There on the thick and shadowy trees, amid the foliage green,
Were the fig and the pomegranate, the pear and apple seen;
And other fruits of various kinds, the tufted leaves between,
None were unpleasant to the taste and none decayed, I ween.

The verdure of the meadow green, the odour of the flowers
The grateful shadows of the trees, tempered with fragrant showers,
Refreshed me in the burning heat of the sultry noontide hours;
Oh, one might live upon the balm and fragrance of those bowers!

Ne'er had I found on earth a spot that had such power to please,
Such shadows from the summer sun, such odours on the breeze;
I threw my mantle on the ground, that I might rest at ease,
And stretched upon the greensward lay in the shadow of the trees.

There soft reclining in the shade, all cares beside me flung,
I heard the soft and mellow notes that through the woodland rung;
Ear never listened to a strain, for instrument or tongue,
So mellow and harmonious as the songs above me sung.

HENRY WADSWORTH LONGFELLOW

Alfonso was responsible for the codification of the laws of Spain in the monumental Siete partidas. *The latter is one of the most important works prepared under his direction. The real beginnings of Spanish prose, however, are more clearly evident in the* Primera crónica general, *which treats of the history of Spain. A universal history was also undertaken, resulting in the* Grande y general historia.

In spite of the fact that he is regarded as 'the father of Spanish prose', Alfonso deserted that language in the field of poetry. He wrote his lyric poems—some four hundred Cantigas de Santa María—*in Galician, considered at the time a more elegant tongue.*

THE SEVEN PARTS

PART II, TITLE I, LAW X

What the Word Tyrant Means, and How a Tyrant Makes Use of His Power in a Kingdom, After He Has Obtained Possession of It.

A tyrant means a lord who has obtained possession of some kingdom, or country, by force, fraud, or treason. Persons of this

tales son de tal natura, que despues que son bien apoderados en la tierra aman mas de facer su pro, maguer sea a daño de la tierra, que la pro comunal de todos, porque siempre viven a mala sospecha de la perder. Et porque ellos pudiesen complir su entendimiento más desembargadamente dixieron los sabios antiguos que usaron ellos de su poder siempre contra los del pueblo en tres maneras de arteria: la primera es que puñan que los de su señorio sean siempre nescios et medrosos, porque cuando atales fuesen non osarien levantarse contra ellos, nin contrastar sus voluntades; la segunda que hayan desamor entre si, de guisa que non se fien unos dotros; ca mientra en tal desacuerdo vivieren non osarán facer ninguna fabla contra él, por miedo que non guardarien entre si fe nin poridat; la tercera razon es que puñan de los facer pobres, et de meterlos en tan grandes fechos que los nunca puedan acabar, porque siempre hayan que veer tanto en su mal que nunca les venga a corazon de cuidar facer tal cosa que sea contra su señorio. Et sobre todo esto siempre puñaron los tiranos de astragar a los poderosos, et de matar a los sabidores, et vedaron siempre en sus tierras confradias et ayuntamientos de los homes: et puñaron todavia de saber lo que se decie o se facie en la tierra: et fian más su consejo et la guarda de su cuerpo en los estraños porquel sirven a su voluntad, que en los de la tierra quel han de facer servicio por premia.

Otrosi decimos que maguer alguno hobiese ganado señorio de regno por alguna de las derechas razones que deximos en las leyes ante desta, que si él usase mal de su poderío en las maneras que dixiemos en esta ley, quel puedan decir las gentes 'tirano', ca tórnase el señorio que era derecho en torticero, así como dixo Aristotiles en el libro que fabla del regimiento de las cibdades et de los regnos.

PARTIDA SEGUNDA, TÍTULO VII, LEY V

Qué cosas deben costumbrar los ayos a los fijos de los reyes para ser limpios et apuestos en el comer.

Sabios y hobo que fablaron de como los ayos deben nodrir a los fijos de los reyes, et mostraron muchas razones por que los deben costumbrar a comer et a beber bien et apuestamente; et porque nos semejó que eran cosas que debien ser sabudas, porque los ayos pudiesen mejor guardar sus criados que non cayesen en yerro por mengua de las non saber, mandámoslas aqui escrebir. Et dixieron que la primera cosa que los ayos deben facer aprender a los mozos es

kind are of such a character, that after they have obtained thorough control of a country, they prefer to act for their own advantage, although it may result in injury to the country, rather than for the common benefit of all, because they always live in the expectation of losing it. And, in order that they might execute their desires more freely, the ancient sages declared that they always employed their power against the people, by means of three kinds of artifice. The first is, that persons of this kind always exert themselves to keep those under their dominion ignorant and timid, because, when they are such, they will not dare to rise up against them, or oppose their wishes. The second is, that they promote disaffection among the people so that they do not trust one another, for while they live in such discord, they will not dare to utter any speech against the king, fearing that neither faith nor secrecy will be kept among them. The third is, that they endeavour to make them poor, and employ them in such great labours that they can never finish them; for the reason that they may always have so much to consider in their own misfortunes, that they will never have the heart to think of committing any act against the government of the tyrant.

In addition to all this, tyrants always endeavour to despoil the powerful, and put the wise to death; always forbid brotherhoods and associations in their dominions; and constantly manage to be informed of what is said or done in the country, trusting more for counsel and protection to strangers, because they serve them voluntarily, than to natives who have to perform service through compulsion. We also decree that although a person may have obtained the sovereignty of a kingdom by any of the methods mentioned in the preceding law, if he should make a bad use of his power in any of the ways above stated in this law, people can denounce him as a tyrant, and his government, which was lawful, will become wrongful; as Aristotle stated in the book which treats of the government of cities and kingdoms.

PARTIDA II, TITLE VII, LAW V

What Should Be Taught the Sons of Kings, in Order That They May Be Elegant and Cleanly.

There were certain wise men who described how tutors should bring up the sons of kings, and who prescribed many ways in which they should be taught how to eat and drink properly and in a well-bred manner. And, for the reason that it seems to us that these are things which should be known, and by means of

que coman et beban limpiamente et apuesto; es maguer el comer et
el beber es cosa que ninguna criatura non la puede escusar, con todo
eso los homes non lo deben facer bestialmente, comiendo et bebiendo
ademas et desapuesto, et mayormente los fijos de los reyes por el
linage onde vienen, et el lugar que han de tener, et de quien los otros
han de tomar enxiemplo. Et esto dixieron por tres razones: la
primera porque del comer et del beber les viniese pro; la segunda por
escusallos del daño que les podrie venir cuando los ficiesen comer o
beber ademas; la tercera por costumbralos a seer limpios et apuestos,
que es cosa que les conviene mucho, ca mientre que los niños comen
et beben cuanto les es menester, son por ende más sanos et más
recios; et si comiesen ademas, serien por ende más flacos et en-
fermizos, et avenirles hie que el comer et el beber, de que les debie
venir vida et salud, se les tornarie en enfermedat o en muerte. Et
apuestamente dixieron que les debien facer comer, non metiendo en
la boca otro bocado fasta que hobiesen comido el primero, porque
sin la desapostura que y ha, podrie ende venir tan grand daño, que se
afogarien a so hora. Et non les deben consentir que tomen el bocado
con todos los cinco dedos de la mano, porque non los fagan grandes;
et otrosí que non coman feamente con toda la boca, mas con la una
parte; ca mostrarse hien en ello por glotones, que es manera de
bestias más que de homes; et de ligero non se podrie guardar el que
lo ficiese que non saliese de fuera de aquello que comiese, si quisiese
fablar. Et otrosi dixieron que los deben acostumbrar a comer de
vagar et non apriesa, por que quien dotra guisa lo usa, non puede
bien mascar lo que come, et por ende non se puede bien moler, et
por fuerza se ha de dañar et tornarse en malos humores, de que
vienen las enfermedades. Et debenles facer lavar las manos antes de
comer, porque sean limpios de las cosas que ante habien tañido,
porque la vianda cuanto mas limpiamente es comida, tanto mejor
sabe, et tanta mayor pro face; et después de comer gelas deben facer
lavar, porque las lleven limpias a la cara et a los ojos. Et alimpiarlas
deben a las tobaias et non a otra cosa, porque sean limpios et
apuestos ca non las deben alimpiar en los vestidos asi como facen
algunas gentes que non saben de limpiedat ninde apostura.

which tutors can the better rear those entrusted to their charge so that they cannot commit faults through want of knowledge, we order them to be written here. They declared the first thing that tutors should teach boys is how to eat and drink in a cleanly and polite manner; for, although this is something that no creature can avoid, nevertheless, men should not do it in a coarse or awkward way: and especially does this apply to the sons of kings, on account of the race from which they spring, and the place which they will have to occupy, and from the fact that others will have to follow their example. They gave three reasons for this: first, in order that they might receive benefit from eating and drinking; second, to enable them to avoid the injury which might result to them from eating or drinking to excess; third, in order to accustom them to be cleanly and graceful, which is something that is very becoming to them. Children who eat and drink when they have need of it, become, for this reason healthier and more vigorous; and if they eat too much they will become, on that account, weaker and ill, and the food and the drink which should give them life and health, will bring upon them sickness and death. They declared that they should teach them to eat and drink in a well-bred manner, not putting a second morsel into their mouths until the first has been swallowed: for, leaving out of consideration the ill-breeding which will result from this, there is a great danger that they will be suddenly suffocated: and that they should not permit them to grasp the morsel with all five fingers of their hand, for fear they will make it too large. Also that they should not permit them to eat inordinately with the entire mouth, but with a part of it: for, by doing so, they show themselves to be gluttons, which is rather a characteristic of beasts, than of men: and he who does this, cannot easily prevent what he is eating from dropping out of his mouth, if he should desire to speak. Moreover, they declared that they should teach them to eat slowly, and not in haste, because whoever adopts the other way, cannot thoroughly chew what he eats; and therefore it cannot be well ground up, and necessarily must cause injury, and produce bad humours, from which sickness arises. And they should compel them to wash their hands before eating, that they may be clean and free from what they have handled, for the cleaner food is when it is eaten, the more beneficial it becomes. After eating, they should also cause them to wash them in order that they may be free to handle the face and the eyes, and that they may be clean and neat they should wipe them on towels and on nothing else; for they should not wipe them on their clothes, like some people do who do not know anything about cleanliness or politeness.

Et aun dixieron que non deben mucho fablar mientra que comieren, por que si lo ficiesen, non podria seer que non menguasen en el comer o en la razon que dexiesen. Et non deben cantar cuando comieren, porque non es lugar conveniente para ello, et semejarie que lo facien más con alegría de vino que por otra cosa. Otrosi dixieron que non los dexasen mucho baxar sobre la escudilla mientre que comiesen, lo uno porque es grant desapostura, lo al porque semejarie que lo querie todo para sí el que lo ficiese, et que otro non hobiese parte en ello.

JUAN MANUEL
[1282–1349?]

Nephew of Alfonso X, the Prince Don Juan Manuel played an important rôle in Spanish affairs during the first half of the fourteenth century. When not entangled in the web of court intrigue, he was out fighting the wars which peppered his age. And when not engaged in these pursuits, he wrote— poetry, history, didactic works, even a book on the art of hunting.

Although his literary production was, like his uncle's, encyclopaedic in nature, his masterpiece is El Conde Lucanor *(also called* El libro de los ejemplos *and* El libro de Patronio). *A collection of fifty tales largely from oriental sources, it is the first great work of Spanish prose fiction. In*

EL CONDE LUCANOR

ENXENPLO XXXV

De lo que contesçió a un mançebo que casó con una mugier muy fuerte e muy brava

Un día fablava el conde Lucanor con Patronio, su consejero, e díxol: 'Patronio, un mi criado me dixo quel traían casamiento con una mugier muy rica, e aunque es más ondrada que non él, e quel casamiento es muy bueno para él, sinon por un embargo que y ha, e el embargo es éste: díxome quel dixieron que aquella mugier que era la más fuerte e la más brava cosa del mundo; e agora ruégovos quem consejedes sil mandaré que case con aquella mugier, pues save de quál manera es, o sil mandaré que lo non faga.'

'Señor conde, dixo Patronio, si él fuere tal commo fué un fijo de un omne bueno que era moro, consejalde que case con ella; mas sinon fuera atal, non gelo consejedes.'

El conde le rogó quel dixiesse cómmo fuera aquello.

They declared, moreover, that they should not talk much while they ate, because where they do so, they must necessarily suffer loss in their food, and be deficient as well with regard to what they discussed. Nor should they sing while they eat, as it is not the proper place for this, and it would appear that they did so, rather through excitement of wine, than for any other reason. They also declared that their tutors should not permit them to bend down over the porringer while they were eating: first, because it is a mark of great ill-breeding; second, since it would appear that he who acts in this way wanted all the food for himself, and desired that no one else should have any share of it.

SAMUEL PARSONS SCOTT

each story the young noble, Count Lucanor, presents a problem to his adviser, Patronio. In each case Patronio solves the problem by recounting an ejemplo *(exemplary tale).*

El Conde Lucanor, *which anticipates Boccaccio's* Decameron *by some fifteen years, provided a rich mine of plot sources for later writers in other European countries as well as in Spain.*

Ejemplo XXXV, *given here, contains the plot of Shakespeare's* The Taming of the Shrew.

COUNT LUCANOR

EJEMPLO XXXV

Of What Happened to a Young Man on His Wedding Day.

One day Count Lucanor was talking to Patronio his counsellor, and said to him, 'Patronio, one of my dependants tells me he can make a very advantageous marriage with a woman much richer and more honourable than himself; but there is one difficulty in the way, which is this, he tells me he has been informed that she is of a very violent and impetuous temper. Now I beg you to counsel me whether I should allow him to marry this woman, knowing such to be her disposition, or whether I should forbid it.'

'Count Lucanor,' replied Patronio, 'if the man is like the son of a good man, a Moor, advise the marriage by all means; but if such be not the case, forbid it.'

The Count begged of him to relate the narrative.

Patronio le dixo que en una villa avía un moro ondrado que avía un fijo, el mejor mançeco quen el mundo podría ser; mas non era tan rico que pudiesse conplir tantos fechos nin tan grandes commo el su coraçón le dava a entender que devía conplir, e por esto era él en grand cuydado, ca avía la voluntad, e non avía el poder.

E en aquella villa mesma avía otro moro muy más ondrado e muy más rico que su padre, e avía una fija e non más, e era muy contraria daquel mançebo, ca quanto aquel mançebo avía de buenas maneras, tanto las avía ella de malas e revessadas; e por ende omne del mundo non quería casar con aquel diablo.

E aquel tan buen mançebo vino un día a su padre e díxol que bien savía él que non era tan rico que pudiesse darle con que él pudiesse vevir a su ondra, e pues quel convenía fazer vida menguada e lazdrada, o irse daquella tierra, que si él por bien toviesse, quel paresçia mejor seso de catar algunt casamiento con que pudiesse aver alguna passada. E el padre le dixo quel plazería ende mucho si pudiesse fallar casamiento quel conpliese. E estonçe le dixo el fijo que si él quisiesse que podería guisar que aquel omne bueno que avía aquella fija, que gela diesse para él.

Quando el padre esto oyó, fué mucho maravillado, e díxol que cómmo cuydaba en tal cosa, que non avía omne que la conosçiesse, que por pobre que fuesse quisiesse casar con ella; e el fijo le dixo quel pidía por merçed quel guisasse aquel casamiento; e tanto lo affincó, que commo quier quel padre lo tovo por estraño, que gelo otorgó.

E fuésse luego para aquel omne bueno, e amos eran mucho amigos, e díxol todo lo que passava con su fijo, e rogol que pues su fijo se atrevía a casar con su fija, quel ploguiesse, e gela diesse para él. Quando el omne bueno esto oyó dezir a aquel su amigo, díxol:

—Por Dios, amigo, si yo tal cosa fiziesse, servos-y-a muy falso amigo; ca vos avedes muy buen fijo, e ternía que fazía muy grant falsedad si yo vos consintiesse su mal nin su muerte, ca só cierto que si con mi fija casasse, que sería muerto, o le valdría más la muerte que la vida. E vos non entendades que vos digo esto por non conplir vuestro talante, ca si la quisiéredes, a mí bien me plaze la dar a vuestro fijo, o a otro quem la saque de casa.

E aquel su amigo díxol que le gradesçía mucho esto quel dezía, e quel rogaba, que pues su fijo quería aquel casamiento, que le ploguiesse.

E el casamiento se fizo, e levaron la novia a casa de su marido. E los moros an por costunbre que adovan de çenar a los novios, e pónenles la mesa, e déxanlos en su casa fasta otro día, e fiziéronlo assí aquéllos; pero estavan los padres e las madres e parientes del

'There lived in a city,' said Patronio, 'a Moor who was much respected, and who had a son, the most promising youth in the world; but, not being rich enough to accomplish the great deeds which he felt in his heart equal to, he was greatly troubled, having the will and not the power.

'Now in the same town there lived another Moor, who held a higher position, and was very much richer than his father, and who had an only daughter, the very reverse in character and appearance of the young man, she being of so very violent a temper that no one could be found willing to marry such a virago.

'One day the young man came to his father, and said, "You know that your means will not allow you to put me in a position to live honourably" adding that, as he desired to live an easy and quiet life, he thought it better to seek to enrich himself by an advantageous marriage, or to leave that part of the country.

'The father told him that he would be very happy if he could succeed in such a union. On this, the son proposed, if it were agreeable to his father, to seek the daughter of their neighbour in marriage. Hearing this, the father was much astonished, and asked how he could think of such a thing, when he knew that no man, however poor, could be induced to marry her.

'Nevertheless, the son insisted; and, although the father thought it a strange whim, in the end he gave his consent. The good man then visited his neighbour, telling him the wish of his son.

'When the good man heard what his friend said, he answered, "By heaven, my friend, were I to do such a thing I should prove myself a very false friend, for you have a worthy son, and it would be base in me to consent to his injury or death; and I know for certain that, were he to live with my daughter, he would soon die, or death, at least, would be preferable to life. Do not think I say this from any objection to your alliance, for I should only be too grateful to any man who would take her out of my house."

'The young man's father was much pleased at this, as his son was so intent on the marriage. All being ultimately arranged, they were in the end married, and the bride taken home, according to the Moorish fashion, to the house of her husband, and left to supper; the friends and relations returning to their respective

novio e de la novia con grand reçelo, cuydando que otro día fallarían el novio muerto o muy maltrecho.

E luego que ellos fincaron solos en casa, assentáronsse a la mesa, e ante que ella oviesse e dezir cosa, cató el novio en derredor de la mesa, e vió un su alano, e díxol ya quanto bravamente: 'Alano, dadnos agua a las manos.' E el alano non lo fizo, e él se començó a ensañar, e díxol más bravamente quel diesse agua a las manos, e el perro non lo fizo. E desque vió que non lo fazía, levantósse muy sañudo de la mesa, e metió mano al espada, e endereçó al alano; e quando el alano le vió venir contra sí comenzó a foir, e él en pos dél saltando amos por la ropa e por la mesa e por el fuego; tanto anduvo en pos dél, fasta que lo alcanzó, e cortól la cabeça e las piernas e los braços, e fízolo todo pieças, e ensangrentó toda la casa e la ropa e la mesa; e assí muy sañudo e ensangrentado tornós a la mesa, e cató en derredor, e vió un gato, e mandól quel diesse del agua a las manos; e porque lo non fizo díxol:

—¿Cómmo, don falso traydor, non vistes lo que fize al alano porque non quiso fazer lo quel mandé? Yo prometo que si un punto más porfías conmigo, que eso mesmo faré a ti que al alano.

E porque lo non fizo levantósse, e tomól por las piernas, e dió con él a la pared, e fízolo más de cient pedaços, mostrando muy mayor saña que contra el alano.

E assí, bravo e sañudo, faziendo malos continentes, tornós a sentar a la mesa, e cató a todas partes; e la mugier, quel vió esto fazer, tovo que estava loco e fuera de seso, e non dezía nada. E desque ovo catado a todas partes vió un su cavallo que estava en casa, e él non avía más daquel, e díxol bravamente quel diesse agua a las manos, e el cavallo non lo fizo. E desque vió que lo non fazía díxol:

—¿Cómmo, don cavallo, cuidades que porque non he otro sinon vos, que por esso vos dexaré si non fiziéredes lo que vos mandare? Que tan mala muerte vos daré commo a los otros, e non ha cosa viva en el mundo que non faga lo que yo mandare, que esso mesmo le non faga.

El cavallo estovo quedo, e desque él vió que non fazía su mandado, fué a él e cortól la cabeça, e con la mayor saña que podía mostrar despedaçávalo todo.

E quando la mugier vió que matara el cavallo non aviendo otro, e que dezía que esto faría a quiquier que su mandado non fiziesse, tovo que esto ya non se fazía por trebejo, e ovo tan grand miedo que non savía si era muerta o viva.

E él assí bravo e sañudo e ensangrentado, tornós a la mesa, jurando que si mil cavallos e omnes e mugieres él oviesse en casa quel saliessen de mandado, que todos serían muertos, assentósse e

homes, waiting anxiously for the following day, when they feared to find the bridegroom either dead or seriously injured.

'Now, being left alone, the young couple sat down to supper, when the bridegroom, looking behind him, saw his mastiff and said to him, "Bring me water wherewith to wash my hands." The dog, naturally taking no notice of this command, the young man became irritated, and ordered the animal more angrily to bring him water for his hands, which the latter not heeding, the young man arose in a great rage, and, drawing his sword, commenced a savage attack on the dog, who, to avoid him ran away; but, finding no retreat, jumped on the table, then to the fireplace, his master still pursuing him, who, having caught him, first cut off his head, then his paws, hewing him to pieces, covering everything with blood. Thus furious and bloodstained, he returned to the table, and, looking round, saw a cat. "Bring me water for my hands," said he to him. The animal not noticing the command, the master cried out, "How, false traitor, did you not see how I treated the mastiff for disobeying me? If you do not as I tell you this instant you shall share his fate." The poor little harmless cat continuing motionless, the master seized him by the paws and dashed him to pieces against the wall. His fury increasing, he again placed himself at the table, looking about on all sides as if for something to attack next. His wife, seeing this, and supposing he had lost his senses, held her peace. At length he espied his horse, the only one he had, and called to him fiercely to bring him water to wash his hands. The animal not obeying, he cried out in a rage, "How is this? Think you that because you are the only horse I have that you dare thus to disobey my orders? Know then that your fate shall be the same as the others, and that anyone living who dares to disobey me shall not escape my vengeance." Saying this, he seized the horse, cut off his head, and hacked him to pieces.

'And when the wife saw this, and knowing he had no other horse, felt that he was really in earnest, she became dreadfully alarmed.

'He again sat down to table, raging and all bloody as he was, swearing he would kill a thousand horses, or even men or women, if they dared to disobey him. Holding at the same time his bloody

cató a toda parte teniendo la espada ensangrentada en el regaço. E desque cató a una parte e a otra e non vió cosa viva, bolvió los ojos contra su mugier muy bravamente e díxol con grand saña, teniendo la espada sacada en la mano: 'Levantadvos e dadme agua a las manos.'

E la mugier, que non esperava otra cosa sinon que la despedaçaría toda, levantósse muy apriessa e diól agua a las manos; e él díxol: '¡Ah! cómmo gradesco a Dios porque fezistes lo que vos mandé; ca de otra guisa, por el pesar que estos locos me fizieron, esso oviera yo fecho a vos que a ellos.' E después mandól quel diesse de comer e ella fízolo; e cada que él dezía alguna cosa, tan bravamente e con tal son gelo dezía, quella cuydava que la cabeça era ida por el polvo; e assí passó el fecho entrellos aquella noche, e nunca ella fabló; mas fazía todo lo quél le mandava.

E desque ovieron dormido una pieça, dixo él a ella: 'Con esta saña que ove esta noche non puedo bien dormir; catad que non me dispierte cras ninguno, e tenedme bien adovado de comer.'

E quando fué grand mañana, los padres e las madres, e los parientes allegáronsse a la puerta e en quanto non fablava ninguno, cuydaron quel novio estava muerto o ferido; e desque vieron entre las puertas a la novia e non al novio, cuydáronlo más; e quando la novia los vió a la puerta llegó muy paso e con grand miedo, e comenzóles luego a dezir: 'Locos traidores, ¿qué fazedes e cómmo osades llegar a la puerta? Non fablad, callad; sinon, también vosotros commo yo, todos somos muertos.'

E en quanto todos esto oyeron fueron muy maravillados; e desque sopieron cómmo passaran en uno aquella noche, presçiaron mucho al mançebo, porque assí sopiera fazer lo que conplía e castigara tan bien su casa; e daquel día adelante fué aquella mugier atan bien mandada, e ovieron muy buena vida.

E dende a pocos días su suegro quiso fazer assí commo fiziera su yerno, e por aquella manera mató un cavallo, e díxol su mugier:

—A la fe, don fulán, tarde vos acordastes, ca ya non vos valdrá nada si matássedes çient cavallos, que ante lo oviérades a començar, ca ya bien nos conosçemos.

'E vos, señor conde, si aquel vuestro criado quiere casar con tal mugier, si fuere él tal commo aquel mançebo, consejalde que case seguramente, ca él savrá commo ha de pasar en su casa; mas si non fuere tal que entienda lo que deve fazer o lo quel cunple. dexadle passar por su ventura. E aun conséjovos que con los omnes que ovierdes a fazer, fazed que siempre dedes a entender en qué manera han de passar convusco.'

sword in his hand, he looked around with glaring eyes until, fixing them on his wife, he ordered her to bring him water to wash his hands.

'The wife, expecting no other fate than to be cut to pieces, if she demurred, immediately arose and brought him the water.

' "Ha! thank God you have done so," said he, "otherwise I am so irritated by these senseless brutes that I should have done by you as by them." He afterwards commanded her to help him to meat. She complied; but he told her, in a fearful tone of voice, to beware, as he felt as if he was going mad.

'Thus passed the night; she not daring to speak, but strictly obeying all his orders. After letting her sleep for a short time, he said to her, "Get up, I have been so annoyed that I cannot sleep; take care that nothing disturbs me, and in the meanwhile prepare me a good and substantial meal."

'While it was yet early the following morning, the fathers, mothers, and other relatives came stealthily to the door of the young people, and, hearing no movement, feared the bridegroom was either dead or wounded; and, seeing the bride approach the door alone, were still more alarmed.

'She, seeing them, went cautiously and tremblingly towards them, and exclaimed : "Traitors, what are you doing? How dare you approach this gate? Speak not—be silent, or all of us, you as well as I, are dead."

'When they heard this they were much astonished, and on learning what had taken place the night previous, they esteemed the young man very much who had made so good a commencement in the management of his household; and from that day forward his wife became tractable and complaisant, so that they led a very happy life.

'A few days later, his father-in-law, wishing to follow the example of his son, likewise killed a horse in order to intimidate his wife, but she said to him, "My friend, it is too late to begin now; it would not avail you to kill a hundred horses; we know each other too well."

'And you, Count Lucanor, if your dependant wishes to marry such a woman, if he be like this young man, advise him that he may do it with safety, for he will know how to rule his house : but if he be not likely to act with resolute determination at the beginning, and to sustain his position in his household, advise him to have nothing to do with her. As also I would counsel you in all cases where you have dealings with men to act with that

El conde tovo éste por buen consejo, e fízol assí, e fallósse ende bien.

E porque don Johán lo tovo por buen enxenplo, fízolo escrevir en este libro, e fizo estos viessos que dizen assí:

Si al comienço non muestras qui eres,
Nunca podrás después quando quisieres.

ARCHPRIEST OF HITA
[1283?–1350?]

The literary masterpiece of fourteenth-century Spain—indeed, one of the greatest works of all Spanish literature—is the rollicking Libro de buen amor *by Juan Ruiz, Archpriest of Hita. What few facts we have of this author's life are largely gathered from references in the poem itself. Juan Ruiz was probably born in Alcalá de Henares, and lived in Guadalajara and Toledo. He became Archpriest of Hita, and was, for reasons now unknown, imprisoned for thirteen years by the Archbishop of Toledo. Apparently while still in jail, Hita completed his only work, the* Libro de buen amor—*in 1330 according to one manuscript, in 1343 according to another.*

LIBRO DE BUEN AMOR

AQUÍ DIZE DE CÓMO EL ACIPRESTE RROGÓ A DIOS QUE LE DIESE
GRAÇIA QUE PODIESE FACER ESTE LIBRO

Dios Padre, Dios Fijo, Dios Spíritu Santo:
El que nasçió de Virgen esfuerçe nos de tanto,
Que sienpre lo loemos en prosa é en canto,
Sea de nuestras almas cobertura é manto.

El que fizo el çielo, la tierra é la mar
Él me dé la su graçia é me quiera alunbrar,
Que pueda de cantares un librete rrimar,
Que los que lo oyeren, puedan soláz tomar.

Tú, Señor é Dios mío, que al ome formeste,
Enforma é ayuda a mí, tu açipreste,
Que pueda facer *Libro de Buen Amor* aqueste,
Que los cuerpos alegre é á las almas preste.

decision which will leave them no room to think that you can be
imposed upon.'

The Count thought this a very good example, and Don Juan
had it written in this book, and made these lines, saying :

> Who would not for life be a henpeck'd fool
> Must show, from the first, that he means to rule.

JAMES YORK

Its seven thousand-odd verses vary greatly both in metrical form and subject-matter. Though he primarily gives a picaresque account of his own amorous adventures (so that, he piously states, others may learn the ways of mundane love and thus avoid its pitfalls), the Archpriest also includes numerous digressions—fables, serious religious poems, love poems, advice on courting, an allegory on Lent, etc. The entire work presents a rich view of fourteenth-century society, seen through the merry, if satirical, eyes of a man who truly loved life.

THE BOOK OF GOOD LOVE

THE ARCHPRIEST'S PRAYER

God the Father, God the Son, and God the Holy Ghost,
May He who was of Virgin born inspire us through His Host
That we in song and spoken word may praise His being most,
And may the mantle of His grace become our bravest boast.

May He who formed the sweeping heavens, made the land and sea,
Upon me concentrate His grace and shine His light on me
'Til I compose a book of songs that will so joyous be
All men who hear them will forget their present misery.

Thou gracious God who first set man upon his earthly march,
Inspire and aid this priest of Thine whom thou createdst arch
For I a book on love divine would write for souls that parch
And I would stiffen up their smocks with love's old-fashioned
  starch.

Sy queredes, señores, oyr un buen soláz,
Ascuchad el rromanze, sosegadvos en paz:
Non vos diré mintira en quanto en él iaz';
Ca por todo el mundo se usa é se faz'.

E porque mijor sea de todos escuchado,
Fablarvos he por trobas é por cuento rrimado:
Es un decir fermoso é saber sin pecado.
Rrazón más plazentera, ffablar más apostado.

Non cuydés que es libro de neçio devaneo
Nin tengades por chufa algo que en él leo:
Ca segund buen dinero yaze en vil correo,
Asy en feo libro yaze saber non feo.

El axenúz de fuera negro más que caldera,
Es de dentro muy blanco, más que la peñavera;
Blanca farina yaze so negra cobertera,
Açucar dulce é blanco yaze en vil cañavera.

So la espina yaze la rrosa, noble flor;
So fea letra yaze saber de grand dotor;
Como so mala capa yaze buen bevedor,
Asy so mal tabardo yaze *El Buen Amor*.

Enxienplo de la propiedat que'l dinero ha

Mucho faz' el dinero, mucho es de amar:
Al torpe faze bueno é ome de prestar,
Ffaze correr el coxo é al mudo fablar,
El que non tiene manos, dyneros quier' tomar.

Sea un ome nesçio é rudo labrador,
Los dyneros le fazen fidalgo é sabydor,
Quanto más algo tiene, tanto es de más valor;
El que non há dineros, non es de sy señor.

Sy tovyeres dyneros, avrás consolaçión,
Plazer é alegría é del papa ración,
Conprarás parayso, ganarás salvaçión:
Do son muchos dineros, es mucha bendiçión.

So, gentlemen, if you would hear a hearty, merry tale,
Come all who heavy laden are and I'll your ears regale,
I shall not tell you silly lies nor spin some romance stale
But sing of things just as they are, of men and women hale.

And that I may the best secure the whole of your attention
I'll trick the story out in rhymes of my supreme invention—
While in its pretty style you'll find no word unfit to mention.
No, you will find my broadest jokes conform to strict convention.

Don't think this is a foolish book replete with giddy verse,
Nor hold the jests therein contained as something even worse;
For oft, as goodly money lies within a filthy purse,
A messy book may likewise hold much wisdom sound and terse.

The fennel seed is kettle-black, as black as poison bane,
But inside all its meat is white as is the marmot's mane.
And whitest flour is wont to lie within the darkest grain,
While sugar sweet and white resides within an ugly cane.

There grows upon the crabbèd thorn the rose's noble bloom,
And parchments writ in strangest script great learning oft entomb.
Full many an honest tippler wears a shoddy cape and plume,
And I to sorry covers cheap this Book of Good Love doom.

ELISHA K. KANE

Certain Examples of the Power Which Sir Money Possesses

Much power, indeed, Sir Money has and much for him we dabble,
He makes the dolt a man of worth and sets him o'er the rabble,
He makes the lame leap up and run, he makes the deaf-mute
    babble;
Why those who have no hands at all will after money scrabble!

Suppose a man's an utter fool, a farmer or a boor,
With money he becomes a sage, a knight with prestige sure,
In fact the greater grows his wealth the greater his allure,
While he not even owns himself who is in money poor.

If you have money you can get the blessed consolation
Of worldly bliss, or from the Pope can gain a lofty station,
Or purchase seats in Paradise and buy yourself salvation—
Where wealth is great, there lies the state of beatification.

Yo vy allá en Roma, do es la santidat,
Que todos al dinero fazianl' omilidat,
Grand onrra le fazían con grand solenidat:
Todos á él se omillan como á la magestat.

.   .   .   .   .

Dava muchos juyzios, mucha mala sentençia;
Con malos abogados era su mantenençia,
En tener malos pleitos é fer mal' abenencia;
En cabo por dineros avya penitençia.

El dinero quebranta las cadenas dañosas,
Tyra çepos é grillos, presiones peligrosas;
Al que non da dineros, échanle las esposas:
Por todo el mundo faze cosas maravillosas.

Vy fazer maravillas a do él mucho usava:
Muchos meresçían muerte, que la vida les dava;
Otros eran syn culpa, que luego los matava:
Muchas almas perdía, muchas almas salvava.

Faze perder al pobre su casa é su vyña;
Sus muebles é rayzes todo lo desalyña,
Por todo el mundo cunde su sarna é su tyña,
Do el dinero juzga, ally el ojo guiña.

Él faze cavalleros de neçios aldeanos,
Condes é ricos omes de algunos vyllanos;
Con el dinero andan todos omes loçanos,
Quantos son en el mundo, le besan oy las manos.

.   .   .   .   .

CANTIGA DE SSERRANA

Cerca la Tablada,
La sierra passada,
Falléme con Alda
Á la madrugada.

Ençima del puerto
Cuydéme ser muerto

I noticed over there in Rome where sanctities abound
That every one to Money bowed and humbly kissed the ground,
And paid him many honours with solemnities profound,
Yes, homaged him upon their knees, as slaves a king surround.

.   .   .   .   .

Sir Money causes sentences and unjust dooms at court,
He urges shysters for his sake to sue on false report
With all the sundry other frauds to which they will resort,
In short, for money, one condemned can cut his penance short.

Sir Money breaks those mortal bonds that chain a man for life,
He empties stocks and prisons grim with noisome vermin rife,
But one who has no gold to give must wear the iron wife;
All up and down throughout the world Sir Money causes strife.

Myself have seen real miracles occur through Money's power
As when a man condemned to die is freed within an hour
Or when those innocent the gallows presently devour
Or when a soul is prayed to heaven or damned in Hell to cower.

Sir Money often confiscates a poor man's goods and lands,
His vines, his furniture, and all the things his toil commands.
The world has got the itch and scab of money on its hands;
When Money winks his golden eye, there justice stock-still stands.

Sir Money makes a knight presumptuous from a village clown,
And out of peasant farmers chooses coronet and crown;
With Money anyone can strut in gilt and broidered gown
While all his neighbours kiss his hands and bow their bodies down.

.   .   .   .   .

ELISHA K. KANE

THE SONG OF THE MOUNTAIN GIRL

Tablada I was near
When, passing mountains sheer,
I met Aldea, dear,
As dawn was breaking drear.

Upon that pass I thought
I'd die, for I was caught

De nieve é de frío
É dese rruçío
 É de grand' elada.

Ya á la decida
Dy una corrida:
Fallé una sserrana
Fermosa, loçana,
 É byen colorada.

Díxel' yo a ella:
'Omíllome, bella'.—
Diz': 'Tú, que bien corres,
Aquí non t' engorres:
 Anda tu jornada'.—

Yo l' dix: 'Frío tengo
É por eso vengo
A vos, fermosura:
Quered, por mesura,
 Oy darme posada'.

  . . .

Diz': 'Vente comigo'.—
Levóme consigo,
Dióme buena lunbre,
Com' era costunbre
 De sierra nevada.

Dióm' pan de çenteno
Tyznado, moreno,
Dióme vino malo,
Agrillo é ralo.
 É carne salada.

Dióm queso de cabras;
Dyz': 'Fidalgo, abras
Ese blaço, toma
Un canto de soma,
 Que tengo guardada'.—

In snow and bitter cold
Since numbing mist uprolled
  That season of the year.

Yet on my long descent
I ran like one Hell-bent
And met a mountain girl
With whom a god would curl,
  She was so pink and clear.

Said I unto the jade,
'I doff my hat, fair maid.'
Said she, 'Since you can hop,
Don't think with me to stop,
  But take yourself from here.'

I answered, 'I've a chill,
And for that reason will
Entreat you, pretty one,
So that God's will be done,
  To lodge and give me cheer.'

    ·   ·   ·

Said she, 'All right, come on.'
So quickly we were gone
And she prepared the fire
Which customs there require
  Of every mountaineer.

She gave me bread of rye,
All grimy, dark, and dry;
She gave me watered wine
And meat besoaked in brine
  So that it tasted queer.

She gave me cheese of goat
And said, 'Sir, let your throat
In this brown bread delight
And in this crust of white
  Which I have hoarded here.

Diz': 'Uéspet, almuerça,
É bev' é esfuerça,
Caliéntat' é paga:
De mal no s' te faga
Fasta la tornada.'

.   .   .

DE LAS PROPIEDADES QUE LAS DUEÑAS CHICAS HAN

Quiero abreviarvos, señores, la mi predicación,
Ca siempre me pagé de pequeño sermón
É de dueña pequeña é de breve rrasón:
Ca lo poco é bien dicho finca en el coraçón.

Del que mucho fabla rríen, quien mucho rríe es loco,
Tyene la dueña chica amor grand é non de poco:
Dueñas dy grandes por chicas, por grandes chicas non troco;
Mas las chicas por las grandes non se rrepiente del troco.

De las chicas, que bien diga, el amor me fiso rruego,
Que diga de sus noblesas é quiérolas dezir luego:
Direvos de dueñas chicas, que lo tenedes en juego.
Son frías como la nieve é arden más que 'l fuego:

Son frías de füera; en el amor ardientes,
En cama solaz, trebejo, plasenteras é rrientes.
En casa cuerdas, donosas, sosegadas, bienfasyentes;
Muncho ál fallaredes, ado byen paredes mientes.

En pequeña girgonça yase grand rresplandor,
En açúcar muy poco yase mucho dulçor:
En la dueña pequeña yase muy gran amor:
Pocas palabras cumple al buen entendedor.

Es pequeño el grano de la buena pimienta;
Pero más que la nués conorta é más calyenta:
Así dueña pequeña, sy todo amor consienta,
Non há plaser del mundo, qu' en ella non se sienta.

Como en chica rrosa está mucha color,
E en oro muy poco grand preçio é grand valor,

'Eat well,' said she, 'my guest,
And drink and take your rest;
Get warm and then be gay,
No harm can come your way
Till your return career.

    .   .   .

ELISHA K. KANE

PRAISE OF LITTLE WOMEN

I wish to make my sermon brief,—to shorten my oration,—
For a never-ending sermon is my utter detestation :
I like short women,—suits at law without procrastination,—
And am always most delighted with things of short duration.

A babbler is a laughing-stock; he's a fool who's always grinning;
But little women love so much, one falls in love with sinning.
There are women who are very tall, and yet not worth the winning,
And in the change of short for long repentance finds beginning.

To praise the little women Love besought me in my musing;
To tell their noble qualities is quite beyond refusing :
So I'll praise the little women, and you'll find the thing amusing;
They are, I know, as cold as snow, whilst flames around diffusing.

They're cold without, whilst warm within the flame of Love is
    raging;
They're gay and pleasant in the street,—soft, cheerful, and
    engaging;
They're thrifty and discreet at home,—the cares of life assuaging :
All this and more;—try, and you'll find how true is my presaging.

In a little precious stone what splendour meets the eyes !
In a little lump of sugar how much of sweetness lies !
So in a little woman love grows and multiplies :
You recollect the proverb says,—*A word unto the wise.*

A pepper-corn is very small, but seasons every dinner
More than all other condiments, although 't is sprinkled thinner :
Just so a little woman is, if Love will let you win her,—
There's not a joy in all the world you will not find within her.

And as within the little rose you find the richest dyes,
And in a little grain of gold much price and value lies,

Como en poco balsamo yase grand buen olor:
Ansy en chica dueña yase muy grand amor.

Como rroby pequeño tyene muncha bondad,
Color, vertud é precio, noblesa é claridad:
Asy dueña pequeña tiene muncha beldad,
Fermosura é donayre, amor é lealtad.

Chica es la calandria é chico el rroysyñor;
Pero más dulçe canta, que otra ave mayor:
La muger, por ser chica, por eso non es pior;
Con doñeo es más dulce, que açucar nin flor.

Son aves pequeñuelas papagayo é orior;
Pero cualquiera dellas es dulçe gritador,
Adonada, fermosa, preçiada cantador:
Bien atal es la dueña pequeña con amor.

En la muger pequeña non ha conparación:
Terrenal parayso es é consolaçión,
Solás é alegría, plaser é bendiçión.
¡Mijor es en la prueva, qu' en la salutaçión!

Syenpre quis' muger chica, mas que grand' nin mayor.
¡Non es desaguisado de grand mal ser foydor!
Del mal, tomar lo menos: díselo el sabidor:
¡Por end' de las mugeres la menor es mijor!

CANTIGA DE LOORES Á SANTA MARÍA

Quiero seguir
A ty ¡flor de las flores!
Sienpre desir,
Cantar de tus loores,
Non me partir
De te servir.
¡Mejor de las mejores!

Gran fyança,
Hé yo en ty, Señora,
La mi esperança
En ty es toda ora:
¡De tribulança,
Syn tardança,
Vénme librar agora!

As from a little balsam much odour doth arise,
So in a little woman there's a taste of paradise.

Even as the little ruby its secret worth betrays,
Colour, and price, and virtue, in the clearness of its rays,—
Just so a little woman much excellence displays,
Beauty, and grace, and love, and fidelity always.

The skylark and the nightingale, though small and light of wing,
Yet warble sweeter in the grove than all the birds that sing :
And so a little woman, though a very little thing,
Is sweeter far than sugar, and flowers that bloom in spring.

The magpie and the golden thrush have many a thrilling note,
Each as a gay musician doth strain his little throat,—
A merry little songster in his green and yellow coat :
And such a little woman is, when Love doth make her dote.

There's naught can be compared to her, throughout the wide
        creation;
She is a paradise on earth,—our greatest consolation,—
So cheerful, gay, and happy, so free from all vexation :
In fine, she's better in the proof than in anticipation.

If as her size increases are woman's charms decreased,
Then surely it is good to be from all the great released.
Now of two evils choose the less,—said a wise man of the East :
By consequence, of woman-kind be sure to choose the least.

HENRY WADSWORTH LONGFELLOW

HYMN TO THE VIRGIN

Thou Flower of Flowers! I'll follow thee,
    And sing thy praise unweariedly :
Best of the best! O, may I ne'er
        From thy pure service flee!

Lady! to thee I turn my eyes,
    On thee my trusting hope relies;
O, let thy spirit, smiling here,
        Chase my anxieties!

¡Virgen santa!
Yo paso atribulado
Pena atanta
Con dolor atormentado,
E me espanta
Coyta atanta,
Que veo ¡mal pecado!

¡Estrella de la mar!
¡Puerto de folgura!
¡De dolor é pesar
É de tristura
Vénme librar
É conortar,
Señora, del altura!

Nunca falleçe
La tu merçed conplida;
Sienpre guaresçe
De coytas é da vida:
¡Nunca peresçe
Nin entristeçe
Quien á ty non olvida!

Sufro grand mal,
Syn meresçer, á tuerto.
Esquivo tal,
Porqué pienso ser muerto:
Mas ¡tú me val'!
Que non veo ál,
Que me saque á puerto.

ARCHPRIEST OF TALAVERA
[1398?–1470?]

Alfonso Martínez de Toledo, Archpriest of Talavera, is the author of one of the best prose works of the fifteenth century. Written in 1438, El Corbacho

EL CORBACHO

De cómo la Muger parlera siempre fabla de fechos agenos

La muger, ser mucho parlera, regla general es dello: que non es muger que non quisiese siempre fablar e ser escuchada. E non es de

Most Holy Virgin! tired and faint,
I pour my melancholy plaint;
Yet lift a tremulous thought to thee,
Even 'midst mortal taint.

Thou Ocean-Star! Thou Port of Joy!
From pain, and sadness, and annoy,
O, rescue me! O, comfort me,
Bright Lady of the Sky!

Thy mercy is a boundless mine;
Freedom from care, and life are thine:
He recks not, faints not, fears not, who
Trusts in thy power divine.

I am the slave of woe and wrong,
Despair and darkness guide my song;
Do thou avail me, Virgin! thou
Waft my weak bark along!

HENRY WADSWORTH LONGFELLOW

(a title borrowed from Boccaccio) contains a lively satirical description of the customs of the time, with special emphasis on the habits of women—and their faults.

THE SCOURGE

Of How the Talkative Woman Always Speaks of That Which Does Not Concern Her

For a woman to be very talkative is the general rule: for there is no woman who does not like to talk endlessly and be heard. And

su costumbre dar logar a que otra fable delante della; e, si el dia vn año durase, nunca se fartaria de fablar e non se enojaria dia nin noche. E, por ende, verás muchas mugeres que de tener mucha continuaçion de fablar, quando non han con quien fablar, están fablando consigo mesmas, entre sí. Por ende, verás vna muger que es vsada de fablar, las bocas de diez ombres atapar e vençerles fablando e maldiziendo.

Quando razon non le vale, ¡bia a porfiar!, e con esto nunca los secrectos de otro a otra podria çelar. Antes te digo que te deves guardar de aver palabras con muger que algund secreto tuyo sepa, como del fuego: que, sabe, como suso dixe, non guarda lo que dize con ira la muger, avnque el tal secreto de muerte fuese, o venial; o lo que más secreto le encomendares, aquello está reptando e escarvando por lo dezir e publicar, en tanto que todavia fallarás las mugeres por rençonçillos, por renconadas e apartados diziendo, fablando de sus vezinas e de sus comadres e de sus fechos, e mayormente de los agenos. Siempre están fablando, librando cosas agenas: aquéllacómo bive, qué tiene, cómo anda, cómo casó e cómo la quieresu marido mal, cómo ella se lo meresçe, cómo en la iglesia oyó dezir tal cosa; e la otra responde otra cosa, e asi pasan su tiempo despendiendolo en locuras e cosas vanas, que aquí espaçificarlas seria imposible. Por ende, general regla es que donde quier que ay mugeres ay de muchas nuevas.

Alleganse las benditas en vn tropel, muchas matronas, otras moças de menor e mayor edad: e comiençan e non acaban, diziendo de fijas agenas, de mugeres estrañas (en el invierno al fuego, en el verano a la frescura) dos o tres oras, sin más estar diziendo: 'Tal, la muger de tal, la fija de tal, a osadas ¿quién se la vee? ¿quién non la conosçe? ¡Ovejuela de Sant Blas, corderuela de Sant Anton, quien en ella se fiase!', etc. Responde luego la otra: '¡O, bien si lo sopiesedes cómo es de mala lengua! ¡ravia, Señor! ¡allá irá! Por Nuestro Señor Dios, embaçada estariades, comadre: ¡quién se la vee, simplezilla!', etc. Todo el dia estarán mal fablando.

E si quieres saber de mugeres nuevas, vete al forno, a las bodas, a la iglesia: que alli nunca verás sinon fablar la vna a la oreja de la otra, e reirse la vna de la otra, e tomar las vnas compañias con las malquerientes de las otras; e afeitarse e arrearse a porfia, avnque sopiesen fazer malbarato de su cuerpo por aver joyas e ir las vnas más arreadas que las otras, diziendo: '¡Pues mal gozo vean de mí si

it is not her wont to give another woman a chance to speak in her presence; and even if each day lasted a year, she would never tire of talking and she would not be displeased day or night. And for that reason you will see many women who, from habit of talking continuously, talk to themselves when they have no one else to talk to. Therefore you will see a woman who is a good talker stop the mouths of ten men and overwhelm them in talking and cursing.

When logic is not on her side she begins to wrangle, and when that happens she cannot keep any secrets. I warn you that as you would guard yourself from fire, so should you beware of having words with a woman who knows some secret of yours: for know, as I have said above, that a woman speaking in anger does not watch what she says. And whether the secret be a matter of life and death or a trivial thing, it cries and gnaws within her to be told and broadcast. Thus you will find women in nooks, on street corners, in secluded spots, talking of their neighbours and friends and of their deeds, and generally of what does not concern them. They are always talking, meddling in other people's affairs: how so and so lives, what she owns, how she behaves, how she married and how her husband does not love her (and for good reason), how in church one heard such-and-such, and the other one answers thus-and-so. And in this way women spend their time, wasting it on nonsense and frivolous things, which it would be impossible to list here. Wherefore it is a general rule that wherever there are women there is a lot of news.

The little darlings throng together—some, matrons, and others, of varying ages—and they start and never finish, talking about other people's daughters, about other women. In winter by the fire, in summer out-of-doors, they go on for two or three hours, without saying more than: 'this one, the wife of that one, the daughter of the other one, upon my word, who looks at her? Who does not know her? Pity the poor lamb who trusts her!' etc. Then another answers: 'And if you only knew what an evil tongue she has! By the Good Lord, my dear, you would blush to hear her, and who even pays attention to her, the little fool!' etc. All day they speak ill of others.

And if you seek news from women, go to the ovens, to a wedding, to church, for there you will find them always whispering in each other's ear, and one making fun of another, and joining those who wish evil to the rest. And they vie with one another in painting and decorating themselves, even if they have to sell their bodies to own jewels, so long as they can be better-dressed than the others, saying: 'May the devil take me if next Sunday you put a better

el otro domingo que viene tú me pasas el pie delante!' Ayuntanse las vnas loçanas de vn barrio contra las otras galanas de la otra vezindad: '¡Pues agora veamos a quáles mirarán más, e quáles serán las más fabladas e presçiadas! ¿quiça si piensan que non somos para plaça? ¡ mejor que non ellas, avnque les pese e mal pese, sí somos, en verdad! ¡ Yuy, amiga! ¿non vedes cómo nos miran de desgaire? ¿quieres que les demos vna corredura e vna ladradura? Riamonos la vna con la otra e fablemonos asi a la oreja mirando fazia ellas, e vereis cómo se correrán; o antes que ellas se levanten, pasemos aina delante dellas, porque los que miraren a ellas, en pasando nosotras, fagan primero a nosotras reverençia antes que non a ellas: e esta les daremos en barva avnque les pese, quanto a lo primero'.

E estas, e otras infinitas cosas largas de escrevir, estudian las mugeres e vrden en tanto que nunca donde van e se ayuntan fazen sino fablar e murmurar, e de agenos fechos contractar. Do podemos dezir la muger ser muy parlera e de secretos muy mal guardadora. Por ende, quien dellas non se fia non sabe qué prenda tiene; e quien de sus fechos se apartare e más las olvidare, bivirá más en seguro: desto yo le aseguro.

MARQUÉS DE SANTILLANA
[1398–1458]

Íñigo López de Mendoza, Marquis of Santillana, was not only one of the most powerful noblemen of his day but also an extraordinarily cultured man and writer of uncommon artistry.

He left a number of didactic works in prose and verse. But the greatest fame of the Marquis of Santillana stems from his short and delicately beautiful lyric poems. His serranillas (mountain songs) are especially

SERRANILLA VI

(De la Finojosa)

Moça tan fermosa
Non vi en la frontera,
Como una vaquera
De la Finojosa.

foot forward than I.' The beauties of one neighbourhood join forces
against the lovelies of another district : 'Well, let us see now at
whom men will look the most, and who will be most discussed and
admired. Do you think we are not good enough to appear in public?
Better than they, whether they like it or not. Oh, my dear, do you
see how angrily they're looking at us? Why do we not put them to
shame and ridicule? Let us laugh among ourselves and whisper into
each other's ear, looking in their direction, and you will see how
they will run away; or before they get up, let us pass quickly in
front of them, because the men who are looking at them will have
to bow to us first when we go by, and we shall throw it in their
teeth about our being first.'

And these and an infinity of other things, too lengthy to relate,
women study and plot, for wherever they go and gather they never
do anything but talk and gossip and meddle in other people's
affairs. Wherefore we may say that woman is very talkative and a
very poor keeper of secrets. Therefore he who puts no trust in them
does not know what security he has, and he who keeps away from
their dealings and most disregards them will live in greatest tran-
quillity, of this I assure you.

SEYMOUR RESNICK

delightful, and the Serranilla de la Finojosa *given here has always been a
popular favourite. He also wrote forty-two sonnets in the Italian manner,
which are thought to be the first of that type in the Spanish language, and
was the author of Spain's first document of literary criticism—the* Proemio
e carta al Condestable de Portugal.

MOUNTAIN SONG VI

(De la Finojosa)

I ne'er on the border
Saw girl fair as Rosa,
The charming milk-maiden
Of Sweet Finojosa.

Faziendo la vía
Del Calatraveño
A Sancta María,
Vencido del sueño,
Por tierra fragosa
Perdí la carrera,
Do vi la vaquera
De la Finojosa.

En un verde prado
De rosas e flores,
Guardando ganado
Con otros pastores,
La vi tan graciosa
Que apenas creyera
Que fuesse vaquera
De la Finojosa.

Non creo las rosas
De la primavera
Sean tan fermosas
Nin de tal manera
(fablando sin glosa),
Si antes sopiera
De aquella vaquera
De la Finojosa.

Non tanto mirara
Su mucha beldad,
Porque me dexara
En mi liberdad.
Mas dixe:—'Donosa'
(por saber quién era),
'¿Dónde es la vaquera
'De la Finojosa?'

Bien como riendo,
Dixo:—'Bien vengades;
'Que ya bien entiendo
'Lo que demandades:
'Non es deseosa
'De amar, nin lo espera,
'Aquessa vaquera
'De la Finojosa.'

Once making a journey
  To Santa Maria
Of Calatraveño,
  From weary desire
Of sleep, down a valley
  I strayed, where young Rosa
I saw, the milk-maiden
  Of lone Finojosa.

In a pleasant green meadow,
  'Midst roses and grasses,
Her herd she was tending,
  With other fair lasses;
So lovely her aspect,
  I could not suppose her
A simple milk-maiden
  Of rude Finojosa.

I think not primroses
  Have half her smile's sweetness,
Or mild, modest beauty—
  I speak with discreetness.
O, had I beforehand
  But known of this Rosa,
The handsome milk-maiden
  Of far Finojosa,—

Her very great beauty
  Had not so subdued,
Because it had left me
  To do as I would!
I have said more, O fair one,
  By learning 'twas Rosa,   JEREMIAH
The charming milk-maiden   HOLMES
  Of sweet Finojosa.   WIFFEN

The shepherdess laughed
  And said: 'Be at rest;
I sense all too well
  What you would request.
Finojosa's shepherdess
  Does not desire
And does not intend
  To yield to love's fire.' NICHOLSON B. ADAMS

CANCIÓN

Si tú deseas a mí
Yo non lo sé;
Pero yo deseo a ti
En buena fe.

E non a ninguna más
Asy lo ten:
Nin es, ni será jamás
Otra mi bien.

En tan buena ora te vi
E te fablé
Que del todo te me di
En buena fe.

Yo soy tuyo, non lo dubdes,
Sin fallir;
E non pienses al, ni cuydes,
Sin mentir.

Después que te conosçí
Me captivé,
E sesso e saber perdí
En buena fe.

A ti amo e amaré
Toda sazón,
E siempre te serviré
Con grand razón:

Pues la mejor escojí
De quantas sé,
E non finjo nin fengí
En buena fe.

POEM

Whether you love me
I cannot tell.
But that I love you,
This I know well.

You and none other
Hold I so dear.
This shall be always,
Year upon year.

When first I saw you,
So it befell.
I gave you all things—
This I know well.

Myself I gave you
Ever in fee.
Doubt then of all things
But doubt not me.

Since first I saw you,
Under your spell,
All my wits wander,
This I know well.

Still have I loved you,
Still shall I love,
Love you and serve you
All things above.

Her I have chosen
None doth excel.
Trust me, I feign not,
This I know well.

                    JOHN PIERREPONT RICE

JORGE MANRIQUE
[1440?–1479]

Jorge Manrique, a young man of illustrious lineage who died fighting for Queen Isabel, achieved immortality in Spanish literature for his Coplas por la muerte de su padre. *This beautiful elegy—worthy of being printed in letters of gold, according to Lope de Vega—was composed upon the death*

COPLAS POR LA MUERTE DE SU PADRE

Recuerde el alma dormida,
Abive el seso y despierte,
   Contemplando
Cómo se passa la vida,
Cómo se viene la muerte
   Tan callando;
Cuán presto se va el plazer,
Cómo después de acordado,
   Da dolor,
Cómo, a nuestro parescer,
Cualquiera tiempo passado
   Fué mejor.

Pues si vemos lo presente
Cómo en un punto se es ido
   Y acabado,
Si juzgamos sabiamente,
Daremos lo no venido
   Por passado.
No se engañe nadie, no,
Pensando que ha de durar
   Lo que espera
Más que duró lo que vió,
Pues que todo ha de passar
   Por tal manera.

Nuestras vidas son los ríos
Que van a dar en la mar,
   Que es el morir:
Allí van los señoríos
Derechos a se acabar
   Y consumir;
Allí los ríos caudales,

of Manrique's valiant father, Don Rodrigo, in 1476. The entire forty stanzas were rendered into English by Henry Wadsworth Longfellow, and the translation, from which the following excerpts are taken, is itself a work of art.

ODE ON THE DEATH OF HIS FATHER

O, Let the soul her slumbers break!
Let thought be quickened, and awake,—
   Awake to see
How soon this life is past and gone,
And death comes softly stealing on,
   How silently!
Swiftly our pleasures glide away :
Our hearts recall the distant day
   With many sighs;
The moments that are speeding fast
We heed not; but the past—the past—
   More highly prize.

Onward its course the present keeps,
Onward the constant current sweeps,
   Till life is done;
And did we judge of time aright,
The past and future in their flight
   Would be as one.
Let no one fondly dream again
That Hope and all her shadowy train
   Will not decay;
Fleeting as were the dreams of old,
Remembered like a tale that's told,
   They pass away.

Our lives are rivers, gliding free
To that unfathomed, boundless sea,
   The silent grave :
Thither all earthly pomp and boast
Roll, to be swallowed up and lost
   In one dark wave.
Thither the mighty torrents stray,

Allí los otros medianos
Y más chicos,
Allegados son iguales,
Los que biven por sus manos
Y los ricos.

. . .

Este mundo es el camino
Para el otro, que es morada
Sin pesar;
Mas cumple tener buen tino
Para andar esta jornada
Sin errar.
Partimos cuando nascemos,
Andamos mientra bivimos,
Y llegamos
Al tiempo que fenescemos;
Assí que cuando morimos
Descansamos.

. . .

Ved de cuán poco valor
Son las cosas tras que andamos
Y corremos,
Que, en este mundo traidor,
Aun primero que muramos
Las perdemos:
Dellas desfaze la edad,
Dellas casos desastrados
Que acaescen,
Dellas, por su calidad,
En los más altos estados
Desfallescen.

Dezidme, la fermosura,
La gentil frescura y tez
De la cara,
La color y la blancura,
Cuando viene la vejez
¿Cuál se para?
Las mañas y ligereza

Thither the brook pursues its way,
    And tinkling rill.
There all are equal. Side by side,
The poor man and the son of pride
    Lie calm and still.

                    .   .   .

This world is but the rugged road
Which leads us to the bright abode
    Of peace above;
So let us choose that narrow way
Which leads no traveller's foot astray
    From realms of love.
Our cradle is the starting-place;
In life we run the onward race,
    And reach the goal;
When, in the mansions of the blest,
Death leaves to its eternal rest
    The weary soul.

                    .   .   .

Behold of what delusive worth
The bubbles we pursue on earth,
    The shapes we chase,
Amid a world of treachery!
They vanish ere death shuts the eye,
    And leave no trace.
Time steals them from us—chances strange,
Disastrous accidents, and change,
    That come to all:
Even in the most exalted state,
Relentless sweeps the stroke of fate;
    The strongest fall.

Tell me—the charms that lovers seek
In the clear eye and blushing cheek,—
    The hues that play
O'er rosy lip and brow of snow,—
When hoary age approaches slow,
    Ah, where are they?
The cunning skill, the curious arts,

Y la fuerça corporal
De joventud,
Todo se torna graveza
Cuando llega al arraval
De senectud.

.   .   .

Los estados y riqueza,
Que nos dexan a desora,
   ¿Quién lo duda?
No les pidamos firmeza
Pues que son de una señora
   Que se muda;
Que bienes son de Fortuna
Que rebuelve con su rueda
   Presurosa,
La cual no puede ser una
Ni estar estable ni queda
   En una cosa.

Pero digo que acompañen
Y lleguen hasta la huessa
   Con su dueño:
Por esso no nos engañen,
Pues se va la vida apriessa
   Como sueño.
Y los deleites de acá
Son, en que nos deleitamos,
   Temporales,
Y los tormentos de allá,
Que por ellos esperamos,
   Eternales.

Los plazeres y dulçores
Desta vida trabajada
   Que tenemos,
¿Qué son sino corredores,
Y la muerte la celada
   En que caemos?
No mirando nuestro daño,
Corremos a rienda suelta
   Sin parar:

The glorious strength that youth imparts
  In life's first stage,—
These shall become a heavy weight,
When Time swings wide his outward gate
  To weary age.

.   .   .

Wealth and the high estate of pride
With what untimely speed they glide,
  How soon depart?
Bid not the shadowy phantoms stay,—
The vassals of a mistress they,
  Of fickle heart.
These gifts in Fortune's hands are found;
Her swift-revolving wheel turns round,
  And they are gone!
No rest the inconstant goddess knows,
But changing, and without repose,
  Still hurries on.

Even could the hand of avarice save
Its gilded bawbles, till the grave
  Reclaimed its prey,
Let none on such poor hopes rely,
Life, like an empty dream, flits by,
  And where are they?
Earthly desires and sensual lust
Are passions springing from the dust,—
  They fade and die;
But, in the life beyond the tomb,
They seal the immortal spirit's doom
  Eternally!

The pleasures and delights which mask
In treacherous smiles life's serious task,
  What are they all,
But the fleet coursers of the chase,—
And death an ambush in the race,
  Wherein we fall?
No foe, no dangerous pass, we heed,
Brook no delay,—but onward speed,
  With loosened rein;

Desque vemos el engaño
Y queremos dar la buelta,
No hay lugar.

.   .   .

Essos reyes poderosos
Que vemos por escrituras
    Ya passadas,
Con casos tristes, llorosos,
Fueron sus buenas venturas
    Trastornadas:
Assí que no hay cosa fuerte,
Que a papas y emperadores
    Y perlados,
Assí los trata la Muerte
Como a los pobres pastores
    De ganados.

Dexemos a los troyanos,
Que sus males no los vimos,
    Ni sus glorias;
Dexemos a los romanos,
Aunque oímos y leímos
    Sus estorias,
No curemos de saber
Lo de aquel siglo passado
    Qué fué dello;
Vengamos a lo de ayer,
Que tan bien es olvidado
    Como aquello.

¿Qué se fizo el rey don Juan?
Los infantes de Aragón,
    ¿Qué se fizieron?
¿Qué fué de tanto galán?
¿Qué fué de tanta invención
    Como truxieron?
Las justas y los torneos,
Paramentos, bordaduras,
    Y cimeras,
¿Fueron sino devaneos?
¿Qué fueron sino verduras
    De las eras?

And when the fatal snare is near,
We strive to check our mad career,
But strive in vain.

     •   •   •

Monarchs, the powerful and the strong,
Famous in history and in song
    Of olden time,
Saw, by the stern decrees of fate,
Their kingdoms lost, and desolate
    Their race sublime.
Who is the champion? who the strong?
Pontiff and priest, and sceptred throng?
    On these shall fall
As heavily the hand of Death,
As when it stays the shepherd's breath
    Beside his stall.

I speak not of the Trojan name,—
Neither its glory nor its shame
    Has met our eyes;
Nor of Rome's great and glorious dead,—
Though we have heard so oft, and read,
    Their histories.
Little avails it now to know
Of ages past so long ago,
    Nor how they rolled;
Our theme shall be of yesterday.
Which to oblivion sweeps away,
    Like days of old.

Where is the king, Don Juan? where
Each royal prince and noble heir
    Of Aragon?
Where are the courtly gallantries?
The deeds of love and high emprise,
    In battle done?
Tourney and joust, that charmed the eye,
And scarf, and gorgeous panoply,
    And nodding plume,—
What were they but a pageant scene?
What, but the garlands, gay and green,
    That deck the tomb?

¿Qué se fizieron las damas,
Sus tocados, sus vestidos,
    Sus olores?
¿Qué se fizieron las llamas
De los fuegos encendidos
    De amadores?
¿Qué se fizo aquel trobar,
Las músicas acordadas
    Que tañían?
¿Qué se fizo aquel dançar,
Aquellas ropas chapadas
    Que traían?

.   .   .

Las dádivas desmedidas,
Los edificios reales
    Llenos de oro,
Las vaxillas tan febridas,
Los enriques y reales
    Del tesoro,
Los jaezes, los cavallos
De su gente, y atavíos
    Tan sobrados,
¿Dónde iremos a buscallos?
¿Qué fueron sino rocíos
    De los prados?

.   .   .

Pues aquel grand condestable,
Maestre que conoscimos
    Tan privado,
No cumple que dél se fable,
Sino sólo que lo vimos
    Degollado.
Sus infinitos tesoros,
Sus villas y sus lugares,
    Su mandar,
¿Qué le fueron sino lloros?
¿Qué fuéron sino pesares
    Al dexar?

.   .   .

Where are the high-born dames, and where
Their gay attire, and jewelled hair,
   And odours sweet?
Where are the gentle knights, that came
To kneel, and breathe love's ardent flame,
   Low at their feet?
Where is the song of Troubadour?
Where are the lute and gay tambour
   They loved of yore?
Where is the mazy dance of old,—
The flowing robes, inwrought with gold,
   The dancers wore?

       •   •   •

The countless gifts,—the stately walls,
The royal palaces, and halls
   All filled with gold;
Plate with armorial bearings wrought,
Chambers with ample treasures fraught
   Of wealth untold;
The noble steeds, and harness bright,
And gallant lord, and stalwart knight,
   In rich array;—
Where shall we seek them now? Alas!
Like the bright dew-drops on the grass,
   They passed away.

       •   •   •

Spain's haughty Constable,—the true
And gallant Master,—whom we knew
   Most loved of all,—
Breathe not a whisper of his pride;
He on the gloomy scaffold died,—
   Ignoble fall!
The countless treasures of his care,
His hamlets green and cities fair,
   His mighty power,—
What were they all but grief and shame,
Tears and a broken heart, when came
   The parting hour?

       •   •   •

Tantos duques excelentes,
Tantos marqueses y condes
    Y varones
Como vimos tan potentes,
Di, Muerte, ¿dó los escondes
    Y traspones?
Y las sus claras hazañas
Que fizieron en las guerras
    Y en las pazes,
Cuando tú, cruda, te ensañas,
Con tu fuerça las atierras
    Y desfazes.

Las huestes innumerables,
Los pendones y estandartes
    Y vanderas,
Los castillos impunables,
Los muros y baluartes
    Y barreras,
La cava honda, chapada,
O cualquier otro reparo,
    ¿Qué aprovecha?
Que si tú vienes airada,
Todo lo passas de claro
    Con tu flecha.

.   .   .

Aquel de buenos abrigo,
Amado por virtuoso
    De la gente,
El maestre don Rodrigo
Manrique, tanto famoso
    Y tan valiente;
Sus grandes fechos y claros
No cumple que los alabe,
    Pues los vieron,
Ni los quiero fazer caros,
Pues el mundo todo sabe
    Cuáles fueron.

¡Qué amigo de sus amigos!
¡Qué señor para criados
    Y parientes!

So many a duke of royal name,
Marquis and count of spotless fame,
    And baron brave,
That might the sword of empire wield,—
All these, O Death, hast thou concealed
    In the dark grave!
Their deeds of mercy and of arms,
In peaceful days, or war's alarms,
    When thou dost show,
O Death, thy stern and angry face,
One stroke of thy all-powerful mace
    Can overthrow!

Unnumbered hosts, that threaten nigh,—
Pennon and standard flaunting high,
    And flag displayed,—
High battlements intrenched around,
Bastion, and moated wall, and mound,
    And palisade,
And covered trench, secure and deep,—
All these cannot one victim keep,
    O Death, from thee,
When thou dost battle in thy wrath,
And thy strong shafts pursue their path
    Unerringly!

.   .   .

And he, the good man's shield and shade,
To whom all hearts their homage paid,
    As Virtue's son,—
Roderick Manrique,—he whose name
Is written on the scroll of Fame,
    Spain's champion;
His signal deeds and prowess high
Demand no pompous eulogy,—
    Ye saw his deeds!
Why should their praise in verse be sung?
The name that dwells on every tongue
    No minstrel needs.

To friends a friend;—how kind to all
The vassals of this ancient hall
    And feudal fief!

¡Qué enemigo de enemigos!
¡Qué maestro de esforçados
    Y valientes!
¡Qué seso para discretos!
¡Qué gracia para donosos!
    ¡Qué razón!
¡Qué benigno a los subjetos!
Y a los bravos y dañosos,
    Un león!

.   .   .

No dexó grandes tesoros,
Ni alcançó muchas riquezas
    Ni vaxillas,
Mas fizo guerra a los moros,
Ganando sus fortalezas
    Y sus villas;
Y en las lides que venció,
Muchos moros y cavallos
    Se perdieron;
Y en este oficio ganó
Las rentas y los vassallos
    Que le dieron.

Después de puesta la vida
Tantas vezes por su ley
    Al tablero,
Después de tan bien servida
La corona de su rey
    Verdadero,
Después de tanta hazaña
A que non puede bastar
    Cuenta cierta,
En la su villa de Ocaña
Vino la Muerte a llamar
    A su puerta.

Diziendo: 'Buen cavallero,
Dexad el mundo engañoso
    Y su halago;
Vuestro coraçón de azero
Muestre su esfuerço famoso
    En este trago;

To foes how stern a foe was he!
And to the valiant and the free
　　How brave a chief!
What prudence with the old and wise!
What grace in youthful gayeties!
　　In all how sage!
Benignant to the serf and slave,
He showed the base and falsely brave
　　A lion's rage.

　　　　　・　　　・　　　・

He left no well filled treasury,
He heaped no pile of riches high,
　　Nor massive plate;
He fought the Moors,—and, in their fall,
City and tower and castled wall
　　Were his estate.
Upon the hard-fought battle-ground
Brave steeds and gallant riders found
　　A common grave;
And there the warrior's hand did gain
The rents, and the long vassal train,
　　That conquest gave.

And when so oft, for weal or woe,
His life upon the fatal throw
　　Had been cast down,—
When he had served, with patriot zeal,
Beneath the banner of Castile,
　　His sovereign's crown,—
And done such deeds of valour strong,
That neither history nor song
　　Can count them all;
Then, on Ocaña's castled rock,
Death at his portal came to knock,
　　With sudden call,—

Saying, 'Good Cavalier, prepare
To leave this world of toil and care
　　With joyful mien;
Let thy strong heart of steel this day
Put on its armour for the fray,—
　　The closing scene.

Y pues de vida y salud
Fezistes tan poca cuenta
   Por la fama,
Esfuércese la virtud
Para sofrir esta afruenta
   Que vos llama.

'No se os faga tan amarga
La batalla temerosa
   Que esperáis,
Pues otra vida más larga
De la fama glorïosa
   Acá dexáis.
Aunque esta vida de onor
Tampoco no es eternal
   Ni verdadera,
Mas, con todo, es muy mejor
Que la otra temporal,
   Perescedera.

'Y pues vos, claro varón,
Tanta sangre derramastes
   De paganos,
Esperad el galardón
Que en este mundo ganastes
   Por las manos;
Y con esta confïança,
Y con la fe tan entera
   Que tenéis,
Partid con buena esperança
Que estotra vida tercera
   Ganaréis.'

—'No gastemos tiempo ya
En esta vida mezquina
   Por tal modo,
Que mi voluntad está
Conforme con la divina
   Para todo;
Y consiento en mi morir
Con voluntad plazentera,
   Clara y pura,
Que querer ombre bivir

Since thou hast been, in battle-strife,
So prodigal of health and life,
   For earthly fame,
Let virtue nerve thy heart again;
Loud on the last stern battle-plain
   They call thy name.

'Think not the struggle that draws near
Too terrible for man, nor fear
   To meet the foe;
Nor let thy noble spirit grieve,
Its life of glorious fame to leave
   On earth below.
A life of honour and of worth
Has no eternity on earth,—
   'Tis but a name;
And yet its glory far exceeds
That base and sensual life which leads
   To want and shame.

And thou, brave knight, whose hand has poured
The life-blood of the pagan horde
   O'er all the land,
In heaven shalt thou receive, at length,
The guerdon of thine earthly strength
   And dauntless hand.
Cheered onward by this promise sure,
Strong in the faith entire and pure
   Thou dost profess,
Depart, thy hope is certainty;—
The third—the better life on high
   Shalt thou possess.'

'O Death, no more, no more delay!
My spirit longs to flee away
   And be at rest :—
The will of Heaven my will shall be,—
I bow to the divine decree,
   To God's behest.
My soul is ready to depart,—
No thought rebels,—the obedient heart
   Breathes forth no sigh;
The wish on earth to linger still

Cuando Dios quiere que muera,
Es locura.

. . .

Assí con tal entender,
Todos sentidos umanos
    Conservados,
Cercado de su muger,'
De sus fijos y hermanos
    Y criados,
Dió el alma a quien gela dió,
El cual la ponga en el cielo
    En su gloria,
Y aunque la vida murió,
Nos dexó harto consuelo
    Su memoria.

JUAN ESCRIVÁ
[c. 1490]

The Comendador Escrivá was the author of some refreshingly melodious lyric poems. Beyond this, little is known of the man or his life. His Ven,

CANCIÓN

Ven muerte tan escondida
Que no te sienta comigo,
Porqu' el gozo de contigo
No me torne a dar la vida.

Ven como rayo que hiere,
Que hasta que ha herido
No se siente su ruydo,
Por mejor herir do quiere:
Assí sea tu venida,
Si no, desde aquí me obligo
Qu' el gozo que avré contigo
Me dará de nuevo vida.

Were vain, when 'tis God's sovereign will
That we shall die.'

. . .

And thus the dying warrior prayed,
Without one gathering mist or shade
    Upon his mind,—
Encircled by his family,
Watched by affection's gentle eye,
    So soft and kind,—
His soul to Him who gave it rose.
God lead it to its long repose,
    Its glorious rest!
And, though the warrior's sun has set,
Its light shall linger round us yet,
    Bright, radiant, blest.

HENRY WADSWORTH LONGFELLOW

muerte, tan escondida, *given here, has been translated many times and has been quoted by Cervantes, Calderón and Edgar Allan Poe, among others.*

WELCOME DEATH

Come, gentle death! come silently,—
    And sound no knell, no warning give,
Lest the sweet bliss of welcoming thee
    Should rouse my wearied soul to live.

Come like the rapid lightning's ray,
    That wounds, but while it wounds is still;
It passes, voiceless, on its way,
    And flings its mortal barb at will.
Thus soft, thus calm, thy coming be,
    Else, death! this warning now I give,
That the sweet bliss of welcoming thee
    Will rouse my weary soul to live.

JOHN BOWRING

ANONYMOUS POEMS

Poetry flourished during the first half of the fifteenth century in the court of the poet-king Juan II. Thousands of verse compositions—almost all lyric love poems written in an artificial, affected tone, and often employing intricate metrical forms—are preserved in several cancioneros *dating from this era.*

EL BESO

Pues por besarte, Minguillo,
  Me riñe mi madre a mí;
Vuélveme presto, carillo,
  Aquel beso que te di.
Vuelve el beso con buen pecho
  Porque no haya más reñir;
  A tal podremos decir
Que hemos deshecho lo hecho.
A ti será de provecho,
  El beso volverme a mí;
Vuélveme presto, carillo,
  Aquel beso que te di.
Vuélveme el beso, por Dios,
  (A madre tan importuno)
  Pensarás volverme uno
Y vendrás a tener dos.
En bien avengámonos
  Que no me riñan a mí.
Vuélveme presto, carillo,
  Aquel beso que te di.

AXA Y FÁTIMA Y MARIÉN

Tres morillas me enamoran
En Jaén:
Axa y Fátima y Marién.

Tres morillas tan garridas
Iban a coger olivas,
Y hallábanlas cogidas
En Jaén:
Axa y Fátima y Marién.

Two of the most important collections are the Cancionero de Baena *(c. 1445) and the* Cancionero general *(1511). While the quality of the works contained in these collections has not been highly valued by critics in general, we include two of the better anonymous poems of the period.*

THE KISS

Since for kissing thee, Minguillo,
    Mother's ever scolding me,
Give me swiftly back, thou dear one!
    Give the kiss I gave to thee.
Give me back the kiss—that one now,
    Let my mother scold no more;
    Let us tell her all is o'er:
What was done is all undone now.
Yes! it will be wise, Minguillo,
    My fond kiss to give to me,—
Give me swiftly back, thou dear one!
    Give the kiss I gave to thee.
Give me back the kiss, for mother
    Is impatient—prithee do!
    For that one thou shalt have two;
Give me that, and take another.
Help me—let them be contented,
    Let them not complain of me;
Give me swiftly back, thou dear one!
    Give the kiss I gave to thee.

                                JOHN BOWRING

AXA, FÁTIMA, AND MARIÉN

Three Moorish girls I loved
In Jaén,
Axa and Fátima and Marién.

Three Moorish girls so gay
Went olive-plucking there,
And found them plucked away
In Jaén,
Axa and Fátima and Marién.

Y hallábanlas cogidas
Y tornaban desmaídas
Y las colores perdidas
En Jaén:
Axa y Fátima y Marién.

Tres moricas tan lozanas,
Tres moricas tan lozanas
Iban a coger manzanas
En Jaén:
Axa y Fátima y Marién.

BALLADS

Of particular renown in Spanish literature is its extensive collection of popular poetry—the romances. *Colourful, spirited, intensely rhythmic, these ballads enchant the reader as they sing of life and love, hero and traitor, Moor and Christian, adventure and misadventure, history and legend.*

The old romances *were anonymous poems, transmitted orally for many years. Their structure is based on sixteen-syllable lines with assonance (rhyme of the vowel). The question of the actual origin of the* romances,

EL CONDE ARNALDOS

¡Quién hubiese tal ventura
Sobre las aguas del mar
Como hubo el conde Arnaldos
La mañana de San Juan!
Con un falcón en la mano
La caza iba a cazar,
Y venir vió una galera
Que a tierra quiere llegar;
Las velas traía de seda,
La jarcia de un cendal.
Marinero que la manda,
Diciendo viene un cantar
Que la mar ponía en calma,
Los vientos hace amainar,
Los peces que andan al hondo,
Arriba los hace andar;
Las aves que andan volando,
Las hace al mástil posar.

And found them plucked away
And turned back in dismay,
And pale and sad were they
In Jaén,
Axa and Fátima and Marién.

Three Moorish girls so fair,
Three Moorish girls so fair
Went apple-plucking there
In Jaén,
Axa and Fátima and Marién.

JEAN ROGERS LONGLAND

however, is one of the most puzzling in Spanish literature. Some scholars maintain that they are as old as the early epics, and indeed might be fragments of epics, while others assert that the first were not composed much before the fifteenth century.

In any case, the Spanish ballads were a literary mine for later authors of all nationalities. The German philosopher Hegel termed them 'a string of pearls'.

COUNT ARNALDOS

Oh, who could have such fortune
On the sea so far away
As once had Count Arnaldos
On the morn of St. John's Day.
He was hunting on that morning,
With a falcon on his hand;
When he saw a small ship coming,
Coming to the land.
Its sails they were all silken,
And its rigging lace, but strong,
And the captain on the foredeck
Was singing such a song
That it made the sea all quiet,
And it lulled the wind to sleep,
And it lured the silver fishes
To swim up from the deep.
It drew the birds from Heaven
To rest upon the mast.

—Galera, la mi galera,
Dios te me guarde de mal.—
Allí habló el conde Arnaldos,
Bien oiréis lo que dirá:
—Por Dios te ruego, marinero,
Dígasme ora ese cantar.—
Respondióle el marinero,
Tal respuesta lo fué a dar:
—Yo no digo mi canción
Sino a quien conmigo va.

ROMANCE DEL PRISIONERO

Que por mayo era, por mayo,
cuando hace la calor,
cuando canta la calandria
y responde el ruiseñor,
cuando los enamorados
van a servir al amor;
sino yo, triste, cuitado,
que vivo en esta prisión;
que ni sé cuándo es de día
ni cuándo las noches son,
sino por una avecilla
que me cantaba al albor.
Matómela un ballestero;
déle Dios mal galardón.

ROMANCE DE LA HIJA DEL REY DE FRANCIA

De Francia partió la niña.
De Francia la bien guarnida:
Íbase para París,
Do padre y madre tenía.

Errado lleva el camino,
Errado lleva la guía:
Arrimárase a un roble
Por esperar compañía.

Then up spoke Count Arnaldos,
  Then up he spoke at last :
'For God's sweet sake, oh, Captain,
  A boon I crave of thee;
For I never heard such singing
  On land or on the sea,
Oh, teach me that strange chantey !'
  Then the Captain said, said he :
'I do not sing that chantey
  Save to him who goes with me.'

NICHOLSON B. ADAMS

THE PRISONER

Oh 'tis May, the month of May,
when the season's heat is high,
and the larks above are singing
and the nightingales reply,
and all lovers are a-running
on love's errands far and nigh;
all but me, afflicted, wretched,
that in prison-house do lie;
neither know I when day cometh,
nor when night is passing by,
were it not for one wee birdie,
singing when the dawn is nigh :
but an archer slew my birdie—
may he earn God's curse thereby !

WILLIAM J. ENTWISTLE

THE FRENCH PRINCESS

Towards France a maiden went,
Towards France her course she bent,
Unto Paris,—there to find
Her father and her mother kind.

Far from any known abode
She had wandered from the road,
And rested on a blasted fir,
Waiting for some passenger.

Vió venir un caballero
Que a París lleva la guía.
La niña, desque lo vido,
De esta suerte le decía:

—Si te place, caballero,
Llévesme en tu compañía.
—Pláceme, dijo, señora;
Pláceme, dijo, mi vida.—

Apeóse del caballo
Por hacelle cortesía;
Puso la niña en las ancas
Y él subiérase en la silla.

En el medio del camino
De amores la requería.
La niña, desque lo oyera,
Díjole con osadía:

—Tate, tate, caballero,
No hagáis tal villanía;
Hija soy de un malato
Y de una malatía;

El hombre que a mí llegase,
Malato se tornaría.—
El caballero, con temor,
Palabra no respondía.

A la entrada de París,
La niña se sonreía.
—¿De qué vos reís, señora?
¿De qué vos reís, mi vida?

—Ríome del caballero
Y de su gran cobardía,
¡Tener la niña en el campo
Y catarle cortesía!—

Caballero con vergüenza
Estas palabras decía:
—Vuelta, vuelta, mi señora,
Que una cosa se me olvida.—

Towards her came a cavalier,
He to Paris, too, did steer;
When he met the maiden's eyes,
She address'd him in this guise :

'Wilt thou guide me, cavalier,
If to Paris thou dost steer?'
'Will I guide thee, maiden fair?
Yes, by all my hopes I swear.'

In the middle of the way,
He spoke to her of love and play;
The maid, when she his suit had heard,
Cool'd him with a single word :

'Hush thee, hush thee, gentle knight!
Tho' I look so fair and bright,
Diseas'd I am,—diseas'd I came
From a tainted sire and dame,

'The mortal who with me shall lie
Will waste away until he die!'
The cavalier grew pale to see,
But not a sentence answer'd he.

The maid, when Paris was in sight,
Smil'd until she laughed outright.
'What makes thee smile?' the warrior said;
'What make thee laugh, my pretty maid?'

'I laugh at the weak cavalier;
I hold in scorn the dastard's fear,
Who led me thro' the desert plains
And yet got nothing for his pains.'

The warrior's face with shame was dy'd;
He stammer'd and at length replied :
'We must return the way we've crost,
For a something I have lost.'

La niña, como discreta,
Dijo:—Yo no volvería,
Ni persona, aunque volviese,
En mi cuerpo tocaría:

Hija soy del rey de Francia
Y de la reina Constantina;
El hombre que a mí llegase,
Muy caro le costaría.

ROMANCE DE FONTE-FRIDA

Fonte-frida, Fonte-frida,
   Fonte-frida y con amor,
Do todas las avecicas
   Van tomar consolación,
Si no es la tortolica,
   Que está viuda y con dolor.

Por allí fuera a pasar
   El traidor de ruiseñor;
Las palabras que le dice
   Llenas son de traición:
—Si tú quisieses, señora,
   Yo sería tu servidor.

—Vete de ahí, enemigo,
   Malo, falso, engañador,
Que ni poso en ramo verde
   Ni en prado que tenga flor;
Que si el agua hallo clara
   Turbia la bebía yo;
Que no quiero haber marido
   Porque hijos no haya, no;

No quiero placer con ellos,
   Ni menos consolación.
¡Déjame, triste enemigo,
   Malo, falso, ruin traidor,
Que no quiero ser tu amiga
   Ni casar contigo, no!

'No,' answer'd she, 'I'll not turn back,
To cross with thee yon desert track;
And even tho' we did return
Yet would treat thy love with scorn.

'Daughter of France's royal line,
I boast my birth from Constantine :
The man that makes me shed a tear
I reckon it will cost him dear.'

GEORGE BORROW

FOUNT OF FRESHNESS

Fount of freshness! fount of freshness!
  Fount of freshness and of love!
Where the little birds of spring-time
  Seek for comfort, as they rove;
All except the widowed turtle,—
  Widowed, sorrowing turtle-dove.

There the nightingale—the traitor!—
  Lingered on his giddy way;
And these words of hidden treachery
  To the dove I heard him say :
'I will be thy servant, lady!
  I will ne'er thy love betray.'

'Off! false-hearted, vile deceiver!
  Leave me, nor insult me so :
Dwell I, then, midst gaudy flowerets?
  Perch I on the verdant bough?
Even the waters of the fountain
  Drink I dark and troubled now.
Never will I think of marriage,—
  Never break the widow-vow.

'Had I children, they would grieve me,
  They would wean me from my woe :
Leave me, false one! thoughtless traitor!
  Base one! vain one! sad one! go!
I can never, never love thee,—
  I will never wed thee,—no!'   JOHN BOWRING

EL REINO PERDIDO

Las huestes de don Rodrigo desmayaban y huían
Cuando en la octava batalla sus enemigos vencían.
Rodrigo deja sus tiendas y del real se salía,
Solo va el desventurado sin ninguna compañía;

El caballo de cansado ya moverse no podía,
Camina por donde quiere sin que él le estorbe la vía.
El rey va tan desmayado que sentido no tenía;
Muerto va de sed y hambre, de velle era gran mancilla;

Iba tan tinto de sangre que una brasa parecía.
Las armas lleva abolladas, que eran de gran pedrería;
La espada lleva hecha sierra de los golpes que tenía;
El almete de abollado en la cabeza se hundía;
La cara llevaba hinchada del trabajo que sufría.

Subióse encima de un cerro, el más alto que veía;
Desde allí mira su gente cómo iba de vencida;
De allí mira sus banderas y estandartes que tenía,
Cómo están todos pisados que la tierra los cubría;

Mira por los capitanes que ninguno parecía;
Mira el campo tinto en sangre, la cual arroyos corría.
El triste de ver aquesto gran mancilla en sí tenía,
Llorando de los sus ojos desta manera decía:

'Ayer era rey de España, hoy no lo soy de una villa;
Ayer villas y castillos, hoy ninguno poseía;
Ayer tenia criados y gente que me servía,
Hoy no tengo ni una almena que pueda decir que es mía.

¡Desdichada fué la hora, desdichado fué aquel día
En que nací y heredé la tan grande señoría,
Pues lo había de perder todo junto y en un día!
¡Oh muerte!, ¿por qué no vienes y llevas esta alma mía
De aqueste cuerpo mezquino, pues se te agradecería?'

THE LAMENTATION OF DON RODERICK

The hosts of Don Rodrigo were scattered in dismay,
When lost was the eighth battle, nor heart nor hope had they—
He, when he saw that field was lost, and all his hope was flown,
He turned him from his flying host, and took his way alone.

His horse was bleeding, blind, and lame—he could no farther go;
Dismounted, without path or aim, the King stepped to and fro;
It was a sight of pity to look on Roderick,
For, sore athirst and hungry, he staggered faint and sick.

All stained and strewed with dust and blood, like to some
    smouldering brand
Plucked from the flame Rodrigo shewed—his sword was in his
    hand,
But it was hacked into a saw of dark and purple tint;
His jewelled mail had many a flaw, his helmet many a dint.

He climbed unto a hill top, the highest he could see,
Thence all about of that wide route his last long look took he;
He saw his royal banners, where they lay drenched and torn,
He heard the cry of victory, the Arab's shout of scorn.

He looked for the brave captains that had led the hosts of Spain,
But all were fled except the dead, and who could count the slain!
Where'er his eye could wander, all bloody was the plain,
And while thus he said, the tears he shed run down his cheeks
    like rain :—

'Last night I was the King of Spain—today no king am I;
Last night fair castles held my train, tonight where shall I lie?
Last night a hundred pages did serve me on the knee;
Tonight not one I call mine own :—not one pertains to me.

'O luckless, luckless was the hour, and cursed was the day,
When I was born to have the power of this great signiory!
Unhappy me, that I should see the sun go down tonight!
O Death, why now so slow art thou, why fearest thou to smite?'

JOHN GIBSON LOCKHART

ABENÁMAR, ABENÁMAR

¡Abenámar, Abenámar,
Moro de la morería,
El día que tú naciste
Grandes señales había!
Estaba la mar en calma,
La luna estaba crecida:
Moro que en tal siglo nace
No debe decir mentira.—
Allí respondiera el moro,
Bien oiréis lo que decía:

Yo te la diré, señor,
Aunque me cueste la vida,
Porque soy hijo de un moro
Y una cristiana cautiva;
Siendo yo niño y muchacho
Mi madre me lo decía:
Que mentira no dijese,
Que era grande villanía:
Por tanto, pregunta, rey,
Que la verdad te diría.

Yo te agradezco, Abenámar,
Aquesa tu cortesía.
¿Qué castillos son aquéllos?
¡Altos son y relucían!

El Alhambra era, señor,
Y la otra la mezquita;
Los otros los Alixares,
Labrados a maravilla.
El moro que los labraba
Cien doblas ganaba al día,
Y el día que no los labra
Otras tantas se perdía.
El otro es Generalife,
Huerta que par no tenía;
El otro, Torres Bermejas,
Castillo de gran valía.—

Allí habló el rey don Juan,
Bien oiréis lo que decía:

ABENAMAR, ABENAMAR

O thou Moor of *Morería*,
There were mighty signs and aspects
On the day when thou wert born,
Calm and lovely was the ocean,
Bright and full the moon above.
Moor, the child of such an aspect
Never ought to answer falsely.
Then replied the Moorish captive,
(You shall hear the Moor's reply) :

Nor will I untruly answer,
Though I died for saying truth.
I am son of Moorish sire.
My mother was a Christian slave.
In my childhood, in my boyhood,
Often would my mother bid me
Never know the liar's shame.
Ask thou, therefore, King, thy question.
Truly will I answer thee.

Thank thee, thank thee, Abenamar,
For thy gentle answer, thanks.
What are yonder lofty castles,
Those that shine so bright on high?

That, O King, is the Alhambra,
Yonder is the Mosque of God.
There you see the Alixares,
Works of skill and wonder they;
Ten times ten doubloons the builder
Daily for his hire received;
If an idle day he wasted
Ten times ten doubloons he paid.
Farther is the Generalife,
Peerless are its garden groves.
Those are the Vermilion Towers,
Far and wide their fame is known.

Then spake up the King Don Juan
(You shall hear the Monarch's speech) :

Si tú quisieses, Granada,
Contigo me casaría; daréte en arras y dote
A Córdoba y a Sevilla.

Casada soy, rey don Juan;
Casada soy, ·que no viuda;
El moro que a mí me tiene
Muy grande bien me quería.

LA PÉRDIDA DE ALHAMA

Paseábase el rey moro
Por la ciudad de Granada,
Desde la puerta de Elvira
Hasta la de Vivarrambla.
      '¡Ay de mi Alhama!'

Cartas le fueron venidas
Que Alhama era ganada;
Las cartas echó en el fuego,
Y al mensajero matara.
      '¡Ay de mi Alhama!'

Descabalga de una mula,
Y en un caballo cabalga;
Por el Zacatín arriba
Subido se había al Alhambra.
      '¡Ay de mi Alhama!'

Como en el Alhambra estuvo,
Al mismo punto mandaba
Que se toquen sus trompetas,
Sus añafiles de plata.
      '¡Ay de mi Alhama!'

Y que las cajas de guerra
Apriesa toquen al arma,
Porque lo oigan sus moriscos,
Los de la Vega y Granada.
      '¡Ay de mi Alhama!'

Wouldst thou marry me, Granada,
Gladly would I for thy dowry
Cordoba and Seville give.

I am married, King Don Juan.
King, I am not yet a widow.
Well I love my noble husband.
Well my wedded lord loves me.

ROBERT SOUTHEY

WOE IS ME, ALHAMA

The Moorish King rides up and down,
Through Granada's royal town;
From Elvira's gates to those
Of Bivarambla on he goes.
            Woe is me, Alhama!

Letters to the monarch tell
How Alhama's city fell;
In the fire the scroll he threw,
And the messenger he slew.
            Woe is me, Alhama!

He quits his mule and mounts his horse,
And through the streets directs his course;
Through the street of Zacatín
To the Alhambra spurring in.
            Woe is me, Alhama!

When the Alhambra's walls he gained
On the moment he ordained
That the trumpet straight should sound
With the silver clarion round.
            Woe is me, Alhama!

And when the hollow drums of war
Beat the loud alarm afar,
That the Moors of town and plain
Might answer to the martial strain,
            Woe is me, Alhama!

Los moros que el son oyeron
Que al sangriento Marte llama,
Uno a uno y dos a dos
Juntado se ha gran batalla.
          '¡Ay de mi Alhama!'

Allí hablo un moro viejo,
De esta manera hablara:
—¿Para qué nos llamas, rey,
Para qué es esta llamada?
          '¡Ay de mi Alhama!'

—Habéis de saber, amigos,
Una nueva desdichada:
Que cristianos de braveza
Ya nos han ganado Alhama.
          '¡Ay de mi Alhama!'

Allí habló un alfaquí
De barba cruda y cana:
—¡Bien se te emplea, buen rey,
Buen rey, bien se te empleara!
          '¡Ay de mi Alhama!'

Mataste los Bencerrajes,
Que eran la flor de Granada;
Cogiste los tornadizos
De Córdoba la nombrada.
          '¡Ay de mi Alhama!'

Por eso mereces, rey,
Una pena muy doblada:
Que te pierdas tú y el reino
Y aquí se pierda Granada.—
          '¡Ay de mi Alhama!'

LA CONSTANCIA

Mis arreos son las armas,
     Mi descanso es pelear,
Mi cama las duras peñas,
     Mi dormir siempre velar.

Then the Moors, by this aware,
That bloody Mars recalled them there,
One by one, and two by two,
To a mighty squadron grew.
        Woe is me, Alhama!

Out then spoke an agèd Moor
In these words the King before,
'Wherefore call on us, O King?
What may mean this gathering?'
        Woe is me, Alhama!

'Friends, ye have, alas, to know
Of a most disastrous blow;
That the Christians, stern and bold,
Have obtained Alhama's hold.'
        Woe is me, Alhama!

Out then spake old Alfaquì,
With his beard so white to see,
'Good King! thou art justly served!
Good King! this thou hast deserved.
        Woe is me, Alhama!

'By thee were slain, in evil hour,
The Abencerrage, Granada's flower;
And strangers were received by thee
Of Cordova the chivalry.
        Woe is me, Alhama!

'And for this, O King, is sent
On thee a double chastisement;
Thee and thine, thy crown and realm,
One last wreck shall overwhelm.
        Woe is me, Alhama!

                    LORD BYRON

MY ORNAMENTS ARE ARMS

My ornaments are arms,
   My bed the flinty stone,
My rest is war's alarms,
   My sleep to watch alone.

Las manidas son escuras,
Los caminos por usar,
El cielo con sus mudanzas
Ha por bien de me dañar,
Andando de sierra en sierra
Por orillas de la mar,
Por probar si mi ventura
Hay lugar donde avadar.
Pero por vos, mi señora,
Todo se ha de comportar.

FERNANDO DE ROJAS
[1465?–1541?]

Next to Don Quixote, *the greatest work in all Spanish literature is the extraordinary dramatized novel by Fernando de Rojas,* La Celestina. *The work first appeared in 1499 as the* Comedia de Calisto y Melibea, *in sixteen acts. Later editions bore the title* Tragicomedia de Calisto y Melibea *and contained twenty-one acts. It is universally known, however, by the name of the principal character,* Celestina, *the cynical and avaricious 'go-between'.*

Beyond the fact that he was a converted Jewish lawyer, there exists almost no biographical data on Rojas himself. Indeed, many scholars have questioned his authorship of the tragicomedy, although an acrostic in the work names him as the author, and he was further identified as such in the records of an

LA CELESTINA

ARGUMENTO DE TODA LA OBRA

Calisto fué de noble linaje, de claro ingenio, de gentil disposición, de linda crianza, dotado de muchas gracias, de estado mediano. Fué preso en el amor de Melibea, mujer moza, muy generosa, de alta y serenísima sangre, sublimada en próspero estado, una sola heredera a su padre Pleberio, y de su madre Alisa muy amada. Por solicitud del pungido Calisto, vencido el casto propósito de ella interviniendo Celestina, mala y astuta mujer, con dos sirvientes del vencido Calisto, engañados y por ésta tornados desleales, presa su fidelidad con anzuelo de codicia y de deleite, vinieron los amantes

Through gloomy paths unknown,
Paths which untrodden be,
From rock to rock I go
Along the dashing sea,
And seek from busy woe
With hurrying steps to flee;
But know, fair lady! know,
All this I bear for thee!

JOHN BOWRING

Inquisition trial of the period. Critics now generally agree, however, that Fernando de Rojas wrote most—if not all—of La Celestina.

In any case, its popularity and influence were immense; the work inspired a flood of imitations, adaptations and translations. We have taken our selections from the classic version by James Mabbe (The Spanish Bawd, *1631), which is famous for its raciness and verbosity—the English is about one and a half times as long as the original.*

The argumento *relates briefly the simple plot: an illicit love affair between two young people of aristocratic background, Calisto and Melibea, which is brought to consummation and tragedy by the wiles of Celestina. The greatness of the book lies in the masterly delineation of its characters both major and minor; its vivid and powerful style; and most of all in the brilliant interplay between two spheres—that of the noble and idealistic lovers with the vulgar, realistic world of Celestina and her cohorts.*

THE CELESTINA

THE ARGUMENT

Calisto, who was of lineage noble, of wit singular, of disposition gentle, of behaviour sweet, with many graceful qualities richly endowed, and of a competent estate, fell in love with *Melibea*, of years young, of blood noble, of estate great, and only daughter and heir to her father *Pleberio* and to her mother *Alisa*, of both exceedingly beloved. Whose chaste purpose conquered by the hot pursuit of amorous *Calisto*, *Celestina* interposing herself in the business, a wicked and crafty woman, and together with her two deluded servants of subdued *Calisto*, and by her wrought to be disloyal, their fidelity being taken with the hook of covetousness and pleasure,—those lovers came, and those that served them, to

y los que les ministraron, en amargo y desastroso fin. Para comienzo de lo cual, dispuso la adversa fortuna lugar oportuno, donde a la presencia de Calisto se presentó la deseada Melibea.

ACTO PRIMERO

. . .
CALISTO. Sempronio.
SEMPRONIO. Señor.
CALISTO. Dame acá el laúd.
SEMPRONIO. Señor, vesle aquí.
CALISTO. ¿Cuál dolor puede ser tal,
Que se iguale con mi mal?
SEMPRONIO. Destemplado está ese laúd.
CALISTO. ¿Cómo templará el destemplado? ¿Cómo sentirá el armonía aquél, que consigo está tan discorde? ¿Aquél en quien la voluntad a la razón no obedece? ¿Quién tiene dentro del pecho aguijones, paz, guerra, tregua, amor, enemistad, injurias, pecados, sospechas, todo a una causa? Pero tañe y canta la más triste canción, que sepas.

SEMPRONIO. Mira Nerón de Tarpeya
A Roma como se ardía:
Gritos dan niños y viejos
Y él nada se dolía.
CALISTO. Mayor es mi fuego y menor la piedad de quien ahora digo.

SEMPRONIO. No me engaño yo, que loco está este mi amo.

CALISTO. ¿Qué estás murmurando, Sempronio?
SEMPRONIO. No digo nada.
CALISTO. Di lo que dices, no temas.
SEMPRONIO. Digo que, ¿cómo puede ser mayor el fuego, que atormenta a un vivo, que el que quemó tal ciudad y tanta multitud de gente?
CALISTO. ¿Cómo? Yo te lo diré. Mayor es la llama que dura ochenta años, que la que en un día pasa, y mayor la que mata un ánima, que la que quema cien mil cuerpos. Como de la apariencia a la existencia, como de lo vivo a lo pintado, como de la sombra a lo real, tanta diferencia hay del fuego, que dices, al que me quema. Por cierto, si el del purgatorio es tal, más querría que mi espíritu fuese con los de los brutos animales, que por medio de aquél ir a la gloria de los santos.

a wretched and unfortunate end. For entrance whereunto, adverse fortune afforded a fit and opportune place, where, to the presence of *Calisto*, the desired *Melibea* presented herself.

. . .   ACT I

CALISTO. Sempronio!

SEMPRONIO. Sir.

CALISTO. Reach me that lute.

SEMPRONIO. Sir, here it is.

CALISTO. Tell me what grief so great can be
     As to equal my misery.

SEMPRONIO. This lute, sir, is out of tune.

CALISTO. How shall he tune it, who himself is out of tune? Or how canst thou hear harmony from him who is at such discord with himself? Or how can he do anything well, whose will is not obedient to reason? Who harbours in his breast needles, peace, war, truce, love, hate, injuries and suspicions; and all these at once and from one and the same cause. Do thou therefore take this lute unto thee, and sing me the most doleful ditty thou canst devise.

SEMPRONIO. Nero from Tarpey doth behold
     How Rome doth burn all on a flame;
     He hears the cries of young and old,
     Yet is not grieved at the same.

CALISTO. My fire is far greater and less her pity, whom now I speak of.

SEMPRONIO. I was not deceived when I said my master had lost his wits.

CALISTO. What's that, Sempronio, thou mutterest to thyself?

SEMPRONIO. Nothing, sir, not I.

CALISTO. Tell me what thou saidst : be not afraid.

SEMPRONIO. Marry I said, how can that fire be greater which but tormenteth one living man than that which burnt such a city as that was and such a multitude of men?

CALISTO. How? I shall tell thee. Greater is that flame which lasteth fourscore years than that which endureth but one day, and greater that fire which burneth one soul than that which burneth an hundred thousand bodies. See what difference there is betwixt apparencies and existencies, betwixt painted shadows and lively substances, betwixt that which is counterfeit and that which is real; so great a difference is there betwixt that fire which thou speakest of and that which burneth me.

SEMPRONIO. ¡Algo es lo que digo! ¡A más ha de ir este hecho! No basta loco, sino hereje.

CALISTO. ¿No te digo que hables alto, cuando hablares? ¿Qué dices?

SEMPRONIO. Digo que nunca Dios quiera tal; que es especie de herejía lo que ahora dijiste.

CALISTO. ¿Por qué?

SEMPRONIO. Porque lo que dices contradice la cristiana religión.

CALISTO. ¿Qué a mí?

SEMPRONIO. ¿Tú no eres cristiano?

CALISTO. ¿Yo? Melibeo soy y a Melibea adoro y en Melibea creo y a Melibea amo.

SEMPRONIO. Tú te lo dirás. Como Melibea es grande, no cabe en el corazón de mi amo, que por la boca le sale a borbollones. No es más menester. Bien sé de qué pie cojeas. Yo te sanaré.

CALISTO. Increíble cosa prometes.

SEMPRONIO. Antes fácil. Que el comienzo de la salud es conocer hombre la dolencia del enfermo.

CALISTO. ¿Cuál consejo puede regir lo que en sí no tiene orden ni consejo?

SEMPRONIO. ¡Ja! ¡ja! ¡ja! ¿Esto es el fuego de Calisto? ¿Estas son sus congojas? ¡Como si solamente el amor contra él asestara sus tiros! ¡Oh soberano Dios, cuán altos son tus misterios! ¡Cuánta premia pusiste en el amor, que es necesaria turbación en el amante! Su límite pusiste por maravilla. Parece al amante que atrás queda. Todos pasan, todos rompen, pungidos y esgarrochados como ligeros toros. Sin freno saltan por las barreras. Mandaste al hombre por la mujer dejar el padre y la madre; ahora no sólo aquello, mas a ti y a tu ley desamparan, como ahora Calisto. Del cual no me maravillo, pues los sabios, los santos, los profetas por él te olvidaron.

CALISTO. Sempronio.

SEMPRONIO. Señor.

CALISTO. No me dejes.

SEMPRONIO. De otro temple está esta gaita.

CALISTO. ¿Qué te parece de mi mal?

SEMPRONIO. Que amas a Melibea.

CALISTO. ¿Y no otra cosa?

SEMPRONIO. Harto mal es tener la voluntad en un solo lugar cautiva.

CALISTO. Poco sabes de firmeza.

SEMPRONIO. La perseverancia en el mal no es constancia; mas dureza o pertinacia la llaman en mi tierra. Vosotros los filósofos de Cupido llamadla como quisiereis.

SEMPRONIO. I see, I did not mistake my bias, which, for aught I perceive, runs worse and worse. Is it not enough to shew thyself a fool, but thou must also speak profanely?

CALISTO. Did not I tell thee, when thou speakest, that thou shouldest speak aloud? Tell me what's that thou mumblest to thyself.

SEMPRONIO. Only I doubted of what religion your lovers are.

CALISTO. I am a Melibean, I adore Melibea, I believe in Melibea, and I love Melibea.

SEMPRONIO. My master is all Melibea : who now but Melibea? whose heart not able to contain her, like a boiling vessel venting its heat, goes bubbling her name in his mouth. Well, I have now as much as I desire : I know on which foot you halt, I shall now heal you.

CALISTO. Thou speakest of matters beyond the moon. It is impossible.

SEMPRONIO. O, sir, exceeding easy; for the first recovery of sickness is the discovery of the disease.

CALISTO. What counsel can order that which in itself hath neither counsel nor order?

SEMPRONIO. Ha, ha, ha, Calisto's fire! these, his intolerable pains! as if love had bent his bow, shot all his arrows only against him. Oh Cupid, how high and unsearchable are thy mysteries! What reward hast thou ordained for love, since that so necessary a tribulation attends on lovers? Thou hast set his bounds as marks for men to wonder at : lovers ever deeming, that they only are cast behind, and that others still outstrip them, that all men break through but themselves, like your light-footed bulls, which being let loose in the place, and galled with darts, take over the bars as soon as they feel themselves pricked.

CALISTO. Sempronio.

SEMPRONIO. Sir.

CALISTO. Do not you go away.

SEMPRONIO. This pipe sounds in another tune.

CALISTO. What dost thou think of my malady?

SEMPRONIO. That you love Melibea.

CALISTO. And nothing else?

SEMPRONIO. It is misery enough to have a man's will captivated and chained to one place only.

CALISTO. Thou wot'st not what constancy is.

SEMPRONIO. Perseverance in ill is not constancy, but obstinacy or pertinacy, so they call it in my country; however it please you philosophers of Cupid to phrase it.

CALISTO. Torpe cosa es mentir el que enseña a otro, pues que tú te precias de loar a tu amiga Elicia.

SEMPRONIO. Haz tú lo que bien digo y no lo que mal hago.

CALISTO. ¿Qué me repruebas?

SEMPRONIO. Que sometes la dignidad del hombre a la imperfección de la flaca mujer.

CALISTO. ¿Mujer? ¡Oh grosero! ¡Dios, Dios!

SEMPRONIO. ¿Y así lo crees? ¿O te burlas?

CALISTO. ¿Que me burlo? Por Dios la creo, por Dios la confieso.

. . .

SEMPRONIO. . . . Y porque no te desesperes, yo quiero tomar esta empresa de cumplir tu deseo.

CALISTO. ¡Oh! ¡Dios te dé lo que deseas! ¡Qué glorioso me es oírte; aunque no espero que lo has de hacer!

SEMPRONIO. Antes lo haré cierto.

CALISTO. Dios te consuele. El jubón de brocado, que ayer vestí, Sempronio, vístetele tú.

SEMPRONIO. Prospérete Dios por este y por muchos más, que me darás. De la burla yo me llevo lo mejor. Con todo, si de estos aguijones me da, traérsela he hasta la cama. ¡Bueno ando! Hácelo esto, que me dió mi amo; que, sin merced, imposible es obrarse bien ninguna cosa.

CALISTO. No seas ahora negligente.

SEMPRONIO. No lo seas tú, que imposible es hacer siervo diligente el amo perezoso.

CALISTO. ¿Cómo has pensado de hacer esta piedad?

SEMPRONIO. Yo te lo diré. Días ha grandes que conozco en fin desta vecindad una vieja barbuda, que se dice Celestina, hechicera, astuta, sagaz en cuantas maldades hay. Entiendo que pasan de cinco mil virgos los que se han hecho y deshecho por su autoridad en esta ciudad. A las duras peñas promoverá y provocará a lujuria, si quiere.

CALISTO. ¿Podríala yo hablar?

SEMPRONIO. Yo te la traeré hasta acá. Por eso, aparéjate, sele

CALISTO. It is a foul fault tor a man to belie that which he preacheth to others: for thou thyself takest pleasure in praising thy Elicia.

SEMPRONIO. Do you that good which I say, but not that ill which I do.

CALISTO. Why dost thou reprove me?

SEMPRONIO. Because thou dost subject the dignity and worthiness of a man to the imperfection and weakness of a frail woman.

CALISTO. A woman? O thou blockhead, she's a goddess.

SEMPRONIO. Are you in earnest, or do you but jest?

CALISTO. Jest? I verily believe she is a goddess.

. . .

SEMPRONIO. . . . Do not you despair; myself will take this business in hand, not doubting but to accomplish your desire.

CALISTO. Jove grant thou mayest: howsoever, I am proud to hear thee, though hopeless of ever obtaining it.

SEMPRONIO. Nay, I will assure it you.

CALISTO. Heav'n be thy good speed; my cloth of gold doublet, which I wore yesterday, it is thine, Sempronio. Take it to thee.

SEMPRONIO. I thank you for this, and for many more which you shall give me. My jesting hath turn'd to my good. I hitherto have the better of it. And if my master clap such spurs to my sides, and give me such good encouragements, I doubt not but I shall bring her to his bed. This which my master hath given me is a good wheel to bring the business about: for without reward it is impossible to go well through with anything.

CALISTO. See you be not negligent now.

SEMPRONIO. Nay, be not you negligent; for it is impossible that a careless master should make a diligent servant.

CALISTO. But tell me, how dost thou think to purchase her pity?

SEMPRONIO. I shall tell you. It is now a good while ago, since at the lower end of this street I fell acquainted with an old bearded woman called Celestina, a witch, subtle as the devil, and well practised in all the rogueries and villainies that the world can afford, one who in my conscience hath marred and made up again a hundred thousand maidenheads in this city: such a power and such authority she hath, what by her persuasions and other her cunning devices, that none can escape her: she will move hard rocks, if she list, and at her pleasure provoke them to luxury.

CALISTO. O that I might but speak with her!

SEMPRONIO. I will bring her hither unto you; and therefore prepare yourself for it, and when she comes, in any case use her kindly, be frank and liberal with her; and whilst I go my ways, do you study

gracioso, sele franco. Estudia, mientras voy yo, de decirle tu pena tan bien como ella te dará el remedio.

CALISTO. ¿Y tardas?

SEMPRONIO. Ya voy. Quede Dios contigo.

CALISTO. Y contigo vaya. ¡Oh todopoderoso, perdurable Dios! Tú, que guías los perdidos y los reyes orientales por el estrella precedente a Belén trujiste y en su patria los redujiste, humilmente te ruego que guíes a mi Sempronio, en manera que convierta mi pena y tristeza en gozo y yo indigno merezca venir en el deseado fin.

ACTO CUARTO

CELESTINA. Ahora, que voy sola, quiero mirar bien lo que Sempronio ha temido deste mi camino. Porque aquellas cosas, que bien no son pensadas, aunque algunas veces hayan buen fin, comúnmente crían desvariados efectos. Así que la mucha especulación nunca carece de buen fruto. Que, aunque yo he disimulado con él, podría ser que, si me sintiesen en estos pasos de parte de Melibea, que no pagase con pena, que menor fuese que la vida, o muy amenguada quedase, cuando matar no me quisiesen, manteándome o azotándome cruelmente. Pues amargas cien monedas serían éstas. ¡Ay cuitada de mí! ¡En qué lazo me he metido! ¡Que por mostrarme solícita y esforzada pongo mi persona al tablero! ¿Qué haré, cuitada, mezquina de mí, que ni el salir afuera es provechoso ni la perseverancia carece de peligro? ¿Pues iré o tornarme he? ¡Oh dudosa y dura perplejidad! ¡No sé cuál escoja por más sano! ¡En el osar, manifiesto peligro; en la cobardía, quedaré denostada, perdida! ¿A dónde irá el buey que no are? Cada camino descubre sus dañosos y hondos barrancos. Si con el hurto soy tomada, nunca de muerta o encorozada falto, a bien librar. Si no voy, ¿qué dirá Sempronio? Que todas estas eran mis fuerzas, saber y esfuerzo, ardid y ofrecimiento, astucia

and devise with yourself, to express your pains as well as, I know, she is able to give you remedy.

CALISTO. O but thou stayest too long.

SEMPRONIO. I am gone, sir.

CALISTO. A good luck with thee! You happy powers that predominate human actions, assist and be propitious to my desires, second my intentions, prosper Sempronio's proceedings and his success, in bringing me such an advocatrix as shall, according to his promise, not only negotiate, but absolutely compass and bring to a wished period the preconceived hopes of an incomparable pleasure.

. . .

ACT IV

CELESTINA. Now that I am all alone, I will, as I walk by myself, weigh and consider that which Sempronio feared concerning my travail in this business. For those things which are not well weighed and considered, though sometimes they take good effect, yet commonly fall out ill, so that much speculation brings forth much good fruit. For, although I dissembled with him and did set a good face on the matter, it may be that, if my drift and intent should chance to be found out by Melibea's father, it would cost me little less than my life: or at least, if they should not kill me, I should rest much impaired in my credit, either by their tossing me in a blanket, or by causing me to be cruelly whipped, so that my sweet meats shall have sour sauce, and my hundred crowns in gold be purchased at too dear a rate. Ay, wretched me! into what a labyrinth have I put myself? What a trap am I like to fall into through mine own folly? For that I might shew myself solicitous and resolute, I have put myself upon the hazard of the dice. Woe is me! What shall I do? To go back is not for my profit, and to go on stands not with my safety. Shall I persist; Or shall I desist? In what a strait am I? In what a doubtful and strange perplexity? I know not which I were best to choose. On my daringness dependeth manifest danger, on my cowardice shameful damage. Which way shall the ox go, but he must needs plough? Every way, go which way I will, discovers to my eyes deep and dangerous furrows, desperate downfalls; if I be taken in the mainour, if the theft be found about me, I shall be either killed, or carted with a paper crown set upon my head, having my fault written in great text-letters. But in case I should not go, what will Sempronio then say? 'Is this all thou canst do? Thy power, thy wisdom, thy stoutness, thy courage, thy large promises, thy fair offers, thy tricks, thy subtleties, and the great care forsooth thou wouldest

y solicitud. Y su amo Calisto, ¿qué dirá? ?qué hará? ¿qué pensará, sino que hay nuevo engaño en mis pisadas y que yo he descubierto la celada, por haber más provecho de esta otra parte, como sofística prevaricadora? O si no se le ofrece pensamiento tan odioso, dará voces como loco. Diráme en mi cara denuestos rabiosos. Propondrá mil inconvenientes, que mi deliberación presta le puso, diciendo: Tú, puta vieja, ¿por qué acrecentaste mis pasiones con tus promesas? Alcahueta falsa, para todo el mundo tienes pies, para mí lengua; para todos obra, para mí palabra; para todos remedio, para mí pena; para todos esfuerzo, para mí te faltó; para todos luz, para mí tiniebla. Pues, vieja traidora, ¿por qué te me ofreciste? Que tu ofrecimiento me puso esperanza; la esperanza dilató mi muerte, sostuvo mi vivir, púsome título de hombre alegre. Pues no habiendo efecto, ni tú carecerás de pena ni yo de triste desesperación. ¡Pues triste yo! ¡Mal acá, mal acullá: pena en ambas partes! Cuando a los extremos falta el medio, arrimarse el hombre al más sano, es discreción. Más quiero ofender a Pleberio, que enojar a Calisto. Ir quiero. Que mayor es la vergüenza de quedar por cobarde, que la pena, cumpliendo como osada lo que prometí, pues jamás al esfuerzo desayudó la fortuna. Ya veo su puerta. En mayores afrentas me he visto. ¡Esfuerza, esfuerza, Celestina! ¡No desmayes! Que nunca faltan rogadores para mitigar las penas. Todos los agüeros se aderezan favorables o yo no sé nada de esta arte. Cuatro hombres, que he topado, a los tres llaman Juanes y los dos son cornudos. La primera palabra, que oí por la calle, fué de achaque de amores. Nunca he tropezado como otras veces. Las piedras parece que se apartan y me hacen lugar que pase. Ni me estorban las haldas ni siento cansancio en andar. Todos me saludan. Ni perro me ha ladrado ni ave negra he visto, tordo ni cuervo ni otras nocturnas. Y lo mejor de todo es que veo a Lucrecia a la puerta de Melibea. Prima es de Elicia: no me será contraria.

take; what? are they all come to this?' And his master Calisto,
what will he say? What will he do? Or what will he think? Save
only this, that there is much deceit in my steps, and that I have
discovered this plot to Pleberio, like a prevaricating sophistress or
cunning ambidexter, playing the traitor on both sides, that I might
gain by both? And if he do not entertain so hateful a thought, he
will rail upon me like a madman; he will upbraid me to my face
with most reproachful terms; he will propose a thousand incon-
veniences, which my hasty deliberation was the cause of, saying,
'Out, you old whore; why didst thou increase my passions with
thy promises? False bawd as thou art, for all the world besides thy
feet can walk, for me only thy tongue; others can have works, I
only words. Others can have remedy at thy hands; I only the
man that must endure torment. To all others thy force can extend
itself; and to me is it only wanting. To all others thou art light, to
me darkness. Out, thou old treacherous, disloyal wretch; why didst
thou offer thyself and service unto me? For it was thy offer that
did put me in hope : and that hope did delay my death, prolonged
my life, and did put upon me the title of a glad man. Now, for
that thy promises have not proved effectual, neither shalt thou
want punishment, nor I woeful despair.' So that, look I on which
side I will (miserable woman that I am), it is ill here, and it is ill
there; pain and grief on either hand : but when extremes shall
want their mean, and no means to avoid either the one or the
other, of two evils it is the wiser course to incline to the lesser. And
therefore I had rather offend Pleberio than displease Calisto. Well
then, I will go. For greater will my shame be, to be condemned
for a coward, than my punishment, in daring to accomplish what
I promised. Besides Fortune still friendeth those that are bold and
valiant. Lo, yonder's the gate; I have seen myself in greater danger
than this in my days. Coraggio, coraggio, Celestina; be of good
cheer; be not dismayed : for there are never suitors wanting for
the mitigating and allaying of punishment. All divinations are in
my favour and shew themselves propitious in my proceedings;
or else I am nobody in this my art, a mere bungler, an idiot, an
ass. Of four men that I met by the way three of them were
Johns; whereof two were cuckolds. The first word that I heard
passing along the street, was a love complaint. I have not stumbled
since I came forth, as at other times I used to do. Methinks the
very stones of the street did sunder themselves one from another
to give me way as I passed. Nor did the skirts of my clothes rumple
up in troublesome folds to hinder my feet. Nor do I feel any faint-
ness or weariness in my legs. Every one saluteth me. Not a dog

. . .

MELIBEA. Pide lo que querrás, sea para quien fuere.

CELESTINA. ¡Doncella graciosa y de alto linaje! Tu suave habla y alegre gesto, junto con el aparejo de liberalidad, que muestras con esta pobre vieja, me dan osadía a decírtelo. Yo dejo un enfermo a la muerte, que con sola una palabra de tu noble boca salida, que le lleve metida en mi seno, tiene por fe que sanará, según la mucha devoción que tiene en tu gentileza.

MELIBEA. Vieja honrada, no te entiendo, si más no declaras tu demanda. Por una parte me alteras y provocas a enojo; por otra me mueves a compasión. No te sabría volver respuesta conveniente, según lo poco, que he sentido de tu habla. Que yo soy dichosa, si de mi palabra hay necesidad para salud de algún cristiano. Porque hacer beneficio es semejar a Dios, y el que le da le recibe, cuando a persona digna de él le hace. Y demás de esto, dicen que el que puede sanar al que padece, no haciéndolo, le mata. Así que no ceses tu petición por empacho ni temor.

CELESTINA. El temor perdí mirando, señora, tu beldad. Que no puedo creer que en balde pintase Dios unos gestos más perfectos que otros, más dotados de gracias, más hermosas facciones; sino para hacerlos almacén de virtudes, de misericordia, de compasión, ministros de sus mercedes y dádivas, como a ti. Y pues como todos seamos humanos, nacidos para morir, sea cierto que no se puede decir nacido el que para sí solo nació. Porque sería semejante a los brutos animales, en los cuales aun hay algunos piadosos, como se dice del

that hath once barked at me; I have neither seen any bird of a black feather, neither thrush nor crow, nor any other of the like unlucky nature; and, which is a better sign of good luck than all these, yonder do I see Lucrecia standing at Melibea's gate, which is kinswoman to Elicia; it cannot but go well with us; it is impossible we should miss of our purpose; all is cock-sure.

. . .

MELIBEA. Ask what thou wilt, be it either for thyself or anybody else, whom it pleaseth thee.

CELESTINA. My most gracious and courteous lady, descended of high and noble parentage, your sweet words and cheerful gesture, accompanied with that kind and free proffer, gives boldness to my tongue, to speak what my heart even longeth to utter. I come lately from one, whom I left sick to the death, who only with one word, which should come from your noble mouth, and entrusted in this my bosom to carry it hence with me—I verily assure myself it will save his life, so great is the devotion which he bears to your gentle disposition, and the comfort he would receive by this so great a kindness.

MELIBEA. Good woman, I understand thee not, unless thou deliver thy mind unto me in plain terms. On the one side thou dost anger me and provoke me to displeasure; on the other thou dost move and stir me to compassion. Neither know I how to return thee a convenient answer, because I have not fully comprehended thy meaning; I should think myself happy, if my words might carry that force, as to save the life of any man, though never so mean. For to do good is to be like unto the Deity. Besides he that doth a benefit, receives it, when it is done to a person that desires it. And he that can cure one that is sick, not doing it is guilty of his death; and therefore give not over thy petition, but proceed and fear nothing.

CELESTINA. All fear fled, fair lady, in beholding your beauty. For I cannot be persuaded that Nature did paint in vain one face fairer than another, more enriched with grace and favour, more fashionable and more beautiful than another, were it not to make them magazines of virtue, mansions of mercy, houses of compassion and pity, ministers of her blessings, and dispensers of those good gifts and graces, which in her bounty she hath bestowed upon them, and upon yourself in a more plentiful manner. Besides, sithence we are all mortal and born to die, as also, that it is most certain that he cannot be said truly to be born, who is only born for himself—for then should men be like unto brute beasts, if not worse, amongst which there are some, that are very pitiful : as

unicornio, que se humilla a cualquiera doncella. El perro con todo su ímpetu y braveza, cuando viene a morder, si se echan en el suelo, no hace mal; esto de piedad. ¿Pues las aves? Ninguna cosa el gallo come que no participe y llame las gallinas a comer de ello. El pelícano rompe el pecho por dar a sus hijos a comer de sus entrañas. Las cigüeñas mantienen otro tanto tiempo a sus padres viejos en el nido, cuanto ellos les dieron cebo siendo pollitos. Pues tal conocimiento dió la natura a los animales y aves, ¿por qué los hombres habemos de ser más crueles? ¿Por qué no daremos parte de nuestras gracias y personas a los prójimos, mayormente, cuando están envueltos en secretas enfermedades y tales que, donde está la melecina, salió la causa de la enfermedad?

MELIBEA. Por Dios, sin más dilatar, me digas quién es ese doliente, que de mal tan perplejo se siente, que su pasión y remedio salen de una misma fuente.

CELESTINA. Bien ternás, señora, noticia en esta ciudad de un caballero mancebo, gentilhombre de clara sangre, que llaman Calisto.

MELIBEA. ¡Ya, ya, ya! Buena vieja, no me digas más, no pases adelante. ¿Ese es el doliente por quien has hecho tantas premisas en tu demanda? ¿Por quien has venido a buscar la muerte para ti? ¿Por quien has dado tan dañosos pasos, desvergonzada barbuda? ¿Qué siente ese perdido, que con tanta pasión vienes? De locura será su mal. ¿Qué te parece? ¡Si me hallaras sin sospecha de ese loco, con qué palabras me entrabas! No se dice en vano que el más empecible miembro del mal hombre o mujer es la lengua. ¡Quemada seas, alcahueta falsa, hechicera, enemiga de honestad, causadora de secretos yerros! ¡Jesús, Jesús! ¡Quítamela, Lucrecia, de delante, que me fino, que no me ha dejado gota de sangre en el cuerpo! Bien se lo merece esto y más, quien a estas tales da oídos. Por cierto, si no mirase a mi honestidad y por no publicar su osadía de ese atrevido, yo te hiciera, malvada, que tu razón y vida acabaran en un tiempo.

your unicorn of whom it is reported that he will humble and
prostrate himself at the feet of a virgin; and your dog, for all his
fierceness and cruelness of nature, when he comes to bite another,
if he throw himself down at his feet, he will let him alone and do
him no harm; and this is all out of pity. Again, to come to your
birds and fowls of the air, your cock eateth not anything, but he
first calleth his hens about him and gives them part of his feeding.
The pelican with her beak breaketh up her own breast, that she
may give her very bowels and entrails to her young ones to eat.
The storks maintain their aged parents as long in the nest, as they
did give them food, when they were young and unable to help
themselves. Now, if God and Nature gave such knowledge unto
beasts and birds, why should we that are men, be more cruel one
to another? Why give we not part of our graces and of our persons
to our neighbours? Especially when they are involved and afflicted
with secret infirmities, and those such that, where the medicine is,
thence was the cause of the malady?

MELIBEA. For God's love, without any more dilating tell me who
is this sick man, who feeling such great perplexity, hath both
his sickness and his cure, flowing from one and the selfsame
fountain.

CELESTINA. You cannot choose, lady, but know a young gentleman
in this city, nobly descended, whose name is Calisto.

MELIBEA. Enough, enough! no more, good old woman! not a
word, not a word more, I would advise you! Is this the sick
patient, for whom thou hast made so many prefaces to come to thy
purpose? For what or whom camest thou hither? Camest thou to
seek thy death? Knowest thou for whom, thou bearded impudent,
thou hast trodden these dangerous steps? What ails this wicked
one, that thou pleadest for him with such passion? He is fool-sick,
is he not? Is he in his wits, I trow? What wouldst thou have
thought, if thou shouldst have found me without some suspicion
and jealousy of this fool? What a windlass hast thou fetched, with
what words hast thou come upon me? I see it is not said in vain
that the most hurtful member in a man or woman is the tongue.
I will have thee burned, thou false witch, thou enemy to honesty,
thou causeress of secret errors; fie upon thee, filth! Lucrecia, out
of my sight with her, send her packing; away with her, I pray,
she makes me ready to swoon; ay me, I faint, I die; she hath not
left me one drop of blood in my body! But I well deserve this and
more, for giving ear to such a paltry housewife as she is. Believe
me, were it not that I regarded mine honour, and that I am unwilling to publish to the world his presumptuous audaciousness and

CELESTINA. (*Aparte.*) ¡En hora mala acá vine, si me falta mi conjuro! ¡Ea pues!: bien sé a quién digo. ¡Ce, hermano, que se va todo a perder!

MELIBEA. ¿Aun hablas entre dientes delante de mí, para acrecentar mi enojo y doblar tu pena? ¿Querrías condenar mi honestidad por dar vida a un loco? ¿Dejar a mí triste por alegrar a él y llevar tú el provecho de mi perdición, el galardón de mi yerro? ¿Perder y destruir la casa y la honra de mi padre por ganar la de una vieja maldita como tú? ¿Piensas que no tengo sentidas tus pisadas y entendido tu dañado mensaje? Pues yo te certifico que las albricias, que de aquí saques, no sean sino estorbarte de ofender más a Dios, dando fin a tus días. Respóndeme, traidora, ¿cómo osaste tanto hacer?

CELESTINA. Tu temor, señora, tiene ocupada mi disculpa. Mi inocencia me da osadía, tu presencia me turba en verla irada y lo que más siento y me pena es recibir enojo sin razón ninguna. Por Dios, señora, que me dejes concluir mi dicho, que ni él quedará culpado ni yo condenada. Y verás cómo es todo más servicio de Dios, que pasos deshonestos; más para dar salud al enfermo, que para dañar la fama al médico. Si pensara, señora, que tan de ligero habías de conjeturar de lo pasado nocibles sospechas, no bastara tu licencia para dar osadía a hablar en cosa, que a Calisto ni a otro hombre tocase.

MELIBEA. ¡Jesús! No oiga yo mentar más ese loco, saltaparedes, fantasma de noche, luengo como cigüeña, figura de paramento malpintado; si no, aquí me caeré muerta. ¡Este es el que el otro día me vió y comenzó a desvariar conmigo en razones, haciendo mucho del galán! Dirásle, buena vieja que, ¿si pensó que ya era todo suyo

boldness, I would so handle thee, thou accursed hag, that thy discourse and thy life should have ended both together.

CELESTINA. In an ill hour came I hither, if my spells and conjuration fail me. Go to, go to; I wot well enough to whom I speak. This poor gentleman, this your brother is at the point of death and ready to die.

MELIBEA. Darest thou yet speak before me and mutter words between thy teeth, for to augment my anger and double thy punishment? Wouldst thou have me soil mine honour, for to give life to a fool, to a madman? Shall I make myself sad to make him merry? Wouldst thou thrive by my loss? And reap profit by my perdition? And receive remuneration by my error? Wouldst thou have me overthrow and ruin my father's house and honour, for to raise that of such an old rotten bawd as thou art? Dost thou think I do not perceive thy drift? That I do not track thee step by step? Or that I understand not thy damnable errand? But I assure thee, the reward that thou shalt get thereby, shall be no other, save, that I may take from thee all occasion of farther offending heaven, to give an end to thy evil days. Tell me, traitor as thou art, how didst thou dare to proceed so far with me?

CELESTINA. My fear of you, madame, doth interrupt my excuse; but my innocency puts new courage into me : your presence again disheartens me, in seeing you so angry. But that which grieves and troubles me most, is that I receive displeasure without any reason, and am hardly thought on without a cause. Give me leave, good lady, to make an end of my speech, and then will you neither blame it nor condemn me : then will you see that I rather seek to do good service, than endeavour any dishonest course; and that I do it more to add health to the patient, than to detract anything from the fame and worth of the physician. And had I thought that your ladyship would so easily have made this bad construction out of your late noxious suspicion, your licence should not have been sufficient warrant to have emboldened me to speak anything, that might concern Calisto, or any other man living.

MELIBEA. Let me hear no more of this madman, name not this fool unto me; this leaper over walls; this hobgoblin; this nightwalker; this fantastical spirit; long-shanked, like a stork; in shape and proportion, like a picture in arras, that is ill-wrought; or an ill-favoured fellow in an old suit of hangings; say no more of him, unless you would have me to fall down dead where I stand! This is he who saw me the other day, and began to court me with I know not what extravagant phrases, as if he had not been well in his wits, professing himself to be a great gallant. Tell him, good

y quedaba por él el campo, porque holgué más de consentir sus necedades, que castigar su yerro, quise más dejarle por loco, que publicar su grande atrevimiento? Pues avísale que se aparte de este propósito y serle ha sano; si no, podrá ser que no haya comprado tan cara habla en su vida. Pues sabe que no es vencido, sino el que se cree serlo, y yo quedé bien segura y él ufano. De los locos es estimar a todos los otros de su calidad. Y tú tórnate con su mesma razón; que respuesta de mí otra no habrás ni la esperes. Que por demás es ruego a quien no puede haber misericordia. Y da gracias a Dios, pues tan libre vas de esta feria. Bien me habían dicho quien tú eras y avisado de tus propriedades, aunque ahora no te conocía.

CELESTINA. (*Aparte.*) ¡Más fuerte estaba Troya y aun otras más bravas he yo amansado! Ninguna tempestad mucho dura.

MELIBEA. ¿Qué dices, enemiga? Habla, que te pueda oír. ¿Tienes disculpa alguna para satisfacer mi enojo y excusar tu yerro y osadía?

CELESTINA. Mientras viviere tu ira, más dañará mi descargo. Que estás muy rigurosa y no me maravillo: que la sangre nueva poca calor ha menester para hervir.

MELIBEA. ¿Poca calor? ¿Poco lo puedes llamar, pues quedaste tú viva y yo quejosa sobre tan gran atrevimiento? ¿Qué palabra podías tú querer para ese tal hombre, que a mí bien me estuviese? Responde, pues dices que no has concluído: ¡quizá pagarás lo pasado!

CELESTINA. Una oración, señora, que le dijeron que sabías de santa Polonia para el dolor de las muelas. Asimismo tu cordón, que es fama que ha tocado todas las reliquias, que hay en Roma y Jeru-

old woman, if he think that I was wholly his and that he had won the field, because it pleased me rather to consent to his folly than correct his fault, and yield to his errand than chastise his error, that I was willing rather to let him go like a fool as he came than to publish this his presumptuous enterprise. Moreover, advise him that the next way to have his sickness leave him is to leave off his loving, and wholly to relinquish his purpose, if he purpose to impart health to himself; which if he refuse to do, tell him from me, that he never bought words all the days of his life at a dearer rate. Besides, I would have him know that no man is overcome, but he that thinks himself so to be. So shall I live secure, and be contented. But it is evermore the nature of fools, to think others like themselves. Return thou with this very answer unto him; for other answer of me shall he none, nor never hope for any : for it is but in vain to entreat mercy of him, of whom thou canst not have mercy. And for thine own part, thou mayest thank God, that thou scapest hence scot-free; I have heard enough of you heretofore and of all your good qualities, though it was not my hap to know you.

CELESTINA. Troy stood out more stoutly, and held out longer. And many fiercer dames have I tamed in my days. Tush! No storm lasteth long.

MELIBEA. You mine enemy, what say you? Speak out, I pray, that I may hear you. Hast thou anything to say in thy excuse, whereby thou mayest satisfy my anger, and clear thyself of this thy error and bold attempt?

CELESTINA. Whilst your choler lives, my cause must needs die. And the longer your anger lasteth, the less shall my excuse be heard. But I wonder not that you should be thus rigorous with me : for a little heat will serve to set young blood a-boiling.

MELIBEA. Little heat, say you? Indeed thou mayest well say little; because thyself yet lives, whilst I with grief endure thy great presumption. What words canst thou demand of me for such a one as he is, that may stand with my good? Answer to my demand, because thou sayest thou hast not yet concluded. And perhaps thou mayest pacify me for that which is past.

CELESTINA. Marry, a certain charm, madame, which as he is informed by many of his good friends, your ladyship hath, which cureth the toothache; as also that same admirable girdle of yours, which is reported to have been found and brought from Cumae the cave there, and was worn, 'tis thought, by the Sibylla or prophetess of that place; which girdle, they say, hath such a singular and peculiar property and power, with the very touch to

salem. Aquel caballero, que dije, pena y muere de ellos. Esta fué mi venida. Pero, pues en mi dicha estaba tu airada respuesta, padézcase él su dolor, en pago de buscar tan desdichada mensajera. Que, pues en tu mucha virtud me faltó piedad, también me faltará agua, si a la mar me enviara. Pero ya sabes que el deleite de la venganza dura un momento y el de la misericordia para siempre.

MELIBEA. Si eso querías, ¿por qué luego no me lo expresaste? ¿Por qué me lo dijiste en tan pocas palabras?

CELESTINA. Señora, porque mi limpio motivo me hizo creer que, aunque en menos lo propusiera, no se había de sospechar mal. Que, si faltó el debido preámbulo, fué porque la verdad no es necesario abundar de muchas colores. Compasión de su dolor, confianza de tu magnificencia ahogaron en mi boca al principio la expresión de la causa. Y pues conoces, señora, que el dolor turba, la turbación desmanda y altera la lengua, la cual había de estar siempre atada con el seso, ¡por Dios! que no me culpes. Y si él otro yerro ha hecho, no redunde en mi daño, pues no tengo otra culpa, sino ser mensajera del culpado. No quiebre la soga por lo más delgado. No seas la telaraña, que no muestra su fuerza sino contra los flacos animales. No paguen justos por pecadores. Imita la divina justicia, que dijo: El ánima que pecare, aquella misma muera; a la humana, que jamás condena al padre por el delito del hijo ni al hijo por el del padre. Ni es, señora, razón que su atrevimiento acarree mi perdición. Aunque, según su merecimiento, no tendría en mucho que fuese él el delincuente y yo la condenada. Que no es otro mi oficio, sino servir a los semejantes: de esto vivo y de esto me arreo. Nunca fué mi voluntad enojar a unos por agradar a otros, aunque hayan dicho a tu merced en mi ausencia otra cosa. Al fin, señora, a la firme verdad el viento del vulgo no la empece. Una sola soy en este limpio trato.

abate and ease any ache or anguish whatsoever. Now this gentleman I told you of, is exceedingly pained with the toothache, and even at death's door with it. And this was the true cause of my coming : but since it was my ill hap to receive so harsh and unpleasing an answer, let him still for me continue in his pain, as a punishment due unto him for sending so unfortunate a messenger. For since in that muchness of your virtue I have found much of your pity wanting, I fear me he would also want water, should he send me to the sea to fetch it. And you know, sweet lady, that the delight of vengeance and pleasure of revenge endureth but a moment, but that of pity and compassion continueth for ever and ever.

MELIBEA. If this be that thou wouldst have, why didst thou not tell me of it sooner? Why wentest thou about the bush with me? What needed all those circumstances? Or why didst thou not deliver it in other words?

CELESTINA. Because my plain and simple meaning made me believe that, though I should have proposed it in any other words whatsoever, had they been worse than they were, yet would you not have suspected any evil in them. For, if I were failing in the fitness of my preface and did not use so due and convenient a preamble as I should have done, it was because truth needeth no colours. The very compassion that I had of his pain, and the confidence of your magnificency did choke in my mouth, when I first began to speak, the expression of the cause. And for that you know, lady, that sorrow works turbation, and turbation doth disorder and alter the tongue, which ought always to be tied to the brain, for heaven's love, lay not the fault on me; and if he hath committed an error, let not that redound to my hurt; for I am no farther blameable of any fault, than as I am the messenger of the faulty. Break not the rope where it is weakest. Be not like the cobweb, which never shows its force but on poor little flies. No human law condemns the father for the son's offence, nor the son for the father's : nor indeed, lady, is it any reason, that his presumption should occasion my perdition; though considering his desert, I should not greatly care that he should be the delinquent and myself be condemned, since that I have no other trade to live by, save to serve such as he is; this is my occupation, this I make my happiness. Yet withal, madame, I would have you to conceive, that it was never in my desire to hurt one, to help another, though behind my back your ladyship hath perhaps been otherwise informed of me. But the best is, it is not the vain breath of the vulgar that can blast the truth; assuredly I mean nothing in this,

En toda la ciudad pocos tengo descontentos. Con todos cumplo, los que algo me mandan, como si tuviese veinte pies y otras tantas manos.
MELIBEA. No me maravillo, que un solo maestro de vicios dicen que basta para corromper un gran pueblo. Por cierto, tantos y tales loores me han dicho de tus falsas mañas, que no sé si crea que pedías oración.
CELESTINA. Nunca yo la rece, y si la rezare no sea oída, si otra cosa de mí se saque, aunque mil tormentos me diesen.
MELIBEA. Mi pasada alteración me impide reír de tu disculpa. Que bien sé que ni juramento ni tormento te torcerá a decir verdad, que no es en tu mano.
CELESTINA. Eres mi señora. Téngote de callar, hete yo de servir, hasme tú de mandar. Tu mala palabra será víspera de una saya.
MELIBEA. Bien la has merecido.
CELESTINA. Si no la he ganado con la lengua, no la he perdido con la intención.
MELIBEA. Tanto afirmas tu ignorancia, que me haces creer lo que puede ser. Quiero pues en tu dudosa disculpa tener la sentencia en peso y no disponer de tu demanda al sabor de ligera interpretación. No tengas en mucho ni te maravilles de mi pasado sentimiento, porque concurrieron dos cosas en tu habla, que cualquiera de ellas era bastante para me sacar de seso: nombrarme ese tu caballero, que conmigo se atrevió a hablar, y también pedirme palabra sin más causa, que no se podía sospechar sino daño para mi honra. Pero pues todo viene de buena parte, de lo pasado haya perdón. Que en alguna manera es aliviado mi corazón, viendo que es obra pía y santa sanar los apasionados y enfermos.
CELESTINA. ¡Y tal enfermo, señora! Por Dios, si bien le conocieses, no le juzgases por el que has dicho y mostrado con tu ira. En Dios y en mi alma, no tiene hiel; gracias, dos mil; en franqueza, Alejandro;

but only plain and honest dealing. I do little harm to any; I have as few enemies in this city, as a woman can have : I keep my word with all men; and what I undertake, I perform as faithfully as if I had twenty feet and so many hands.

MELIBEA. I now wonder not that your ancients were wont to say that one only teacher of vice was sufficient to mar a great city. For I have heard such and so many tales of thy false and cunning tricks, that I know not whether I may believe thy errand was for this charm.

CELESTINA. Never let me pray, or if I pray, let me never be heard, if you can draw any other thing from me, though I were to be put to a thousand torments!

MELIBEA. My former late anger will not give me leave to laugh at thy excuse. For I wot very well that neither oath nor torment shall make thee to speak the truth. For it is not in thy power to do it.

CELESTINA. You are my good lady and mistress, you may say what you list, and it is my duty to hold my peace; you must command, and I must obey, but your rough language, I hope, will cost your ladyship an old petticoat.

MELIBEA. And well hast thou deserved it.

CELESTINA. If I have not gained it with my tongue, I hope I have not lost it with my intention.

MELIBEA. Thou dost so confidently plead thy ignorance, that thou makest me almost ready to believe thee; yet will I in this thy so doubtful an excuse hold my sentence in suspense, and will not dispose of thy demand upon the relish of so light an interpretation. Neither for all this would I have thee to think much of it, nor make it any such wonder that I was so exceedingly moved; for two things did concur in thy discourse, the least of which was sufficient to make me run out of my wits. First, in naming this gentleman unto me, who thus presumed to talk with me : then, that thou shouldst entreat me for him, without any further cause given; which could not but engender a strong suspicion of hurt to my honour. But since all is well meant and no harm intended, I pardon all that is past; for my heart is now somewhat lightened, sithence it is a pious and a holy work to cure the sick and help the distressed.

CELESTINA. Ay, and so sick, madame, and so distressed, that, did you know it as well as I, you would not judge him the man, which in your anger you have censured him to be. By my fay, the poor gentleman hath no gall at all, no ill meaning in his heart. He is endued with thousands of graces; for bounty he is an Alexander;

en esfuerzo, Héctor; gesto, de un rey; gracioso, alegre; jamás reina en él tristeza. De noble sangre, como sabes. Gran justador, pues verlo armado, un san Jorge. Fuerza y esfuerzo, no tuvo Hércules tanta. La presencia y facciones, disposición, desenvoltura, otra lengua había menester para las contar. Todo junto semeja ángel del cielo. Por fe tengo que no era tan hermoso aquel gentil Narciso, que se enamoró de su propa figura, cuando se vió en las aguas de la fuente. Ahora, señora, tiénele derribado una sola muela, que jamás cesa de quejarse.
MELIBEA. ¿Y qué tanto tiempo ha?
CELESTINA. Podrá ser, señora, de veinte y tres años: que aquí está Celestina, que le vió nacer y le tomó a los pies de su madre.
MELIBEA. Ni te pregunto eso ni tengo necesidad de saber su edad; sino qué tanto ha que tiene el mal.
CELESTINA. Señora, ocho días. Que parece que ha un año en su flaqueza. Y el mayor remedio que tiene es tomar una vihuela y tañe tantas canciones y tan lastimeras, que no creo que fueron otras las que compuso aquel emperador y gran músico Adriano, de la partida del ánima, por sufrir sin desmayo la ya vecina muerte. Que aunque yo sé poco de música, parece que hace aquella vihuela hablar. Pues, si acaso canta, de mejor gana se paran las aves a oírle, que no aquel antiguo, de quien se dice que movía los árboles y piedras con su canto. Siendo éste nacido no alabaran a Orfeo. Mirá, señora, si una pobre vieja, como yo, si se hallará dichosa en dar la vida a quien tales gracias tiene. Ninguna mujer le ve, que no alabe a Dios, que así le pintó. Pues, si le habla acaso, no es más señora de sí, de lo que él ordena. Y pues tanta razón tengo, juzgá, señora, por bueno mi propósito, mis pasos saludables y vacíos de sospecha.

for strength an Hector; he has the presence of a prince; he is fair in his carriage, sweet in his behaviour, and pleasant in his conversation; there is no melancholy or other bad humour, that reigneth in him; nobly descended, as yourself well knows; a great tilter; and to see him in his armour, it becomes him so well, that you would take him to be another Saint George. Hercules had not that force and courage as he hath; his deportment, his person, his feature, his disposition, his agility and activeness of body, had need of another manner of tongue to express it than mine. Take him all together and for all in all, you shall not find such another; and for admired form, a miracle : and I am verily persuaded that that fair and gentle Narcissus, who was enamoured with his own proper beauty, when, as in a glass, he viewed himself in the water, was nothing so fair as he, whom now one poor tooth with the extremity of its pain doth so torment, that he doth nothing but complain.

MELIBEA. The age, I pray, how long hath he had it?

CELESTINA. His age, madame? Marry, I think he is about some three and twenty. For here stands she, who saw him born, and took him up from his mother's feet.

MELIBEA. This is not that which I ask thee; nor do I care to know his age. I ask thee how long he hath been troubled with his toothache?

CELESTINA. Some eight days, madame, but you would think he had had it a year, he is grown so weak with it, and the greatest ease and best remedy he hath, is to take his viol, whereto he sings so many songs, and in such doleful notes, that I verily believe they did far exceed those which that great emperor and musician Hadrian composed concerning the soul's departure from the body, the better to endure without dismayment his approaching death. For, though I have but little skill in music, methinks he makes the viol, when he plays thereon, to speak; and when he sings thereunto, the birds with a better will listen unto him than to that musician of old, which made the trees and stones to move. Had he been born then, Orpheus had lost his prey. Weigh then with yourself, sweet lady, if such a poor old woman as I am, have not cause to count myself happy, if I may give life unto him, to whom the heavens have given so many graces? Not a woman that sees him, but praiseth Nature's workmanship, whose hand did draw so perfect a piece; and, if it be their hap to talk with him, they are no more mistresses of themselves, but are wholly at his disposing; and of commanders, desire to be commanded by him. Wherefore, seeing I have so great reason to do for him, conceive, good lady,

MELIBÉA. ¡Oh cuánto me pesa con la falta de mi paciencia! Porque siendo él ignorante y tú inocente, habéis padecido las alteraciones de mi airada lengua. Pero la mucha razón me releva de culpa, la cual tu habla sospechosa causó. En pago de tu buen sufrimiento, quiero cumplir tu demanda y darte luego mi cordón. Y porque para escribir la oración no habrá tiempo sin que venga mi madre, si esto no bastare, ven mañana por ella muy secretamente.

LUCRECIA (*Aparte.*) ¡ Ya, ya, perdida es mi ama! ¿Secretamente quiere que venga Celestina? ¡Fraude hay! ¡Más le querrá dar, que lo dicho! . . .

GIL VICENTE
[1470?–1539?]

Gil Vicente, Portuguese poet and dramatist, is one of the glories of the literature of that country and the founder of Portugal's national drama. He also stands high, however, in Spanish literature, for he wrote eleven of his

MUY GRACIOSA ES LA DONCELLA

Muy graciosa es la doncella,
¡Cómo es bella y hermosa!

Digas tú, el marinero
Que en las naves vivías,
Si la nave o la vela o la estrella
Es tan bella.

Digas tú, el caballero
Que las armas vestías,
Si el caballo o las armas o la guerra
Es tan bella.

Digas tú, el pastorcico
Que el ganadico guardas,
Si el ganado o las valles o la sierra
Es tan bella.

my purpose to be fair and honest, my courses commendable and free from suspicion and jealousy.

MELIBEA. O how I am fallen out with mine own impatience! How angry with myself that, he being ignorant and thou innocent of any intended ill, thou hast endured the distemperature of my enraged tongue! But the great reason I had for it, frees me from any fault of offence, urged thereunto by thy suspicious speeches : but in requital of thy sufferance, I will forthwith fulfil thy request and likewise give thee my girdle. And, because I have not the leisure to write the charm, till my mother comes home, if this will not serve the turn, come secretly for it tomorrow morning.

LUCRECIA. Now, now, is my mistress quite undone. All the world cannot save her; she will have Celestina come secretly tomorrow. I smell a rat; there is a pad in the straw; I like not this *come secretly tomorrow*; I fear me she will part with something more than words. . . .

JAMES MABBE

forty-three plays in Spanish. Indeed he frequently introduced some Spanish even into his Portuguese plays. Almost all of Gil Vicente's works are based on popular themes, and his poetry is noteworthy for its lyric charm and richness of language.

GRACE AND BEAUTY HAS THE MAID

Grace and beauty has the maid;
Could anything more lovely be?

Sailor, you who live on ships,
Did you ever see
Any ship or sail or star
As beautiful as she?

Knight of war, in armour clad,
Did you ever see
Horse or arms or battle-field
As beautiful as she?

Shepherd, you who guard youɪ flock,
Did you ever see
Cattle, vale, or mountain range
As beautiful as she?

ALICE JANE McVAN

DICEN QUE ME CASE YO

Dicen que me case yo:
No quiero marido, no.
Más quiero vivir segura
N'esta sierra a mi soltura
Que no estar en ventura
  Si casaré bien o no.
Dicen que me case yo:
No quiero marido, no.

Madre, no seré casada
Por no ver vida cansada,
Y quizá mal empleada
  La gracia que Dios me dió.
Dicen que me case yo:
No quiero marido, no.

No será ni es nacido
Tal para ser mi marido;
Y pues que tengo sabido
  Que la flor yo me la só,
Dicen que me case yo:
No quiero marido, no.

GARCILASO DE LA VEGA
[1503?–1536]

To Garcilaso and his friend Juan Boscán, Spanish poetry owes the introduction of certain Italian metres, notably the eleven-syllable line and the sonnet. Boscán is important only as an innovator, but Garcilaso was, in addition, the finest poet of the first half of the sixteenth century. His total

ÉGLOGA PRIMERA

El dulce lamentar de dos pastores,
Salicio juntamente y Nemoroso,
He de contar, sus quejas imitando;
Cuyas ovejas al cantar sabroso
Estaban muy atentas, los amores,
De pacer olvidadas, escuchando . . .

.   .   .

CASSANDRA'S SONG OF CELIBACY

They say, ' 'Tis time, go, marry! go!'
But I'll no husband! Not I! no!
For I would live all carelessly,
Amidst these hills, a maiden free,
And never ask, nor anxious be,
    Of wedded weal or woe.
Yet still they say, 'Go, marry! go!'
But I'll no husband! not I! no!

So, mother, think not I shall wed,
And through a tiresome life be led,
Or use, in folly's ways instead,
    What grace the heavens bestow.
Yet still they say, 'Go, marry! go!'
But I'll no husband! not I! no!

The man has not been born, I ween,
Who as my husband shall be seen;
And since what frequent tricks have been
    Undoubtedly I know,
In vain they say, 'Go, marry! go!'
For I'll no husband! not I! no!

                          GEORGE TICKNOR

*literary production is slight, but highly polished, and his poetry was held
in the highest esteem by the writers of the Golden Age. In contrast to his
turbulent life as courtier and soldier (he died on the battlefield), Garcilaso's
verse deals only with the theme of love.*

ECLOGUE I

The sweet lament of two Castilian swains,
Salicio's love and Nemoroso's tears,
In sympathy I sing, to whose loved strains
Their flocks, of food forgetful, crowding round,
Were most attentive. . . .

            .   .   .

Saliendo de las ondas encendido,
Rayaba de los montes el altura
El sol, cuando Salicio, recostado
Al pie de un alta haya, en la verdura,
Por donde un agua clara con sonido
Atravesaba el fresco y verde prado;
Él, con canto acordado
Al rumor que sonaba,
Del agua que pasaba,
Se quejaba tan dulce y blandamente
Como si no estuviera de allí ausente
La que de su dolor culpa tenía;
Y así, como presente,
Razonando con ella, le decía.

Salicio

¡Oh más dura que mármol a mis quejas,
Y al encendido fuego en que me quemo
Más helada que nieve, Galatea!
Estoy muriendo, y aun la vida temo;
Témola con razón, pues tú me dejas;
Que no hay, sin ti, el vivir para qué sea.
Vergüenza he que me vea
Ninguno en tal estado,
De ti desamparado,
Y de mí mismo yo me corro agora.
¿De un alma te desdeñas ser señora,
Donde siempre moraste, no pudiendo
Della salir un hora?
Salid sin duelo, lágrimas, corriendo.

Por ti el silencio de la selva umbrosa,
Por ti la esquividad y apartamiento
Del solitario monte me agradaba;
Por ti la verde hierba, el fresco viento,
El blanco lirio y colorada rosa
Y dulce primavera deseaba.

The sun, from rosy billows risen, had rayed
With gold the mountain tops, when at the foot
Of a tall beech romantic, whose green shade
Fell on a brook, that, sweet-voiced as a lute,
Through lively pastures wound its sparkling way,
Sad on the daisied turf Salicio lay;
And with a voice in concord to the sound
Of all the many winds, and waters round,
As o'er the mossy stones they swiftly stole,
Poured forth in melancholy song his soul
Of sorrow with a fall
So sweet, and aye so mildly musical,
None could have thought that she whose seeming guile
Had caused his anguish, absent was the while,
But that in very deed the unhappy youth
Did, face to face, upbraid her questioned truth.

Salicio

More hard than marble to my mild complaints,
And to the lively flame with which I glow,
Cold, Galatea, cold as winter snow!
I feel that I must die, my spirit faints,
And dreads continuing life; for, alienate
From thee, life sinks into a weary weight,
To be shook off with pleasure; from all eyes
I shrink, ev'n from myself despised I turn,
And left by her for whom alone I yearn,
My cheek is tinged with crimson; heart of ice!
Dost thou the worshipped mistress scorn to be
Of one whose cherished guest thou ever art;
Not being able for an hour to free
Thine image from my heart?
This dost thou scorn? in gentleness of woe
Flow forth, my tears, 'tis meet that ye should flow!

.   .   .

Through thee the silence of the shaded glen,
Through thee the horror of the lonely mountain
Pleased me no less than the resort of men;
The breeze, the summer wood, and lucid fountain,
The purple rose, white lily of the lake,
Were sweet for thy sweet sake;

¡Ay, cuánto me engañaba!
¡Ay, cuán diferente era
Y cuán de otra manera
Lo que en tu falso pecho se escondía!
Bien claro con su voz me lo decía
La siniestra corneja repitiendo
La desventura mía.
Salid sin duelo, lágrimas, corriendo.

.   .   .

Tu dulce habla ¿en cúya oreja suena?
Tus claros ojos ¿a quién los volviste?
¿Por quién tan sin respeto me trocaste?
Tu quebrantada fe ¿dó la pusiste?
¿Cuál es el cuello que, como en cadena,
De tus hermosos brazos anudaste?
No hay corazón que baste,
Aunque fuese de piedra,
Viendo mi amada hiedra,
De mí arrancada, en otro muro asida,
Y mi parra en otro olmo entretejida,
Que no se esté con llanto deshaciendo
Hasta acabar la vida.
Salid sin duelo, lágrimas, corriendo.

.   .   .

Con mi llorar las piedras enternecen
Su natural dureza y la quebrantan;
Los árboles parece que se inclinan;
Las aves que me escuchan, cuando cantan,
Con diferente voz se condolecen,
Y mi morir cantando me adivinan.
Las fieras que reclinan
Su cuerpo fatigado,
Dejan el sosegado
Sueño por escuchar mi llanto triste.

For thee the fragrant primrose, dropt with dew,
Was wished when first it blew !
Of how completely was I in all this
Myself deceiving ! oh the different part
That thou wert acting, covering with a kiss
Of seeming love, the traitor in thy heart !
This is my severe misfortune, long ago,
Did the soothsaying raven, sailing by
On the black storm, with hoarse sinister cry,
Clearly presage; in gentleness of woe,
Flow forth, my tears, 'tis meet that ye should flow.

      •   •   •

In the charmed ear of what beloved youth
Sounds thy sweet voice? on whom revolvest thou
Thy beautiful blue eyes? on whose proved truth
Anchors thy broken faith? who presses now
Thy laughing lip, and hopes thy heaven of charms,
Locked in the embraces of thy two white arms?
Say thou, for whom hast thou so rudely left
My love, or stolen, who triumphs in the theft?
I have not yet a bosom so untrue
To feeling, nor a heart of stone, to view
My darling ivy, torn from me, take root
Against another wall or prosperous pine,
To see my virgin vine
Around another elm in marriage hang
Its curling tendrils and empurpled fruit,
Without the torture of a jealous pang,
Ev'n to the loss of life; in gentle woe,
Flow forth, my tears, 'tis meet that ye should flow !

      •   •   •

Over my griefs the mossy stones relent
Their natural durity, and break; the trees
Bend down their weeping boughs without a breeze,
And full of tenderness, the listening birds,
Warbling in different notes, with me lament,
And warbling prophesy my death; the herds
That in the green meads hang their heads at eve,
Wearied, and worn, and faint,
The necessary sweets of slumber leave,
And low, and listen to my wild complaint.

Tú sola contra mí te endureciste,
Los ojos aun siquiera no volviendo
A lo que tú heciste.
Salid sin duelo, lágrimas, corriendo.

Mas ya que a socorrer aquí no vienes,
No dejes el lugar que tanto amaste,
Que bien podrás venir de mí segura.
Yo dejaré el lugar do me dejaste;
Ven, si por sólo esto te detienes.
Ves aquí un prado lleno de verdura,
Ves aquí un espesura,
Ves aquí un agua clara,
En otro tiempo cara,
A quien de ti con lágrimas me quejo.
Quizá aquí hallarás, pues yo me alejo,
Al que todo mi bien quitarme puede;
Que pues el bien le dejo,
No es mucho que el lugar también le quede.—

.   .   .

Nemoroso

Corrientes aguas, puras, cristalinas;
Árboles que os estáis mirando en ellas,
Verde prado de fresca sombra lleno,
Aves que aquí sembráis vuestras querellas,
Hiedra que por los árboles caminas,
Torciendo el paso por su verde seno;
Yo me vi tan ajeno
Del grave mal que siento,
Que de puro contento
Con vuestra soledad me recreaba,
Donde con dulce sueño reposaba,
O con el pensamiento discurría
Por donde no hallaba
Sino memorias llenas de alegría;

Thou only steel'st thy bosom to my cries,
Not ev'n once rolling thine angelic eyes
On him thy harshness kills; in gentle woe,
Flow forth, my tears, 'tis meet that ye should flow!

But though thou wilt not come for my sad sake,
Leave not the landscape thou hast held so dear;
Thou may'st come freely now, without the fear
Of meeting me, for though my heart should break,
Where late forsaken I will now forsake.
Come then, if this alone detains thee, here
Are meadows full of verdure, myrtles, bays,
Woodlands, and lawns, and running waters clear,
Beloved in other days,
To which, bedewed with many a bitter tear,
I sing my last of lays.
These scenes perhaps, when I am far removed,
At ease thou wilt frequent
With him who rifled me of all I loved;
Enough! my strength is spent;
And leaving thee in his desired embrace,
It is not much to leave him this sweet place.

.   .   .

Nemoroso

Smooth-sliding waters, pure and crystalline!
Trees, that reflect your image in their breast!
Green pastures, full of fountains and fresh shades!
Birds, that here scatter your sweet serenades!
Mosses, and reverend ivies serpentine,
That wreathe your verdurous arms round beech and pine,
And, climbing, crown their crest!
Can I forget, ere grief my spirit changed,
With what delicious ease and pure content
Your peace I wooed, your solicitudes I ranged,
Enchanted and refreshed where'er I went!
How many blissful noons I here have spent
In luxury of slumber, couched on flowers,
And with my own fond fancies, from a boy,
Discoursed away the hours,
Discovering nought in your delightful bowers,
But golden dreams and memories fraught with joy!

Y en este mismo valle, donde agora
Me entristesco y me canso, en el reposo
Estuve ya contento y descansado.
¡Oh bien caduco, vano y presuroso!
Acuérdome durmiendo aquí algún hora,
Que despertando, a Elisa vi a mi lado.
¡Oh miserable hado!
¡Oh tela delicada,
Antes de tiempo dada
A los agudos filos de la muerte!
Más convenible suerte
A los cansados años de mi vida,
Que es más que el hierro fuerte,
Pues no la ha quebrantado tu partida.

.   .   .

¿Quién me dijera, Elisa, vida mía,
Cuando en aqueste valle al fresco viento
Andábamos cogiendo tiernas flores,
Que había de ver con largo apartamiento
Venir el triste y solitario día
Que diese amargo fin a mis amores?
El cielo en mis dolores
Cargó la mano tanto,
Que a sempiterno llanto
Y a triste soledad me ha condenado;
Y lo que siento más es verme atado
A la pesada vida y enojosa,
Solo, desamparado,
Ciego sin lumbre en cárcel tenebrosa.

Divina Elisa, pues agora el cielo
Con inmortales pies pisas y mides,
Y su mudanza ves, estando queda,
¿Por qué de mí te olvidas, y no pides
Que se apresure el tiempo en que este velo
Rompa del cuerpo, y verme libre pueda,
Y en la tercera rueda
Contigo mano a mano
Busquemos otro llano,
Busquemos otros montes y otros ríos,

And in this very valley where I now
Grow sad, and droop, and languish, have I lain
At ease, with happy heart and placid brow;
Oh pleasure fragile, fugitive, and vain!
Here, I remember, waking once at noon,
I saw Eliza standing at my side;
Oh cruel fate! of finespun web, too soon
By Death's sharp scissors clipt! sweet, suffering bride,
In womanhood's most interesting prime,
Cut off, before thy time!
How much more suited had his surly stroke
Been to the strong thread of my weary life!
Stronger than steel, since in the parting strife
From thee, it has not broke.

      .   .   .

Who would have said, my love, when late through this
Romantic valley, we from bower to bower
Went gathering violets and primroses,
That I should see the melancholy hour
So soon arrive that was to end my bliss,
And of my love destroy both fruit and flower?
Heaven on my head has laid a heavy hand;
Sentencing, without hope, without appeal,
To loneliness and ever-during tears
The joyless remnant of my future years;
But that which most I feel,
Is to behold myself obliged to bear
This condemnation to a life of care;
Lone, blind, forsaken, under sorrow's spell,
A gloomy captive in a gloomy cell.

      .   .   .

Divine Eliza! since the sapphire sky
Thou measurest now on angel-wings, and feet
Sandalled with immortality, oh why
Of me forgetful? Wherefore not entreat
To hurry on the time when I shall see
The veil of mortal being rent in twain,
And smile that I am free?
In the third circle of that happy land,
Shall we not seek together, hand in hand,
Another lovelier landscape, a new plain,
Other romantic streams and mountains blue,

Otros valles floridos y sombríos,
Donde descanse y siempre pueda verte
Ante los ojos míos,
Sin miedo y sobresalto de perderte?—

Nunca pusieran fin al triste lloro
Los pastores, ni fueran acabadas
Las canciones que sólo el monte oía
Si mirando las nubes coloradas,
Al tramontar del sol bordadas de oro,
No vieran que era ya pasado el día.
La sombra se veía
Venir corriendo apriesa
Ya por la falda espesa
Del altísimo monte, y recordando
Ambos como de sueño, y acabando
El fugitivo sol, de luz escaso,
Su ganado llevando,
Se fueron recogiendo paso a paso.

SONETO X

¡Oh dulces prendas, por mi mal halladas,
Dulces y alegres cuando Dios quería!
Juntas estáis en la memoria mía,
Y con ella en mi muerte conjuradas.

¿Quién me dijera, cuando en las pasadas
Horas en tanto bien por vos me vía,
Que me habíades de ser en algún día
Con tan grave dolor representadas?

Pues en un hora junto me llevastes
Todo el bien que por términos me distes,
Llevadme junto el mal que me dejastes.

Si no, sospecharé que me pusistes
En tantos bienes, porque deseastes
Verme morir entre memorias tristes.

Fresh flowery vales, and a new shady shore,
Where I may rest, and ever in my view
Keep thee, without the terror and surprise
Of being sundered more!

Ne'er had the shepherds ceased these songs, to which
The hills alone gave ear, had they not seen
The sun in clouds of gold and crimson rich
Descend, and twilight sadden o'er the green;
But noting now, how rapidly the night
Rushed from the hills, admonishing to rest,
The sad musicians, by the blushful light
Of lingering Hesperus, themselves addressed
To fold their flocks, and step by step withdrew,
Through bowery lawns and pastures wet with dew.

JEREMIAH HOLMES WIFFEN

SONNET X

O precious locket, found by luckless me,
Precious and pleasing when the Lord hath willed;
Thou art made one with mine own memory,
And with my death thou too shalt be stilled.

Who could foresee in the so recent past,
When thou wert a source of true joy to me,
That our delightful bliss would not long last,
But would turn to heartache and misery?

For in one sole hour thou didst remove
All the joy and good thou didst ever bring;
Take too the grief left by thee with me.

If not, I shall think thou didst falsely love,
And didst leave me a victim to Remorse's sting
That I might die with thy sad memory.

SEYMOUR RESNICK

GUTIERRE DE CETINA
[1518?–1554?]

The author of many charming poems, Gutierre de Cetina was born in Seville of well-to-do parents. He spent much of his brief life as a military man and courtier, finally going in 1546 to the New World. There, in Mexico, he died—the story goes—as the result of wounds inflicted by the

MADRIGAL

Ojos claros, serenos,
Si de un dulce mirar sois alabados,
¿Por qué, si me miráis, miráis airados?
Si cuanto más piadosos
Más bellos parecéis a aquel que os mira,
No me miréis con ira,
Porque no parezcáis menos hermosos.
¡Ay tormentos rabiosos!
Ojos claros, serenos,
Ya que así me miráis, miradme al menos

LAZARILLO DE TORMES
[1554]

Perhaps the most characteristic of literary genres in Spain is its own native product, the picaresque novel. Although the ancestry of the pícaro *or rogue may be traced back to characters in folklore, and to* La Celestina *in Spanish literature, the birth of the first important picaresque novel took place in 1554 with the publication—in three different editions—of* Lazarillo de Tormes.
In contrast to the types of novels then prevalent—the chivalrous, pastoral and sentimental—the picaresque novel is marked by a down-to-earth, highly satirical portrayal of real life, and most generally the life of the lower classes. Its structure is uncomplicated. The pícaro *recounts, in autobiographical*

LAZARILLO DE TORMES

Tratado Primero

CUENTA LÁZARO SU VIDA Y CUYO HIJO FUÉ

Pues sepa vuestra merced ante todas cosas, que a mí me llaman Lázaro de Tormes, hijo de Tomé González y de Antonia Pérez, naturales de Tejares, aldea de Salamanca.

*jealous friend of a woman to whom Cetina paid court. If true, this was a
sad but appropriate end, for Cetina has been called the 'poet of love'.
His exquisite madrigal* Ojos claros, serenos *is one of the most frequently
quoted poems in the Spanish language.*

MADRIGAL

Clear eyes, sweet and serene,
If for your gentle looks you are so praised,
Why, seeing me, are you in anger raised?
Since for their pitying glance
They lovelier seem to him on whom they gaze,
Dispel their angry haze
Lest beauty's eyes thus look at you askance,
Oh, rage and torture keen!
Clear eyes, sweet and serene,
E'en though your look be harsh, by you let me be seen.

NICHOLSON B. ADAMS

*form, his experiences with a variety of masters, and his tricks, both harrowing
and amusing, in the struggle to survive.*

*Lazarillo de Tormes itself was enormously popular, inspiring many
translations and imitations throughout Europe. The author is unknown,
although for many years the book was attributed to the noted poet and historian
Don Diego Hurtado de Mendoza (1503–1575). There is negative evidence
however, plus the fact that Hurtado de Mendoza was of noble family.
Critics now generally believe that to have written so intimately of the picaresque
life, the author must have been himself, at one time or another, a penniless
rogue.*

LAZARILLO DE TORMES

Treatise First

WITH A BLIND MAN

Then know Your Worship, before anything else that my name
is Lazaro of Tormes, son of Thome Gonçales and Antona Perez,
natives of Tejares, a hamlet near Salamanca. My birth took place

Mi nacimiento fué dentro del río Tormes, por la cual causa tomé el sobrenombre, y fué de esta manera. Mi padre, que Dios perdone, tenía a cargo de proveer una molienda de una aceña, que está ribera de aquel río, en la cual fué molinero más de quince años. Y estando mi madre una noche en la aceña, preñada de mí, tomóla el parto y parióme allí. De manera, que con verdad me puedo decir nacido en el río.

Pues siendo yo niño de ocho años, achacaron a mi padre ciertas sangrías mal hechas en los costales de los que allí a moler venían, por lo cual fué preso y confesó y no negó y padeció persecución por justicia. Espero en Dios que está en la gloria, pues el Evangelio los llama bienaventurados.

En este tiempo se hizo cierta armada contra moros, entre los cuales fué mi padre, que a la sazón estaba desterrado por el desastre ya dicho, con cargo de acemilero de un caballero que allá fué. Y con su señor, como leal criado, feneció su vida.

Mi viuda madre, como sin marido y sin abrigo se viese, determinó arrimarse a los buenos por ser uno de ellos y vínose a vivir a la ciudad y alquiló una casilla y metióse a guisar de comer a ciertos estudiantes y lavaba la ropa a ciertos mozos de caballos ... se fué a servir a los que al presente vivían en el mesón de la Solana. Y allí, padeciendo mil importunidades, se acabó de criar mi hermanico, hasta que supo andar y a mí hasta ser buen mozuelo, que iba a los huéspedes por vino y candelas y por lo demás que me mandaban.

En este tiempo vino a posar al mesón un ciego, el cual, pareciéndole que yo sería para adestrarle, me pidió a mi madre y ella me encomendó a él, diciéndole cómo era hijo de un buen hombre, el cual, por ensalzar la fe, había muerto en la de los Gelves, y que ella confiaba en Dios no saldría peor que mi padre, y que le rogaba me tratase bien, y mirase por mí, pues era huérfano.

El respondió que así lo haría, y que me recibía no por mozo, sino por hijo.

Y así, le comencé a servir y adestrar a mi nuevo y viejo amo.

Como estuvimos en Salamanca algunos días, pareciéndole a mi amo que no era la ganancia a su contento, determinó irse de allí, y cuando nos hubimos de partir, yo fuí a ver a mi madre, ambos llorando, me dió su bendición, y dijo:

—Hijo, ya sé que no te veré más. Procura de ser bueno, y Dios te guíe. Criado te he, y con buen amo te he puesto. Válete por ti.

Y así me fuí para mi amo, que esperándome estaba.

in the river Tormes, for which reason I had the surname, and it was in this manner. My father (whom God forgive) had the job of overseeing the grinding of a water-mill, which is by the bank of that river, wherein he was miller more than fifteen years; and my mother being one night in the water-mill, big with me, her pains took her and she delivered me there; so that I can truthfully say I was born in the river. Well, when I was a child of eight, they imputed to my father certain awkward bleedings in the sacks of those who came there to grind, for which he was taken, and he confessed, and denied not, and suffered persecution for justice' sake. I trust in God that he is in glory, for the Gospel calls them blessed. At this time there was an expedition made against the Moors, in the which went my father, who had been banished for the misfortune abovesaid, serving as muleteer to a knight; and with his lord, like a loyal servant, he ended his life.

My widow mother when she found herself without husband or support determined to get among worthy people and be one of them, and betook herself to live in the city, and hired a little house, and undertook to do the cooking for some students, and washed clothes for certain stable-boys . . . [later] she went into service with those who were then living at the inn of La Solana; and there suffering a thousand annoyances, she managed to bring up my small brother to the point where he knew how to walk, and me to where I was a good-sized little fellow, who fetched wine and candles for the guests, or whatever else they bade me.

At this time there came a blind man to lodge at the inn; and as it seemed to him that I would be suitable for leading him, he begged me of my mother, and she turned me over to him, telling him how I was the son of a good man, who had died to exalt the faith in the affair of Los Gelves, and that she had trust in God I should not turn out a worse man than my father, and she begged him to treat me well and look after me, for I was an orphan. He answered that he would do so, and that he was receiving me not as his boy but as his son. And so I began to serve and to lead my new old master.

After we had remained in Salamanca several days and it appeared to my master that the profits were not to his satisfaction, he determined to leave there; and when we were about to depart I went to see my mother, and both weeping she gave me her blessing and said : 'Son, now I know that I shall never see thee more; try to be good, and God guide thee; I have reared thee and placed thee with a good master, take care of thyself.' And so I went along to my master who was waiting for me.

Salimos de Salamanca, y llegando a la puente, está a la entrada de ella un animal de piedra, que casi tiene forma de toro, y el ciego mandóme que llegase cerca del animal, y allí puesto, me dijo:

—Lázaro, llega el oído a este toro, y oirás gran ruido dentro de él.

Yo simplemente llegué, creyendo ser así; y como sintió que tenía la cabeza par de la piedra, afirmó recio la mano y dióme una gran calabazada en el diablo del toro, que más de tres días me duró el dolor de la cornada, y díjome:

—Necio, aprende. Que el mozo del ciego un punto ha de saber más que el diablo.

Y rió mucho la burla.

Parecióme que en aquel instante desperté de la simpleza en que como niño dormido estaba, y dije entre mí:

—Verdad dice éste, que me cumple avivar el ojo y avisar, pues soy solo, y pensar cómo me sepa valer.

Comenzamos nuestro camino, y en muy pocos días me mostró jerigonza. Y como me viese de buen ingenio, holgábase mucho y decía:

—Yo oro ni plata no te lo puedo dar; mas avisos para vivir muchos te mostraré.

Y fué así, que después de Dios éste me dió la vida, y siendo ciego, me alumbró y adestró en la carrera de vivir.

Huelgo de contar a vuestra merced estas niñerías, para mostrar cuánta virtud sea saber los hombres subir siendo bajos, y dejarse bajar siendo altos cuánto vicio.

Pues tornando al bueno de mi ciego y contando sus cosas, vuestra merced sepa que, desde que Dios crió el mundo, ninguno formó más astuto ni sagaz. En su oficio era un águila. Ciento y tantas oraciones sabía de coro. Un tono bajo, reposado y muy sonable, que hacía resonar la iglesia donde rezaba. Un rostro humilde y devoto, que con muy buen continente ponía, cuando rezaba, sin hacer gestos, ni visajes con boca ni ojos, como otros suelen hacer. Allende de esto, tenía otras mil formas y maneras para sacar el dinero. Decía saber oraciones para muchos y diversos efectos: para mujeres que no parían, para las que estaban de parto, para las que eran mal casadas, que sus maridos las quisiesen bien. Echaba pronósticos a las preñadas, si traía hijo o hija. Pues en caso de medicina, decía, Galeno no supo la mitad que él para muelas, desmayos, males de madre. Finalmente, nadie le decía padecer alguna pasión, que luego no le decía:

—Haced esto, haréis estotro, coged tal yerba, tomad tal raíz.

Con esto andábase todo el mundo tras él, especialmente mujeres, que cuanto les decía creían. De éstas sacaba él grandes provechos

We went out of Salamanca, and as you approach the bridge there is a stone animal at the entrance, almost in the shape of a bull, and the blind man bade me go close to the animal, and when I was there, said to me : 'Lazaro, put thine ear close to this bull and shalt hear a great noise inside.' Naïvely I went, believing this to be so; and when he perceived that I had my head close to the stone, he swung out his hand hard and gave my head a great blow against the devil of a bull, so that for three days the pain of the butting remained, and said to me : 'Silly fool, learn that the blind man's boy has to know one point more than the devil,' and laughed a great deal at the joke. It seemed to me that in that instant I awoke from the childish simplicity in which I had always been asleep. I said to myself : 'This man says the truth, for it behooves me to open mine eyes and look about, since I am alone, and to consider how to take care of myself.'

We began our journey, and in a very few days he taught me thieves' jargon, and when he saw me to be of a good wit, was well pleased, and used to say : 'Gold or silver I cannot give thee, but I will show thee many pointers about life.' And it was so; for after God this man gave me my life, and although blind lighted and guided me in the career of living. I enjoy relating these puerilities to Your Worship in order to show how much virtue there is in men's knowing how to rise when they are low, and in their letting themselves lower when they are high, how much vice! To return to my good blind man and his affairs, Your Worship must know that since God created the world, He never formed any one more astute or sagacious. In his trade he was an eagle; he knew a hundred and odd prayers by heart; had a bass voice, tranquil and very sonorous, which made the church where he prayed resound, a humble and devout countenance which he put on with very good effect when he prayed, without making faces or grimaces with his mouth or eyes, as others wont to do. Besides, he had a thousand other modes and fashions for getting money : he said he knew prayers to many and divers effects : for women that did not bear, for those that were in travail, for those badly married to make their husbands love them; he cast prognostications for the pregnant whether they were carrying son or daughter. Then in regard to medicine, he used to say that Galen didn't know the half of what he knew about grinders, swoons, the vapours; in a word, nobody could tell him that he was suffering any illness, but straightway he would reply : 'Do this, you will do that, pluck such an herb, take such a root.' Accordingly he had all the world marching after him, especially the women, for they believed whatever he told

con las artes que digo y ganaba más en un mes que cien ciegos en un año.

Mas también quiero que sepa vuestra merced que, con todo lo que adquiría y tenía, jamás tan avariento ni mezquino hombre no vi, tanto, que me mataba a mí de hambre y así no me demediaba de lo necesario. Digo verdad. Si con mi sutileza y buenas mañas no me supiera remediar, muchas veces me finara de hambre. Mas con todo su saber y aviso le contraminaba de tal suerte, que siempre, o las más veces, me cabía lo más y mejor.

Para esto le hacía burlas endiabladas, de las cuales contaré algunas, aunque no todas a mi salvo.

El traía el pan y todas las otras cosas en un fardel de lienzo, que por la boca se cerraba con una argolla de hierro y su candado y su llave, y al meter de todas las cosas y sacarlas, era con tanta gran vigilancia y tanto por contadero, que no bastara hombre en todo el mundo hacerle menos una migaja. Mas yo tomaba aquella laceria, que él me daba, la cual en menos de dos bocados era despachada.

Después que cerraba el candado y se descuidaba, pensando que yo estaba entendiendo en otras cosas, por un poco de costura, que muchas veces del un lado del fardel descosía y tornaba a coser, sangraba el avariento fardel, sacando no por tasa pan, mas buenos pedazos, torreznos y longaniza.

Y así buscaba conveniente tiempo para rehacer, no la chaza, sino la endiablada falta, que el mal ciego me faltaba.

Todo lo que podía sisar y hurtar traía en medias blancas, y cuando le mandaban rezar, y le daban blancas, como él carecía de vista, no había el que se la daba amagado con ella, cuando yo la tenía lanzada en la boca y la media aparejada, que por presto que él echaba la mano, ya iba de mi cambio aniquilada en la mitad del justo precio.

Quejábaseme el mal ciego, porque al tiento luego conocía y sentía que no era blanca entera, y decía:

—¿Qué diablo es esto, que después que conmigo estás no me dan sino medias blancas, y de antes una blanca, y un maravedí hartas veces me pagaban? En ti debe estar esta desdicha.

También él abreviaba el rezar, y la mitad de la oración no acababa, porque me tenía mandado que, en yéndose el que la mandaba rezar, le tirase por cabo del capuz. Yo así lo hacía. Luego él tornaba a dar voces, diciendo:

—¿Mandan rezar tal y tal oración? como suelen decir.

them; from them he extracted large profits by the arts I tell you of, and used to gain more in a month than a hundred blind men in a year.

But also I wish Your Worship to know, that with all he acquired and possessed, never did I see so miserly or mean a man, to such a point that he was killing me with hunger, and didn't share even the necessaries with me. I am telling the truth : if I had not known how to cure myself by my slyness and good devices, many times I should have died of hunger; but with all his experience and vigilance I worked against him in such fashion, that the biggest and best part, always or more generally, fell to me. To this end I played him devilish tricks, some of which I shall relate, though not all to my advantage.

He used to carry bread and everything else in a linen sack which closed at the mouth with an iron ring and a padlock and key, and when he put things in and took them out, it was with so much attention, so well counted, that the whole world wouldn't have been equal to making it a crumb less. But I would take what stingy bit he gave me, and finish it in less than two mouthfuls. After he had fastened the lock and stopped worrying about it, thinking me to be engaged in other things, by a little seam, which I unsewed and sewed up again many times in the side of the sack, I used to bleed the miserly sack, taking out bread,—not measured quantities but good pieces,—and slices of bacon and sausage; and thus would seek a convenient time to make good the devilish state of want which the wicked blind man left me in.

All I could filch and steal I carried in half-farthings; and when they bade him pray and gave him a farthing, it was no sooner proffered than I had it popped into my mouth and a half-farthing ready, so that however soon he held out his hand, his remuneration was already reduced by my money-changing to half its real value. The wicked blind man used to complain to me, for he at once perceived by the feeling that it was not a whole farthing, and would say : 'Why the devil is it that since thou art with me they don't give me but half-farthings, and before, they paid me a farthing and oftentimes a maravedi? This bad luck must come through thee.' He used also to shorten his prayers and not half finish them, having ordered me that when the person went away who had ordered him to pray, I should pluck him by the end of his hood. And so I used to do; and at once he began again to lift his voice, saying : 'Who would like to have me say a prayer?' as the custom is,

Usaba poner cabe sí un jarrillo de vino, cuando comíamos y yo muy de presto le asía y daba un par de besos callados y tornábale a su lugar. Mas duróme poco; que en los tragos conocía la falta, y por reservar su vino a salvo, nunca después desamparaba el jarro, antes lo tenía por el asa asido. Mas no había piedra imán que así trajese a sí como yo con una paja larga de centeno, que para aquel menester tenía hecha, la cual, metiéndola en la boca del jarro, chupando el vino, lo dejaba a buenas noches.

Mas como fuese el traidor tan astuto, pienso que me sintió y dende en adelante mudó propósito y asentaba su jarro entre las piernas y atapábale con la mano y así bebía seguro. Yo, como estaba hecho al vino, moría por él. Y viendo que aquel remedio de la paja no me aprovechaba ni valía, acordé en el suelo del jarro hacerle una puentecilla y agujero sutil y delicadamente con una muy delgada tortilla de cera taparlo y al tiempo de comer, fingiendo haber frío, entrábame entre las piernas del triste ciego a calentarme en la pobrecilla lumbre que teníamos, y al calor de ella luego derretida la cera, por ser muy poca, comenzaba la fuentecilla a destilarme en la boca, la cual yo de tal manera ponía, que maldita la gota se perdía.

Cuando el pobrete iba a beber, no hallaba nada.

Espantábase, maldecíase, daba al diablo el jarro y el vino, no sabiendo qué podía ser.

—No diréis, tío, que os lo bebo yo—decía—, pues no lo quitáis de la mano.

Tantas vueltas y tientos dió al jarro, que halló la fuente y cayó en la burla. Mas así lo disimuló como si no lo hubiera sentido. Y luego otro día, teniendo yo rezumando mi jarro como solía, no pensando el daño, que me estaba aparejado, ni que el mal ciego me sentía, sentéme como solía, estando recibiendo aquellos dulces tragos, mi cara puesta hacia el cielo, un poco cerrados los ojos por mejor gustar el sabroso licor, sintió el desesperado ciego que ahora tenía tiempo de tomar de mí venganza, y con toda su fuerza, alzando con dos manos aquel dulce y amargo jarro, le dejó caer sobre mi boca, ayudándose —como digo—con todo su poder, de manera que el pobre Lázaro que de nada de esto se guardaba, antes, como otras veces, estaba descuidado y gozoso, verdaderamente me pareció que el cielo, con todo lo que en él hay, me había caído encima.

Fué tal el golpecillo, que me desatinó y sacó de sentido, y el jarrazo tan grande, que los pedazos de él se me metieron por la cara, rompiéndomela por muchas partes, y me quebró los dientes, sin los cuales hasta hoy día me quedé.

Desde aquella hora quise mal al mal ciego, y aunque me quería y regalaba y me curaba, bien vi que se había holgado del cruel castigo.

When we ate he used to put a little jug of wine near him. I would quickly seize it and give it a couple of silent kisses and return it to its place; but this plan didn't work long, for he noticed the deficiency in his draughts, and in order to keep his wine safe, he never after let go the jug, but kept hold of the handle. But there is no lode-stone that draws things to it so strongly as I with a long rye straw, which I had prepared for that purpose, and placing which in the mouth of the jug, I would suck up the wine to a fare-ye-well. But the villain was so clever that I think he heard me; and from then on he changed procedure and set his jug between his legs and covered it with his hand, and thus drank secure. Now that I had grown accustomed to wine, I was dying for it; and seeing that the straw-cure was no longer helping me, I decided to make a tiny hole in the bottom of the jug for a little drain, and to bung it neatly with a very thin cake of wax, and at dinner-time, pretending to be cold, I got between the wretched blind man's legs to warm me at the miserable fire we had, in whose heat the wax being soon melted, for there was very little, the streamlet began to drain into my mouth, which I held in such a way that devil a drop was lost. When the poor creature went to drink, he found nothing : he was astounded, damned himself, and sent the jug and the wine to the devil, not knowing what it all could mean. 'You won't say, uncle, that I drank it for you,' said I, 'for you haven't let it out of your hand.' He turned and felt the jug so much, that he found the outlet and fell on to the trick; but made as though he had not perceived it. And the next day, when I had my jug leaking as before, and was not dreaming of the injury in store for me, or that the wicked blind man heard me, I sat as before, in the act of receiving those sweet draughts, my faced turned toward heaven, my eyes partly closed, the better to enjoy the delicious liquid, when the desperate blind man perceived that now was his time to take vengeance of me, and with all his might, raising that sweet and bitter jug with both hands, he let it fall upon my mouth, making use (as I say) of all his strength, so that poor Lazaro, who was expecting none of this, but, as at other times, was careless and joyful, verily it seemed to me that the heavens, with all that in them is, had fallen on top of me. Such was the gentle tap he gave me that it stupefied and knocked me senseless, and the blow so hard that the pieces of the jug stuck in my face, breaking it in many places, and cracked off my teeth which I remain without until this very day. From that hour forth I hated the wicked blind man; and although he liked and caressed me and cared for me, well I saw that the cruel chastisement had diverted him. He washed with wine

Lavóme con vino las roturas que con los pedazos del jarro me había hecho, y sonriéndose decía:

—¿Qué te parece, Lázaro? Lo que te enfermó te sana y da salud. Y otros donaires que a mi gusto no lo eran.

Ya que estuve medio bueno de mi negra trepa y cardenales, considerando que a pocos golpes tales el cruel ciego ahorraría de mí, quise yo ahorrar de él. Mas no lo hice tan presto por hacerlo más a mi salvo y provecho. Aunque yo quisiera asentar mi corazón y perdonalle el jarrazo, no daba lugar el mal tratamiento que el mal ciego desde allí adelante me hacía; que sin causa ni razón me hería, dándome coscorrones y repelándome.

Y si alguno le decía por qué me trataba tan mal, luego contaba el cuento del jarro, diciendo:

—¿Pensaréis que éste mi mozo es algún inocente? Pues oíd si el demonio ensayara otra tal hazaña.

Santiguándose los que le oían, decían:

—¡Mirad quién pensara de un muchacho tan pequeño tal ruindad!

Y reían mucho el artificio, y decíanle:

—¡Castigadlo, castigadlo, que de Dios lo habréis!

Y él con aquello nunca otra cosa hacía.

Y en esto yo siempre le llevaba por los peores caminos y adrede, por le hacer mal daño. Si había piedras, por ellas. Si lodo, por lo más alto, que aunque yo no iba por lo más enjuto, holgábame a mí de quebrar un ojo por quebrar dos al que ninguno tenía. Con esto siempre con el cabo alto del tiento me tentaba el colodrillo, el cual siempre traía lleno de tolondrones y pelado de sus manos. Y aunque yo juraba no lo hacer con malicia, sino por no hallar mejor camino, no me aprovechaba ni me creía más. Tal era el sentido y grandísimo entendimiento del traidor.

Y porque vea vuestra merced a cuánto se extendía el ingenio de este astuto ciego, contaré un caso de muchos, que con él me acaescieron, en el cual me parece dió bien a entender su gran astucia.

Cuando salimos de Salamanca, su motivo fué venir a tierra de Toledo, porque decía ser la gente más rica, aunque no muy limosnera. Arrimábase a este refrán: 'Más da el duro que el desnudo'. Y venimos a este camino por los mejores lugares. Donde hallaba buena acogida y ganancia, deteníamonos; donde no, a tercero día hacíamos San Juan.

Acaeció que en llegando a un lugar que llaman Almoroz, al tiempo que cogían las uvas, un vendimiador le dió un racimo de ellas en

the wounds he had made me with the pieces of the jug, and smiling, said : 'How seems it to thee, Lazaro? That which made thee sick cures thee and gives thee health,' and other pleasantries which to my taste were none.

Once I was half well of my horrid bumps and bruises, considering that with a few such blows the cruel blind man would be rid of me, I was anxious to be rid of him; but I did not manage it too quickly, in order to do it with more safety and profit. Even though I should have been willing to soften my heart and forgive him the blow with the jug, the ill-treatment the wicked blind man gave me from this point on, left no chance for that; for he abused me without cause or reason, beating me over the head and pulling my hair. And if anybody asked him why he treated me so badly, he at once retailed the story of the jug, saying : 'Would you take this boy of mine for an innocent? Then listen, whether the devil himself could teach another such exploit.' Those that listened would say, making the sign of the cross : 'Well, now, who would expect such badness from a lad so small!' and would laugh heartily at the trick, and say to him : 'Chastise him, chastise him, for you'll get your reward from God,' and on that he never did anything else.

And meantime I always led him by the worst roads, and purposely, to do him harm and damage; if there were stones, through them, if mud, through the deepest; for although I didn't go through the dryest part, it pleased me to put out one of my own eyes in order to put out two for him, who had none. Therefore he used always to keep the upper end of his staff against the back of my head, which was continually full of bumps, and the hair pulled out by his hands; and although I swore I didn't do it of malice, but because I found no better road, that didn't help me, nor did he believe me any more for that; such was the perspicacity and the vast intelligence of the traitor.

And that Your Worship may see how far the cleverness of this astute blind man extended, I will relate one instance of many that befel me with him, wherein it seems to me he made his great astuteness very manifest. When we left Salamanca his intention was to go to the region around Toledo, because he said the people were richer, although not very charitable; he pinned his faith to the proverb : The hard give more than the poor. And we came along that route through the best places : where he found good welcome and profit, we would stop, where not, on the third day, we would move away. It happened that on arriving at a place called Almorox at the time when the grapes are gathered, a vintager gave him a bunch for alms. And as the paniers generally get

limosna. Y como suelen ir los cestos maltratados y también porque la uva en aquel tiempo está muy madura, desgranábasele el racimo en la mano; para echarlo en el fardel tornábase mosto y lo que a él se llegaba. Acordó de hacer un banquete, así por no lo poder llevar, como por contentarme. Que aquel día me había dado muchos rodillazos y golpes.

Sentámonos en un valladar, y dijo:

—Ahora quiero yo usar contigo de una liberalidad y es que ambos comamos este racimo de uvas y que hayas de él tanta parte como yo. Partillo hemos de esta manera: tú picarás una vez, y yo otra, con tal que me prometas no tomar cada vez más de una uva; yo haré lo mismo hasta que lo acabemos y de esta suerte no habrá engaño.

Hecho así el concierto, comenzamos. Mas luego al segundo lance el traidor mudó propósito y comenzó a tomar de dos en dos, considerando que yo debría hacer lo mismo. Como vi que él quebraba la postura, no me contenté ir a la par con él, mas aun pasaba adelante dos a dos, y tres a tres. Y como podía las comía.

Acabado el racimo, estuvo un poco con el escobajo en la mano, y meneando la cabeza, dijo:

—Lázaro, engañado me has. Juraré yo a Dios que has tú comido las uvas tres a tres.

—No comí—dije yo.—Mas, ¿por qué sospecháis eso?

Respondió el sagacísimo ciego:

—¿Sabes en qué veo que las comiste tres a tres? En que comía yo dos a dos y callabas.

Reíme entre mí, y—aunque muchacho—noté mucho la discreta consideración del ciego.

Mas, por no ser prolijo, dejo de contar muchas cosas, así graciosas como de notar, que con este mi primer amo me acaecieron, y quiero decir el despidiente, y con él acabar.

Estábamos en Escalona—villa del duque de ella—en un mesón, y dióme un pedazo de longaniza que le asase. Ya que la longaniza había pringado y comídose las pringadas, sacó un maravedí de la bolsa, y mandó que fuese por él de vino a la taberna.

Púsome el demonio el aparejo delante los ojos, el cual—como suelen decir—hace al ladrón. Y fué, que había cabe el fuego un nabo pequeño, larguillo y ruinoso y tal que, por no ser para la olla, debió ser echado allí. Y como al presente nadie estuviese sino él y yo solos, como me vi con apetito goloso, habiéndome puesto dentro el sabroso olor de la longaniza, del cual solamente sabía que había de gozar, no mirando qué me podría suceder, pospuesto todo el temor, por cumplir con el deseo, en tanto que el ciego sacaba de la bolsa el dinero, saqué la longaniza y muy presto metí el sobredicho nabo en

hard treatment, and the grapes at that time are very ripe, the bunch fell apart in his hand : if put into the sack, it would turn to must, and so he decided on this : he resolved to have a banquet, as much because we could not carry it, as to comfort me, for that day he had given me many kicks and blows. We sat down on a wall and he said : 'Now I wish to be generous with thee : we will both eat this bunch of grapes, and thou shalt have as big a share as I; we will divide in this way : thou shalt pick once and I once; provided thou promise me not to take more than one grape each time. I shall do the same until we finish, and in this way there will be no cheating.' The agreement thus made, we began; but directly at the second turn the traitor changed his mind and began to take two at a time, supposing that I must be doing likewise. As I saw he was breaking the agreement, I was not content to keep even with him, but went still farther : I ate them two at a time, three at a time, and as I could. The bunch finished, he waited awhile with the stem in his hand and shaking his head said : 'Lazaro, thou hast cheated : I will swear to God that thou hast eaten the grapes by threes.' 'I have not,' said I; 'but why do you suspect that?' The clever blind man replied : 'Knowest how I see that thou wast eating them by threes? Because I ate by twos and thou saidst nothing.' I laughed inwardly, and although only a lad noted well the blind man's just reasoning.

But not to be prolix, I omit an account of many things, as funny as they are worthy of note, which befel me with this my first master, but I wish to tell our leave-taking and with that to finish. We were at Escalona, town of the Duke of that ilk, in an inn, and he gave me a piece of sausage to roast. When he had basted the sausage and eaten the bastings, he took a maravedi from his purse and bade me fetch wine from the tavern. The devil put the occasion before my eyes, which, as the saying is, makes the thief; and it was this : there lay by the fire a small turnip, rather long and bad, and which must have been thrown there because it was not fit for the stew. And as nobody was there at the time but him and me alone, as I had an appetite whetted by having got the toothsome odour of the sausage inside me (the only part, as I knew, that I had to enjoy myself with), not considering what might follow, all fear set aside in order to comply with desire,—while the blind man was taking the money out of his purse, I took the sausage, and quickly put the above-mentioned turnip on the spit, which my

el asador, el cual mi amo, dándome el dinero para el vino, tomó y comenzó a dar vueltas al fuego, queriendo asar al que de ser cocido por sus deméritos había escapado.

Yo fuí por el vino, con el cual no tardé en despachar la longaniza, y cuando vine, hallé al pecador del ciego que tenía entre dos rebanadas apretado el nabo, al cual aún no había conocido, por no lo haber tentado con la mano. Como tomase las rebanadas y mordiese en ellas, pensando también llevar parte de la longaniza, hallóse en frío con el frío nabo.

Alteróse, y dijo:

—¿Qué es esto, Lazarillo?

—Lacerado de mí—dije yo—. ¿Si queréis a mí echar algo? ¿Yo no vengo de traer el vino? Alguno estaba ahí y por burla haría eso.

—No, no—dijo él; —que yo no he dejado el asador de la mano, no es posible.

Yo torné a jurar y perjurar que estaba libre de aquel trueco y cambio. Mas poco me aprovechó, pues a las astucias del maldito ciego nada se le escondía.

Levantóse y asióme por la cabeza, y llegóse a olerme. Y como debió sentir el huelgo, a uso de buen podenco, por mejor satisfacerse de la verdad y con la gran agonía que llevaba, asiéndome con las manos, abrióme la boca más de su derecho. Y desatentadamente metía la nariz, la cual él tenía luenga y afilada, y a aquella sazón con el enojo se había aumentado un palmo: con el pico de la cual me llegó a la gulilla.

Y con esto y con el gran miedo que tenía y con la brevedad del tiempo, la negra longaniza aún no había hecho asiento en el estómago, y lo más principal, con el destiento de la cumplidísima nariz, medio casi ahogándome, todas estas cosas se juntaron y fueron causa que el hecho y golosina se manifestase y lo suyo fuese vuelto a su dueño. De manera que antes que el mal ciego sacase de mi boca su trompa, tal alteración sintió mi estómago, que le dió con el hurto en ella, de suerte que su nariz y la negra mal mascada longaniza, a un tiempo salieron de mi boca.

¡Oh, gran Dios! ¡Quién estuviera aquella hora sepultado!, que muerto ya lo estaba.

Fué tal el coraje del perverso ciego, que si al ruido no acudieran, pienso no me dejara con la vida.

Sacáronme de entre sus manos, dejándoselas llenas de aquellos pocos cabellos que tenía, arañada la cara y rasguñado el pescuezo y la garganta. Y esto bien lo merecía, pues por su maldad me venían tantas persecuciones.

Contaba el mal ciego a todos cuantos allí se llegaban mis desastres

master grasped, when he had given me the money for the wine, and began to turn before the fire, trying to roast what through its demerit had escaped being boiled. I went for the wine, and on the way did not delay in despatching the sausage, and when I came back I found the sinner of a blind man holding the turnip ready between two slices of bread, for he had not yet recognized it, because he had not tried it with his hand. When he took the slices of bread and bit into them, thinking to get part of the sausage too, he found himself chilled by the chilly turnip; he grew angry and said : 'What is this, Lazarillo?' 'Poor Lazaro,' said I, 'if you want to blame me for anything. Haven't I just come back with the wine? Somebody was here, and must have done this for a joke.' 'No, no,' said he, 'for I've not let the spit out of my hand. It's not possible.' I again swore and forswore that I was innocent of the exchange, but little did it avail me, for nothing was hid from the sharpness of the confounded blind man. He got up and seized me by the head and came close up to smell me; and since he must have caught the scent like a good hound, the better to satisfy himself of the truth in the great agony he was suffering, he seized me with his hands, opened my mouth wider than it ought to go, and unconsideringly thrust in his nose,—which was long and sharp, and at that crisis a palm longer from rage,—with the point of which he reached my gorge; what with this and with the great fright I was in, and the short time the black sausage had had to get settled in my stomach, and most of all, with the tickling of his huge nose nearly half-choking me,—all these things conjointly were the cause that my misconduct and gluttony were made evident, and his own returned to my master; for before the wicked blind man withdrew his bugle from my mouth, my stomach was so upset that it abandoned its stolen goods, and thus his nose and the wretched, half-masticated sausage went out of my mouth at the same time. O great God, that I had been buried at that hour ! for dead I already was. Such was the depraved blind man's fury, that if they had not come to my assistance at the noise, I think he had not left me alive. They dragged me from out his hands, leaving them full of what few hairs I had, my face scratched and my neck and throat clawed; and well my throat deserved this, for such abuse befel me through its viciousness. The wicked blind man related my disgraceful actions

y dábales cuenta una y otra vez, así de la del jarro como de la del racimo y ahora de lo presente. Era la risa de todos tan grande, que toda la gente que por la calle pasaba entraba a ver la fiesta; mas con tanta gracia y donaire contaba el ciego mis hazañas, que aunque yo estaba tan maltratado y llorando, me parecía que hacía sinjusticia en no se las reír.

Y en cuanto esto pasaba, a la memoria me vino una cobardía y flojedad que hice por qué me maldecía, y fué no dejarle sin narices, pues tan buen tiempo tuve para ello que la mitad del camino estaba andado. Que con sólo apretar los dientes se me quedaran en casa, y con ser de aquel malvado, por ventura lo retuviera mejor mi estómago que tuvo la longaniza . . .

Visto esto y las malas burlas, que el ciego burlaba de mí, determiné de todo en todo dejarle, y como lo traía pensado y lo tenía en voluntad, con este postrer juego que me hizo, afirmélo más.

Y fué así, que luego otro día salimos por la villa a pedir limosna y había llovido mucho la noche antes. Y porque el día también llovía y andaba rezando debajo de unos portales, que en aquel pueblo había, donde no nos mojamos; mas como la noche se venía y el llover no cesaba, díjome el ciego.

—Lázaro, esta agua es muy porfiada, y cuanto la noche más cierra, más recia. Acojámonos a la posada con tiempo.

Para ir allá habíamos de pasar un arroyo, que con la mucha agua iba grande. Yo le dije:

—Tío, el arroyo va muy ancho. Mas si queréis, yo veo por dónde atravesemos más aína sin nos mojar, porque se estrecha allí mucho, y saltando pasaremos a pie enjuto.

Parecióle buen consejo, y dijo:

—Discreto eres, por esto te quiero bien. Llévame a ese lugar, donde el arroyo se ensangosta, que ahora es invierno y sabe mal el agua, y más llevar los pies mojados.

Yo que vi el aparejo a mi deseo, saquéle debajo de los portales y llevélo derecho de un pilar o poste de piedra que en la plaza estaba, sobre el cual y sobre otros cargaban saledizos de aquellas casas, y dígole:

—Tío, éste es el paso más angosto, que en el arroyo hay.

Como llovía recio y el triste se mojaba y con la priesa que llevábamos de salir del agua, que encima de nos caía, y lo más principal, porque Dios le cegó aquella hora el entendimiento por darme de él venganza, creyóse de mí, y dijo:

—Ponme bien derecho y salta tú el arroyo.

to all that approached, and gave them the history once and again, both of the wine-jug and of the bunch of grapes, and now of the actual trouble. Everybody laughed so much that all the passers-by came in to see the fun; for the blind man related my doings with so much wit and sprightliness that although I was thus abused and weeping, it seemed to me that I was doing him injustice not to laugh. And while this was going on, I remembered a piece of cowardly weakness I had been guilty of, and I cursed myself for it; and that was my leaving him with a nose, when I had such a good chance, half the distance being gone, for by only clinching my teeth it would have remained in my house, and because it belonged to that villain, perhaps my stomach would have retained it better than the sausage. . . .

In view of this and the evil tricks the blind man played me, I decided to leave him once and for all, and as I had everything thought out and in my mind, on his playing me this last game I determined on it more fully. And so it was that the next day we went out about time to beg alms, and it had rained a great deal the night before; and as it was still raining that day he walked in prayer under some arcades which there were in that town, where we didn't get wet; but as night was coming on and the rain didn't stop, the blind man said to me: 'Lazaro, this water is very persistent, and the more night shuts down, the heavier it is: let us get back to the inn in time.' To go there we had to cross a gutter which was running full because of all the water; I said to him: 'Uncle, the gutter runs very wide; but if you wish, I see where we can get over more quickly without wetting us, for there it becomes much narrower, and by jumping we can cross with dry feet.' This seemed good advice to him, and he said: 'Thou art clever, I like thee for that. Bring me to the place where the gutter contracts, for it is winter now and water is disagreeable, and going with wet feet still more so.' Seeing the scheme unfolding as I desired, I led him out from the arcades and brought him in front of a pillar or stone post which was in the square, and upon which and others like it projections of the houses rested, and said to him: 'Uncle, this is the narrowest crossing there is in the gutter.' As it was raining hard, and the poor creature was getting wet, and what with the haste we made to get out of the water that was falling on us, and most of all because God blinded his intelligence in that hour,—it was to give me revenge on him,—he trusted me, and said: 'Place me quite straight, and do thou jump the gutter.' I placed him

Yo le puse bien derecho enfrente del pilar y doy un salto y
póngome detrás del poste, como quien espera tope de toro, y díjele:
—¡Sus! ¡Saltad todo lo que podáis, porque deis de este cabo del
agua!
Aun apenas lo había acabado de decir, cuando se abalanza el
pobre ciego como cabrón y de toda su fuerza arremete, tomando un
paso atrás de la corrida para hacer mayor salto, y da con la cabeza
en el poste, que sonó tan recio como si diera con una gran calabaza,
y cayó luego para atrás medio muerto y hendida la cabeza.
—¿Cómo y olistes la longaniza y no el poste? ¡Huele, huele!—le
dije yo.
Y dejéle en poder de mucha gente que lo había ido a socorrer, y
tomé la puerta de la villa en los pies de un trote, y antes que la noche
viniese, di conmigo en Torrijos.
No supe más lo que Dios dél hizo ni curé de lo saber.

LUIS DE LEÓN
[1528?–1591]

*The question—Who is the greatest of all Spanish lyric poets?—is as
highly debatable in that country as in any nation which has produced a like
treasure of fine poetry. Many critics place at the top of the list an Augustinian
professor at the University of Salamanca—Fray Luis de León. A provoking
and erudite teacher, known throughout Spain during his lifetime for his
translations and prose writings, Fray Luis himself gave little importance
to his original poems. They are relatively few in number. But each is distinguished for the polished, classic style in which Fray Luis phrases his*

VIDA RETIRADA

¡Qué descansada vida
La del que huye el mundanal ruido,
Y sigue la escondida
Senda por donde han ido
Los pocos sabios que en el mundo han sido!

Que no le enturbia el pecho
De los soberbios grandes el estado,
Ni del dorado techo
Se admira, fabricado
Del sabio moro, en jaspes sustentado.

quite straight in front of the pillar, and gave a jump, and put myself behind the post like one who awaits the charge of a bull, and said to him : 'Hey, jump all you can, so as to get to this side of the water.' Scarcely had I finished saying it, when the poor blind man charged like a goat and with all his might came on, taking a step back before he ran, for to make a bigger jump, and struck the post with his head, which sounded as loud as if he had struck it with a big gourd, and fell straight down backwards half dead and with his head split open. 'What, thou smeltest the sausage and not the post? Smell, smell!' said I, and left him in charge of many folk who had come to help him, and took the town-gate on foot in a trot, and before night had struck into Torrijos. I knew no more of what God did with him, nor cared to know.

LOUIS HOW

yearning towards peace both celestial and earthly, and for the lyric beauty of his language and sentiment.

Fray Luis also left two valuable prose works, De los nombres de Cristo, *a theological treatise on the names of Christ, and* La perfecta casada, *a guide to the Christian wife. His Spanish translation of the* Song of Solomon *was a factor cited by jealous associates who denounced him to the Inquisition. Fray Luis thereupon spent almost five years in prison until his acquittal in 1576. It is said that when he returned to the University, amid tumultuous acclaim, he began his first lecture with the simple statement 'We were saying yesterday . . .'*

ODE TO RETIREMENT

O, happy, happy he, who flies
　　Far from the noisy world away,—
Who, with the worthy and the wise,
　　Hath chosen the narrow way,—
The silence of the secret road
That leads the soul to virtue and to God !

No passions in his breast arise;
　　Calm in his own unaltered state,
He smiles superior, as he eyes
　　The splendour of the great;
And his undazzled gaze is proof
Against the glittering hall and the gilded roof.

No cura si la fama
Canta con voz su nombre pregonera,
Ni cura si encarama
La lengua lisonjera
Lo que condena la verdad sincera.

¿Qué presta a mi contento
Si soy del vano dedo señalado,
Si en busca de este viento
Ando desalentado
Con ansias vivas y mortal cuidado?

¡Oh campo, oh monte, oh río!
¡Oh secreto seguro deleitoso!
Roto casi el navío,
A vuestro almo reposo
Huyo de aqueste mar tempestuoso.

.   .   .

ODA A FRANCISCO SALINAS

El aire se serena
Y viste de hermosura y luz no usada,
Salinas, cuando suena
La música extremada
Por vuestra sabia mano gobernada.

A cuyo son divino
Mi alma que en olvido está sumida,
Torna a cobrar el tino,
Y memoria perdida
De su origen primera esclarecida.

.   .   .

Traspasa el aire todo
Hasta llegar a la más alta esfera,
Y oye allí otro modo
De no perecedera
Música, que es de todas la primera.

He heeds not, though the trump of fame
　　Pour forth the loudest of its strains,
To spread the glory of his name;
　　And his high soul disdains
That flattery's voice should varnish o'er
The deed that truth or virtue would abhor.

Such lot be mine : what boots to me
　　The cumbrous pageantry of power;
To court the gaze of crowds, and be
　　The idol of the hour;
To chase an empty shape of air,
That leaves me weak with toil and worn with care?

O streams, and shades, and hills on high,
　　Unto the stillness of your breast
My wounded spirit longs to fly,—
　　To fly, and be at rest!
Thus from the world's tempestuous sea,
O gentle Nature, do I turn to thee!

　　　　.　　　.　　　.

ANONYMOUS

ODE TO FRANCISCO SALINAS

The air grows pure and clear,
Steeped in unearthly loveliness and light,
When we, Salinas, hear
Thy music take its flight,
Pressed from the keys by hands of magic might;

And, at that wondrous sound,
My soul, that long in apathy had lain,
New wisdom now hath found;
And taught by thee would fain
Of her high origin take thought again.

　　　　.　　　.　　　.

So, journeying through the air,
Till in the highest sphere in joy immersed,
She hears that music rare
Stilling the Spirit's thirst,
That music, of all harmonies the first;

Ve como el gran maestro,
A aquesta inmensa cítara aplicado,
Con movimiento diestro
Produce el son sagrado,
Con que este eterno templo es sustentado.

.   .   .

Aquí la alma navega
Por un mar de dulzura, y finalmente
En él así se anega,
Que ningún accidente
Extraño o peregrino oye o siente.

¡Oh desmayo dichoso!
¡Oh muerte que das vida, oh dulce olvido!
¡Durase en tu reposo,
Sin ser restituido
Jamás a aqueste bajo y vil sentido!

.   .   .

¡Oh suene de contino,
Salinas, vuestro son en mis oídos!
Por quien al bien divino
Despiertan los sentidos,
Quedando a lo demás amortecidos.

MORADA DEL CIELO

Alma región luciente,
Prado de bienandanza, que ni al hielo
Ni con el rayo ardiente
Falleces, fértil suelo
Producido eterno de consuelo;

De púrpura y de nieve
Florida la cabeza coronado,
A dulces pastos mueve,
Sin honda ni cayado,
El buen Pastor en ti su hato amado.

And with enraptured gaze
She sees the Master, Who o'er all hath reign;
He His great cithern plays,
Striking those chords amain,
Whereby He doth the universe sustain.

*   *   *

Here in this sea of sound
Floats the tired soul in endless ecstasy,
Till, therein wholly drowned
She's lost to things that be.
From all that fetters her, divinely free.

O thou most blessed swoon!
O death that givest life, O gentle peace!
Would that thy gracious boon
Of joy might never cease,
And from low earth-born cares bestow release!

*   *   *

Let then the glorious stream
Of thy grand music, my Salinas, flow,
That to the Good Supreme
My senses wake, and so
Remain for ever dead to things below.

IDA FARNELL

THE LIFE OF THE BLESSED

Region of life and light!
Land of the good whose earthly toils are o'er!
Nor frost nor heat may blight
Thy vernal beauty, fertile shore,
Yielding thy blessed fruits for evermore!

There, without crook or sling,
Walks the Good Shepherd; blossoms white and red
Round his meek temples cling;
And, to sweet pastures led,
His own loved flock beneath his eye is fed.

El va, y en pos dichosas
Le siguen sus ovejas, do las pace
Con inmortales rosas,
Con flor que siempre nace,
Y cuanto más se goza más renace.

Ya dentro a la montaña
Del alto bien las guía; ya en la vena
Del gozo fiel las baña,
Y les da mesa llena,
Pastor y pasto él solo, y suerte buena.

Y de su esfera cuando
La cumbre toca altísimo subido
El sol, él sesteando,
De su hato ceñido,
Con dulce son deleita el santo oído.

Toca el rabel sonoro,
Y el inmortal dulzor al alma pasa,
Con que envilece el oro,
Y ardiendo se traspasa
Y lanza en aquel bien libre de tasa.

¡Oh son, oh voz, siquiera
Pequeña parte alguna descendiese
En mi sentido, y fuera
De sí el alma pusiese
Y toda en ti, oh amor, la convirtiese!

Conocería dónde
Sesteas, dulce Esposo, y desatada
De esta prisión a donde
Padece, a tu manada
Junta, no ya andará perdida, errada.

EN LA ASCENSIÓN

¿Y dejas, Pastor santo,
Tu grey en este valle hondo, escuro,
Con soledad y llanto,
Y tú rompiendo el puro
Aire, te vas al inmortal seguro?

He guides, and near him they
Follow delighted; for he makes them go
    Where dwells eternal May,
    And heavenly roses blow,
Deathless, and gathered but again to grow.

He leads them to the height
Named of the infinite and long-sought Good,
    And fountains of delight;
    And where his feet have stood,
Springs up, along the way, their tender food.

And when, in the mid skies,
The climbing sun has reached his highest bound,
    Reposing as he lies,
    With all his flock around,
He witches the still air with numerous sound.

From his sweet lute flow forth
Immortal harmonies, of power to still
    All passions born of earth,
    And draw the ardent will
Its destiny of goodness to fulfil.

Might but a little part,
A wandering breath, of that high melody
    Descend into my heart,
    And change it till it be
Transformed and swallowed up, O love! in thee:

Ah! then my soul should know,
Beloved! where thou liest at noon of day;
    And from this place of woe
    Released, should take its way
To mingle with thy flock, and never stray.

                              WILLIAM CULLEN BRYANT

HYMN ON THE ASCENSION

And dost thou, holy Shepherd, leave
    Thine unprotected flock alone,
Here, in this darksome vale, to grieve,
    While thou ascend'st thy glorious throne?

Los antes bienhadados,
Y los ahora tristes y afligidos,
A tus pechos criados,
De ti desposeídos,
¿A dó convertirán ya sus sentidos?

¿Qué mirarán los ojos
Que vieron de tu rostro la hermosura,
Que no les sea enojos?
Quién oyó tu dulzura,
¿Qué no tendrá por sordo y desventura?

Aqueste mar turbado
¿Quién le pondrá ya freno? ¿quién concierto
Al viento fiero airado?
Estando tu encubierto,
¿Qué norte guiará la nave al puerto?

¡Ay!, nube envidiosa
Aun de este breve gozo, ¿qué te aquejas?
¿Dó vuelas presurosa?
¡Cuán rica tú te alejas!
¡Cuán pobres y cuan ciegos ay, nos dejas!

AL SALIR DE LA CÁRCEL

Aquí la envidia y mentira
Me tuvieron encerrado.
Dichoso el humilde estado
Del sabio que se retira
De aqueste mundo malvado;
Y con pobre mesa y casa,
En el campo deleitoso,
Con solo Dios se compasa.
Y a solas su vida pasa
Ni envidiado ni envidioso.

O, where can they their hopes now turn,
Who never lived but on thy love?
Where rest the hearts for thee that burn,
When thou art lost in light above?

How shall those eyes now find repose
That turn, in vain, thy smile to see?
What can they hear save mortal woes,
Who lose thy voice's melody?

And who shall lay his tranquil hand
Upon the troubled ocean's might?
Who hush the winds by his command?
Who guide us through this starless night?

For thou art gone!—that cloud so bright,
That bears thee from our love away,
Springs upward through the dazzling light,
And leaves us here to weep and pray!

GEORGE TICKNOR

ON LEAVING PRISON

Falsehood and hatred here
Held me in this prison pent :
Happy whose life is spent
In learning's humble sphere,
Far from the world malevolent;
He, with poor house and fare,
Communing with God alone,
Doth in the country fair
Dwell solitary, there
By none envied, envying none.

AUBREY F. G. BELL

SANTA TERESA DE JESÚS
[1515-1582]

Few men have won the eminence in religious and literary spheres which was achieved almost unwillingly by Teresa de Cepeda y Ahumada, the renowned Santa Teresa de Jesús. This extraordinary woman, founder against enormous odds of the Spanish Order of Discalced Carmelites, composed most of her works reluctantly. Indeed, she wrote at the express order of her superiors, for she declared that she had 'neither health nor head' for writing. Santa Teresa became nevertheless one of Spain's greatest mystic authors in prose and verse.

VIVO SIN VIVIR EN MÍ

Vivo sin vivir en mí,
Y de tal manera espero,
Que muero porque no muero.

Vivo ya fuera de mí,
Después que muero de amor;
Porque vivo en el Señor,
Que me quiso para sí.
Cuando el corazón le di
Puse en él este letrero:
Que muero porque no muero.

Esta divina prisión
Del amor con que yo vivo
Ha hecho a Dios mi cautivo,
Y libre mi corazón;
Y causa en mí tal pasión
Ver a Dios mi prisionero,
Que muero porque no muero.

¡Ay, qué larga es esta vida!
¡Qué duros estos destierros!
Esta cárcel, estos hierros
En que el alma está metida.
Sólo esperar la salida
Me causa dolor tan fiero,
Que muero porque no muero.

The ecstasy of the divine visions which she experienced permeate her prose works, although some also include very down-to-earth details of her life and duties. The style is spontaneous and unaffected, reflecting both the vivacious personality and brilliant mind for which she was famous. Religious intensity also marks her verse.

Santa Teresa's finest prose is found in El castillo interior, *a mystic description of the prayerful means by which the soul reaches its divine essence.*

I DIE BECAUSE I DO NOT DIE

I live, yet no true life I know,
And, living thus expectantly,
I die because I do not die.

Since this new death-in-life I've known,
Estrang'd from self my life has been,
For now I live a life unseen :
The Lord has claim'd me as His own.
My heart I gave Him for His throne,
Whereon He wrote indelibly :
'*I die because I do not die.*'

Within this prison-house divine,
Prison of love whereby I live,
My God Himself to me doth give,
And liberate this heart of mine.
And, as with love I yearn and pine,
With God my prisoner, I sigh :
'*I die because I do not die.*'

How tedious is this life below,
This exile, with its griefs and pains,
This dungeon and these cruel chains
In which the soul is forced to go !
Straining to leave this life of woe,
With anguish sharp and deep I cry :
'*I die because I do not die.*'

¡Ay, qué vida tan amarga
Do no se goza el Señor!
Porque si es dulce el amor,
No lo es la esperanza larga;
Quíteme Dios esta carga,
Más pesada que el acero,
Que muero porque no muero.

Sólo con la confianza
Vivo de que he de morir,
Porque muriendo el vivir
Me asegura mi esperanza;
Muerte do el vivir se alcanza,
no te tardes, que te espero,
Que muero porque no muero.

Mira que el amor es fuerte;
Vida, no me seas molesta,
Mira que sólo te resta
Para ganarte, perderte;
Venga ya la dulce muerte,
El morir venga ligero,
Que muero porque no muero.

Aquella vida de arriba,
Que es la vida verdadera,
Hasta que esta vida muera,
No se goza estando viva;
Muerte, no me seas esquiva;
Viva muriendo primero,
Que muero porque no muero.

Vida, ¿qué puedo yo darle
A mi Dios, que vive en mí,
Si no es el perderte a ti
Para merecer ganarte?
Quiero muriendo alcanzarte,
Pues tanto a mi Amado quiero,
Que muero porque no muero.

How bitter our existence ere
We come at last the Lord to meet !
For, though the soul finds loving sweet,
The waiting-time is hard to bear.
Oh, from this leaden weight of care,
My God, relieve me speedily,
Who die because I do not die.

I only live because I know
That death's approach is very sure,
And hope is all the more secure
Since death and life together go.
O death, thou life-creator, lo !
I wait upon thee, come thou nigh :
I die because I do not die.

Consider, life, love's potency,
And cease to cause me grief and pain.
Reflect, I beg, that, thee to gain,
I first must lose thee utterly.
Then, death, come pleasantly to me.
Come softly : undismay'd am I
Who die because I do not die.

That life, with life beyond recall,
Is truly life for evermore :
Until this present life be o'er
We cannot savour life at all.
So, death, retreat not at my call,
For life through death I can descry
Who die because I do not die.

O life, what service can I pay
Unto my God Who lives in me
Save if I first abandon thee
That I may merit thee for aye?
I'd win thee dying day by day,
Such yearning for my Spouse have I,
Dying because I do not die.

E. ALLISON PEERS

NADA TE TURBE

Nada te turbe,
Nada te espante,
Todo se pasa,
Dios no se muda;
La paciencia
Todo lo alcanza;
Quien a Dios tiene
Nada le falta:
Sólo Dios basta.

SAN JUAN DE LA CRUZ
[1542–1591]

Santa Teresa's disciple and assistant, San Juan de la Cruz, wrote only about one thousand lines of poetry. But in them, and their accompanying prose commentaries, he achieves the highest expression of Spanish mysticism. Indeed he is considered by many the greatest poet Spain has produced. The eminent Spanish

NOCHE OSCURA DEL ALMA

En una noche oscura,
Con ansias en amores inflamada,
¡Oh dichosa ventura!
Salí sin ser notada,
Estando ya mi casa sosegada.

A escuras, y segura,
Por la secreta escala disfrazada,
¡Oh dichosa ventura!
A escuras, y en celada,
Estando ya mi casa sosegada.

En la noche dichosa
En secreto, que nadie me veía,
Ni yo miraba cosa,
Sin otra luz y guía,
Sino la que en el corazón ardía.

LET NOTHING DISTURB THEE

Let nothing disturb thee,
Nothing affright thee;
All things are passing;
God never changeth;
Patient endurance
Attaineth to all things;
Who God possesseth
In nothing is wanting;
Alone God sufficeth.

HENRY WADSWORTH LONGFELLOW

*critic Menéndez y Pelayo calls his poetry 'angelic, celestial and divine', and
E. Allison Peers refers to it as 'the sweetest music in the Spanish language'.
San Juan's most famous poems are the* Noche oscura, Llama de
amor viva *and the* Cántico espiritual.

SONGS OF THE SOUL

*Songs of the soul that rejoices at having reached the high
estate of perfection, which is union with God, by the road of
spiritual negation.*

Upon a darksome night,
Kindling with love in flame of yearning keen
—O moment of delight !—
I went, by all unseen,
New-hush'd to rest the house where I had been.

Safe sped I through that night,
By the secret stair, disguisèd and unseen
—O moment of delight !—
Wrapt in that night serene,
New-hush'd to rest the house where I had been.

O happy night and blest !
Secretly speeding, screen'd from mortal gaze,
Unseeing, on I prest,
Lit by no earthly rays,
Nay, only by heart's inmost fire ablaze.

Aquesta me guiaba
Más cierto que la luz del mediodía,
Adonde me esperaba,
Quien yo bien me sabía,
En parte donde nadie parecía.

¡Oh noche, que guiaste,
Oh noche amable más que el alborada:
Oh noche, que juntaste
Amado con amada,
Amada en el Amado transformada!

En mi pecho florido,
Que entero para él sólo se guardaba,
Allí quedó dormido,
Y yo le regalaba,
Y el ventalle de cedros aire daba.

El aire de la almena,
Cuando yo sus cabellos esparcía,
Con su mano serena
En mi cuello hería,
Y todos mis sentidos suspendía.

Quedéme, y olvidéme,
El rostro recliné sobre el Amado,
Cesó todo, y dejéme,
Dejando mi cuidado
Entre las azucenas olvidado.

LLAMA DE AMOR VIVA

¡Oh llama de amor viva,
Que tiernamente hieres
De mi alma en el más profundo centro!
Pues ya no eres esquiva,
Acaba ya si quieres,
Rompe la tela deste dulce encuentro.

¡Oh cauterio suave!
¡Oh regalada llaga!
¡Oh mano blanda! ¡Oh toque delicado,
Que a vida eterna sabe,

'Twas that light guided me,
More surely than the noonday's brightest glare,
To the place where none would be
Save one that waited there—
Well knew I whom or ere I forth did fare.

O night that led'st me thus!
O night more winsome than the rising sun!
O night that madest us,
Lover and lov'd, as one,
Lover transform'd in lov'd, love's journey done!

Upon my flowering breast,
His only, as no man but he might prove,
There, slumbering, did he rest,
'Neath my caressing love,
Fann'd by the cedars swaying high above.

When from the turret's height,
Scattering his locks, the breezes play'd around,
With touch serene and light
He dealt me love's sweet wound,
And with the joyful pain thereof I swoon'd.

Forgetful, rapt, I lay,
My face reclining on my lov'd one fair.
All things for me that day
Ceas'd, as I slumber'd there,
Amid the lilies drowning all my care.

E. ALLISON PEERS

O FLAME OF LIVING LOVE

O flame of living love,
That dost eternally
Pierce through my soul with so consuming heat,
Since there's no help above,
Make thou an end of me,
And break the bond of this encounter sweet.

O burn that burns to heal!
O more than pleasant wound!
And O soft hand, O touch most delicate,
That dost new life reveal,

Y a toda deuda paga!
Matando, muerte en vida la has trocado.

¡Oh lámparas de fuego,
En cuyos resplandores
Las profundas cavernas del sentido,
Que estaba obscuro y ciego,
Con extraños primores
Calor y luz dan junto a su querido!

¡Cuán manso y amoroso
Recuerdas en mi seno,
Donde secretamente solo moras:
Y en tu aspirar sabroso
De bien y gloria lleno
Cuán delicadamente me enamoras!

COPLAS HECHAS SOBRE UN ÉXTASIS DE ALTA CONTEMPLACIÓN

Entréme donde no supe,
Y quedéme no sabiendo,
Toda sciencia trascendiendo.

Yo no supe dónde entraba,
Pero, cuando allí me ví,
Sin saber dónde me estaba,
Grandes cosas entendí;
No diré lo que sentí,
Que me quedé no sabiendo,
Toda sciencia trascendiendo.

De paz y de piedad
Era la sciencia perfecta,
En profunda soledad,
Entendida vía recta;
Era cosa tan secreta,
Que me quedé balbuciendo,
Toda sciencia trascendiendo.

Estaba tan embebido,
Tan absorto y ajenado,

That dost in grace abound,
And, slaying, dost from death to life translate!

O lamps of fire that shined
With so intense a light
That those deep caverns where the senses live,
Which were obscure and blind,
Now with strange glories bright,
Both heat and light to His belovèd give!

With how benign intent
Rememberest thou my breast,
Where thou alone abidest secretly;
And in thy sweet ascent,
With glory and good possessed,
How delicately thou teachest love to me!

ARTHUR SYMONS

VERSES WRITTEN AFTER AN ECSTASY
OF HIGH EXALTATION

I entered in, I know not where,
And I remained, though knowing naught,
Transcending knowledge with my thought.

Of when I entered I know naught,
But when I saw that I was there
(Though where it was I did not care)
Strange things I learned with greatness fraught.
Yet what I heard I'll not declare.
But there I stayed, though knowing naught,
Transcending knowledge with my thought.

Of peace and piety interwound
This perfect science had been wrought,
Within the solitude profound
A straight and narrow path it taught,
Such secret wisdom there I found
That there I stammered, saying naught,
But topped all knowledge with my thought.

So borne aloft, so drunken-reeling,
So rapt was I, so swept away,

Que se quedó mi sentido
De todo sentir privado;
Y el espíritu dotado
De un entender no entendiendo,
Toda sciencia trascendiendo.

El que allí llega de vero,
De sí mismo desfallesce;
Cuanto sabía primero
Mucho bajo le paresce;
Y su sciencia tanto cresce,
Que se queda no sabiendo,
Toda sciencia trascendiendo.

Cuanto más alto se sube,
Tanto menos entendía
Qué es la tenebrosa nube
Que a la noche esclarecía;
Por eso quien la sabía
Queda siempre no sabiendo
Toda sciencia trascendiendo.

Este saber no sabiendo
Es de tan alto poder,
Que los sabios arguyendo
Jamás le pueden vencer;
Que no llega su saber
A no entender entendiendo,
Toda sciencia trascendiendo.

Y es de tan alta excelencia
Aqueste sumo saber,
Que no hay facultad ni sciencia
Que le puedan emprender;
Quien se supiere vencer
Con un no saber sabiendo,
Irá siempre trascendiendo.

Y si lo queréis oír,
Consiste esta suma sciencia
En un subido sentir
De la divinal Esencia;
Es obra de su clemencia
Hacer quedar no entendiendo
Toda sciencia trascendiendo.

Within the scope of sense or feeling
My sense or feeling could not stay.
And in my soul I felt, revealing,
A sense that, though its sense was naught,
Transcended knowledge with my thought.

The man who truly there has come
Of his own self must shed the guise;
Of all he knew before the sum
Seems far beneath that wondrous prize :
And in this lore he grows so wise
That he remains, though knowing naught,
Transcending knowledge with his thought.

The farther that I climbed the height
The less I seemed to understand
The cloud so tenebrous and grand
That there illuminates the night
For he who understands that sight
Remains for aye, though knowing naught,
Transcending knowledge with his thought.

This wisdom without understanding
Is of so absolute a force
No wise man of whatever standing
Can ever stand against its course,
Unless they tap its wondrous source,
To know so much, though knowing naught,
They pass all knowledge with their thought.

This summit all so steeply towers
And is of excellence so high
No human faculties or powers
Can ever to the top come nigh.
Whoever with its steep could vie,
Though knowing nothing, would transcend
All thought, forever, without end.

If you would ask, what is its essence—
This summit of all sense and knowing :
It comes from the Divinest Presence—
The sudden sense of Him outflowing,
In His great clemency bestowing
The gift that leaves men knowing naught,
Yet passing knowledge with their thought.

ROY CAMPBELL

LOPE DE RUEDA
[1510–1565]

In the introduction to his Ocho comedias, Cervantes *speaks admiringly
of Lope de Rueda, one of the forerunners of the Spanish drama.* Director
and principal actor of a comic troupe, Lope de Rueda was the author—among

LAS ACEITUNAS

TORUBIO, *simple, viejo*
ÁGUEDA DE TORUÉGANO, *su mujer*
MENCIGÜELA, *su hija*
ALOJA, *vecino*

TOR. ¡Válgame Dios y qué tempestad ha hecho desde el requebrajo
del monte acá, que no pareció sino que el cielo se quería hundir y las
nubes venir abajo! Pues decid ahora: ¿qué os tendrá aparejado de
comer la señora de mi mujer? ¡así mala rabia la mate! (*Llamando.*)
¿Oíslo? ¡Muchacha Mencigüela! Si todos duermen en Zamora.
¡Águeda de Toruégano! ¡oíslo!

MEN. ¡Jesús, padre! ¿y habéisnos de quebrar las puertas?
TOR. ¡Mirad qué pico, mirad qué pico! ¿Y adónde está vuestra
madre, señora?
MEN. Allá está en casa de la vecina, que le ha ido a ayudar a coser
unas madejillas.
TOR. ¡Malas madejillas vengan por ella y por vos! Andad y llamadla.

AGU. Ya, ya, el de los misterios, ya viene de hacer una negra car-
guilla de leña, que no hay quien se averigüe con él.
TOR. ¿Sí? ¿carguilla de leña le parece a la señora? Juro al cielo de
Dios que éramos yo y vuestro ahijado a cargarla y no podíamos.

other dramatic pieces—of delightful one-act farces called pasos. *These developed into the* entremeses *of the Golden Age, and the* sainetes *of the eighteenth century.*

The paso *presented here is his famous* Las aceitunas.

THE OLIVES

TORUVIO .... an old man
AGUEDA DE TORUÉGANO ... his wife
MENCIGÜELA ...... their daughter
ALOJA .... a neighbour

Scene: Outside the door of Toruvio's house. It has been raining, but has cleared.

(*Enter* Toruvio, *dripping wet, and carrying firewood.*)

TOR. Good Heavens, what a storm raged through the ravines of that wooded hill out yonder. Every minute I expected the sky to fall and the clouds to come down on top of me. And am I hungry? I wonder what my wife has ready to eat. (*He tries the door and finds it locked. He throws down his load.*) Plague take her! Wife! Where's that daughter of mine, Mencigüela? Is everybody fast asleep! Agueda de Toruégano! Wife!

(Mencigüela *comes to the door.*)

MEN. For goodness' sake, father, are you going to break down the door?

TOR. What a chatterbox! What a regular magpie! And where is your mother, young lady?

MEN. She's next door at the neighbour's, for she's gone to help her wind some skeins.

TOR. May evil skeins carry her away, and you, too! Go and call her.

(*Enter* Agueda, *his wife.*)

AGUE. Well, well, here's the frequenter of witches' revels just come back from hauling a little bit of wood, and so grouchy that nobody can get along with him.

TOR. Maybe you think it's only a little bit of wood, but I swear to heaven that I and your godchild were both hauling it, and it was all we could handle.

AGUE. Ya, noramaza sea, marido, ¡y qué mojado que venís!

TOR. Vengo hecho una sopa de agua. Mujer, por vida vuestra, que me deis algo que cenar.

ÁGUE. ¿Yo qué diablos os tengo de dar, si no tengo cosa ninguna?

MEN. ¡Jesús, padre, y qué mojada que venía aquella leña!

TOR. Sí, despуés dirá tu madre que es el alba.

ÁGUE. Corre, muchacha, aderézale un par de huevos para que cene tu padre, y hazle luego la cama. Y os aseguro, marido, que nunca se os acordó de plantar aquel renuevo de aceitunas que rogué que plantaseis.

TOR. ¿Pues en qué me he detenido sino en plantarle como me rogasteis?

ÁGUE. Callad, marido, ¿y adónde lo plantasteis?

TOR. Allí junto a la higuera breval, adonde, si se os acuerda, os di un beso.

MEN. Padre, bien puede entrar a cenar, que ya está aderezado todo.

ÁGUE. Marido, ¿no sabéis qué he pensado?: que aquel renuevo de aceitunas que plantasteis hoy, que de aquí a seis o siete años llevará cuatro o cinco fanegas de aceitunas, y que poniendo plantas acá y plantas acullá, de aquí a veinte y cinco o treinta años, tendréis un olivar hecho y derecho.

TOR. Eso es la verdad, mujer, que no puede dejar de ser lindo.

ÁGUE. Mirad, marido, ¿sabéis qué he pensado?: que yo cogeré la aceituna y vos la acarrearéis con el asnillo, y Mencigüela la venderá en la plaza. Y mira, muchacha, que te mando que no me des menos el celemín de a dos reales castellanos.

TOR. ¿Cómo a dos reales castellanos? ¿No veis que es cargo de conciencia y nos llevará al almotacén cada día la pena, que basta pedir a catorce o quince dineros por celemín?

ÁGUE. Callad, marido, que es el veduño de la casta de los de Córdoba.

TOR. Pues aunque sea de la casta de los de Córdoba, basta pedir lo que tengo dicho.

ÁGUE. Hora no me quebréis la cabeza. Mira, muchacha, que te mando que no las des menos el celemín de a dos reales castellanos.

TOR. ¿Cómo 'a dos reales castellanos'? Ven acá, muchacha: ¿a cómo has de pedir?

MEN. A como quisiereis, padre.

TOR. A catorce o quince dineros.

AGUE. But, bad luck to you, husband, how wet you are!

TOR. Indeed I'm wet as sop. Wife, as you value your life, get me something to eat.

AGUE. And what the devil am I to give you, if I haven't anything?

MEN. Dear me, father, how wet the wood is!

TOR. Yes, your mother will be saying next 'Fiddlesticks!'

AGUE. Hurry, daughter. Cook a couple of eggs for your father to eat and then make up the bed. (Mencigüela *goes into the house.*) I'm sure, husband, that it never once entered your head to plant that olive sapling as I asked you to.

TOR. Well, what made me so late, if it wasn't planting it as you wanted?

AGUE. Really, husband? And where did you plant it?

TOR. Out there near the early fig tree where, if you remember, I once gave you a kiss.

(Mencigüela *opens the door.*)

MEN. Dad, come in and eat now, for everything is ready.

AGUE. Husband, you don't know what I'm thinking, do you? That in six or seven years that olive tree you planted today will bear four or five bushels of olives, and that setting out trees here and there, twenty or thirty years from now you'll have a really and truly olive grove.

TOR. That's true, wife, and won't that be fine!

AGUE. See here, husband, do you know what I've thought? That I'll pick the olives and you'll take them in the donkey cart and Mencigüela will sell them in the main square. And look here, child, I tell you not to bring me back less than two Castilian reales a peck!

TOR. What do you mean, two reales? Why, my conscience will trouble me, and besides, the clerk of the market who regulates prices will fine us every day. A third of that is plenty to ask for a peck.

AGUE. Nonsense, husband, for they are the very best quality, as good as the horses of Cordoba.

TOR. Well, even if they are better than the best that Cordoba can show, you sell them for what I say, because that's plenty.

AGUE. Go away and don't bother me. See here, daughter, I order you not to sell a peck for less than two Castilian reales.

TOR. What are you talking about with your two reales? Come here, child. How much are you going to ask? (*He tugs at her.*)

MEN. Whatever you want, father.

TOR. Seven or eight maravedis.

MEN. Así lo haré, padre.

ÁGUE. ¿Cómo 'así lo haré, padre'? Ven acá, muchacha: ¿a cómo has de pedir?

MEN. A como mandareis, madre.

ÁGUE. A dos reales castellanos.

TOR. ¿Cómo 'a dos reales castellanos'? Yo os prometo que si no hacéis lo que yo os mando, que os tengo de dar más de doscientos correonazos. ¿A cómo has de pedir?

MEN. A como decís vos, padre.

TOR. A catorce o quince dineros.

MEN. Así lo haré, padre.

ÁGUE. ¿Cómo 'así lo haré, padre'? Tomad, tomad, haced lo que yo os mando.

TOR. Deja la muchacha.

MEN. ¡Ay, madre! ¡ay, padre, que me mata!

ALO. ¿Qué es esto, vecinos? ¿por qué maltratáis así la muchacha?

ÁGUE. ¡Ay, señor!, este mål hombre que me quiere dar las cosas a menos precio y quiere echar a perder mi casa: ¡unas aceitunas que son como nueces!

TOR. Yo juro a los huesos de mi linaje que no son ni aun como piñones.

ÁGUE. ¡Sí son!

TOR. ¡No son!

ALO. Hora, señora vecina, hacedme tamaño placer que os entréis allá dentro, que yo lo averiguaré todo.

ÁGUE. Averigüe o póngase todo del quebranto.

ALO. Señor vecino, ¿qué son de las aceitunas? Sacadlas acá fuera, que yo las compraré, aunque sean veinte fanegas.

TOR. Que no, señor; que no es de esa manera que vuestra merced se piensa, que no están las aceitunas aquí en casa, sino en la heredad.

ALO. Pues traedlas aquí, que yo las compraré todas al precio que justo fuere.

MEN. A dos reales quiere mi madre que se venda el celemín.

ALO. Cara cosa es ésa.

TOR. ¿No le parece a vuestra merced?

MEN. Y mi padre a quince dineros.

ALO. Tenga yo una muestra de ellas.

TOR. ¡Válgame Dios, señor!, vuestra merced no me quiere entender.

MEN. Yes, sir, that's what I'll do.

AGUE. What do you mean : 'That's what I'll do'? Come here, girl. How much are you going to ask? (*She pulls* Mencigüela *away.*)

MEN. Whatever you tell me, mother.

AGUE. Two Castilian reales.

TOR. Two reales, bosh! I promise you that if you don't do as I tell you, I'm going to give you more than two hundred lashes. Now, how much are you going to sell a peck for?

MEN. Just what you say, father.

TOR. Eight maravedis.

MEN. That's what I'll do.

AGUE. There you go again with your : 'That's what I'll do.' Take that and that (*beating her*) and do what I tell you.

TOR. Let that girl alone. (*He pulls* Mencigüela *and tries to push* Agueda *away.*)

MEN. Ouch, mother! Oh, father, you're pulling me apart.

(*Enter* Aloja, *a neighbour.*)

ALO. What's the matter, neighbours? Why are you maltreating the girl that way?

AGUE. Oh, sir, this bad man wants to sell things for less than they're worth, and wants to ruin us all. And olives as big as walnuts!

TOR. I vow by the bones of my ancestors that they're not even as big as hickory nuts.

AGUE. They are, too!

TOR. They are not!

ALO. Now, good madame, my neighbour, be kind enough to go in there and I'll find out everything.

AGUE. Find out, or let everything go to smash. (Agueda *goes into the house.*)

ALO. Now, sir, what's all this about olives? Bring them out for me. Even if there are twenty bushels, I'll buy them.

TOR. You can't, because things aren't the way you think. The olives aren't here in the house. They're out on the farm.

ALO. Well, go fetch them, then, because I'll buy all of them at what will be a just price.

MEN. At two reales a peck, my mother wants to sell them.

ALO. That's pretty expensive.

TOR. Yes, don't you think so?

MEN. And my father at a third of that.

ALO. May I have a sample of them?

TOR. Bless us, sir! You don't try to understand me. Today I

Hoy he yo plantado un renuevo de aceitunas, y dice mi mujer que de aquí a seis o siete años llevará cuatro o cinco fanegas de aceituna, y que ella la cogería, y que yo la acarrease y la muchacha la vendiese, y que a fuerza de derecho había de pedir a dos reales por cada celemín; yo que no, y ella que sí, y sobre esto ha sido la cuestión.

ALO. ¡Oh, qué graciosa cuestión, nunca tal se ha visto! Las aceitunas no están plantadas, y ha llevado la muchacha tarea sobre ellas!

MEN. ¡Qué le parece, señor!

TOR. No llores, rapaza. La muchacha, señor, es como un oro. Hora andad, hija, y ponedme la mesa, que yo os prometo de hacer un sayuelo de las primeras aceitunas que se vendieren.

ALO. Ahora andad, vecino, entraos allá adentro y tened paz con vuestra mujer.

TOR. Adiós, señor.

ALO. Hora, por cierto, ¡qué cosas vemos en esta vida que ponen espanto! Las aceitunas no están plantadas, y ya las habemos visto reñidas. Razón será que dé fin a mi embajada.

MIGUEL DE CERVANTES SAAVEDRA
[1547–1616]

Beyond his pre-eminence as Spain's foremost writer, Miguel de Cervantes Saavedra ranks among the true giants of world literature. His magnificent work Don Quixote *is considered one of the greatest literary creations ever produced by a single human mind. It is certainly the world's finest novel.*

Cervantes was born in Alcald de Henares in 1547. During the famous naval battle of Lepanto in 1571 he was maimed in the left hand, 'for the greater glory of the right'. On his way back to Spain in 1575, Cervantes was captured by pirates, and held prisoner in Algiers until freed by ransom in 1580.

*Between 1582 and 1587, Cervantes claims to have composed some twenty or thirty dramas, of which group only two—*El trato de Argel *and* La Numancia—*have come down to us. In 1585 he wrote the pastoral novel* La Galatea, *which remained his favourite work; throughout his life, Cervantes promised to write a second part but never did so.*

For many years he worked as a Government tax agent, and was several times imprisoned for irregularities caused by his financial ineptitude and dishonest associates.

In 1605 the first part of the immortal Don Quixote *appeared. It met with overwhelming success. The* Novelas ejemplares, *twelve charming novelettes, were published in 1613. The following year marked the publication of* Viaje del Parnaso, *a long verse work whose theme is poets and poetry. (Cervantes had always liked to write poetry, although aware of his limitations.)*

planted an olive shoot, and my wife says that six or seven years from now it will bear four or five bushels of olives and that she'll pick them, and for me to cart them and the girl to sell them, and that by all rights she ought to ask two reales a peck. I say 'no' and she says 'yes', and that's what the argument has been about.

ALO. Oh, what a funny argument! Who ever heard of anything like that before! The olives aren't even planted, and has the girl got to be brought to task for them?

MEN. Yes, isn't that awful?

TOR. Don't cry, girl! That child, sir, is as good as gold. Now go, dear, and set the table for me, and I promise to get you a pretty frock from the first olives that are sold. (Mencigüela *goes into the house.*)

ALO. Go on, sir. Go in and make peace with your wife.

TOR. Goodbye, neighbour. (Toruvio *goes into the house.*)

ALO. Well, I swear, life is full of surprises. The olives aren't planted and yet we see them quarrelled over. But I guess I've done my job in settling things.

WILLIS KNAPP JONES

He was working at a leisurely pace on a second part of Don Quixote *when one Alonso Fernández de Avellaneda published an apocryphal continuation in 1614. Cervantes then hastened to finish his own second part, and it appeared in 1615.*

During the same year his Ocho comedias y ocho entremeses *were published. The all-verse* comedias, *however, cannot be compared with the plays of the outstanding Golden Age dramatists. In contrast, his* entremeses *(interludes), written mostly in prose, are clever, fast-moving farces which may still be staged or read with pleasure.*

Cervantes did not live to see the publication of his last work, Los trabajos de Persiles y Sigismunda, *a dream-like novel of fantastic adventures and wanderings. Indeed, recognizing that his days were numbered by illness, he had rushed to complete its final chapters. He wrote the prologue only a few days before his death in 1616.*

The Quixote, *his masterpiece, inspired countless volumes of comment and interpretation. Some critics see in it a study of all humanity; others believe Cervantes' expressed intention—that he wanted to write a parody ridiculing books of chivalry, and thus provide entertainment for his readers. It seems most likely that Cervantes started to write a novelette—another* novela ejemplar—*about a mad knight, but finding that he had not exhausted his subject, expanded its scope.*

In the first part, Don Quixote and his squire Sancho Panza are caricatured

*types, one representing illogical idealism—'quixotism'—the other, hard-
headed materialism. The adventures of the poor knight are mainly farcical,
intended simply to provoke laughter. Part II is superior in its organization,
style, universality and character development. Don Quixote's madness is less
obvious, and Sancho becomes more idealistic. By the end of the novel the two
characters are almost entirely blended.*

DON QUIJOTE

PRIMERA PARTE

*Capítulo primero. Que trata de la condición y ejercicio del famoso hidalgo
Don Quijote de la Mancha.*

En un lugar de la Mancha, de cuyo nombre no quiero acordarme,
no ha mucho tiempo que vivía un hidalgo de los de lanza en astillero,
adarga antigua, rocín flaco y galgo corredor. Una olla de algo más
vaca que carnero, salpicón las más noches, duelos y quebrantos los
sábados, lentejas los viernes, y algún palomino de añadidura los
domingos, consumían las tres partes de su hacienda. El resto de ella
concluían sayo de velarte, calzas de velludo para las fiestas con sus
pantuflas de lo mismo, y los días de entre semana se honraba con su
vellorí de lo más fino. Tenía en su casa un ama que pasaba de los
cuarenta, y una sobrina que no llegaba a los veinte, y un mozo de
campo y plaza, que así ensillaba el rocín como tomaba la podadera.
Frisaba la edad de nuestro hidalgo con los cincuenta años: era de
complexión recia, seco de carnes, enjuto de rostro, gran madrugador
y amigo de la caza. Quieren decir que tenía el sobrenombre de
Quijada o Quesada (que en esto hay alguna diferencia en los autores
que de este caso escriben), aunque por conjeturas verosímiles se deja
entender que se llamaba Quejana. Pero esto importa poco a nuestro
cuento: basta que en la narración de él no se salga un punto de la
verdad.
Es, pues, de saber que este sobredicho hidalgo, los ratos que estaba
ocioso (que eran los más del año) se daba a leer libros de caballerías
con tanta afición y gusto, que olvidó casi de todo punto el ejercicio
de la caza, y aun la administración de su hacienda; y llegó a tanto
su curiosidad y desatino en esto, que vendió muchas fanegas de tierra
de sembradura para comprar libros de caballerías en que leer, y así,
llevó a su casa todos cuantos pudo haber de ellos; y de todos, nin-

Don Quixote *has become the most widely published of all books with the exception of the Bible. Editions and translations in all languages are innumerable. The first English translation, by Thomas Shelton, appeared in 1612 (Part I) and 1620 (Part II). Of the many subsequent English translations, the three best are by John Ormsby, London, 1885; Samuel Putnam, New York, 1948; and J. M. Cohen, London, 1950.*

DON QUIXOTE

PART I

Chapter I. Which treats of the quality and way of life of the famous knight Don Quixote de la Mancha.

In a certain village in La Mancha, which I do not wish to name, there lived not long ago a gentleman—one of those who have always a lance in the rack, an ancient shield, a lean hack and a greyhound for coursing. His habitual diet consisted of a stew, more beef than mutton, of hash most nights, boiled bones on Saturdays, lentils on Fridays, and a young pigeon as a Sunday treat; and on this he spent three-quarters of his income. The rest of it went on a fine cloth doublet, velvet breeches and slippers for holidays, and a homespun suit of the best in which he decked himself on weekdays. His household consisted of a housekeeper of rather more than forty, a niece not yet twenty, and a lad for the field and market, who saddled his horse and wielded the pruning-hook.

Our gentleman was verging on fifty, of tough constitution, lean-bodied, thin-faced, a great early riser and a lover of hunting. They say that his surname was Quixada or Quesada—for there is some difference of opinion amongst authors on this point. However, by very reasonable conjecture we may take it that he was called Quexana. But this does not much concern our story; enough that we do not depart by so much as an inch from the truth in the telling of it.

The reader must know, then, that this gentleman, in the times when he had nothing to do—as was the case for most of the year—gave himself up to the reading of books of knight errantry; which he loved and enjoyed so much that he almost entirely forgot his hunting, and even the care of his estate. So odd and foolish, indeed, did he grow on this subject that he sold many acres of cornland to buy these books of chivalry to read, and in this way brought home every one he could get. And of them all he considered none

gunos le parecían tan bien como los que compuso el famoso Feliciano de Silva, porque la claridad de su prosa y aquellas intrincadas razones suyas le parecían de perlas y más cuando llegaba a leer aquellos requiebros y cartas de desafíos, donde en muchas partes hallaba escrito: 'La razón de la sinrazón que a mi razón se hace, de tal manera mi razón enflaquece, que con razón me quejo de la vuestra hermosura.' Y también cuando leía: 'Los altos cielos que de vuestra divinidad divinamente con las estrellas os fortifican, y os hacen merecedora del merecimiento que merece la vuestra grandeza.'

Con estas razones perdía el pobre caballero el juicio, y desvelábase por entenderlas y desentrañarles el sentido, que no se lo sacara ni las entendiera el mismo Aristóteles, si resucitara para sólo ello. No estaba muy bien con las heridas que don Belianís daba y recibía, porque se imaginaba que por grandes maestros que le hubiesen curado, no dejaría de tener el rostro y todo el cuerpo lleno de cicatrices y señales. Pero, con todo, alababa en su autor aquel acabar su libro con la promesa de aquella inacabable aventura, y muchas veces le vino deseo de tomar la pluma y darle fin al pie de la letra, como allí se promete; y sin duda alguna lo hiciera y aun saliera con ello, si otros mayores y continuos pensamientos no se lo estorbaran.

Tuvo muchas veces competencia con el cura de su lugar (que era hombre docto, graduado en Sigüenza), sobre cuál había sido mejor caballero, Palmerín de Inglaterra o Amadís de Gaula; mas maese Nicolás, barbero del mismo pueblo, decía que ninguno llegaba al Caballero del Febo, y que si alguno se le podía comparar era don Galaor, hermano de Amadís de Gaula, porque tenía muy acomodada condición para todo, que no era caballero melindroso, ni tan llorón como su hermano, y que en lo de valentía no le iba en zaga.

En resolución, él se enfrascó tanto en su lectura, que se le pasaban las noches leyendo de claro en claro, y los días de turbio en turbio; y así, del poco dormir y del mucho leer se le secó el cerebro de manera que vino a perder el juicio. Llenósele la fantasía de todo aquello que leía en los libros, así de encantamientos como de pendencias, batallas, desafíos, heridas, requiebros, amores, tormentas y disparates imposibles; y asentósele de tal modo en la imaginación que era verdad toda aquella máquina de aquellas sonadas invenciones que leía, que para él no había otra historia más cierta en el mundo. Decía él que el Cid Ruy Díaz había sido muy buen caballero, pero que no tenía que ver con el caballero de la Ardiente Espada, que de sólo un revés había partido por medio dos fieros y

so good as the works of the famous Feliciano de Silva. For his brilliant style and those complicated sentences seemed to him very pearls, especially when he came upon those love-passages and challenges frequently written in the manner of : 'The reason for the unreason with which you treat my reason, so weakens my reason that with reason I complain of your beauty'; and also when he read : 'The high heavens that with their stars divinely fortify you in your divinity and make you deserving of the desert that your greatness deserves.'

These writings drove the poor knight out of his wits; and he passed sleepless nights trying to understand them and disentangle their meaning, though Aristotle himself would never have unravelled or understood them, even if he had been resurrected for that sole purpose. He did not much like the wounds that Sir Belianis gave and received, for he imagined that his face and his whole body must have been covered with scars and marks, however skilful the surgeons who tended him. But, for all that, he admired the author for ending his book with the promise to continue with that interminable adventure, and often the desire seized him to take up the pen himself and write the promised sequel for him. No doubt he would have done so, and perhaps successfully, if other greater and more persistent preoccupations had not prevented him.

Often he had arguments with the priest of his village, who was a scholar and a graduate of Siguenza, as to which was the better knight—Palmerin of England or Amadis of Gaul. But Master Nicholas, the barber of that village, said that no one could compare with the Knight of the Sun. Though if anyone could, it was Sir Galaor, brother of Amadis of Gaul. For he had a very accommodating nature, and was not so affected nor such a sniveller as his brother, though he was not a bit behind him in the matter of bravery.

In short, he so buried himself in his books that he spent the nights reading from twilight till daybreak and the days from dawn till dark; and so from little sleep and much reading, his brain dried up and he lost his wits. He filled his mind with all that he read in them, with enchantments, quarrels, battles, challenges, wounds, wooings, loves, torments and other impossible nonsense; and so deeply did he steep his imagination in the belief that all the fanciful stuff he read was true, that to his mind no history in the world was more authentic. He used to say that the Cid Ruy Diaz must have been a very good knight, but that he could not be compared to the Knight of the Burning Sword, who with a single backstroke had cleft a pair of fierce and monstrous giants in two. And he had

descomunales gigantes. Mejor estaba con Bernardo del Carpio, porque en Roncesvalles había muerto a Roldán el encantado, valiéndose de la industria de Hércules cuando ahogó a Anteo, el hijo de la Tierra, entre los brazos. Decía mucho bien del gigante Morgante, porque, con ser de aquella generación gigantea, que todos son soberbios y descomedidos, él solo era afable y bien criado. Pero, sobre todos, estaba bien con Reinaldos de Montalbán, y más cuando lo veía salir de su castillo, y robar cuantos topaba, y cuando en allende robó aquel ídolo de Mahoma, que era todo de oro, según dice su historia. Diera él, por dar una mano de coces al traidor de Galalón, al ama que tenía y aun a su sobrina de añadidura.

En efecto, rematado ya su juicio, vino a dar en el más extraño pensamiento que jamás dió loco en el mundo, y fué que le pareció convenible y necesario, así para el aumento de su honra como para el servicio de su república, hacerse caballero andante e irse por todo el mundo con sus armas y caballo a buscar las aventuras, y a ejercitarse en todo aquello que él había leído que los caballeros andantes se ejercitaban, deshaciendo todo género de agravio, y poniéndose en ocasiones y peligros, donde acabándolos, cobrase eterno nombre y fama. Imaginábase el pobre ya coronado por el valor de su brazo, por lo menos del imperio de Trapisonda y así, con estos tan agradables pensamientos, llevado del extraño gusto que en ellos sentía, se dió prisa a poner en efecto lo que deseaba. Y lo primero que hizo fué limpiar unas armas que habían sido de sus bisabuelos, que, tomadas de orín y llenas de moho, luengos siglos había que estaban puestas y olvidadas en un rincón. Limpiólas y aderezólas lo mejor que pudo; pero vió que tenían una gran falta, y era que no tenían celada de encaje, sino morrión simple; mas a esto suplió su industria, porque de cartones hizo un modo de media celada, que, encajada con el morrión, hacía una apariencia de celada entera. Es verdad que para probar si era fuerte y podía estar al riesgo de una cuchillada, sacó su espada y le dió dos golpes, y con el primero y en un punto deshizo lo que había hecho en una semana; y no dejó de parecerle mal. la facilidad con que la había hecho pedazos, y por asegurarse de este peligro, la tornó a hacer de nuevo poniéndole unas barras de hierro por de dentro, de tal manera que él quedó satisfecho de su fortaleza y sin querer hacer nueva experiencia de ella, la diputó y tuvo por celada finísima de encaje.

Fué luego a ver a su rocín, y aunque tenía más cuartos que un real, y más tachas que el caballo de Gonela, que *tantum pellis et ossa fuit*, le pareció que ni el Bucéfalo de Alejandro, ni Babieca el del Cid, con él se igualaban.

an even better opinion of Bernardo del Carpio for slaying the enchanted Roland at Roncesvalles, by making use of Hercules' trick when he throttled the Titan Antaeus in his arms.

He spoke very well of the giant Morgante; for, though one of that giant brood who are all proud and insolent, he alone was affable and well-mannered. But he admired most of all Reynald of Montalban, particularly when he saw him sally forth from his castle and rob everyone he met, and when in heathen lands overseas he stole that idol of Mahomet, which history says was of pure gold. But he would have given his housekeeper and his niece into the bargain, to deal the traitor Galaon a good kicking.

In fact, now that he had utterly wrecked his reason he fell into the strangest fancy that ever a madman had in the whole world. He thought it fit and proper, both in order to increase his renown and to serve the state, to turn knight errant and travel through the world with horse and armour in search of adventures, following in every way the practice of the knights errant he had read of, redressing all manner of wrongs, and exposing himself to chances and dangers, by the overcoming of which he might win eternal honour and renown. Already the poor man fancied himself crowned by the valour of his arm, at least with the empire of Trebizond; and so, carried away by the strange pleasure he derived from these agreeable thoughts, he hastened to translate his desires into action.

The first thing that he did was to clean some armour which had belonged to his ancestors, and had lain for ages forgotten in a corner, eaten with rust and covered with mould. But when he had cleaned and repaired it as best he could, he found that there was one great defect: the helmet was a simple head-piece without a visor. So he ingeniously made good this deficiency by fashioning out of pieces of pasteboard a kind of half-visor which, fitted to the helmet, gave the appearance of a complete head-piece. However, to see if it was strong enough to stand up to the risk of a sword-cut, he took out his sword and gave it two strokes, the first of which demolished in a moment what had taken him a week to make. He was not too pleased at the ease with which he had destroyed it, and to safeguard himself against this danger, reconstructed the visor, putting some strips of iron inside, in such a way as to satisfy himself of his protection; and, not caring to make another trial of it, he accepted it as a fine jointed head-piece and put it into commission.

Next he went to inspect his hack, but though, through leanness, he had more quarters than there are pence in a groat, and more blemishes than Gonella's horse, which was nothing but skin and bone, he appeared to our knight more than the equal of Alexander's

Cuatro días se le pasaron en imaginar qué nombre le pondría porque (según se decía él a sí mismo) no era razón que caballo de caballero tan famoso, y tan bueno él por sí, estuviese sin nombre conocido; y así procuraba acomodársele de manera que declarase quién había sido antes que fuese de caballero andante, y lo que era entonces; pues estaba muy puesto en razón que mudando su señor estado, mudase él también el nombre, y lo cobrase famoso y de estruendo, como convenía a la nueva orden y al nuevo ejercicio que ya profesaba; y así, después de muchos nombres que formó, borró y quitó, añadió, deshizo y tornó a hacer en su memoria e imaginación, al fin le vino a llamar Rocinante, nombre a su parecer alto, sonoro y significativo de lo que había sido cuando fué rocín, antes de lo que ahora era, que era antes y primero de todos los rocines del mundo. Puesto nombre y tan a su gusto a su caballo, quiso ponérselo a sí mismo y en este pensamiento duró otros ocho días, y al cabo se vino a llamar don Quijote; de donde, como queda dicho, tomaron ocasión los autores de esta tan verdadera historia, que sin duda se debía llamar Quijada, y no Quesada, como otros quisieron decir. Pero acordándose que el valeroso Amadís no sólo se había contentado con llamarse Amadís a secas, sino que añadió el nombre de su reino y patria por hacerla famosa, y se llamó Amadís de Gaula, así quiso, como buen caballero, añadir al suyo el nombre de la suya, y llamarse don Quijote de la Mancha, con que, a su parecer, declaraba muy al vivo su linaje y patria, y la honraba con tomar el sobrenombre de ella.

Limpias, pues, sus armas, hecho del morrión celada, puesto nombre a su rocín, y confirmándose a sí mismo, se dió a entender que no le faltaba otra cosa sino buscar una dama de quien enamorarse; porque el caballero andante sin amores era árbol sin hojas y sin fruto, y cuerpo sin alma. Decíase él: 'Si yo por males de mis pecados, o por mi buena suerte, me encuentro por ahí con algún gigante, como de ordinario les acontece a los caballeros andantes, y lo derribo de un encuentro, o lo parto por mitad del cuerpo, o finalmente lo venzo y lo rindo, ¿no será bien tener a quien enviarlo presentado, y que entre y se hinque de rodillas ante mi dulce señora, y diga con voz humilde y rendida: 'Yo, señora, soy el gigante Caraculiambro, señor de la ínsula Malindrania, a quien venció en singular batalla el jamás como se debe alabado caballero don Quijote de la Mancha, el cual me mandó que me presentase ante la vuestra merced para que la vuestra

Bucephalus and the Cid's Babieca. He spent four days pondering what name to give him; for, he reflected, it would be wrong for the horse of so famous a knight, a horse so good in himself, to be without a famous name. Therefore he tried to fit him with one that would signify what he had been before his master turned knight errant, and what he now was; for it was only right that as his master changed his profession, the horse should change his name for a sublime and high-sounding one, befitting the new order and the new calling he professed. So, after many names invented, struck out and rejected, amended, cancelled and remade in his fanciful mind, he finally decided to call him Rocinante, a name which seemed to him grand and sonorous, and to express the common horse he had been before arriving at his present state : the first and foremost of all hacks in the world.

Having found so pleasing a name for his horse, he next decided to do the same for himself, and spent another eight days thinking about it. Finally he resolved to call himself Don Quixote. And that is no doubt why the authors of this true history, as we have said, assumed that his name must have been Quixada and not Quesada, as other authorities would have it. Yet he remembered that the valorous Amadis had not been content with his bare name, but had added the name of his kingdom and native country in order to make it famous, and styled himself Amadis of Gaul. So, like a good knight, he decided to add the name of his country to his own and call himself Don Quixote de la Mancha. Thus, he thought, he very clearly proclaimed his parentage and native land and honoured it by taking his surname from it.

Now that his armour was clean, his helmet made into a complete head-piece, a name found for his horse, and he confirmed in his new title, it struck him that there was only one more thing to do : to find a lady to be enamoured of. For a knight errant without a lady is like a tree without leaves or fruit and a body without a soul. He said to himself again and again : 'If I for my sins or by good luck were to meet with some giant hereabouts, as generally happens to knights errant, and if I were to overthrow him in the encounter, or cut him down the middle or, in short, conquer him and make him surrender, would it not be well to have someone to whom I could send him as a present, so that he could enter and kneel down before my sweet lady and say in tones of humble submission : "Lady, I am the giant Caraculiambro, lord of the island of Malindrania, whom the never-sufficiently-to-be-praised knight, Don Quixote de la Mancha, conquered in single combat and ordered to appear before your Grace, so that your Highness might

grandeza disponga de mí a su talante'? ¡Oh, cómo se holgó nuestro buen caballero cuando hubo hecho este discurso, y más cuando halló a quien dar nombre de su dama! Y fué, a lo que se cree, que en un lugar cerca del suyo había una moza labradora de muy buen parecer, de quien él un tiempo anduvo enamorado, aunque según se entiende, ella jamás lo supo ni se dió cata de ello. Llamábase Aldonza Lorenzo, y a ésta le pareció ser bien darle título de señora de sus pensamientos; y buscándole nombre que no desdijese mucho del suyo, y que tirase y se encaminase al de princesa y gran señora, vino a llamarla Dulcinea del Toboso, porque era natural del Toboso: nombre, a su parecer músico y peregino, y significativo, como todos los demás que a él y a sus cosas había puesto.

Capítulo II. Que trata de la primera salida que de su tierra hizo el ingenioso Don Quijote.

Hechas, pues, estas prevenciones, no quiso aguardar más tiempo a poner en efecto su pensamiento, apretándole a ello la falta que él pensaba que hacía en el mundo su tardanza, según eran los agravios que pensaba deshacer, tuertos que enderezar, sinrazones que enmendar, y abusos que mejorar, y deudas que satisfacer. Y así, sin dar parte a persona alguna de su intención y sin que nadie lo viese, una mañana, antes del día (que era uno de los calurosos del mes de julio) se armó de todas sus armas, subió sobre Rocinante, puesta su mal compuesta celada, embrazó su·adarga, tomó su lanza y por la puerta falsa de un corral salió al campo con grandísimo contento y alborozo de ver con cuánta facilidad había dado principio a su buen deseo. Mas apenas se vió en el campo, cuando lo asaltó un pensamiento terrible, y tal que por poco lo hiciera dejar la comenzada empresa, y fué que le vino a la memoria que no era armado caballero, y que conforme a la ley de caballería ni podía ni debía tomar armas con ningún caballero; y puesto que lo fuera, había de llevar armas blancas como novel caballero, sin empresa en el escudo, hasta que por su esfuerzo la ganase. Estos pensamientos lo hicieron titubear en su propósito; mas pudiendo más su locura que otra razón alguna, propuso de hacerse armar caballero del primero que topase, a imitación de otros muchos que así lo hicieron, según él había leído en los libros que tal le tenían. En lo de las armas blancas, pensaba limpiarlas de manera, en teniendo lugar, que lo fuesen más que un armiño; y con esto se quietó y prosiguió su camino, sin llevar otro que aquel que su caballo quería, creyendo que en aquello consistía la fuerza de las aventuras.

dispose of me according to your will"?' Oh, how pleased our knight was when he had made up this speech, and even gladder when he found someone whom he could call his lady. It happened, it is believed, in this way : in a village near his there was a very good-looking farm girl, whom he had been taken with at one time, although she is supposed not to have known it or had proof of it. Her name was Aldonza Lorenzo, and she it was he thought fit to call the lady of his fancies; and, casting around for a name which should not be too far away from her own, yet suggest and imply a princess and great lady, he resolved to call her Dulcinea del Toboso —for she was a native of El Toboso—a name which seemed to him as musical, strange and significant as those others that he had devised for himself and his possessions.

Chapter II. Which treats of the First Expedition which the ingenious Don Quixote made from his village.

Once these preparations were completed, he was anxious to wait no longer before putting his ideas into effect, impelled to this by the thought of the loss the world suffered by his delay, seeing the grievances there were to redress, the wrongs to right, the injuries to amend, the abuses to correct, and the debts to discharge. So, telling nobody of his intention, and quite unobserved, one morning before dawn—it was on one of those sweltering July days—he armed himself completely, mounted Rocinante, put on his badly-mended head-piece, slung on his shield, seized his lance and went out into the plain through the back gate of his yard, pleased and delighted to see with what ease he had started on his fair design. But scarcely was he in open country when he was assailed by a thought so terrible that it almost made him abandon the enterprise he had just begun. For he suddenly remembered that he had never received the honour of knighthood, and so, according to the laws of chivalry, he neither could nor should take arms against any knight, and even if he had been knighted he was bound, as a novice, to wear plain armour without a device on his shield until he should gain one by his prowess. These reflections made him waver in his resolve, but as his madness outweighed any other argument, he made up his mind to have himself knighted by the first man he met, in imitation of many who had done the same, as he had read in the books which had so influenced him. As to plain armour, he decided to clean his own, when he had time, till it was whiter than ermine. With this he quieted his mind and went on his way, taking whatever road his horse chose, in the belief that in this lay the essence of adventure.

Yendo, pues, caminando nuestro flamante aventurero, iba hablando consigo mismo y diciendo: '¿Quién duda sino que en los venideros tiempos, cuando salga a luz la verdadera historia de mis famosos hechos, que el sabio que los escribiere no ponga, cuando llegue a contar esta mi primera salida tan de mañana, de esta manera?: 'Apenas había el rubicundo Apolo tendido por la faz de la ancha y espaciosa tierra las doradas hebras de sus hermosos cabellos, y apenas los pequeños y pintados pajarillos con sus arpadas lenguas habían saludado con dulce y meliflua armonía la venida de la rosada aurora, que dejando la blanda cama del celoso marido, por las puertas y balcones del manchego horizonte a los mortales se mostraba, cuando el famoso caballero don Quijote de la Mancha, dejando las ociosas plumas, subió sobre su famoso caballo Rocinante, y comenzó a caminar por el antiguo y conocido campo de Montiel'. (Y era la verdad que por él caminaba). Y añadió diciendo: '¡Dichosa edad y siglo dichoso aquel adonde saldrán a luz las famosas hazañas mías, dignas de entallarse en bronces, esculpirse en mármoles y pintarse en tablas para memoria en lo futuro! ¡Oh tú, sabio encantador, quienquiera que seas, a quien ha de tocar ser cronista de esta peregrina historia!, ruégote que no te olvides de mi buen Rocinante, compañero eterno mío en todos mis caminos y carreras.' Luego volvía diciendo, como si verdaderamente fuera enamorado: '¡Oh, princesa Dulcinea, señora de este cautivo corazón!, mucho agravio me habéis hecho en despedirme y reprocharme con el riguroso afincamiento de mandarme no parecer ante la vuestra hermosura. Plégaos, señora, de membraros de este vuestro sujeto corazón, que tantas cuitas por vuestro amor padece'.

Con estos iba ensartando otros disparates, todos al modo de los que sus libros le habían enseñado, imitando en cuanto podía su lenguaje; y con esto caminaba tan despacio, y el sol entraba tan aprisa y con tanto ardor, que fuera bastante a derretirle los sesos si algunos tuviera. Casi todo aquel día caminó sin acontecerle cosa que de contar fuese, de lo cual se desesperaba, porque quisiera topar luego, luego, con quien hacer experiencia del valor de su fuerte brazo. Autores hay que dicen que la primera aventura que le avino fué la del Puerto Lápice, otros dicen que la de los molinos de viento; pero lo que yo he podido averiguar en este caso, y lo que he hallado escrito en los anales de la Mancha, es que él anduvo todo aquel día, y al anochecer su rocín y él se hallaron cansados y muertos de hambre; y que, mirando a todas partes por ver si descubría algún castillo o alguna majada de pastores donde recogerse, y adonde pudiese remediar su mucha hambre y necesidad, vió no lejos del camino por donde iba una venta, que fué como si viera una estrella

As our brand-new adventurer journeyed along, he talked to himself, saying: 'Who can doubt that in ages to come, when the authentic story of my famous deeds comes to light, the sage who writes of them will say, when he comes to tell of my first expedition so early in the morning: "Scarce had the ruddy Apollo spread the golden threads of his lovely hair over the broad and spacious face of the earth, and scarcely had the forked tongues of the little painted birds greeted with mellifluous harmony the coming of the rosy Aurora who, leaving the soft bed of her jealous husband, showed herself at the doors and balconies of the Manchegan horizon, when the famous knight, Don Quixote de la Mancha, quitting the slothful down, mounted his famous steed Rocinante and began to journey across the ancient and celebrated plain of Montiel"?' That was, in fact, the road that our knight actually took, as he went on: 'Fortunate the age and fortunate the times in which my famous deeds shall come to light, deeds worthy to be engraved in bronze, carved in marble and painted on wood, as a memorial for posterity. And you, sage enchanter, whoever you may be, to whose lot it falls to be the chronicler of this strange history, I beg you not to forget my good Rocinante, my constant companion on all my rides and journeys!' And presently he cried again, as if he had really been in love: 'O Princess Dulcinea, mistress of this captive heart! You did me great injury in dismissing me and inflicting on me the cruel rigour of your command not to appear in your beauteous presence. Deign, lady, to be mindful of your captive heart, which suffers such griefs for love of you.'

He went on stringing other nonsense on to this, all after the fashion he had learnt in his reading, and imitating the language of his books at best he could. And all the while he rode so slowly and the sun's heat increased so fast that it would have been enough to turn his brain, if he had had any. Almost all that day he rode without encountering anything of note, which reduced him to despair, for he longed to meet straightway someone against whom he could try the strength of his strong arm.

There are authors who say that the first adventure he met was that of the pass of Lapice. Others say it was the windmills. But what I have been able to discover of the matter and what I have found written in the annals of La Mancha, is that he rode all that day, and that at nightfall his horse and he were weary and dying of hunger. Looking in all directions to see if he could discover any castle or shepherd's hut where he could take shelter and supply his urgent needs, he saw, not far from the road he was travelling on, an inn, which seemed to him like a star to guide him to the gates,

que, no a los portales, sino a los alcázares de su redención lo encaminaba. Dióse prisa a caminar, y llegó a ella a tiempo que anochecía. Estaban acaso a la puerta dos mujeres mozas, de estas que llaman 'del partido', las cuales iban a Sevilla con unos arrieros, que en la venta aquella noche acertaron a hacer jornada; y como a nuestro aventurero todo cuanto pensaba, veía o imaginaba le parecía ser hecho y pasar al modo de lo que había leído, luego que vió la venta se le representó que era un castillo con sus cuatro torres y chapiteles de luciente plata, sin faltarle su puente levadizo y honda cava, con todos aquellos adherentes que semejantes castillos se pintan. Fuése llegando a la venta (que a él le parecía castillo), y a poco trecho de ella detuvo las riendas a Rocinante, esperando que algún enano se pusiese entre las almenas a dar señal con alguna trompeta de que llegaba caballero al castillo. Pero, como vió que se tardaban, y que Rocinante se daba prisa por llegar a la caballeriza, se llegó a la puerta de la venta, y vió a las dos distraídas mozas que allí estaban que a él le parecieron dos hermosas doncellas o dos graciosas damas, que delante de la puerta del castillo se estaban solazando.

En esto sucedió acaso que un porquero que andaba recogiendo de unos rastrojos una manada de puercos (que, sin perdón, así se llaman), tocó un cuerno, a cuya señal ellos se recogen, y al instante se le representó a don Quijote lo que deseaba, que era que algún enano hacía señal de su venida, y así con extraño contento llegó a la venta y a las damas, las cuales, como vieron venir a un hombre de aquella suerte armado, y con lanza y adarga, llenas de miedo se iban a entrar en la venta; pero don Quijote, coligiendo por su huída su miedo, alzándose la visera de papelón y descubriendo su seco y polvoroso rostro, con gentil talante y voz reposada les dijo:

—No huyan las vuestras mercedes, ni teman desaguisado alguno, que a la Orden de caballería que profeso no toca ni atañe hacerlo a ninguno, cuanto más a tan altas doncellas como vuestras presencias demuestran.

Mirábanle las mozas, y andaban con los ojos buscándole el rostro que la mala visera le encubría; mas, como se oyeron llamar doncellas, cosa tan fuera de su profesión, no pudieron tener la risa, y fué de manera que don Quijote vino a correrse y a decirles:

—Bien parece la mesura en las hermosas, y es mucha sandez, además, la risa que de leve causa procede, pero no os lo digo porque os acuitéis ni mostréis mal talante, que el mío no es de más que de serviros.

El lenguaje no entendido de las señoras y el mal talle de nuestro caballero acrecentaba en ellas la risa y en él el enojo, y pasara muy adelante, si a aquel punto no saliera el ventero, hombre que por ser

if not to the palace, of his redemption. So he hurried on, and reached it just as night was falling. Now there chanced to be standing at the inn door two young women *of easy virtue,* as they are called, who were on the way to Seville with some carriers who happened to have taken up their quarters at the inn that evening. As everything that our adventurer thought, saw or imagined seemed to follow the fashion of his reading, as soon as he saw the inn he convinced himself that it was a fortress with its four towers and pinnacles of shining silver, complete with a drawbridge, a deep moat and all those appurtenances with which such castles are painted. So he approached the inn, which to his mind was a castle, and when still a short distance away reined Rocinante in, expecting some dwarf to mount the battlements and sound a trumpet to announce that a knight was approaching the fortress. But when he saw that there was some delay, and that Rocinante was in a hurry to get to the stable, he went up to the inn door and, seeing the two young women standing there, took them for two beauteous maidens or graceful ladies taking the air at the castle gate. Now at that very moment, as chance would have it, a swineherd was collecting from the stubble a drove of hogs—pardon me for naming them—and blew his horn to call them together. But Don Quixote immediately interpreted this in his own way, as some dwarf giving notice of his approach. So with rare pleasure he rode up, whereupon those ladies, thoroughly frightened at seeing a man come towards them dressed in armour with lance and shield, turned to go back into the inn. But Don Quixote, gathering from their flight that they were afraid, raised his pasteboard visor, partly revealing his lean and dusty face, and addressed them with a charming expression and in a calm voice : 'I beg you, ladies, not to fly, nor to fear any outrage; for it ill fits or suits the order of chivalry which I profess to injure any-one, least of all maidens of such rank as your appearance proclaims you to be.'

The girls stared at him, trying to get a look at his face, which was almost covered by the badly made visor. But when they heard themselves called maidens—a title ill-suited to their profession—they could not help laughing, which stung Don Quixote into replying : 'Civility befits the fair; and laughter arising from trivial causes, is, moreover, great folly. I do not say this to offend you nor to incur your displeasure, for I have no other wish than to serve you.'

His language, which was unintelligible to them, and the uncouth figure our knight cut, made the ladies laugh the more. Whereat he flew into a rage, and things would have gone much farther, had not

muy gordo era muy pacífico, el cual viendo aquella figura contrahecha, armada de armas tan desiguales, como eran la brida, lanza, adarga y coselete, no estuvo en nada en acompañar a las doncellas en las muestras de su contento. Mas, en efecto, temiendo la máquina de tantos pertrechos, determinó de hablarle comedidamente, y así le dijo:

—Si vuestra merced, señor caballero, busca posada, amén del lecho—porque en esta venta no hay ninguno—todo lo demás se hallará en ella en mucha abundancia.

Viendo don Quijote la humildad del alcaide de la fortaleza—que tal le pareció a él el ventero y la venta—respondió:

—Para mí, señor castellano, cualquier cosa basta, porque mis arreos son las armas, mi descanso el pelear, etcétera.

Pensó el huésped que el haberle llamado castellano había sido por haberle parecido de los sanos de Castilla, aunque él era andaluz y de los de la playa de Sanlúcar, no menos ladrón que Caco, ni menos maleante que estudiante o paje, y así le respondió:

—Según eso, las camas de vuestra merced serán duras peñas, y su dormir siempre velar, y siendo así, bien se puede apear con seguridad de hallar en esta choza ocasión y ocasiones para no dormir en todo un año, cuanto más en una noche.

Y diciendo esto, fué a tener del estribo a don Quijote, el cual se apeó con mucha dificultad y trabajo, como aquel que en todo aquel día no se había desayunado.

Dijo luego al huésped que le tuviese mucho cuidado de su caballo, porque era la mejor pieza que comía pan en el mundo. Mirólo el ventero, y no le pareció tan bueno como don Quijote decía, ni aun la mitad; y acomodándolo en la caballeriza, volvió a ver lo que su huésped mandaba, al cual estaban desarmando las doncellas—que ya se habían reconciliado con él,—las cuales, aunque le habían quitado el peto y el espaldar, jamás supieron ni pudieron desencajarle la gola, ni quitarle la contrahecha celada, que traía atada con unas cintas verdes y era menester cortarlas por no poderse quitar los nudos; mas él no lo quiso consentir en ninguna manera; y así se quedó toda aquella noche con la celada puesta, que era la más graciosa y extraña figura que se pudiera pensar; y al desarmarlo, como él se imaginaba que aquellas traídas y llevadas que le desarmaban eran algunas principales señoras y damas de aquel castillo, les dijo con mucho donaire:

—Nunca fuera caballero
De damas tan bien servido,
Como fuera Don Quijote

the innkeeper, a very fat man and therefore very peaceable, emerged at this moment. Now when he saw this grotesque figure in his equipment of lance, shield and coat of armour, which sorted so ill with his manner of riding, he was on the point of joining the young women in their demonstrations of amusement. But, fearing such a collection of armaments, he decided to speak politely, and addressed him thus : 'If your worship is looking for lodging, Sir Knight, except for a bed—we have none in this inn—you will find plenty of everything.'

And Don Quixote replied, seeing the humility of the warden of the fortress—for such he took the innkeeper to be : 'For me, Sir Castellan, whatever you have is enough. My ornaments are arms, my rest the bloody fray.'

The host thought that he had called him castellan because he took him for a safe man from Castile, though he was an Andalusian from the Strand of San Lucar, as thievish as Cacus and as tricky as a student or a page. So he replied : 'At that rate, your bed shall be the cruel rock, your sleep to watch till day, and that being so, you can safely dismount here in the certainty that you will find in this house ample reason for lying awake not only for one night but for a whole year.'

As he spoke he went to take Don Quixote's stirrup, and our knight dismounted with great labour and difficulty, as he had fasted all day. He then bade the host take good care of his steed, saying that no better piece of horseflesh munched oats in all the world. The innkeeper stared at the beast, which did not seem as good as Don Quixote said, not by a half. However, he put him up in the stable and, when he came back for his guest's orders, he found that the maidens had made it up with him and were taking off his armour. But although they had got off his breast-plate and back-piece, they had no idea how to get him out of his gorget, nor how to take off his counterfeit head-piece, which was tied with green ribbons that would have to be cut, as they could not undo the knot. But to this he would on no account agree, and so he stayed all that night with his helmet on, cutting the strangest and most ridiculous figure imaginable. And whilst he was being dis-armed, imagining that these draggled and loose creatures were illustrious ladies and the mistresses of that castle, he addressed them most gracefully :

'Never was there knight
By ladies so attended
As was Don Quixote

Cuando de su aldea vino:
Doncellas curaban de él,
Princesas de su rocino

o Rocinante, que éste es el nombre, señoras mías, de mi caballo, y don Quijote de la Mancha el mío; que puesto que no quisiera descubrirme hasta que las hazañas hechas en vuestro servicio y pro me descubrieran, la fuerza de acomodar al propósito presente este romance viejo de Lanzarote, ha sido causa que sepáis mi nombre antes de toda sazón; pero tiempo vendrá en que las vuestras señorías me manden y yo obedezca, y el valor de mi brazo descubra el deseo que tengo de serviros.

Las mozas, que no estaban hechas a oír semejantes retóricas, no respondían palabra; sólo le preguntaron si quería comer alguna cosa.

—Cualquiera yantaría yo—respondió don Quijote—, porque, a lo que entiendo, me haría mucho al caso.

A dicha acertó a ser viernes aquel día, y no había en toda la venta sino unas raciones de un pescado que en Castilla llaman abadejo, y en Andalucía bacalao, y en otras partes curadillo, y en otras truchuela. Preguntáronle si por ventura comería su merced truchuela, que no había otro pescado que darle a comer.

—Como haya muchas truchuelas—respondió don Quijote—, podrán servir de una trucha; porque eso se me da que me den ocho reales en sencillos, que una pieza de a ocho. Cuanto más que podría ser que fuesen estas truchuelas como la ternera, que es mejor que la vaca, y el cabrito que el cabrón. Pero, sea lo que fuere, venga luego; que el trabajo y peso de las armas no se puede llevar sin el gobierno de las tripas.

Pusiéronle la mesa a la puerta de la venta por el fresco, y trájole el huésped una porción del mal remojado y peor cocido bacalao, y un pan tan negro y mugriento como sus armas; pero era materia de grande risa verlo comer, porque como tenía puesta la celada y alzada la visera, no podía poner nada en la boca con sus manos si otro no se lo daba y ponía, y así, una de aquellas señoras servía de este menester. Mas al darle de beber, no fué posible, ni lo fuera, si el ventero no horadara una caña, y puesto el un cabo en la boca, por el otro le iba echando el vino; y todo esto lo recibía en paciencia a trueque de no romper las cintas de la celada. Estando en esto, llegó acaso a la venta un castrador de puercos, y así como llegó, sonó su silbato de cañas cuatro o cinco veces, con lo cual acabó de confirmar don Quijote que estaba en algún famoso castillo, y que le servían con

When he left his village.
Maidens waited on him,
On his horse, princesses—

or Rocinante, which, dear ladies, is the name of my horse, and Don
Quixote de la Mancha is mine. For, although I did not wish to
reveal myself till deeds done in your service and for your benefit do
so for me, the need to adapt this old ballad of Lancelot to the
present occasion has betrayed my name to you before the due
season. But the time will come when your ladyships may command
me and I shall obey; and the valour of my arms will then disclose
the desire I have to serve you.'

The girls, who were not used to hearing such high-flown
language, did not say a word in reply, but only asked whether he
would like anything to eat.

'I would gladly take some food,' replied Don Quixote, 'for I
think there is nothing that would come more opportunely.'

That day happened to be a Friday, and there was no food in the
inn except some portions of a fish that is called pollack in Castile
and cod in Andalusia, in some parts ling and in others troutlet.
They asked whether his worship would like some troutlet, as there
was no other fish to eat.

'So long as there are plenty of troutlet they may serve me for
one trout,' replied Don Quixote, 'for I had just as soon be paid
eight separate *reals* as an eight *real* piece. What is more, these
troutlet may be like veal, which is better than beef, or kid, which
is better than goats' meat. But, however that may be, let me have
it now, for the toil and weight of arms cannot be borne without due
care for the belly.'

They set the table for him at the inn door for coolness' sake, and
the host brought him a portion of badly soaked and worse cooked
salt cod with some bread as black and grimy as his armour. It made
them laugh a great deal to see him eat because, as he kept his
helmet on and his visor up, he could get nothing into his mouth
with his own hands, and required someone's assistance to put it in;
and so one of those ladies performed this task for him. But to give
him anything to drink would have been impossible if the innkeeper
had not bored a reed, put one end into his mouth and poured the
wine into the other. All this he bore with patience rather than
break the ribbons of his helmet.

While they were thus occupied there happened to come to the
inn a sow-gelder, and as he arrived he blew his reed whistle four or
five times; which finally convinced Don Quixote that he was at

música, y que el abadejo eran truchas, el pan candeal, y las rameras damas, y el ventero, castellano del castillo; y con esto daba por bien empleada su determinación y salida. Mas lo que más le fatigaba, era el no verse armado caballero, por parecerle que no se podría poner legítimamente en aventura alguna sin recibir la orden de caballería.

Capítulo III. Donde se cuenta la graciosa manera que tuvo Don Quijote en armarse caballero.

Y así, fatigado de este pensamiento, abrevió su venteril y limitada cena, la cual acabada, llamó al ventero, y encerrándose con él en la caballeriza, se hincó de rodillas ante él, diciéndole:

—No me levantaré jamás de donde estoy, valeroso caballero, hasta que la vuestra cortesía me otorgue un don que pedirle quiero, el cual redundará en alabanza vuestra y en pro del género humano.

El ventero, que vió a su huésped a sus pies, y oyó semejantes razones, estaba confuso mirándolo, sin saber qué hacerse ni decirle, y porfiaba con él que se levantase, y jamás quiso, hasta que le hubo de decir que él le otorgaba el don que le pedía.

—No esperaba yo menos de la gran magnificencia vuestra, señor mío—respondió don Quijote—y así, os digo que el don que os he pedido y de vuestra liberalidad me ha sido otorgado, es que mañana en aquel día me habéis de armar caballero, y esta noche en la capilla de este vuestro castillo velaré las armas, y mañana, como tengo dicho, se cumplirá lo que tanto deseo, para poder, como se debe, ir por todas las cuatro partes del mundo buscando las aventuras en pro de los menesterosos, como está a cargo de la caballería y de los caballeros andantes, como yo soy, cuyo deseo a semejantes hazañas es inclinado.

El ventero que, como está dicho, era un poco socarrón y ya tenía algunos barruntos de la falta de juicio de su huésped, acabó de creerlo cuando acabó de oírle semejantes razones, y por tener que reír aquella noche, determinó seguirle el humor; y así le dijo que andaba muy acertado en lo que deseaba y pedía, y que tal prosupuesto era propio y natural de los caballeros tan principales como él parecía y como su gallarda presencia mostraba; y que él asimismo, en los años de su mocedad, se había dado a aquel honroso ejercicio andando por diversas partes del mundo buscando sus aventuras, sin que hubiese dejado los Percheles de Málaga, islas de Riarán, Compás

some famous castle, that they were entertaining him with music, that the pollack was trout, the black bread of the whitest flour, the whores ladies and the innkeeper warden of the castle. This made him feel that his resolution and his expedition had been to good purpose, but what distressed him most deeply was that he was not yet knighted, for he believed that he could not rightfully embark on any adventure without first receiving the order of knighthood.

Chapter III. Which tells of the pleasant method by which Don Quixote chose to be knighted.

So, troubled by these thoughts, he cut short his scanty pothouse supper, and when he was done called the host. Then, shutting the stable door on them both, he fell on his knees before him and said : 'Never will I arise from where I am, valiant knight, till you grant me of your courtesy the boon I am going to beg of you; it is one which will redound to your praise and to the benefit of the human race.'

Seeing his guest at his feet and hearing such language, the innkeeper stared in confusion, not knowing what to do or say, and pressed him to get up; but in vain, for the knight refused to rise until his host had promised to grant him the boon he begged.

'I expected no less from your great magnificence, dear sir,' replied Don Quixote. 'So I will tell you that the boon I begged of you, and you in your generosity granted, is that you will knight me on the morning of tomorrow. This night I will watch my arms in the chapel of this castle of yours, and tomorrow, as I said, my dearest wish will be fulfilled, and I shall have the right to ride through all quarters of the world in search of adventures, for the benefit of the distressed, according to the obligations of knighthood and of knights errant like myself, whose minds are given to such exploits.'

The innkeeper, who, as we have said, was pretty crafty and had already a suspicion that his guest was wrong in the head, was confirmed in his belief when he heard this speech, and, to make some sport for that night, decided to fall in with his humour. So he told him that he was doing a very proper thing in craving the boon he did, and that such a proposal was right and natural in a knight as illustrious as he seemed and his gallant demeanour showed him to be. He added that he, too, in the day of his youth had devoted himself to that honourable profession and travelled in divers parts of the world in search of adventures, not omitting to visit the Fish Market of Malaga, the Isles of Riaran, the Compass of Seville, the

de Sevilla, Azoguejo de Segovia, la Olivera de Valencia, Rondilla de Granada, playa de Sanlúcar, Potro de Córdoba y las ventillas de Toledo, y otras diversas partes, donde había ejercitado la ligereza de sus pies y sutileza de sus manos, haciendo muchos tuertos, recuestando muchas viudas, deshaciendo algunas doncellas y engañando algunos pupilos, y finalmente dándose a conocer por cuantas audiencias y tribunales hay casi en toda España; y que a lo último se había venido a recoger a aquel su castillo, donde vivía con su hacienda y con las ajenas, recogiendo en él a todos los caballeros andantes de cualquiera calidad y condición que fuesen, sólo por la mucha afición que les tenía, y porque partiesen con él de sus haberes en pago de su buen deseo.

Díjole también, que en aquel su castillo no había capilla alguna donde poder velar las armas, porque estaba derribada para hacerla de nuevo; pero que en caso de necesidad él sabía que se podían velar dondequiera, y que aquella noche las podría velar en un patio del castillo; que a la mañana, siendo Dios servido, se harían las debidas ceremonias, de manera que él quedase armado caballero, y tan caballero que no pudiese ser más en el mundo.

Preguntóle si traía dineros; respondió don Quijote que no traía blanca, porque él nunca había leído en las historias de los caballeros andantes que ninguno los hubiese traído.

A esto dijo el ventero que se engañaba; que, puesto caso que en las historias no se escribía por haberles parecido a los autores de ellas que no era menester escribir una cosa tan clara y tan necesaria de traerse, como eran dineros y camisas limpias, no por eso se había de creer que no los trajeron; y así, tuviese por cierto y averiguado que todos los caballeros andantes (de que tantos libros están llenos y atestados) llevaban bien herradas las bolsas por lo que pudiese sucederles; y que asimismo llevaban camisas y una arqueta pequeña llena de ungüentos para curar las heridas que recibían, porque no todas veces en los campos y desiertos donde se combatían y salían heridos había quien los curase, si ya no era que tenían algún sabio encantador por amigo, que luego los socorría trayendo por el aire en alguna nube alguna doncella o enano con alguna redoma de agua de tal virtud, que, en gustando alguna gota de ella, luego al punto quedaban sanos de sus llagas y heridas, como si mal alguno hubiesen tenido; mas que, en tanto que esto no hubiese, tuvieron los pasados caballeros por cosa acertada que sus escuderos fuesen proveídos de dineros y de otras cosas necesarias, como eran hilas y ungüentos para curarse; y cuando sucedía que los tales caballeros no tenían escuderos (que eran pocas y raras veces), ellos mismos lo llevaban todo en unas alforjas muy sutiles, que casi no se parecían, a las ancas del

Little Market Place at Segovia, the Olive Grove at Valencia, the Circle of Granada, the Strand of San Lucar, the Colt-fountain of Cordova, the Taverns of Toledo and sundry other places, where he had exercised the agility of his heels and the lightness of his fingers, doing many wrongs, wooing many widows, ruining sundry maidens and cheating a few minors—in fact, making himself well known in almost all the police-courts and law-courts in Spain. Finally he had retired to this castle, where he lived on his own estate and other people's, welcoming all knights errant of whatever quality and condition, only for the great love he bore them—and to take a share of their possessions in payment for his kindness.

He added that there was no chapel in the castle where he could watch his arms, for it had been pulled down to be rebuilt. But he knew that a vigil might be kept in any place whatever in case of need. So that night he might watch his arms in a courtyard of the castle, and in the morning, God willing, the due ceremonies might be performed, and he emerge a full knight, as much a knight as any in the whole world. He asked him if he had any money with him, and Don Quixote replied that he had not a penny, since he had never read in histories concerning knights errant of any knight that had. At this the innkeeper said that he was wrong: for, granted that it was not mentioned in the histories, because their authors could see no need of mentioning anything so obvious and necessary to take with one as money and clean shirts, that was no reason for supposing that knights did not carry them. In fact, he might take it for an established fact that all knights errant, of whom so many histories were stuffed full, carried purses well lined against all eventualities, and also took with them clean shirts and a little box full of ointments to cure the wounds they got. For on the plains and deserts where they fought and got their wounds they had not always someone at hand to cure them, unless of course they had some magician for a friend. A sorcerer, of course, might relieve them at once by bearing through the air on a cloud some maiden or dwarf with a flask of water of such virtue that after tasting a single drop they were immediately cured of their sores and wounds, and it was as if they had never had any injuries. However, in default of this, the knights of old made certain that their squires were provided with money and other necessaries, such as lint and ointment, to dress their wounds. But when such knights chanced to have no squires—there were only a few rare instances— they carried it all themselves on the cruppers of their horses in bags so very thin that they hardly showed, as though they contained

caballo, como que era otra cosa de más importancia; porque, no siendo por ocasion semejante, esto de llevar alforjas no fué muy admitido entre los caballeros andantes; y por esto le daba por consejo (pues aun se lo podía mandar como a su ahijado, que tan presto lo había de ser) que no caminase de allí adelante sin dineros y sin las prevenciones referidas, y que vería cuán bien se hallaba con ellas, cuando menos se pensase.

Prometióle don Quijote de hacer lo que se le aconsejaba con toda puntualidad; y así se dió luego orden como velase las armas en un corral grande que a un lado de la venta estaba, y recogiéndolas don Quijote todas, las puso sobre una pila que junto a un pozo estaba, y embrazando su adarga asió de su lanza, y con gentil continente se comenzó a pasear delante de la pila; y cuando comenzó el paseo comenzaba a cerrar la noche.

Contó el ventero a todos cuantos estaban en la venta la locura de su huésped, la vela de las armas y la armazón de caballería que esperaba. Admiráronse de tan extraño género de locura, fuéronselo a mirar desde lejos, y vieron que con sosegado ademán unas veces se paseaba, otras arrimado a su lanza ponía los ojos en las armas, sin quitarlos por un buen espacio de ellas. Acabó de cerrar la noche, pero con tanta claridad de la luna, que podía competir con el que se la prestaba; de manera que cuanto el novel caballero hacía era bien visto de todos. Antojósele en esto a uno de los arrieros que estaban en la venta ir a dar agua a su recua, y fué menester quitar las armas de don Quijote, que estaban sobre la pila, el cual viéndolo llegar, en voz alta le dijo:

—¡Oh tú, quienquiera que seas, atrevido caballero, que llegas a tocar las armas del más valeroso andante que jamás se ciñó espada, mira lo que haces, y no las toques, si no quieres dejar la vida en pago de tu atrevimiento!

No se curó el arriero de estas razones (y fuera mejor que se curara, porque fuera curarse en salud), antes trabando de las correas las arrojó gran trecho de sí. Lo cual visto por don Quijote, alzó los ojos al cielo, y puesto el pensamiento (a lo que pareció) en su señora Dulcinea, dijo: 'Acorredme, señora mía, en esta primera afrenta que a este vuestro avasallado pecho se le ofrece; no me desfallezca en este primero trance vuestro favor y amparo.' Y diciendo estas y otras semejantes razones, soltando la adarga, alzó la lanza a dos manos, y dió con ella tan gran golpe al arriero en la cabeza que lo derribó en el suelo tan maltrecho, que, si segundara con otro, no tuviera necesi-

something of even more importance. For, except for such purposes, the carrying of bags was not tolerated among knights errant. So he advised Don Quixote—though as his godson, which he was so soon to be, he might even command him—not to travel in future without money and the other requisites he had mentioned, and he would see how useful they would prove when he least expected it.

Don Quixote promised to do exactly as he recommended, and promptly received his instructions as to keeping watch over his armour in a great yard which lay on one side of the inn. He gathered all the pieces together and laid them on a stone trough, which stood beside a well. Then, buckling on his shield, he seized his lance and began to pace jauntily up and down before the trough. And just as he began his watch, night began to fall.

The innkeeper told everyone staying in the inn of his guest's craziness, of the watching of the armour, and of the knighting he was expecting; and, wondering at this strange form of madness, they came out to observe him from a distance, and watched him, sometimes pacing up and down with a peaceful look and some-times leaning on his lance and gazing on his armour, without taking his eyes off it for a considerable time. Night had now fallen, but the moon was so bright that she might have rivalled the orb that lent her his light; so that whatever the novice knight did was clearly visible to all. Just then it occurred to one of the carriers who was staying at the inn to go and water his mules, and to do this he found it necessary to remove Don Quixote's armour, which lay on the trough. But the knight, seeing him draw near, addressed him in a loud voice : 'You, whoever you are, rash knight, who come to touch the armour of the most valorous errant that ever girt on a sword, take heed what you do. Do not touch it unless you wish to lose your life in payment for your temerity.'

The carrier paid no attention to this speech—it would have been better if he had regarded it, for he would have been regarding his own safety—but, laying hold of the straps, threw the armour some distance from him. At this sight Don Quixote raised his eyes to heaven, and addressing his thoughts, as it seemed, to his lady Dulcinea, cried : 'Assist me, lady, in the first affront offered to this enraptured heart ! Let not your favour and protection fail me in this first trial !'

And, uttering these words and others like them, he loosened his shield and, raising his lance in both hands, dealt his adversary a mighty blow on the head with it, which threw him to the ground so injured that, if it had been followed by a second, the carrier would have had no use for a surgeon to cure him. This done, Don

dad de maestro que lo curara. Hecho esto, recogió sus armas y tornó a pasearse con el mismo reposo que primero.

Desde allí a poco, sin saberse lo que había pasado (porque aun estaba aturdido el arriero) llegó otro con la misma intención de dar agua a sus mulos, y llegando a quitar las armas para desembarazar la pila, sin hablar don Quijote palabra, y sin pedir favor a nadie, soltó otra vez la adarga, y alzó otra vez la lanza, y sin hacerla pedazos, hizo más de tres la cabeza del segundo arriero, porque se la abrió por cuatro. Al ruido acudió toda la gente de la venta y entre ellos el ventero. Viendo esto don Quijote, embrazó su adarga y, puesta mano a su espada, dijo:

—¡Oh, señora de la hermosura, esfuerzo y vigor del debilitado corazón mío! Ahora es tiempo que vuelvas los ojos de tu grandeza a este tu cautivo caballero, que tamaña aventura está atendiendo.

Con esto cobró, a su parecer, tanto ánimo, que si le acometieran todos los arrieros del mundo, no volviera el pie atrás. Los compañeros de los heridos, que tales los vieron, comenzaron desde lejos a llover piedras sobre don Quijote, el cual lo mejor que podía se reparaba con su adarga, y no se osaba apartar de la pila por no desamparar las armas. El ventero daba voces que lo dejasen, porque ya les había dicho como era loco, y que por loco se libraría aunque los matase a todos. También don Quijote las daba mayores, llamándolos de alevosos y traidores, y que el señor del castillo era un follón y mal nacido caballero, pues de tal manera consentía que se tratasen los andantes caballeros, y que si él hubiera recibido la Orden de caballería que él le diera a entender su alevosía; 'pero de vosotros, soez y baja canalla, no hago caso alguno; tirad, llegad, venid, y ofendedme en cuanto pudiereis, que vosotros veréis el pago que lleváis de vuestra sandez y demasía'. Decía esto con tanto brío y denuedo, que infundió un terrible temor en los que lo acometían; y así por esto, como por las persuasiones del ventero, le dejaron de tirar, y él dejó retirar a los heridos, y tornó a la vela de sus armas con la misma quietud y sosiego que primero.

No le parecieron bien al ventero las burlas de su huésped, y determinó abreviar y darle la negra Orden de caballería luego, antes que otra desgracia sucediese; y así, llegándose a él, se disculpó de la insolencia que aquella gente baja con él había usado, sin que él supiese

Quixote gathered his arms together again and paced up and down once more with the same composure as before.

A little later a second carrier, not knowing what had happened since the first man still lay stunned, came out with the same intention of watering his mules. But, just as he was going to clear the armour from the trough, Don Quixote, without uttering word or begging anyone's favour, loosened his shield again, once more raised his lance and made more than three pieces of the second carrier's head—for he opened it in four places—without damage to his weapon. At the noise all the people in the inn rushed out, among them the innkeeper. Whereupon Don Quixote buckled on his shield and, putting his hand to his sword, cried : 'O beauteous lady, strength and vigour of this enfeebled heart! Now is the time to turn your illustrious eyes on this your captive knight, who is awaiting so great an adventure.'

With this it seemed to him that he gained so much courage that if all the carriers in the world had attacked him he would not have yielded a foot. When the fellows of the wounded men saw them in that plight they began to shower stones on Don Quixote from some way off. He protected himself from them as best he could with his shield, but dared not leave the trough, for fear of abandoning his armour. And the innkeeper shouted to them to leave him alone, for he had already told them that he was a madman and, being mad, would go scot-free, even though he killed them all.

Don Quixote shouted also, even louder, calling them cowards and traitors, and swearing that the lord of the castle must be a despicable and base-born knight for allowing knights errant to be so treated, and that if he had received the order of knighthood he would have made him sensible of his perfidy.

'But of you, base and vile rabble, I take no account,' he cried. 'Throw stones! Come on, attack! Assail me as hard as you can, and you will see what penalty you have to pay for your insolent folly!'

He spoke with such spirit and boldness that he struck a lively terror into all who heard him; and for that reason, as much as for the innkeeper's persuasions, they stopped pelting him. Then Don Quixote allowed them to remove the wounded, and returned to watch his arms with the same quiet assurance as before.

Now the innkeeper had begun to dislike his guest's pranks, and decided to cut the matter short and give him his wretched order of knighthood immediately, before anything else could go wrong. So he apologized for the insolence with which those low fellows had behaved without his knowledge, adding, however, that they had

cosa alguna; pero que bien castigados quedaban de su atrevimiento. Díjole como ya le había dicho, que en aquel castillo no había capilla, y para lo que restaba de hacer tampoco era necesaria; que todo el toque de quedar armado caballero consistía en la pescozada y en el espaldarazo, según él tenía noticia del ceremonial de la Orden, y que aquello en mitad de un campo se podía hacer; y que ya había cumplido con lo que tocaba al velar de las armas, que con solas dos horas de vela se cumplía, cuanto más que él había estado más de cuatro.

Todo se lo creyó don Quijote, y dijo que él estaba allí pronto para obedecerle, y que concluyese con la mayor brevedad que pudiese; porque si fuese otra vez acometido, y se viese armado caballero, no pensaba dejar persona viva en el castillo, excepto aquellas que él le mandase, a quien, por su respeto, dejaría. Advertido y medroso de esto el castellano, trajo luego un libro donde asentaba la paja y cebada que daba a los arrieros, y con un cabo de vela que le traía un muchacho, y con las dos ya dichas doncellas, se vino adonde don Quijote estaba, al cual mandó hincar de rodillas, y leyendo en su manual (como que decía alguna devota oración), en mitad de la leyenda alzó la mano, y dióle sobre el cuello un gran golpe y tras él con su misma espada un gentil espaldarazo, siempre murmurando entre dientes como que rezaba. Hecho esto, mandó a una de aquellas damas que le ciñese la espada, la cual lo hizo con mucha desenvoltura y discreción, porque no fué menester poca para no reventar de risa a cada punto de las ceremonias; pero las proezas que ya habían visto del novel caballero les tenían la risa a raya. Al ceñirle la espada, dijo la buena señora:

—Dios haga a vuestra merced muy venturoso caballero y le dé ventura en lides.

Don Quijote le preguntó cómo se llamaba, porque él supiese de allí adelante a quién quedaba obligado por la merced recibida, porque pensaba darle alguna parte de la honra que alcanzase por el valor de su brazo. Ella respondió con mucha humildad que se llamaba la Tolosa y que era hija de un remendón natural de Toledo, que vivía en las tendillas de Sancho Bienaya, y que dondequiera que ella estuviese lo serviría y lo tendría por señor. Don Quijote le replicó que por su amor le hiciese merced que de allí adelante se pusiese don y se llamase doña Tolosa. Ella se lo prometió, y la otra le calzó la espuela, con la cual le pasó casi el mismo coloquio que con la de la espada. Preguntóle su nombre, y dijo que se llamaba la

been soundly punished for their audacity. And seeing, as he had said before, that there was no chapel in that castle, there was no need, he declared, for the rest of the ceremony; for, according to his knowledge of the ceremonial of the order, the whole point of conferring knighthood lay in the blow on the neck and the stroke on the shoulder, and that could be performed in the middle of a field. And Don Quixote had already more than fulfilled the duty of the watching of arms, for he had been more than four hours on vigil, whereas all that was required was a two hours' watch.

Don Quixote believed all this, and said he was ready to obey him. He begged him to conclude the matter as briefly as possible; for if he were again attacked, once knighted, he was resolved to leave no one alive in the castle, except such as he might spare at the castellan's bidding, and out of regard for him.

Forewarned and apprehensive, the castellan then brought out the book in which he used to enter the carriers' accounts for straw and barley. Then, followed by a boy carrying a candle-end and by the two maidens already mentioned, he went up to Don Quixote and ordered him to kneel. Next, reading out of his manual, as if he were reciting some devout prayer, in the middle of his reading he raised his hand and dealt the knight a sound blow on the neck, followed by a handsome stroke on the back with the Don's own sword, all the while muttering in his teeth as if in prayer. When this was over he bade one of the ladies gird on Don Quixote's sword, which she did with great agility and some discretion, no small amount of which was necessary to avoid bursting with laughter at each stage of the ceremony. But what they had already seen of the new knight's prowess kept their mirth within bounds. And as she girt on his sword the good lady said : 'God make your worship a fortunate knight and give you good luck in your battles.'

Don Quixote asked her to tell him her name, as he wished to know in future days to whom he owed the favour received, for he meant to confer on her some part of the honour he was to win by the strength of his arm. She replied very humbly that her name was La Tolosa, and that she was the daughter of a cobbler in Toledo who lived among the stalls of Sancho Bienaya, adding that, wherever she might be, she was at his service and he should be her master. Don Quixote begged her, in reply, as a favour to him, henceforth to take the title of lady and call herself Doña Tolosa, which she promised to do. The other lady then put on his spurs, and his conversation with her was almost the same as with the lady of the sword. He asked her her name, and she replied

Molinera y que era hija de un honrado molinero de Antequera; a la cual también rogó don Quijote que se pusiese don, y se llamase doña Molinera, ofreciéndole nuevos servicios y mercedes. Hechas, pues, de galope y aprisa las hasta allí nunca vistas ceremonias, no vió Ia hora don Quijote de verse a caballo, y salir buscando las aventuras; y ensillando luego a Rocinante subió en él, y abrazando a su huésped le dijo cosas tan extrañas, agradeciéndole la merced de haberlo armado caballero, que no es posible acertar a referirlas. El ventero, por verlo ya fuera de la venta, con no menos retóricas, aunque con más breves palabras, respondió a las suyas, y, sin pedirle la costa de la posada, lo dejó ir a la buen hora.

Capítulo VIII. Del buen suceso que el valeroso Don Quijote tuvo en la espantable y jamás imaginada Aventura de los Molinos de Viento, con otros sucesos dignos de feliz recordación.

En esto descubrieron treinta o cuarenta molinos de viento que hay en aquel campo; y así como don Quijote los vió, dijo a su escudero:

—La ventura va guiando nuestras cosas mejor de lo que acertáramos a desear; porque ves allí, amigo Sancho Panza, donde se descubren treinta o pocos más desaforados gigantes con quien pienso hacer batalla y quitarles a todos las vidas, con cuyos despojos comenzaremos a enriquecer; que ésta es buena guerra, y es gran servicio de Dios quitar tan mala simiente de sobre la faz de la tierra.

—¿Qué gigantes?—dijo Sancho Panza.

—Aquellos que allí ves—respondió su amo,—de los brazos largos, que los suelen tener algunos de casi dos leguas.

—Mire vuestra merced—respondió Sancho,—que aquellos que allí se parecen, no son gigantes, sino molinos de viento, y lo que en ellos parecen brazos son las aspas, que volteadas del viento hacen andar la piedra del molino.

—Bien parece—respondió don Quijote,—que no estás cursado en esto de las aventuras; ellos son gigantes, y si tienes miedo, quítate de ahí y ponte en oración en el espacio que yo voy a entrar con ellos en fiera y desigual batalla.

Y diciendo esto, dió de espuelas a su caballo Rocinante, sin atender a las voces que su escudero Sancho le daba, advirtiéndole que sin duda alguna eran molinos de viento y no gigantes aquellos que iba a acometer. Pero él iba tan puesto en que eran gigantes, que ni oía las voces de su escudero Sancho, ni echaba de ver,

that she was called La Molinera, and that she was the daughter of an honest miller in Antequera. The Don requested her also to take the title of lady and call herself Doña Molinera, renewing his offers of service and favours.

Now that these unprecedented ceremonies had been hurried through post-haste and at top speed, Don Quixote was impatient to be on horseback and to ride out in search of adventures. So, saddling Rocinante at once, he mounted; then, embracing his host, he thanked him for the favour of knighting him in such extravagant terms that it is impossible to write them down faithfully. The innkeeper, once he saw him safely out of the inn, replied to his speech rather more briefly but in no less high-flown terms and, without even asking him to pay the cost of his lodging, was heartily glad to see him go.

Chapter VIII. Of the valorous Don Quixote's success in the dreadful and never before imagined Adventure of the Windmills, with other events worthy of happy record.

At that moment they caught sight of some thirty or forty windmills, which stand on that plain, and as soon as Don Quixote saw them he said to his squire : 'Fortune is guiding our affairs better than we could have wished. Look over there, friend Sancho Panza, where more than thirty monstrous giants appear. I intend to do battle with them and take all their lives. With their spoils we will begin to get rich, for this is a fair war, and it is a great service to God to wipe such a wicked brood from the face of the earth.'

'What giants?' asked Sancho Panza.

'Those you see there,' replied his master, 'with their long arms. Some giants have them about six miles long.'

'Take care, your worship,' said Sancho; 'those things over there are not giants but windmills, and what seem to be their arms are the sails, which are whirled round in the wind and make the millstone turn.'

'It is quite clear,' replied Don Quixote, 'that you are not experienced in this matter of adventures. They are giants, and if you are afraid, go away and say your prayers, whilst I advance and engage them in fierce and unequal battle.'

As he spoke, he dug his spurs into his steed Rocinante, paying no attention to his squire's shouted warning that beyond all doubt they were windmills and no giants he was advancing to attack. But he went on, so positive that they were giants that he neither listened to Sancho's cries nor noticed what they were, even when

aunque estaba ya bien cerca, lo que eran, antes iba diciendo en voces altas:

—No huyáis, cobardes y viles criaturas, que un solo caballero es el que os acomete.

Levantóse en esto un poco de viento, y las grandes aspas comenzaron a moverse, lo cual visto por don Quijote, dijo:

—Pues aunque mováis más brazos que los del gigante Briareo, me lo habéis de pagar.

Y en diciendo esto, y encomendándose de todo corazón a su señora Dulcinea, pidiéndole que en tal trance lo socorriese, bien cubierto de su rodela, con la lanza en el ristre, arremetió a todo el galope de Rocinante, y embistió con el primer molino que estaba delante, y dándole una lanzada en el aspa, la volvió el viento con tanta furia, que hizo la lanza pedazos, llevándose tras sí al caballo y al caballero, que fué rodando muy maltrecho por el campo. Acudió Sancho Panza a socorrerlo a todo el correr de su asno, y cuando llegó halló que no se podía menear: tal fué el golpe que dió con él Rocinante.

—¡Válgame Dios!—dijo Sancho:—¿No le dije yo a vuestra merced que mirase bien lo que hacía, que no eran sino molinos de viento, y no lo podía ignorar sino quien llevase otros tales en la cabeza?

—Calla, amigo Sancho—respondió don Quijote,—que las cosas de la guerra, más que otras están sujetas a continua mudanza; cuanto más que yo pienso, y es así verdad, que aquel sabio Frestón que me robó el aposento y los libros, ha vuelto estos gigantes en molinos por quitarme la gloria de su vencimiento: tal es la enemistad que me tiene; más al cabo al cabo, han de poder poco sus malas artes contra la bondad de mi espada.

—Dios lo haga como puede—respondió Sancho Panza—. Y ayudándolo a levantar, tornó a subir sobre Rocinante, que medio despaldado estaba . . .

SEGUNDA PARTE

Capítulo XLII. De los consejos que dió don Quijote a Sancho Panza, antes que fuese a gobernar la ínsula, con otras cosas bien consideradas.

. . . En esto llegó don Quijote, y sabiendo lo que pasaba, y la celeridad con que Sancho se había de partir a su gobierno, con licencia del duque, lo tomó por la mano, y se fué con él a su estancia, con intención de aconsejarlo cómo se había de haber en su oficio. Entrados, pues, en su aposento, cerró tras sí la puerta, e hizo casi por fuerza que Sancho se sentase junto a él, y con reposada voz le dijo:

he got near them. Instead he went on shouting in a loud voice : 'Do not fly, cowards, vile creatures, for it is one knight alone who assails you.'

At that moment a slight wind arose, and the great sails began to move. At the sight of which Don Quixote shouted : 'Though you wield more arms than the giant Briareus, you shall pay for it!' Saying this, he commended himself with all his soul to his Lady Dulcinea, beseeching her aid in his great peril. Then, covering himself with his shield and putting his lance in the rest, he urged Rocinante forward at a full gallop and attacked the nearest windmill, thrusting his lance into the sail. But the wind turned it with such violence that it shivered his weapon in pieces, dragging the horse and his rider with it, and sent the knight rolling badly injured across the plain. Sancho Panza rushed to his assistance as fast as his ass could trot, but when he came up he found that the knight could not stir. Such a shock had Rocinante given him in their fall.

'O my goodness!' cried Sancho. 'Didn't I tell your worship to look what you were doing, for they were only windmills? Nobody could mistake them, unless he had windmills on the brain.'

'Silence, friend Sancho,' replied Don Quixote. 'Matters of war are more subject than most to continual change. What is more, I think—and that is the truth—that the same sage Friston who robbed me of my room and my books has turned those giants into windmills, to cheat me of the glory of conquering them. Such is the enmity he bears me; but in the very end his black arts shall avail him little against the goodness of my sword.'

'God send it as He will,' replied Sancho Panza, helping the knight to get up and remount Rocinante, whose shoulders were half dislocated . . .

PART II

Chapter XLII. Of Don Quixote's advice to Sancho Panza before he went to govern his Isle, and other grave matters.

. . . At this moment Don Quixote came up, and when he learned what was happening and how soon Sancho was to leave for his governorship, by the Duke's permission he took his squire by the hand and led him to his apartment to give him advice as to his behaviour in office. Then, having entered, he shut the door after him and, almost forcing Sancho to sit down beside him, addressed him with great deliberation :

—Infinitas gracias doy al cielo, Sancho amigo, de que antes y primero que yo haya encontrado con alguna buena dicha, te haya salido a ti a recibir y a encontrar la buena ventura. Yo, que en mi buena suerte te tenía librada la paga de tus servicios, me veo en los principios de aventajarme, y tú antes de tiempo, contra la ley del razonable discurso, te ves premiado de tus deseos. Otros cohechan, importunan, solicitan, madrugan, ruegan, porfían, y no alcanzan lo que pretenden; y llega otro, y sin saber cómo ni cómo no, se halla con el cargo y oficio que otros muchos pretendieron; y aquí entra y encaja bien el decir que hay buena y mala fortuna en las pretensiones. Tú, que para mí sin duda alguna eres un porro, sin madrugar ni trasnochar, y sin hacer diligencia alguna, con sólo el aliento que te ha tocado de la andante caballería, sin más ni más te ves gobernador de una ínsula, como quien no dice nada. Todo esto digo, ¡oh Sancho!, para que no atribuyas a tus merecimientos la merced recibida, sino que des gracias al cielo, que dispone suavemente las cosas; y después las darás a la grandeza que en sí encierra la profesión de la caballería andante. Dispuesto, pues, el corazón a creer lo que te he dicho, está, ¡oh hijo!, atento a este tu Catón, que quiere aconsejarte, y ser norte y guía que te encamine y saque a seguro puerto de este mar proceloso donde vas a engolfarte; que los oficios y grandos cargos no son otra cosa sino un golfo profundo de confusiones.

'Primeramente, ¡oh hijo!, has de temer a Dios; porque en el temerlo está la sabiduría, y siendo sabio no podrás errar en nada.

'Lo segundo, has de poner los ojos en quien eres, procurando conocerte a ti mismo, que es el más difícil conocimiento que puede imaginarse. Del conocerte saldrá el no hincharte, como la rana que quiso igualarse con el buey; que si esto haces, vendrá a ser feos pies de la rueda de tu locura la consideración de haber guardado puercos en tu tierra.' 'Así es la verdad—respondió Sancho—, pero fué cuando muchacho; pero después, algo hombrecillo, gansos fueron los que guardé que no puercos. Pero esto paréceme a mí que no hace al caso, que no todos los que gobiernan vienen de casta de reyes.' 'Así es verdad—replicó don Quijote—, por lo cual los no de principios nobles deben acompañar la gravedad del cargo que ejercitan con una blanda suavidad, que, guiada por la prudencia, los libre de la murmuración maliciosa, de quien no hay estado que se escape.

'Haz gala, Sancho, de la humildad de tu linaje, y no te desprecies de decir que vienes de labradores: porque viendo que no te corres, ninguno se pondrá a correrte; y préciate más de ser humilde virtuoso,

'I give infinite thanks to Heaven, Sancho my friend, that first and foremost, before I strike any good luck myself, prosperity has come out to meet and receive you. I who had staked the payment for your services on my own success find myself at the beginning of my advancement; while you find yourself rewarded with your heart's desire before your time and contrary to all reasonable expectations. Some bribe, importune, solicit, rise early, entreat, pester, and yet fail to achieve their aims; then there comes another, and without knowing how or why he finds himself with the place and office which many others have sought for. Here the proverb comes in pat, that there is good and bad luck in petitionings. You are, in my opinion, most certainly a dullard. Yet without rising early or working late or putting yourself to great pains, with only the breath of knight errantry which has touched you, you find yourself without more ado governor of an isle, as if that were nothing. I say all this, Sancho, so that you shall not attribute this favour to your own merits, but shall give thanks to God, who disposes things so kindly, and afterwards to the greatness implicit in the profession of knight errantry.

'With your heart disposed to believe my words, be attentive, my son, to this your Cato, who will advise you and be the pole-star and guide to direct you and bring you to a safe port, out of this stormy sea in which you are likely to drown. For offices and great places are nothing but a deep gulf of confusion.

'Firstly, my son, you must fear God; for in fearing Him is wisdom and, being wise, you can make no mistake.

'Secondly, you must consider what you are, seeking to know yourself, which is the most difficult task conceivable. From self-knowledge you will learn not to puff yourself up, like the frog who wanted to be as big as an ox. If you achieve this, the memory that you kept hogs in your own country will come to be like the peacock's ugly feet to the tail of your folly.'

'True enough,' answered Sancho, 'but that was when I was a boy. Afterwards, when I was more of a man, it was geese I kept, not hogs. But this doesn't seem to me to the point, for not all governors come from royal stock.'

'True,' replied Don Quixote, 'and therefore those who are not of noble origin must accompany the gravity of the office they exercise with a mild suavity which, guided by prudence, may save them from malicious slanderers, from whom no station is free.

'Rejoice, Sancho, in the humbleness of your lineage, and do not think it a disgrace to say you come of peasants; for, seeing that you are not ashamed, no one will attempt to shame you. Consider it

que pecador soberbio. Innumerables son aquellos que de baja estirpe nacidos, han subido a la suma dignidad pontificia e imperatoria; y de esta verdad te pudiera traer tantos ejemplos, que te cansaran.

'Mira, Sancho: si tomas por medio a la virtud, y te precias de hacer hechos virtuosos, no hay para qué tener envidia a los que los tienen príncipes y señores; porque la sangre se hereda, y la virtud se aquista, y la virtud vale por sí sola lo que la sangre no vale.

'Siendo esto así, como lo es, que si acaso viniere a verte cuando estés en tu ínsula alguno de tus parientes, no lo deseches ni lo afrentes, antes lo has de acoger, agasajar y regalar, que con esto satisfarás al cielo, que gusta que nadie se desprecie de lo que él hizo, y corresponderás a lo que debes a la naturaleza bien concertada.

'Si trajeres a tu mujer contigo (porque no es bien que los que asisten a gobiernos de mucho tiempo estén sin las propias), enséñala, doctrínala y desbástala de su natural rudeza; porque todo lo que suele adquirir un gobernador discreto, suele perder y derramar una mujer rústica y tonta.

'Si acaso enviudares (cosa que puede suceder), y con el cargo mejorares de consorte, no la tomes tal que te sirva de anzuelo y de caña de pescar y del no quiero de tu capilla; porque en verdad te digo que de todo aquello que la mujer del juez recibiere, ha de dar cuenta el marido en la residencia universal, donde pagará con el cuatro tanto en la muerte las partidas de que no se hubiere hecho cargo en la vida.

'Nunca te guíes por la ley del encaje, que suele tener mucha cabida con los ignorantes que presumen de agudos.

'Hallen en ti más compasión las lágrimas del pobre; pero no más justicia que las informaciones del rico.

'Procura descubrir la verdad por entre las promesas y dádivas del rico, como por entre los sollozos e importunidades del pobre.

'Cuando pudiere y debiere tener lugar la equidad, no cargues todo el rigor de la ley al delincuente; que no es mejor la fama del juez riguroso que la del compasivo.

'Si acaso doblares la vara de la justicia, no sea con el peso de la dádiva, sino con el de la misericordia.

'Cuando te sucediere juzgar algún pleito de algún tu enemigo aparta las mientes de tu injuria, y ponlas en la verdad del caso.

'No te ciegue la pasión propia en la causa ajena; que los yerros que en ella hicieres las más veces serán sin remedio, y si lo tuvieren, será a costa de tu crédito y aun de tu hacienda.

more meritorious to be virtuous and poor than noble and a sinner. Innumerable men there are, born of low stock, who have mounted to the highest dignities, pontifical and imperial; and of this truth I could weary you with examples.

'Remember, Sancho, that if you take virtue for your means, and pride yourself on performing virtuous deeds, you will have no reason to envy those who were born princes and lords. For blood is inherited but virtue acquired, and virtue has an intrinsic worth, which blood has not.

'This being so, if any of your relations should chance to come and visit you when you are in your isle, do not reject them or insult them. On the contrary, you must receive them, make much of them and entertain them. In that way you will please God, who would have no one disdain His creation; and what is more, you will be complying with your duty to the order of nature.

'If you should take your wife with you—for it is not right that those engaged in government should be for long without wives of their own—instruct her, indoctrinate her and pare her of her native rudeness; for often everything a wise governor gains is lost and wasted by an ill-mannered and foolish wife.

'If you should chance to be widowed—a thing which may happen—and wish to make a better match to suit your office, do not choose a wife to serve you as a bait and a fishing-rod and take bribes in her hood; for I tell you truly that whatever a judge's wife receives her husband will have to account' for at the Last Judgment, where he will have to pay fourfold in death for the statutes of which he has taken no account in his lifetime.

'Never be guided by arbitrary law, which has generally great influence with the ignorant who set up to be clever.

'Let the poor man's tears find more compassion in you, but not more justice, than the pleadings of the rich.

'Try to discover the truth behind the rich man's promises and gifts, as well as behind the poor man's sobbings and importunities.

'Where equity may justly temper the rigour of the law do not pile the whole force of it on to the delinquent; for the rigorous judge has no higher reputation than the merciful.

'If you should chance to bend the rod of justice, do not let it be with the weight of a bribe, but with that of pity.

'When you happen to judge the case of some enemy of yours, turn your mind away from your injury and apply it to the truth of the case.

'Do not let personal passion blind you in another's case, for most of the errors you make will be irremediable, and if you should

'Si alguna mujer hermosa viniere a pedirte justicia, quita los ojos de sus lágrimas y tus oídos de sus gemidos, y considera despacio la sustancia de lo que pide, si no quieres que se anegue tu razón en su llanto y tu bondad en sus suspiros.

'Al que has de castigar con obras, no trates mal con palabras, pues le basta al desdichado la pena del suplicio, sin la añadidura de las malas razones.

'Al culpado que cayere debajo de tu jurisdicción, considéralo hombre miserable, sujeto a las condiciones de la depravada naturaleza nuestra, y en todo cuanto fuere de tu parte, sin hacer agravio a la contraria, muéstratele piadoso y clemente; porque aunque los atributos de Dios todos son iguales, más resplandece y campea, a nuestro ver, el de la misericordia que el de la justicia.

'Si estos preceptos y estas reglas sigues, Sancho, serán luengos tus días, tu fama será eterna, tus premios colmados, tu felicidad indecible, casarás tus hijos como quisieres, títulos tendrán ellos y tus nietos, vivirás en paz y beneplácito de las gentes, y en los últimos pasos de la vida te alcanzará el de la muerte en vejez suave y madura, y cerrarán tus ojos las tiernas y delicadas manos de tus terceros netezuelos. Esto que hasta aquí te he dicho son documentos que han de adornar tu alma; escucha ahora los que han de servir para adorno del cuerpo.

Capítulo XLV. De cómo el gran Sancho Panza tomó la posesión de su ínsula, y del modo que comenzó a gobernar.

¡Oh, perpetuo descubridor de los antípodas, hacha del mundo, ojo del cielo, meneo dulce de las cantimploras! ¡ Timbrio aquí, Febo allí, tirador acá, médico acullá, padre de la poesía, inventor de la música! ¡Tú que siempre sales, y aunque lo parece nunca te pones! A ti digo, ¡oh sol!, con cuya ayuda el hombre engendra al hombre. A ti digo, que me favorezcas y alumbres la oscuridad de mi ingenio, para que pueda discurrir por sus puntos en la narración del gobierno del gran Sancho Panza; que sin ti yo me siento tibio, desmazalado y confuso.

Digo, pues, que con todo su acompañamiento llegó Sancho a un lugar de hasta mil vecinos, que era de los mejores que el duque tenía. Diéronle a entender que se llamaba la ínsula Barataria, o ya porque el lugar se llamaba Baratario, o ya por el barato con que se le había

find a remedy it will cost you your reputation, or even your fortune.

'If a beautiful woman comes to beg you for justice, turn your eyes from her tears and your ears from her groans, and consider the substance of her plea at leisure, if you do not want your reason to be drowned in her sobs and your honour in her sighs.

'Do not revile with words the man you must punish with deeds, since the pain of the punishment is sufficient for the wretch without adding ill-language.

'Consider the culprit who comes before you for judgment as a wretched man, subject to the conditions of our depraved nature, and so far as in you lies without injury to the contrary party, show yourself pitiful and lenient; for although all godlike attributes are equal, mercy is more precious and resplendent in our sight than justice.

'If you follow these precepts and rules, Sancho, your days will be long, your fame eternal, your rewards abundant, your happiness indescribable. You will marry your children as you wish to; they and your grandchildren will have titles; you will live in peace and good-will among men, and in your life's last stages you will arrive at the hour of death in a mild and ripe old age, and the tender and delicate hands of your great-grandchildren will close your eyes.

'The instructions I have so far given you are for the embellishment of your soul. Listen now to some which will serve you for the adornment of your body.'

Chapter XLV. Of how the great Sancho Panza took possession of his Isle and of the fashion in which he began to govern.

O perpetual discoverer of the Antipodes! Torch of the world! Eye of Heaven! Sweet stirrer of wine coolers! Here Thymbrius, there Phoebus, now archer, now physician! Father of Poetry, inventor of Music, you who always rise and—though you seem to —never set! On you I call, sun, by whose aid man engenders man. On you I call to favour me and to light the darkness of my mind, that I may be scrupulous in the narration of the great Sancho Panza's government; for without you I feel myself timid, faint-hearted and confused.

I must tell you then that Sancho Panza with all his escort arrived at a village of about a thousand inhabitants, which was one of the best in the Duke's dominions. They gave him to understand that this was called the Isle Barataria, either because the

dado el gobierno. Al llegar a las puertas de la villa, que era cercada, salió el regimiento del pueblo a recibirlo; tocaron las campanas y todos los vecinos dieron muestras de general alegría, y con mucha pompa lo llevaron a la iglesia mayor a dar gracias a Dios; y luego con algunas ridículas ceremonias le entregaron las llaves del pueblo, y lo admitieron por perpetuo gobernador de la ínsula Barataria.

El traje, las barbas, la gordura y pequeñez del nuevo gobernador, tenía admirada a toda la gente que el busilis del cuento no sabía, y aun a todos los que lo sabían, que eran muchos. Finalmente, en sacándolo de la iglesia, lo llevaron a la silla del juzgado, y lo sentaron en ella, y el mayordomo del duque le dijo: 'Es costumbre antigua en esta ínsula, señor gobernador, que el que viene a tomar posesión de esta famosa ínsula está obligado a responder a una pregunta que se le hiciere, que sea algo intrincada y dificultosa; de cuya respuesta el pueblo toma y toca el pulso del ingenio de su nuevo gobernador; y así, o se alegra o se entristece con su venida.'

En tanto que el mayordomo decía esto a Sancho, estaba él mirando unas grandes y muchas letras que en la pared frontera de su silla estaban escritas; y como él no sabía leer, preguntó que qué eran aquellas pinturas que en aquella pared estaban. Fuéle respondido: 'Señor, allí está escrito y anotado el día en que vuestra señoría tomó posesión de esta ínsula, y dice el epitafio: 'Hoy, día a tantos de tal mes y de tal año, tomó la posesión de esta ínsula el señor don Sancho Panza, que muchos años la goce'. '¿Y a quién llaman don Sancho Panza?'—preguntó Sancho—. 'A vuestra señoría—respondió el mayordomo—; que en esta ínsula no ha entrado otro Panza, sino el que está sentado en esa silla'. 'Pues advertid, hermano—dijo Sancho—, que yo no tengo don, ni en todo mi linaje lo ha habido: Sancho Panza me llaman a secas, y Sancho se llamó mi padre, y Sancho mi abuelo, y todos fueron Panzas sin añadiduras de dones ni donas; y yo imagino que en esta ínsula debe de haber más dones que piedras; pero basta: Dios me entiende, y podrá ser que si el gobierno me dura cuatro días, yo escardaré estos dones, que por la muchedumbre deben de enfadar como los mosquitos. Pase adelante con su pregunta el señor mayordomo, que yo responderé lo mejor que supiere, ora se entristezca o no se entristezca el pueblo.'

. . . Ante el cual se presentaron dos hombres ancianos: el uno traía una cañaheja por báculo, y el sin báculo dijo: 'Señor, a este buen hombre, le presté días ha diez escudos de oro en oro por

town's name was *Baratario*, or because of the '*barato*,' or low price, at which he had got the government. When they reached the gates of the place, which was walled, the town-council came out to receive him. They rang the bells, and all the inhabitants demonstrated their general rejoicing and conducted him in great pomp to the principal church to give thanks to God. Then with some comical ceremonies they delivered him the keys of the town, and admitted him as perpetual governor of the Isle Barataria. The new governor's apparel, his beard, his fatness and his smallness surprised everyone who was not in the secret, and even those many who were. Next they bore him from the church to the judge's throne and seated him upon it, where the Duke's steward thus addressed him :

'It is an ancient custom in this famous isle, Lord Governor, that everyone who comes to take possession of it is obliged to reply to a question, and this must be a rather intricate and difficult one. By this reply the town touches and feels the pulse of its new governor's understanding and, accordingly, is either glad or grieved at his coming.'

Whilst the steward was thus addressing him, Sancho was gazing at a number of large letters inscribed on the wall facing his seat. Now, as he could not read, he asked what those paintings were on that wall, and the answer came : 'Sir, yonder is written and recorded the day on which your Lordship took possession of this isle, and the inscription says : "*This day, such a date of such a month in such a year, there took possession of the isle the Lord Don Sancho Panza; may he enjoy it for many years.*" '

'Who are they calling Don Sancho Panza?' asked Sancho.

'Your Lordship,' answered the steward, 'for no other Panza has entered this isle but the one seated on that seat.'

'Then take notice, brother,' said Sancho, 'that I'm no Don, and there has never been a Don in my whole family. Plain Sancho Panza's my name, and Sancho my father was called, and Sancho my grandfather, and they were all Panzas without the addition of Dons or Doñas. I fancy there are more Dons than stones in this isle. But enough. God knows my meaning, and perhaps if my government lasts four days I may weed out these Dons, for judging by their numbers they must be as tiresome as gnats. Go on with your question, Master Steward, for I'll reply as best I can, whether the town be sorry or rejoice.' . . .

Next there came before him two old men, one of them carrying a cane for a walking-stick. 'Sir,' said the one without the stick, 'some time ago I lent this fellow ten crowns in gold, as a favour

hacerle placer y buena obra, con condición que me los volviese cuando se los pidiese; pasáronse muchos días sin pedírselos, por no ponerlo en mayor necesidad de volvérmelos, que la que él tenía cuando yo se los presté; pero por parecerme que se descuidaba en la paga, se los he pedido una y muchas veces; y no solamente no me los vuelve, pero me los niega, y dice que nunca tales diez escudos le presté; y que si se los presté, que ya me los ha vuelto. Yo no tengo testigos ni del prestado ni de la vuelta, porque no me los ha vuelto; querría que vuestra merced le tomase juramento, y si jurare que me los ha vuelto yo se los perdono para aquí y para adelante de Dios.' '¿Qué decís vos a esto, buen viejo del báculo?'—dijo Sancho—. A lo que dijo el viejo: 'Yo, señor, confieso que me los prestó; y baje vuestra merced esa vara; y pues él lo deja en mi juramento, yo juraré cómo se los he vuelto y pagado real y verdaderamente.' Bajó el gobernador la vara, y en tanto el viejo del báculo dió el báculo al otro viejo que se le tuviese en tanto que juraba, como si le embarazara mucho; y luego puso la mano en la cruz de la vara, diciendo que era verdad que se le habían prestado aquellos diez escudos que se le pedían; pero que él se los había vuelto de su mano a la suya, y que por no caer en ello se los volvía a pedir por momentos.

Viendo lo cual, el gran gobernador preguntó al acreedor qué respondía a lo que decía su contrario, y dijo que sin duda alguna su deudor debía de decir verdad, porque lo tenía por hombre de bien y buen cristiano, y que a él se le debía de haber olvidado el cómo y cuándo se los había vuelto, y que desde allí en adelante jamás le pediría nada. Tornó a tomar su báculo el deudor, y bajando la cabeza, se salió del juzgado. Visto lo cual por Sancho, y que sin más ni más se iba, y viendo también la paciencia del demandante, inclinó la cabeza sobre el pecho, y poniéndose el índice de la mano derecha sobre las cejas y las narices, estuvo como pensativo un pequeño espacio, y luego alzó la cabeza y mandó que le llamasen al viejo del báculo, que ya se había ido. Trajéronselo, y en viéndolo Sancho le dijo: 'Dame, buen hombre, ese báculo, que lo he menester.' 'De muy buena gana—respondió el viejo—: helo aquí, señor'. Y púsoselo en la mano. Tomólo Sancho, y dándoselo al otro viejo, le dijo: 'Andad con Dios, que ya vais pagado.' '¿Yo, señor?—

and a service to him, on condition that he should repay me on demand. I didn't ask him for them for a long time, so as not to put him into greater difficulties through repaying than he was in when I lent him them. But as he didn't seem to me to be troubling about his debt, I asked him for them, not once but many times. Now not only does he not repay me but he denies the debt, saying that I never lent him these ten crowns, or that if I did he has returned them. I have no witnesses of the loan—nor he of the repayment, for he never made it. So I want your worship to put him under oath, and if he swears that he has repaid me I will let him off the debt here, before God.'

'What do you say to this, you fellow with the stick?' asked Sancho.

'I confess that he lent them to me, sir,' answered the old man. 'Hold down your wand of justice, your worship, and since he leaves it to my oath, I'll swear that I really and truly returned them to him.'

The Governor lowered his wand, and at the same time this old man gave his stick, as if it were very much in his way, to the other old man to hold whilst he took his oath. Then he put his hand on the cross of the wand and declared that he had truly borrowed the ten crowns demanded of him, but that he had returned them into the plaintiff's own hands, and that it was only the other man's forgetfulness that made him continually demand them back.

At this the great Governor asked the creditor what answer he had to give to his adversary. For beyond all doubt the debtor must be speaking the truth since, in his opinion, he was an honest man and a good Christian. It must, in fact, have been the plaintiff who had forgotten how and when the money had been returned, and thenceforward he must never ask for repayment again. The debtor took back his stick, bowed and went out of the court. Now when Sancho saw the defendant depart without more ado and also observed the plaintiff's resignation, he bowed his head on his breast and, placing the first finger of his right hand over his brows and his nose, remained as if in thought for a short while. Then he raised his head and ordered the old man with the stick, who had already left the building, to be recalled; and when he was brought back into his presence, Sancho said: 'Give me that stick, my fellow. I've need of it.'

'With great pleasure,' replied the old man, putting it into Sancho's hand. 'Here it is, sir.' Sancho then took it and, handing it to the other old man, said to him: 'Go, in God's name. You're repaid now.'

respondió el viejo—, ¿pues vale esta cañaheja diez escudos de oro?'
'Sí—dijo el gobernador—, o si no, yo soy el mayor porro del mundo.
Y ahora se verá si tengo yo caletre para gobernar todo un reino.' Y
mandó que allí delante de todos se rompiese y abriese la caña.
Hízose así, y en el corazón de ella hallaron diez escudos en oro.
Quedaron todos admirados, y tuvieron a su gobernador por un
nuevo Salomón. Preguntáronle de dónde había colegido que en
aquella cañaheja estaban aquellos diez escudos, y respondió que de
haberlo visto dar el viejo que juraba a su contrario aquel báculo en
tanto que hacía el juramento y jurar que se los había dado real y
verdaderamente, y que en acabando de jurar le tornó a pedir el
báculo, y le vino a la imaginación que dentro de él estaba la paga de
lo que pedía. De donde se podía colegir que los que gobiernan,
aunque sean unos tontos, tal vez los encamina Dios en sus juicios; y
más que él había oído contar otro caso como aquél al cura de su
lugar, y que él tenía tan gran memoria, que a no olvidársele todo
aquello de que quería acordarse, no hubiera tal memoria en toda
la ínsula. Finalmente, el un viejo corrido y el otro pagado se fueron
y los presentes quedaron admirados, y el que escribía las palabras,
hechos y movimientos de Sancho no acababa de determinarse si lo
tendría y pondría por tonto o por discreto.

Luego, acabado este pleito, entró en el juzgado una mujer asida
fuertemente de un hombre vestido de ganadero rico, la cual venía
dando grandes voces diciendo: '¡Justicia, señor gobernador, justicia!
Y si no la hallo en la tierra la iré a buscar al cielo. Señor gobernador
de mi ánima: este mal hombre me ha cogido en la mitad de ese
campo, y se ha aprovechado de mi cuerpo como si fuera trapo mal
lavado, y, ¡desdichada de mí! me ha llevado lo que yo tenía
guardado más de veintitrés años ha, defendiéndolo de moros y
cristianos, de naturales y extranjeros, y yo siempre dura como un
alcornoque, conservándome entera como la salamanquesa en el
fuego, o como la lana entre las zarzas, para que este buen hombre
llegase ahora con sus manos limpias a manosearme'. 'Aun eso está
por averiguar si tiene limpias o no las manos este galán'—dijo
Sancho—. Y volviéndose al hombre le dijo que qué decía y respondía
a la querella de aquella mujer. El cual, todo turbado, respondió:
'Señores, yo soy un pobre ganadero de ganado de cerda, y esta
mañana salía desde el lugar, de vender (con perdón sea dicho)
cuatro puercos, que me llevaron de alcabalas y socaliñas poco menos
de lo que ellos valían; volvíame a mi aldea, topé en el camino a esta

'What, sir?' replied the old man. 'Is this stick worth ten gold crowns then?'

'Yes,' said the Governor. 'If it isn't I'm the greatest dolt in the world. And now you'll see whether I haven't the gumption to govern a whole kingdom.'

Then he ordered the cane to be broken open in the presence of everyone; and when this was done they found ten gold crowns inside. Whereupon everyone expressed astonishment, and hailed the governor as a new Solomon. And when asked how he had deduced that the ten crowns were inside the cane, he answered that he had watched the defendant give the stick to the plaintiff whilst he took his oath that he had really and truly returned the money; and when the fellow had completed his oath and asked for the stick back, it had occurred to him that the sum in dispute must be inside. From this, he added, they might see that sometimes God directs the judgments of governors, even if some of them are fools. Besides, he had heard the priest of his village tell of a similar case, and he had so good a memory that, if it weren't that he forgot everything he wanted to remember, there would not be a better in the whole isle. Finally they departed, one abashed and the other satisfied. The audience was flabbergasted, and the secretary who noted down Sancho's words, acts and gestures was unable to decide whether to write him down a wise man or a fool.

But no sooner was this case over than a woman came into the court, stoutly clinging to a man dressed like a rich herdsman, and crying out loudly as she came : 'Justice, Lord Governor! Justice! If I don't find it on earth, I'll go and seek it in Heaven! Sweet governor, this wicked man sprang on me in the middle of a field, and abused my body like a dirty dish-rag and, poor wretch that I am, he robbed me of a treasure I've kept for more than twenty-three years, and defended from Moors and Christians, natives and foreigners. I've always been as resistant as a cork-tree and pre-served myself as pure as the salamander in the fire, or as wool on the briars, for this fellow now to come and handle me with his clean hands!'

'We have still to discover whether this fine fellow has clean hands or not,' said Sancho.

Then, turning to the man, he asked him what answer he had to offer to the woman's complaint. And the man replied in great confusion : 'Sirs, I am a poor herdsman with a herd of swine, and this morning I left this place to sell—saving your presence—four pigs, and what with dues and exactions they took from me very nearly their full value. Now as I was coming back to my village I

buena dueña, y el diablo, que todo lo añasca y todo lo cuece, hizo que yogásemos juntos; paguéle lo suficiente, y ella mal contenta asió de mí, y no me ha dejado hasta traerme a este puesto. Dice que la forcé, y miente para el juramento que hago o pienso hacer; y ésta es toda la verdad sin faltar miaja.

Entonces el gobernador le preguntó si traía consigo algún dinero en plata; él dijo que hasta veinte ducados tenía en el seno en una bolsa de cuero. Mandó que la sacase, y se la entregase así como estaba a la querellante; él lo hizo temblando; tomóla la mujer, y haciendo mil zalemas a todos, y rogando a Dios por la vida y salud del señor gobernador, que así miraba por las huérfanas menesterosas y doncellas, con esto se salió del juzgado llevando la bolsa asida con entrambas manos; aunque primero miró si era de plata la moneda que llevaba dentro. Apenas salió, cuando Sancho dijo al ganadero, que ya se le saltaban las lágrimas, y los ojos y el corazón se le iban tras su bolsa: 'Buen hombre, id tras aquella mujer, y quitadle la bolsa aunque no quiera, y volved aquí con ella.' Y no lo dijo a. tonto ni a sordo; porque luego partió como un rayo, y fué a lo que se le mandaba. Todos los presentes estaban suspensos esperando el fin de aquel pleito, y de allí a poco volvieron el hombre y la mujer más asidos y aferrados que la vez primera: ella la saya levantada, y en el regazo puesta la bolsa, y el hombre pugnando por quitársela; mas no era posible según la mujer la defendía, la cual daba voces diciendo. '¡Justicia de Dios y del mundo! Mire vuestra merced, señor gobernador, la poca vergüenza y el poco temor de este desalmado, que en mitad de poblado, en mitad de la calle me ha querido quitar la bolsa que vuestra merced mandó darme.' '¿Y háosla quitado?'—preguntó el gobernador—'¿Cómo quitar?—respondió la mujer—; antes me dejara yo quitar la vida, que me quiten la bolsa. ¡Bonita es la niña! ¡Otros gatos me han de echar a las. barbas, que no este desventurado y asqueroso! ¡Tenazas y martillos, mazos y escoplos no serán bastantes a sacármela de las uñas, ni aun garras de leones: antes el ánima de mitad en mitad de las carnes!' 'Ella tiene razón—dijo el hombre—, y yo me doy por rendido y sin fuerzas, y confieso que las mías no son bastantes para quitársela, y déjola.' Entonces el gobernador dijo a la mujer: 'Mostrad, honrada y valiente, esa bolsa.' Ella se la dió luego y el gobernador se la volvió

met this good woman on the way, and the Devil, the author of all mischief, made us couple together. I paid her sufficient, but she wasn't content and caught hold of me and wouldn't let me go until she had dragged me to this place. She says I forced her, and that's a lie, as I'll swear on oath; and that's the whole truth, to the last crumb.'

Then the Governor asked him if he had any silver money on him, and he replied he had about twenty ducats inside his shirt in a leather purse. This the governor ordered him to take out and hand over to the plaintiff just as it was. He obeyed trembling, and the woman took it, making a thousand curtseys to the company, and praying God for the life and health of the good governor, who thus looked after needy orphans and maidens. With this she left the court, grasping the purse tightly with both hands, although she looked first to see if the money in it was really silver. Then, no sooner was she gone than Sancho said to the herdsman, who was on the point of tears, for his eyes and his heart yearned after his purse, 'Run after that woman, my good fellow, and take the purse away from her, whether she likes it or not. Then come back here with her.'

It was not a fool or a deaf man he spoke to, for the man dashed out at once like lightning and ran to obey. All the audience were in suspense as they awaited the outcome of the case. Then shortly afterwards the man and woman came back, more close entwined and locked together than before, she with her skirt tucked up and the purse in the fold, and the man struggling to get it away from her. But it was impossible, so stoutly did she defend it, crying out loudly: 'Justice, in God's name! Justice! See, Lord worshipful Governor, the shamelessness of this bold, godless fellow. In the middle of the town, in the middle of the street, he's been trying to rob me of the purse your worship made him give me.'

'And did he rob you?' asked the Governor.

'How rob me?' replied the woman. 'I had rather lose my life than this purse. A pretty babe I should be! You must set other cats at my chin than this miserable, filthy fellow. Pincers and hammers, mallets and chisels, won't be enough to get it out of my clutches, nor lion's claws either. They shall sooner have my soul from the very heart of my body!'

'She's right,' said the man. 'I'm beaten, I admit, and tired out. I confess I haven't the strength to take it from her. I give up.'

Then the Governor said to the woman: 'Show me that purse, honest and valiant woman.'

al hombre, y dijo a la esforzada y no forzada: 'Hermana mía, si el mismo aliento y valor que habéis mostrado para defender esta bolsa lo mostrarais, y aun la mitad menos, para defender vuestro cuerpo, las fuerzas de Hércules no os hicieran fuerza. Andad con Dios y mucho de enhoramala, y no paréis en toda esta ínsula, ni en seis leguas a la redonda, so pena de doscientos azotes. Andad luego, digo, churrillera, desvergonzada y embaidora.' Espantóse la mujer y fué cabizbaja y mal contenta, y el gobernador dijo al hombre: 'Buen hombre, andad con Dios a vuestro lugar con vuestro dinero, y de aquí adelante si no lo queréis perder, procurad que no os venga en voluntad de yogar con nadie.' El hombre le dió las gracias lo peor que supo, y fuése. Y los circunstantes quedaron admirados de nuevo de los juicios y sentencias de su nuevo gobernador. Todo lo cual, notado de su cronista, fué luego escrito al duque que con gran deseo lo estaba esperando. Y quédese aquí el buen Sancho . . .

FRANCISCO GÓMEZ DE QUEVEDO
[1580–1645]

One of the outstanding men of Spain's Golden Age was the prolific and energetic Francisco de Quevedo. Born in Madrid of a family which enjoyed marked royal favour, Quevedo reached eminence both in court and literary circles before he was twenty-five. He engaged actively and often unhappily in the politics of early seventeenth-century Spain, seesawing from high posts to exile in the turbulent intrigues of the day. Towards the end of his life his alleged criticism of King Philip IV's favourite, the Conde-duque of Olivares, netted him four years' imprisonment, much of which time he passed in the dank horror of a subterranean cell.

A writer of keen perception and enormous skill, Quevedo cultivated almost all genres of literature. His prose works include serious treatises on philosophy, religion, politics, history and literary criticism. They all reveal encyclopaedic erudition. His forte, however, is wit and satire, and he is at his best in his picaresque novel La vida del Buscón (*written 1608, published 1626*),

She gave it to him at once, and the Governor returned it to the man, saying to the forcible but unforced woman : 'Sister, if you'd shown the same valorous spirit you've displayed in defending that purse, or even half as much, in defending your body, the strength of Hercules couldn't have forced you. Get out, confound you, and ill luck go with you. Don't stay anywhere in this isle, nor within twenty miles of it, under pain of two hundred lashes. Get out at once, I say, you loose-tongued, shameless swindler.'

The woman was thrown into confusion, and went off hanging her head, in high dudgeon, and the Governor said to the man : 'Good fellow, go back home, in God's name, with your money, and in future, if you don't want to lose it, try not to get a fancy for coupling with anyone.'

The man thanked him with the worst possible grace and departed, and the audience were once more astonished at their new governor's judicious decisions. All this, duly recorded by his chronicler, was straightway written down for the Duke, who was most eagerly waiting for news. But here let good Sancho rest.

J. M. COHEN

and in his masterpiece, Los sueños. In the latter work, under the guise of recording his dreams, Quevedo presents a trenchant, bitter satire of the corruption and degeneracy of seventeenth-century Spain.

Quevedo is also one of the country's finest poets. He explored all forms of verse with remarkable facility, but, as in his prose works, he excelled in witty satire. His Poderoso caballero es Don Dinero *is one of the most popular poems in the Spanish language.*

In both prose and verse Quevedo is a master of language, dazzling the reader with verbal pirouettes and a seemingly inexhaustible vocabulary. His style helped fashion the school of writing called conceptismo, *in contrast to the elegantly obscure* culteranismo *developed by Góngora. Ironically,* conceptismo *became almost as involved as the* culteranismo *which Quevedo despised, and it had a deleterious effect on Spanish letters of the second half of the seventeenth century.*

LA VIDA DEL BUSCÓN

De cómo fuí a un pupilaje por criado de Don Diego Coronel

Determinó, pues, don Alonso de poner a su hijo en pupilaje: lo uno por apartarle de su regalo, y lo otro por ahorrar de cuidado. Supo que había en Segovia un licenciado Cabra que tenía por oficio de criar hijos de caballeros, y envió allá el suyo y a mí para que le acompañase y sirviese. Entramos primer domingo después de Cuaresma en poder de la hambre viva, porque tal lacería no admite encarecimiento.

El era un clérigo cerbatana, largo sólo en el talle, una cabeza pequeña, pelo bermejo. No hay más que decir para quien sabe el refrán que dice: 'Ni gato ni perro de aquella color.' Los ojos avecinados en el cogote, que parecía que miraba por cuévanos; tan hundidos y obscuros, que era buen sitio el suyo para tiendas de mercaderes; la nariz, entre Roma y Francia, porque se le había comido de unas búas de resfriado, que aun no fueron de vicio, porque cuestan dinero; las barbas, descoloridas de miedo de la boca vecina, que, de pura hambre, parecía que amenazaba a comérselas; los dientes, le faltaban no sé cuántos, y pienso que por holgazanes y vagamundos se los habían desterrado; el gaznate, largo como avestruz, con una nuez tan salida, que parecía se iba a buscar de comer, forzada de la necesidad; los brazos, secos; las manos, como un manojo de sarmientos cada una. Mirado de media abajo, parecía tenedor, o compás con dos piernas largas y flacas; su andar, muy despacio; si se descomponía algo, se sonaban los huesos como tablillas de San Lázaro; la habla, ética; la barba, grande, por nunca se la cortar por no gastar, y él decía que era tanto el asco que le daba ver las manos del barbero por su cara, que antes se dejaría matar que tal permitiese; cortábale los cabellos un muchacho de los otros.

Traía un bonete los días de sol, ratonado con mil gateras, y guarniciones de grasa; era de cosa que fué paño, con los fondos de caspa. La sotana, según decían algunos, era milagrosa, porque no se sabía de qué color era. Unos, viéndola tan sin pelo, la tenían por de cuero de rana; otros decían que era ilusión. Desde cerca parecía negra y desde lejos entre azul; llevábala sin ceñidor; no traía cuello ni puños: parecía, con los cabellos largos y la sotana mísera y corta, lacayuelo de la muerte. Cada zapato podía ser tumba de un filisteo. Pues ¿ su aposento? Aun arañas no había en él. Conjuraba los

PAUL, THE SPANISH SHARPER

How I went to a boarding school to wait on Don Diego Coronel

Don Alonzo determined to send his son to a boarding school, both to wean him from his tender treatment at home, and also to ease himself of that care. He was informed there was a master of arts in Segovia, whose name was Cabra, and who made it his business to educate *gentlemen's* sons; thither accordingly he sent his, and me to wait upon him. It was the first Sunday after Lent we were brought into the house of famine, for it is impossible to convey a just idea of the penury of such a place.

The master was himself a skeleton, a mere shotten herring, or like a long cane with a little head upon it. He was red-haired, and no more need be said to those who know the proverb, 'that neither cat nor dog of that colour are good'; his eyes almost sunk into his head, as if he had looked through a perspective glass, or the deep windows in a linen-draper's shop; his nose turned up and was somewhat flat, the bridge being almost carried away by an inundation of cold rheum, for he never incurred any worse disorder because it would cost money. His beard had lost its colour from fear of his mouth, which being so near, seemed to threaten to eat it out of mere hunger; his teeth had many of them deserted him from want of employment; his neck was as long as a crane's, with the gullet sticking out so far that it seemed as if compelled by necessity to start out for sustenance; his arms withered; his hands like a bundle of twigs, each of them, hanging downwards, looking like a pair of compasses, with long slender legs. His voice was weak and hollow; his beard shaggy, for he never shaved in order to save soap and razor; besides, it was odious, he said, to feel the barber's hands all over his face, and he would rather die than endure it; but he let one of the boys cut his hair.

In fair weather he wore a threadbare cap, an inch thick in grease and dirt, made of a thing that was once cloth, and lined with scurf and dandruff. His cassock, some said, was really miraculous, for no man knew what colour it was of; some, seeing no hair on it, concluded it was made of frogs' skins; others that it was a mere shadow; near at hand it looked somewhat black, and at a distance bluish. He wore no girdle, cuffs, or band, so that his long hair and scanty short cassock made him look like the messenger of death. Each shoe might have served for an ordinary coffin. As for his chamber, there was not so much as a cobweb in it, the spiders being all starved to death. He put spells upon the mice, for fear

ratones de miedo que no le royesen algunos mendrugos que guardaba. La cama tenía en el suelo, y dormía siempre de un lado, por no
gastar las sábanas. Al fin, era archipobre y protomiseria.

A poder, pues, déste vine y en su poder estuve con don Diego, y
la noche que llegamos nos señaló nuestro aposento y nos hizo una
plática corta, que, por no gastar tiempo, no duró más. Díjonos lo
que habíamos de hacer: estuvimos ocupados en esto hasta la hora
del comer. Fuimos allá. Comían los amos primero, y servíamos los
criados. El refitorio era un aposento como un medio celemín. Susten-
tábanse a una mesa hasta cinco caballeros. Yo miré lo primero por
los gatos, y como no los vi, pregunté que cómo no los había a un
criado antiguo, el cual, de flaco, estaba ya con la marca del pupilaje.

Comenzó a enternecerse, y dijo:

—¿Cómo gatos? Pues, ¿quién os ha dicho a vos que los gatos son
amigos de ayunos y penitencias? En lo gordo se os echa de ver que
sois nuevo.

Yo con esto me comencé a afligir, y más me asusté cuando advertí
que todos los que de antes vivían en el pupilaje estaban como leznas,
con unas caras que parecían se afeitaban con diaquilón.

Sentóse el licenciado Cabra y echó la bendición. Comieron una
comida eterna, sin principio ni fin. Trajeron caldo en unas escudillas
de madera, tan claro, que en comer una dellas peligraba Narciso
más que en la fuente. Noté con la ansia que los macilentos dedos se
echaban a nado tras un garbanzo huérfano y solo que estaba en el
suelo.

Decía Cabra a cada sorbo:

—Cierto que no hay tal cosa como la olla, digan lo que dijeren.
Todo lo demás es vicio y gula.

Acabando de decirlo, echóse su escudilla a pechos, diciendo:

—Todo esto es salud y otro tanto ingenio.

—¡Mal ingenio te acabe!—decía yo entre mí—, cuando vi un
mozo medio espíritu y tan flaco, con un plato de carne en las manos,
que parecía la había quitado de sí mismo.

Venía un nabo aventurero a vueltas, y dijo el maestro:

—¿Nabos hay? No hay para mí perdiz que se le iguale. Coman;
que me huelgo de verlos comer.

Repartió a cada uno tan poco carnero, que en lo que se les pegó
a las uñas y se les quedó entre los dientes pienso que se consumió todo,
dejando descomulgadas las tripas de participantes.

Cabra los miraba, y decía:

—¡Coman; que mozos son, y me huelgo de ver sus buenas ganas!
Mire vuesa merced qué buen aliño para los que bostezaban de

they should gnaw some scraps of bread he treasured up. His bed was on the floor, and he always lay upon one side, from fear of wearing out the sheets; in short, he was the superlative degree of the word avarice, and the very *ne plus ultra* of want.

Into this prodigy's hands I fell, and lived under him along with Don Diego. On the night we came he showed us our room, and made us a short speech,—not longer out of sheer love of economy of words. He told us how we were to behave. The next morning we were engaged till dinner time; we went to it; the masters dined first and the servants waited. The dining-room was as big as a half-peck; five gentlemen ate in it at one table; I looked about for the cat, and seeing none, asked a servant, an old stager, who in his leanness bore the mark of a boarding-school, how it came they had none? The tears stood in his eyes, and he said :

'Why do you talk of cats? Pray who told you that cats loved penance and mortification? Ah, your fat sides show you are a new comer.'

This to me was an augury of sorrow, but I was worse scared when I observed that all those who were before us in the house looked like so many pictures of death on the white horse. Master Cabra said grace, then sat down, and they ate a meal which had neither beginning nor end. They brought the broth in wooden dishes, but it was so clear that a man might have seen to the bottom had it been ten fathoms deep. I observed how eagerly they all dived down after a single pea that was in every dish. Every sip he gave, Cabra cried :

'By my troth, there is no dainty like the *olla*, or boiled meat and broth. Let the world say what it will, all the rest is mere gluttony and extravagancy; this is good for the health, while it sharpens the wits.'

'A curse on thee and thy wit,' thought I, and at the same time I saw a servant, like a walking ghost, bring in a dish of meat, which looked as if he had picked it off his own bones. Among it was one poor stray turnip, at sight of which the master exclaimed :

'What, have we turnips today; no partridge is in my opinion to compare with them. Eat heartily, for I love to see you eat.'

He gave every one such a wretched bit of mutton that it stuck to their nails and in their teeth so that not a shred of it could reach their stomachs. Cabra looked on, and repeated :

'Eat heartily, for it is a pleasure to me to see what good stomachs you have.'

Now just think what comfort this was for them that were pining with hunger. When dinner was over, there remained some scraps

hambre. Acabaron de comer, y quedaron unos mendrugos en la mesa y en el plato unos pellejos y unos huesos, y dijo el pupilero:

—Quede esto para los criados, que también han de comer, no lo queramos todo.

—¡Mal te haga Dios y lo que has comido, lacerado—decía yo— que tal amenaza has hecho a mis tripas!

Echó la bedición, y dijo:

—Ea, demos lugar a los criados, y váyanse hasta las dos a hacer ejercicio, no les haga mal lo que han comido.

Entonces yo no pude tener la risa, abriendo toda la boca. Enojóse mucho y díjome que aprendiese modestia y tres o cuatro sentencias viejas, y fuése.

Sentámonos nosotros, y yo, que vi el negocio mal parado, y que mis tripas pedían justicia, como más cano y más fuerte que los otros, arremetí al plato, como arremetieron todos, y emboquéme de tres mendrugos los dos y el un pellejo. Comenzaron los otros a gruñir.

Al ruido entró Cabra, diciendo:

—Coman como hermanos, pues Dios les da con qué. No riñan; que para todos hay.

Volvióse al sol, y dejónos solos.

Certifico a vuesa merced que había uno dellos que se llamaba Surre, vizcaíno, tan olvidado ya de cómo y por dónde se comía, que una cortecilla que le cupo la llevó dos veces a los ojos, y entre tres no la acertaba a encaminar de las manos a la boca. Y pedí yo de beber, que los otros por estar casi ayunos no lo hacían, y diéronme un vaso con agua, y no le hube bien llegado a la boca, cuando, como si fuera lavatorio de comunión, me le quitó el mozo espiritado que dije. Levantéme con grande dolor de mi ánima, viendo que estaba en casa donde se brindaba a las tripas, y no hacían la razón.

. . .

—¿Cómo encareceré yo mi tristeza y pena? Fué tanta, que considerando lo poco que había de entrar en mi cuerpo, no osé, aunque tenía gana, echar nada dél.

Entretuvímonos hasta la noche. Decíame don Diego que qué haría él para persuadir a las tripas que habían comido, porque no lo querían creer. Andaban vaguidos en aquella casa, como en otra ahitos.

Llegó la hora del cenar. Pasóse la merienda en blanco. Cenamos mucho menos, y no carnero, sino un poco del nombre del maestro:

of bread on the table, and a few bits of skin and bone, and the master said :

'Let this be left for the servants; they must dine as well as we.'

'Perdition seize thee, ruthless wretch,' thought I, 'and may what thou hast eaten stick in thy gizzard for evermore! What a consternation you have thrown my stomach into!'

He next returned thanks, saying, 'Come, let us make way for the servants, and you go and exercise until two o'clock, lest your dinner should be too heavy for you.'

I could no longer forbear laughing aloud for my life, on which he grew very angry, and bade me conduct myself like a modest youth, quoting two or three mouldy old proverbs, and then took himself off. We sat down to this mournful spectacle, and hearing my great guns roar for provender, and as a new comer having more strength than the rest, I seized by force upon two scraps of bread, and bolted them down along with one piece of skin. The others began to mutter, for they were too weak to speak aloud; on which in came Cabra once more, observing :

'Come, come, eat quietly together, since God provides for you, be thankful; there is enough for all.'

Now, I declare it solemnly, there was one of these servants, a Biscayan, named Surre, who had so completely forgotten the way to his mouth, that he put a small bit of crust that was given him into his eye, as if happy that he was thus saved the trouble of swallowing. I asked for drink; the rest who had hardly broken fast never thought of it, and they gave a dish with some water, which I no sooner put to my lips, before the sharp-set lad I spoke of snatched it away, as if I had been Tantalus, and that the flitting river he stands in up to the chin. I got up from table with a sigh, perceiving for truth that I was in a house where they drank to a good appetite, but would not permit it to pledge. It is impossible to express my trouble and concern; and considering how little was likely to go into my belly, I was actually afraid, though hard pressed, of feeling the process of digestion going on.

Thus we passed on till night. Don Diego asked me how he should do to persuade himself that he had dined, for his stomach could not be made to submit, and only grumbled when he alluded to the subject. The house, in short, was a hospital of dizzy heads, proceeding from empty insides,—a different kind of dizziness to that incurred by surfeits.

Supper time came, for afternoon meals were never dreamed of. It was still shorter than the dinner, and consisted of a little roasted

cabra asada. Mire vuesa merced si inventara el diablo tal cosa. —Es cosa muy saludable y provechosa—decía—cenar poco para tener el estómago desocupado. Y citaba una retahila de médicos infernales. Decía alabanzas de la dieta, y que ahorraba un hombre sueños pesados, sabiendo que en su casa no se podía soñar otra cosa sino que comían. Cenaron, y cenamos todos, y no cenó ninguno. Fuímonos a acostar, y en toda la noche yo ni don Diego pudimos dormir; él trazando de quejarse a su padre y pedir que le sacase de allí, y yo aconsejándole que lo hiciese . . .

Entre estas pláticas, y un poco que dormimos se llegó la hora del levantar; dieron las seis, y llamó Cabra a lección. Fuimos, y oímosla todos. Ya mis espaldas e ijadas nadaban en el jubón, y las piernas daban lugar a otras siete calzas; los dientes sacaba con tobas, amarillos, vestidos de desesperación. Mandáronme leer el primer nominativo a los otros, y era de manera mi hambre, que me desayuné con la mitad de las razones, comiéndomelas . . .

Pasamos este trabajo hasta la cuaresma que vino, y a la entrada della estuvo malo un compañero. Cabra, por no gastar, detuvo el llamar médico, hasta que ya él pedía confesión más que otra cosa. Llamó entonces un platicante, el cual le tomó el pulso, y dijo que la hambre le había ganado por la mano en matar aquel hombre. . .

Imprimiéronsele estas razones en el corazón; murió el pobre mozo; enterrámosle muy pobremente, por ser forastero, y quedamos todos asombrados. Divulgóse por el pueblo el caso atroz; llegó a oídos de don Alonso Coronel, y como no tenía otro hijo, desengañóse de las crueldades de Cabra, y comenzó a dar más crédito a las razones de dos sombras, que ya estábamos reducidos a tan miserable estado. Vino a sacarnos del pupilaje, y teniéndonos delante, nos preguntaba por nosotros, y tales nos vió, que sin aguardar a más, trató muy mal de palabra al licenciado Vigilia. Nos mandó llevar en dos sillas a casa; despedímonos de los compañeros, que nos seguían con los deseos y con los ojos, haciendo las lástimas que hace el que queda en Argel viendo venir rescatados sus compañeros.

goat instead of mutton. Surely the devil could never have contrived a worse little beast. Our starving master Cabra said : 'It is very wholesome and beneficial to eat light suppers, that the stomach may not be overwhelmed'; and then he quoted some cursed physician who has been long in hell. He extolled spare diet, alleging that it prevented uneasy dreams, though he knew that in his house it was impossible to dream of anything but eating. Our master and we supped, but in reality we had none of us supped. On going to bed, neither Diego nor I could sleep a wink, for he lay contriving how to complain to his father, that he might remove him, and I advising him so to do. . . .

Having spent the whole night in this discourse, we got a little nap towards morning, till it was time to rise; six o'clock struck, Cabra called, and we all went to school, but when I went to dress me, my doublet was two handfuls too big, and my breeches, which before were close, now hung as loose as if they had been none of my own. In fact, when I was ordered to decline some nouns, such was my hunger that I ate half of my words, for want of more substantial diet. . . .

In this misery we continued till the next Lent, at the beginning of which one of our companions fell sick; Cabra, to save charges, delayed sending for a physician till the patient was just giving up the ghost, and desired to prepare for another world; then he called a young quack, who felt his pulse, and said hunger had been beforehand with him, and prevented his killing that man. These were his last words; the poor lad died, and was buried meanly, because he was a stranger. This struck a terror into all that lived in the house; the dismal story flew all about the town, and came at last to Don Alonzo Coronel's ears, who having no other son, began to be convinced of Cabra's inhumanity, and to give credit to the words of two mere shadows, for we were no better at that time. He came to take us from the boarding-school, and asked for us, though we stood before him; till at length, seeing us with some difficulty, and in so deplorable a condition, he gave our master some hard words. We were carried away in two chairs, taking leave of our famished companions, who followed us with their eyes and wishes, lamenting like those who remain slaves at Algiers, when their other associates are ransomed.

JOHN STEVENS
(Revised by Thomas Roscoe)

LETRILLA

Poderoso caballero
Es don Dinero.

Madre, yo al oro me humillo;
Él es mi amante y mi amado,
Pues de puro enamorado,
De contino anda amarillo;
Que pues, doblón o sencillo,
Hace todo cuanto quiero,
Poderoso caballero
Es don Dinero.

Nace en las Indias honrado,
Donde el mundo lo acompaña;
Viene a morir en España,
Y es en Génova enterrado.
Y pues quien le trae al lado
Es hermoso, aunque sea fiero,
Poderoso caballero
Es don Dinero.

Es galán y es como un oro,
Tiene quebrado el color,
Persona de gran valor,
Tan cristiano como moro.
Pues que da y quita el decoro
Y quebranta cualquier fuero,
Poderoso caballero
Es don Dinero.

Son sus padres principales,
Y es de nobles descendiente,
Porque en las venas de Oriente
Todas las sangres son reales;
Y pues es quien hace iguales
Al rico y al pordiosero,
Poderoso caballero
Es don Dinero

. . .

THE LORD OF DOLLARS

Over kings and priests and scholars
Rules the mighty Lord of Dollars.

Mother, unto gold I yield me,
  He and I are ardent lovers;
  Pure affection now discovers
How his sunny rays shall shield me!
  For a trifle more or less
  All his power will confess,—
Over kings and priests and scholars
Rules the mighty Lord of Dollars.

In the Indies did they nurse him,
  While the world stood round admiring;
  And in Spain was his expiring;
And in Genoa did they hearse him;
  And the ugliest at his side
  Shines with all of beauty's pride;
Over kings and priests and scholars
Rules the mighty Lord of Dollars.

He's a gallant, he's a winner,
  Black or white be his complexion;
  He is brave without correction
As a Moor or Christian sinner.
  He makes cross and medal bright,
  And he smashes laws of right,—
Over kings and priests and scholars
Rules the mighty Lord of Dollars.

Noble are his proud ancestors
  For his blood-veins are patrician;
  Royalties make the position
Of his Orient investors;
  So they find themselves preferred
  To the duke or country herd,—
Over kings and priests and scholars,
Rules to mighty Lord of Dollars.

. . .

THOMAS WALSH

SONETO: AVISOS DE LA MUERTE

Miré los muros de la patria mía,
Si un tiempo fuertes, ya desmoronados,
De la carrera de la edad cansados,
Por quien caduca ya su valentía.
Salíme al campo, vi que el Sol bebía
Los arroyos del yelo desatados,
Y del monte quejosos los ganados,
Que con sombras hurtó su luz al día.

Entré en mi casa; vi que, amancillada,
De anciana habitación era despojos;
Mi báculo, más corvo y menos fuerte.
Vencida de la edad sentí mi espada,
Y no hallé cosa en que poner los ojos
Que no fuese recuerdo de la muerte.

LUIS DE GÓNGORA Y ARGOTE
[1561–1627]

A Cordovan priest who attained the post of royal chaplain, Luis de Góngora began his poetic career in a traditional, popular vein. He wrote many charming lyrics, ballads, sonnets and other verse. Góngora became, however, one of the most controversial figures in Spanish literature. In an attempt to refine his poetry he developed an obscure style characterized by loose syntax and an abundance of foreign words, metaphors and mythological references. This rhetorical exuberance—called 'cultism' and 'Gongorism'— has been termed 'poetic nihilism' by Menéndez y Pelayo, and earned for Góngora the dubious title, 'Angel of Darkness'.

ANDE YO CALIENTE

Ande yo caliente,
Y ríase la gente.

Traten otros del gobierno
Del mundo y sus monarquías,
Mientras gobiernan mis días
Mantequillas y pan tierno,

DEATH WARNINGS

I saw the ramparts of my native land
One time so strong, now dropping in decay,
Their strength destroyed by this new age's way
That has worn out and rotted what was grand.
I went into the fields; there I could see
The sun drink up the waters newly thawed;
And on the hills the moaning cattle pawed,
Their miseries robbed the light of day for me.

I went into my house; I saw how spotted,
Decaying things made that old home their prize;
My withered walking-staff had come to bend.
I felt the age had won; my sword was rotted;
And there was nothing on which to set my eyes
That was not a reminder of the end.

JOHN MASEFIELD

*A host of outstanding writers of the Golden Age, including Lope de Vega
and Quevedo, attacked* culteranismo *with scornful passion. It was widely
adopted by numerous mediocre imitators of Góngora, who hastened the
decay of Spanish letters in the second half of the seventeenth century.*

*Many critics today, however, consider Góngora a rare poetic genius, and
he is greatly esteemed by modernist writers.*

Góngora's two longest works, Polifemo y Galatea *and the* Soledades,
best exemplify—to his detractors—the involved artificiality of culteranismo.
*To his partisans, they represent the highest expression of a polished and brilliant
artist.*

LET ME GO WARM

Let me go warm and merry still;
And let the world laugh, an' it will.

Let others muse on earthly things,—
The fall of thrones, the fate of kings,
   And those whose fame the world doth fill;
Whilst muffins sit enthroned in trays,

Y las mañanas de invierno
Naranjada y aguardiente,
Y ríase la gente.

Coma en dorada vajilla
El príncipe mil cuidados
Como píldoras dorados;
Que yo en mi pobre mesilla
Quiero más una morcilla
Que en el asador reviente,
Y ríase la gente.

Cuando cubra las montañas
De plata y nieve el enero
Tenga yo lleno el brasero
De bellotas y castañas,
Y quien las dulces patrañas
Del rey que rabió me cuente,
Y ríase la gente.

Busque muy en hora buena
El mercader nuevos soles;
Yo conchas y caracoles
Entre la menuda arena,
Escuchando a Filomena
Sobre el chopo de la fuente,
Y ríase la gente.

Pase a media noche el mar,
Y arda en amorosa llama
Leandro por ver su dama;
Que yo más quiero pasar
De Yepes a Madrigar
La regalada corriente,
Y ríase la gente.

Pues Amor es tan cruel
Que de Píramo y su amada
Hace tálamo una espada,
Do se junten ella y él,
Sea mi Tisbe un pastel,
Y la espada sea mi diente,
Y ríase la gente.

And orange-punch in winter sways
The merry sceptre of my days;—
    And let the world laugh, an' it will.

He that the royal purple wears,
From golden plate a thousand cares
    Doth swallow as a gilded pill;
On feasts like these I turn my back,
Whilst puddings in my roasting-jack
Beside the chimney hiss and crack;—
    And let the world laugh, an' it will.

And when the wintry tempest blows,
And January's sleets and snows
    Are spread o'er every vale and hill,
With one to tell a merry tale
O'er roasted nuts and humming ale,
I sit, and care not for the gale;—
    And let the world laugh, an' it will.

Let merchants traverse seas and lands
For silver mines and golden sands;
    Whilst I beside some shadowy rill
Just where its bubbling fountain swells
Do sit and gather stones and shells,
And hear the tale the blackbird tells;—
    And let the world laugh, an' it will.

For Hero's sake the Grecian lover
The stormy Hellespont swam over;
    I cross without the fear of ill
The wooden bridge that slow bestrides
The Madrigal's enchanting sides,
Or barefoot wade through Yepes's tides;—
    And let the world laugh, an' it will.

But since the Fates so cruel prove,
That Pyramus should die of love,
    And love should gentle Thisbe kill;
My Thisbe be an apple-tart,
The sword I plunge into her heart
The tooth that bites the crust apart,—
    And let the world laugh, an' it will.

HENRY WADSWORTH LONGFELLOW

LETRILLA

La más bella niña
De nuestro lugar,
Hoy viuda y sola
Y ayer por casar,
Viendo que sus ojos
A la guerra van,
A su madre dice
Que escucha su mal.
Dejadme llorar
Orillas del mar.

Pues me distes, madre,
En tan tierna edad,
Tan corto el placer,
Tan largo el pesar,
Y me cautivastes
De quien hoy se va
Y lleva las llaves
De mi libertad,
Dejadme llorar
Orillas del mar.

En llorar conviertan
Mis ojos de hoy más
El sabroso oficio
Del dulce mirar,
Pues que no se pueden
Mejor ocupar,
Yéndose a la guerra
quien era mi paz:
Dejadme llorar
Orillas del mar.

No me pongáis freno
ni queráis culpar,
Que lo uno es justo,
Lo otro por demás;
Si me queréis bien
No me hagáis mal,

THE LOVELIEST GIRL

The loveliest girl in all our country-side,
Today forsaken, yesterday a bride,
Seeing her love ride forth to join the wars,
With breaking heart and trembling lips implores:
'My hope is dead, my tears are blinding me,
Oh let me walk alone where breaks the sea!'

'You told me, Mother, what too well I know,
How grief is long, and joy is quick to go,
But you have given him my heart that he
Might hold it captive with love's bitter key,—
My hope is dead, my tears are blinding me.

'My eyes are dim, that once were full of grace,
And ever bright with gazing on his face,
But now the tears come hot and never cease,
Since he is gone in whom my heart found peace,
My hope is dead, my tears are blinding me.

'Then do not seek to stay my grief, nor yet
To blame a sin my heart must needs forget;
For though blame were spoken in good part,

Harto peor fuera
Morir y callar,
Dejadme llorar
Orillas del mar.

Dulce madre mía,
¿quién no llorará,
Aunque tenga el pecho
Como un pedernal,
Y no dará voces
Viendo marchitar,
Los más verdes años
De mi mocedad?
Dejadme llorar
Orillas del mar.

Váyanse las noches,
Pues ido se han
Los ojos que hacían
Los míos velar.
Váyanse, y no vean
Tanta soledad,
Después qué en mi lecho
Sobra la mitad:
Dejadme llorar
Orillas del mar.

LETRILLA

Oveja perdida, ven
Sobre mis hombros, que hoy
No sólo tu pastor soy,
Sino tu pasto también.

Por descubrirte mejor,
Cuando balabas perdida,
Dejé en un árbol la vida,
Donde me subió el amor,
Si prenda quieres mayor,
Mis obras hoy te la den.

Yet speak it not, lest you should break my heart.
My hope is dead, my tears are blinding me.

'Sweet Mother mine, who would not weep to see
The glad years of my youth so quickly flee,
Although his heart were flint, his breast a stone?
Yet here I stand, forsaken and alone,
My hope is dead, my tears are blinding me.

'And still may night avoid my lonely bed,
Now that my eyes are dull, my soul is dead.
Since he is gone for whom they vigil keep,
Too long is night, I have no heart for sleep.
My hope is dead, my tears are blinding me,
Oh let me walk alone where breaks the sea !'

JOHN PIERREPONT RICE

COME, WANDERING SHEEP, O COME!

Come, wandering sheep, O come!
  I'll bind thee to my breast,
I'll bear thee to thy home,
  And lay thee down to rest.

I saw thee stray forlorn,
  And heard thee faintly cry,
And on the tree of scorn,
  For thee I deign'd to die—

Oveja perdida, ven
Sobre mis hombros, que hoy
No sólo tu pastor soy,
Sino tu pasto también.

Pasto, al fin, hoy tuyo hecho,
¿Cuál dará mayor asombro,
O el traerte yo en el hombro,
O el traerme tú en el pecho?
Prendas son de amor estrecho,
Que aun los más ciegos las ven.
Oveja perdida, ven
Sobre mis hombros, que hoy
No sólo tu pastor soy,
Sino tu pasto también.

DE LA SOLEDAD PRIMERA

Era del año la estación florida
En que el mentido robador de Europa
—Media luna las armas de su frente,
Y el Sol todos los rayos de su pelo—,
Luciente honor del cielo,
En campos de zafiro pace estrellas;

Cuando el que ministrar podía la copa
A Júpiter mejor que el garzón de Ida,
—Náufrago y desdeñado, sobre ausente—
Lagrimosas de amor dulces querellas
Da al mar; que condolido,
Fué a las ondas, fué al viento
El mísero gemido,
Segundo de Arión dulce instrumento.
. . . .

LOPE DE VEGA
[1562–1635]

Lope Félix de Vega Carpio astonished his own contemporaries by his productivity—Cervantes called him the 'prodigy of nature'—and his accomplishments evoke no less amazement in our own day. An impassioned genius, Lope cultivated every literary genre with phenomenal ease. His works

What greater proof could I
Give,—than to seek the tomb?
Come, wandering sheep, O come!

I shield thee from alarms,
    And wilt thou not be blest?
I bear thee in my arms,
    Thou bear me in thy breast!
O this is love—come, rest—
This is blissful doom.
Come, wandering sheep, O come!

JOHN BOWRING

From SOLITUDES

'Twas now the blooming season of the year,
And in disguise Europa's ravisher
(His brow arm'd with a crescent, with such beams
Encompast as the sun unclouded streams
The sparkling glory of the zodiac!) led
His numerous herd along the azure mead.

When he, whose right to beauty might remove
The youth of Ida from the cup of Jove,
Shipwreck't, repuls'd, and absent, did complain
Of his hard fate and mistress's disdain;
With such sad sweetness that the winds, and sea,
In sighs and murmurs kept him company. . . .

THOMAS STANLEY

*include a dramatic novel, a pastoral novel, long narrative poems, innumerable
lyric poems, some four hundred religious autos and the formidable total of
over 1,800 plays.*

*With all this, Lope found time not only to live, but to live in such a
fashion as to inspire scandalized tongue-wagging and venomous jibes from his
enemies. He plunged into love as naturally and deeply as his pen into ink;*

*his years were crowded with a succession of mistresses and children in
addition to his two marriages. Lope was not, however, a man of casual
affections. Intense sincerity marked each romantic attachment, and the
happiness and tragedy which often accompanied them inspired some of his
finest poetry.*

*Lope's multitudinous dramatic works cover all themes—the classics,
religion, mythology, history, comedy, intrigue, adventure. Written entirely
in verse, they contain a plot and sub-plot, and are divided into three acts.*

FUENTEOVEJUNA

Sala del concejo en Fuenteovejuna. Salen ESTEBAN, ALONSO *y* BARRILDO.

ESTEBAN.	¿No han venido a la junta?
BARRILDO.	No han venido.
ESTEBAN.	Pues más a priesa nuestro daño corre.
BARRILDO.	Ya está lo más del pueblo prevenido.
ESTEBAN.	Frondoso con prisiones en la torre,
	y mi hija Laurencia en tanto aprieto,
	si la piedad de Dios no los socorre . . .

Salen JUAN ROJO *y el* REGIDOR.

JUAN.	¿De qué dais voces, cuando importa tanto
	a nuestro bien, Esteban, el secreto?
ESTEBAN.	Que doy tan pocas es mayor espanto.

Sale MENGO.

MENGO.	También vengo yo a hallarme en esta junta.
ESTEBAN.	Un hombre cuyas canas baña el llanto,
	labradores honrados, os pregunta
	qué obsequias debe hacer toda esa gente
	a su patria sin honra, ya perdida.
	Y si se llaman honras justamente,
	¿cómo se harán, si no hay entre nosotros
	hombre a quien este bárbaro no afrente?
	Respondedme: ¿hay alguno de vosotros
	que no esté lastimado en honra y vida?
	¿No os lamentáis los unos de los otros?
	Pues si ya la tenéis todos perdida
	¿a qué aguardáis? ¿Qué desventura es ésta?

Except for action, Lope disregarded the classical unities. He frankly wrote to please his audiences. And to the vast and enthusiastic public which jammed the theatres of his day, Lope was an idol. His plays, however, had more than transitory success; their structure set the pattern for the Spanish national drama which had so many excellent exponents in the seventeenth century.

The moving excerpt presented here is from Act III of one of. Lope's best plays, Fuenteovejuna, in which the people of that town take the law into their own hands against the persecution of a local tyrant.

FUENTEOVEJUNA

A room in the Town Hall at Fuenteovejuna. Esteban, Alonso, *and* Barrildo *enter.*

ESTEBAN. Is the Town Board assembled?
BARRILDO. Not a person can be seen.
ESTEBAN. Bravely we face danger!
BARRILDO. All the farms had warning.
ESTEBAN. Frondoso is a prisoner in the tower and my daughter Laurencia in such plight that she is lost save for the direct interposition of heaven.

(Juan Rojo *enters with the* Second Regidor.)

JUAN ROJO. Who complains aloud when silence is salvation? Peace, in God's name, peace!
ESTEBAN. I will shout to the clouds till they re-echo my complaints while men marvel at my silence.

(*Enter* Mengo *and* peasants.)

MENGO. We came to attend the meeting.
ESTEBAN. Farmers of this village, an old man whose grey beard is bathed in tears, inquires what rites, what obsequies we poor peasants, assembled here, shall prepare for our ravished homes, bereft of honour? And if life be honour, how shall we fare since there breathes not ǫne among us whom this savage has not offended? Speak? Who but has been wounded deeply, poisoned in respect? Lament now, yes, cry out! Well? If all be ill, how then say well? Well, there is work for men to do.

JUAN.	La mayor que en el mundo fué sufrida.
	Mas pues ya se publica y manifiesta
	que en paz tienen los reyes a Castilla
	y su venida a Córdoba se apresta,
	vayan dos regidores a la villa
	y echándose a sus pies pidan remedio.
BARRILDO.	En tanto que Fernando, aquel que humilla
	a tantos enemigos, otro medio
	será mejor, pues no podrá, ocupado,
	hacernos bien, con tanta guerra en medio.
REGIDOR.	Si mi voto de vos fuera escuchado,
	desamparar la villa doy por voto.
JUAN.	¿Cómo es posible en tiempo limitado?
MENGO.	A la fe, que si entiende el alboroto,
	que ha de costar la junta alguna vida.
REGIDOR.	Ya, todo el árbol de paciencia roto,
	corre la nave de temor perdida.
	La hija quitan con tan gran fiereza
	a un hombre honrado, de quien es regida
	la patria en que vivís, y en la cabeza
	la vara quiebran tan injustamente.
	¿Qué esclavo se trató con más bajeza?
JUAN.	¿Qué es lo que quieres tú que el pueblo intente?
REGIDOR.	Morir, o dar la muerte a los tiranos,
	pues somos muchos, y ellos poca gente.
BARRILDO.	¡Contra el señor las armas en las manos!
ESTEBAN.	El rey solo es señor después del cielo,
	y no bárbaros hombres inhumanos,
	Si Dios ayuda nuestro justo celo
	¿qué nos ha de costar?
MENGO.	Mirad, señores,
	que vais en estas cosas con recelo.
	Puesto que por los simples labradores
	estoy aquí que más injurias pasan,
	más cuerdo represento sus temores.
JUAN.	Si nuestras desventuras se compasan,
	para perder las vidas ¿qué aguardamos?
	Las casas y las viñas nos abrasan:
	tiranos son; a la venganza vamos.

Sale LAURENCIA, *desmelenada.*

LAURENCIA.	Dejadme entrar, que bien puedo,
	en consejo de los hombres;

JUAN ROJO. The direst that can be. Since by report it is published that Castile is subject now to a King, who shall presently make his entrance into Cordoba, let us despatch two Regidors to that city to cast themselves at his feet and demand remedy.

BARRILDO. King Ferdinand is occupied with the overthrow of his enemies, who are not few, so that his commitments are warlike entirely. It were best to seek other succour.

REGIDOR. If my voice have any weight, I declare the independence of the village.

JUAN ROJO. How can that be?

MENGO. On my soul, my back tells me the Town Board will be informed as to that directly.

REGIDOR. The tree of our patience has been cut down, the ship of our joy rides storm-tossed, emptied of its treasure. They have rept the daughter from one who is Alcalde of this town in which we dwell, breaking his staff over his aged head. Could a slave be scorned more basely?

JUAN ROJO. What would you have the people do?

REGIDOR. Die or rain death on tyrants! We are many while they are few.

BARRILDO. Lift our hands against our Lord and Master?

ESTEBAN. Only the King is our master, save for God, never these devouring beasts. If God be with us, what have we to fear?

MENGO. Gentlemen, I advise caution in the beginning and ever after. Although I represent only the very simplest labourers, who bear the most, believe me we find the bearing most unpleasant.

JUAN ROJO. If our wrongs are so great, we lose nothing with our lives. An end, then! Our homes and vineyards burn. Vengeance on the tyrants!

(*Enter* Laurencia, *her hair dishevelled.*)

LAURENCIA. Open, for I have need of the support of men! Deeds, or I cry out to heaven! Do you know me?

que bien puede una mujer,
si no a dar voto, a dar voces.
¿Conocéisme?

ESTEBAN.   ¡Santo cielo!
¿No es mi hija?

JUAN.   ¿No conoces
a Laurencia?

LAURENCIA.   Vengo tal,
que mi diferencia os pone
en contingencia quién soy.

ESTEBAN.   ¡Hija mía!

LAURENCIA.   No me nombres
tu hija.

ESTEBAN.   ¿Por qué, mis ojos?
¿Por qué?

LAURENCIA.   Por muchas razones,
y sean las principales:
porque dejas que me roben
tiranos sin que me vengues,
traidores sin que me cobres.
Aún no era yo de Frondoso,
para que digas que tome,
como marido, venganza;
que aquí por tu cuenta corre;
que en tanto que de las bodas
no haya llegado la noche,
del padre, y no del marido,
la obligación presupone;
que en tanto que no me entregan
una joya, aunque la compren,
no han de correr por mi cuenta
las guardas ni los ladrones.
Llevóme de vuestros ojos
a su casa Fernán Gómez:
la oveja al lobo dejáis
como cobardes pastores.
¿Qué dagas no vi en mi pecho?
¡Qué desatinos enormes,
qué palabras, qué amenazas,
y qué delitos atroces,
por rendir mi castidad
a sus apetitos torpes!

ESTEBAN. Martyr of God, my daughter?

JUAN ROJO. This is Laurencia.

LAURENCIA. Yes, and so changed that, gazing, you doubt still!

ESTEBAN. My daughter!
LAURENCIA. No, no more! Not yours.

ESTEBAN. Why, light of my eyes, why, pride of the valley?

LAURENCIA. Ask not, reckon not,
    Here be it known
    Tyrants reign o'er us,
    We are ruled by traitors,
    Justice is there none.
    I was not Frondoso's,
    Yours to avenge me,
    Father, till the night
    I was yours
    Though he was my husband,
    You the defender
    Guarding the bride.

As well might the noble pay for the jewel lost in the merchant's hand!
    I was lost to Fernán Gómez,
    Haled to his keep,
    Abandoned to wolves.
    A dagger at my breast
    Pointed his threats,
    His flatteries, insults, lies,
    To overcome my chastity
    Before his fierce desires.

Mis cabellos ¿no lo dicen?
¿No se ven aquí los golpes
de la sangre y las señales?
¿Vosotros sois hombres nobles?
¿Vosotros padres y deudos?
¿Vosotros, que no se os rompen
las entrañas de dolor,
de verme en tantos dolores?
Ovejas sois, bien lo dice
de Fuenteovejuna el nombre.
Dadme unas armas a mí,
pues sois piedras, pues sois broncas,
pues sois jaspes, pues sois tigres . . .
— Tigres no, porque feroces
siguen quien roba sus hijos,
matando los cazadores
antes que entren por el mar
y por sus ondas se arrojen.
Liebres cobardes nacistes;
bárbaros sois, no españoles.
Gallinas, ¡ vuestras mujeres
sufrís que otros hombres gocen!
Poneos ruecas en la cinta.
¿Para qué os ceñís estoques?
¡Vive Dios, que he de trazar
que solas mujeres cobren
la honra de estos tiranos,
la sangre de estos traidores,
y que os han de tirar piedras,
hilanderas, maricones,
amujerados, cobardes,
y que mañana os adornen
nuestras tocas y basquiñas,
solimanes y colores!
A Frondoso quiere ya,
sin sentencia, sin pregones,
colgar el Comendador
del almena de una torre;
de todos hará lo mismo;
y yo me huelgo, medio-hombres,
por que quede sin mujeres
esta villa honrada, y torne

My face is bruised and bloody in this court of honest men. Some of you are fathers, some have daughters. Do your hearts sink within you, supine and cowardly crew? You are sheep, sheep! Oh, well-named, Village of Fuenteovejuna, the Sheep Well! Sheep, sheep, sheep! Give me iron, for senseless stones can wield none, nor images, nor pillars—jasper though they be—nor dumb living things that lack the tiger's heart that follows him who steals its young, rending the hunter limb from limb upon the very margin of the raging sea, seeking the pity of the angry waves.

> But you are rabbits, farmers,
> Infidels in Spain,
> Your wives strut before you
> With the cock upon their train!
> Tuck your knitting in your belts,
> Strip off your manly swords,
> For, God living, I swear
> That your women dare
> Pluck these fearsome despots,
> Beard the traitors there!
> No spinning for our girls;
> Heave stones and do not blench.
> Can you smile, men?
> Will you fight?
> Caps we'll set upon you,
> The shelter of a skirt,
> Be heirs, boys, to our ribbons,
> The gift of the maidenry,

For now the Commander will hang Frondoso from a merlon of the tower, without let or trial, as presently he will string you all, you race of half-men, for the women will leave this village, nor one

	aquel siglo de amazonas,
	eterno espanto del orbe.
ESTEBAN.	Yo, hija, no soy de aquellos
	que permiten que los nombres
	con esos títulos viles.
	Iré solo, si se pone
	todo el mundo contra mí.
JUAN.	Y yo, por más que me asombre
	la grandeza del contrario.
REGIDOR.	Muramos todos.
BARRILDO.	Descoge
	un lienzo al viento en un palo,
	y mueran estos inormes.
JUAN.	¿Qué orden pensáis tener?
MENGO.	Ir a matarle sin orden.
	Juntad el pueblo a una voz;
	que todos están conformes
	en que los tiranos mueran.
ESTEBAN.	Tomad espadas, lanzones,
	ballestas, chuzos y palos.
MENGO.	¡Los reyes nuestros señores
	₋vivan!
TODOS.	¡Vivan muchos años!
MENGO.	¡Mueran tiranos traidores!
TODOS.	¡Traidores tiranos mueran!

.   .   .

CANTARCILLO DE LA VIRGEN

Pues andáis en las palmas,
    Ángeles santos,
Que se duerme mi niño,
    Tened los ramos.

Palmas de Belén
    Que mueven airados
Los furiosos vientos
    Que suenan tanto:
No le hagáis ruido,
    Corred más paso,
Que se duerme mi niño,
    Tened los ramos.

remain behind! Today the age of amazons returns, we lift our arms and strike against this villainy, and the crash of our blows shall amaze the world!

ESTEBAN. Daughter, I am no man to bear names calmly, opprobrious and vile. I will go and beard this despot, though the united spheres revolve against me.

JUAN ROJO. So will I, for all his pride and knavery.

REGIDOR. Let him be surrounded and cut off.

BARRILDO. Hang a cloth from a pike as our banner and cry 'Death to Monsters!'

JUAN ROJO. What course shall we choose?

MENGO. To be at them, of course. Raise an uproar and with it the village, for every man will take an oath and be with you that to the last traitor the oppressors shall die.

ESTEBAN. Seize swords and spears, cross-bows, pikes and clubs.

MENGO. Long live the King and Queen!

ALL. Live our lords and masters!

MENGO. Death to cruel tyrants!

ALL. To cruel tyrants, death!

.   .   .

JOHN GARRETT UNDERHILL

LULLABY OF THE VIRGIN

Holy angels and blest,
  Through these palms as ye sweep,
Hold their branches at rest,
  For my babe is asleep.

And ye Bethlehem palm-trees,
  As stormy winds rush
In tempest and fury,
  Your angry noise hush;—
Move gently, move gently,
  Restrain your wild sweep;
Hold your branches at rest,—
  My babe is asleep.

El niño divino,
   Que está cansado
De llorar en la tierra
   Por su descanso,
Sosegar quiere un poco
   Del tierno llanto.
Que se duerme mi niño,
   Tened los ramos.

Rigurosos yelos
   Le están cercando;
Ya veis que no tengo
   Con qué guardarlo.
Ángeles divinos
   Que váis volando,
Que se duerme mi niño,
   Tened los ramos.

SONETO

¿Qué tengo yo que mi amistad procuras?
   ¿Qué interés se te sigue, Jesús mío,
   Que a mi puerta, cubierto de rocío
Pasas las noches del invierno escuras?

¡Oh, cuánto fueron mis entrañas duras
   Pues no te abrí! ¡Qué extraño desvarío
   Si de mi ingratitud el yelo frío
Secó las llagas de tus plantas puras!

¡Cuántas veces el ángel me decía:
   Alma, asómate agora a la ventana,
   Verás con cuanto amor llamar porfía!

¡Y cuántas, hermosura soberana,
   'Mañana le abriremos' respondía,
   Para lo mismo responder mañana!

My babe all divine,
  With earth's sorrows oppressed,
Seeks in slumber an instant
  His grievings to rest;
He slumbers,—he slumbers,—
  O, hush, then, and keep
Your branches all still,—
  My babe is asleep!

Cold blasts wheel about him,—
  A rigorous storm,—
And ye see how, in vain,
  I would shelter his form;—
Holy angels and blest,
  As above me ye sweep,
Hold these branches at rest,—
  My babe is asleep!

GEORGE TICKNOR

TOMORROW

Lord, what am I, that with unceasing care
  Thou did'st seek after me, that Thou did'st wait
  Wet with unhealthy dews before my gate,
And pass the gloomy nights of winter there?

Oh, strange delusion, that I did not greet
  Thy blest approach, and oh, to heaven how lost
  If my ingratitude's unkindly frost
Has chilled the bleeding wounds upon Thy feet.

How oft my guardian angel gently cried,
  'Soul, from thy casement look, and thou shalt see
  How he persists to knock and wait for thee!'

And oh, how often to that Voice of sorrow,
'Tomorrow we will open,' I replied,
  And when the morrow came I answered still 'Tomorrow'.

HENRY WADSWORTH LONGFELLOW

SONETO

Un soneto me manda hacer Violante,
Que en mi vida me he visto en tanto aprieto;
Catorce versos dicen, que es soneto;
Burla burlando van los tres delante.

Yo pensé que no hallara consonante,
Y estoy a la mitad de otro cuarteto,
Mas si me veo en el primer terceto,
No hay cosa en los cuartetos que me espante.

Por el primer terceto voy entrando,
Y parece que entré con pie derecho,
Pues fin con este verso le voy dando.

Ya estoy en el segundo, y aun sospecho
Que voy los trece versos acabando;
Contad si son catorce, y está hecho.

TIRSO DE MOLINA
[1584–1648]

Fray Gabriel Téllez, who wrote under the pseudonym of Tirso de Molina, was a most enthusiastic follower of Lope de Vega. Like his master, Tirso produced numerous dramas (about four hundred) of many types—historical, religious, Biblical, 'cloak and sword'. His character-analysis, however, especially his portrayal of women, is superior to Lope's.

Tirso is best known for his creation of the dramatic character of the libertine Don Juan in El burlador de Sevilla. *Don Juan has become a*

EL BURLADOR DE SEVILLA

ESCENA XIV   *Sale* DON JUAN TENORIO *y* CATALINÓN.

D. JUAN.   Esas dos yeguas prevén,
Pues acomodadas son.
CATAL.   Aunque soy Catalinón,
Soy, señor, hombre de bien,
    Que no se dijo por mí:
'Catalinón es el hombre'
Que sabes; que aquese nombre
Me asienta al revés a mí.

SONNET ON A SONNET

To write a sonnet doth Juana press me,
   I've never found me in such stress and pain;
   A sonnet numbers fourteen lines 'tis plain,
And three are gone ere I can say, God bless me!

I thought that spinning rhymes might sore oppress me,
   Yet here I'm midway in the last quatrain;
   And, if the foremost tercet I can gain,
The quatrains need not any more distress me.

To the first tercet I have got at last,
   And travel through it with such right good-will,
   That with this line I've finished it, I ween.

I'm in the second now, and see how fast
   The thirteenth line comes tripping from my quill—
   Hurrah, 'tis done! Count if there be fourteen!

                              JAMES YOUNG GIBSON

universal type and has inspired hundreds of imitations. Among the outstanding
authors and composers indebted to Tirso de Molina are Molière, Goldoni,
Mozart, Byron, Pushkin and Shaw. In Spanish literature, the most famous
imitation is the romantic melodrama Don Juan Tenorio (1844), by José
Zorrilla, in which Don Juan attains salvation through last-minute repentance.
   The selections here presented come from the lively 'transmutation' by
Harry Kemp.

THE LOVE-ROGUE

ACT I

SCENE XIV

Don Juan and Catalinón come in.

DON JUAN. Get the two mares; have them ready to gallop away.
CATALINON. Yes, as I'm Catalinón and a true man,
   I'll see to it that there's exactly two
   So that they shan't fall on me with their clubs
   And pay me doubly for the lack of you.

D. JUAN   Mientras que los pescadores
            Van de regocijo y fiesta,
            Tú las dos yeguas apresta;
            Que de sus pies voladores
            Sólo nuestro engaño fío.
CATAL.   Al fin, ¿ pretendes gozar
            A Tisbea ?
D. JUAN.   Si burlar
            Es hábito antiguo mío,
              ¿ Qué me preguntas, sabiendo
            Mi condición ?
CATAL.   Ya sé que eres
            Castigo de las mujeres.
D. JUAN.   Por Tisbea estoy muriendo,
            Que es buena moza.
CATAL.   ¡ Buen pago
            A su hospedaje deseas !
D. JUAN.   Necio, lo mismo hizo Eneas
            Con la reina de Cartago.
CATAL.   Los que fingís y engañáis
            Las mujeres desa suerte
            Lo pagaréis en la muerte.
D. JUAN.   ¡ Qué largo me lo fiáis !
            Catalinón con razón
            Te llaman.
CATAL.   Tus pareceres
            Sigue, que en burlar mujeres
            Quiero ser Catalinón.
            Ya viene la desdichada.
D. JUAN.   Vete, y las yeguas prevén.
CATAL.   ¡ Pobre mujer !   Harto bien
            Te pagamos la posada.

Vase CATALINÓN *y sale* TISBEA.

ESCENA XV

TISBEA.   El rato que sin ti estoy
            Estoy ajena de mí.
D. JUAN.   Por lo que finges ansí,
            Ningún crédito te doy.
TISBEA.   ¿ Por qué ?
D. JUAN.   Porque, si me amaras,
            Mi alma favorecieras.

DON JUAN. While the fishers dance and play
  Take two mares whose flying feet
  Will whisk us off at break of day
  And add the sauce to my deceit.
CATALINON. And so you hold your purpose still
  To cozen Tisbea to your will?
DON JUAN. To turn this trick with women has become
  A habit of my very blood,—you know
  My nature, then why ask me foolish questions?
CATALINON. Yes, yes, I know by now
  You are a scourge for women.
DON JUAN. Ah, I die
  For Tisbea . . . she'll make a dainty morsel.
CATALINON. Fine payment for their hospitality,
  I must say.
DON JUAN. You ninny, I've a classic precedent
  In what Aeneas did to royal Dido.
CATALINON. Some day you'll find your death in fooling women.
DON JUAN. You're generous, I must say,
  In your prognostications, and, thereby,
  You live up to your name
  Of Catalinón, 'the cautious one'.
CATALINON. Unless you twist that edge of irony
  Against yourself, and also grow more cautious
  At your grand game of cozening and deceit,
  You'll surely pay with some most monstrous ill.
DON JUAN. You've talked enough . . . go, get the two mares ready.
CATALINON. Poor little woman, you'll be well rewarded!

(*He goes out.* Tisbea *enters.*)

SCENE XV

TISBEA. When I am not with you time is a sick thing.
DON JUAN. Don't speak that way—because—I don't believe you.
TISBEA. You don't—believe me?
DON JUAN. If it is true you love me
  You'd fill my empty heart with more than words.

TISBEA.   Tuya soy.
D. JUAN.   Pues di, ¿ qué esperas,
    O en qué, señora, reparas ?
TISBEA.   Reparo que fué castigo
    De amor, el que he hallado en ti.
D. JUAN.   Si vivo, mi bien, en ti,
    A cualquier cosa me obligo.
    Aunque yo sepa perder
    En tu servicio la vida,
    La diera por bien perdida,
    Y te prometo de ser
      Tu esposo.
TISBEA.   Soy desigual
    A tu ser.
D. JUAN.   Amor es rey
    Que iguala con justa ley
    La seda con el sayal.
TISBEA.   Casi te quiero creer. . . .
    Mas sois los hombres traidores.
D. JUAN.   ¿Posible es, mi bien, que ignores
    Mi amoroso proceder?
    Hoy prendes por tus cabellos
    Mi alma.
TISBEA.   Yo a ti me allano
    Bajo la palabra y mano
    De esposo.
D. JUAN.   Juro, ojos bellos
    Que mirando me matáis,
    De ser vuestro esposo.
TISBEA.   Advierte,
    Mi bien, que hay Dios y que hay muerte.
D. JUAN.   ¡Qué largo me lo fiáis!
    Y mientras Dios me dé vida
    Yo vuestro esclavo seré.
    Esta es mi mano y mi fe.
TISBEA.   No seré en pagarte esquiva.
D. JUAN.   Ya en mí mismo no sosiego.
TISBEA.   Ven, y será la cabaña
    Del amor que me acompaña
    Tálamo de nuestro fuego.
    Entre estas cañas te esconde
    Hasta que tenga lugar.
D. JUAN.   ¿Por dónde tengo de entrar?

TISBEA. I am all yours. What more can you require?
DON JUAN. Then why withhold the love we both desire?
TISBEA. Because that same love tears my life apart!
DON JUAN. Accept the full devotion of my heart. . . .
  I lay my life in service at your feet . . .
  Now give me all, and make your gift complete.
  Then—we'll get married!
TISBEA. No, my place in life
  Is low, as yours is high . . . that could not be!
DON JUAN. Rank clad in silk and beauty clad in wool
  Are equal in love's kingdom . . . beautiful
  Are you!
TISBEA. I almost make myself believe
  That what you say is true—yet—men deceive!
DON JUAN. Oh, can't you see I love as I declare . . .
  Look deep into my eyes . . . my soul waits there
  That you could trammel with a single hair. . . .
TISBEA. Give me your solemn word, your hand, that you
  Will wed me, then, as you—you promise to!
DON JUAN. I swear by your sweet eyes that madden me
  Marriage shall seal our stolen ecstasy.
TISBEA. Remember, if you lie, there's God and Death.
DON JUAN. I swear again that while God gives me breath
  I'll be the servant of your least command;
  Here is my solemn word, and here's my hand.
  You can put your utmost faith in me.
TISBEA. Then take me; do with me as you desire.
DON JUAN. Only the uttermost can quench this fire.
TISBEA. Come then, my little fisher hut will be
  Our bridal bower . . . stay hidden in these reeds
  Until the hour of opportunity.
DON JUAN. What way shall I get in?

TISBEA.   Ven y te diré por dónde.
D. JUAN.   Gloria al alma, mi bien, dais.
TISBEA.   Esa voluntad te obligue,
    Y si no, Dios te castigue.
D. JUAN.   ¡Qué largo me lo fiáis!

                                          (*Vanse.*)

ESCENA XVIII

Sale TISBEA.

TISBEA.   ¡Fuego, fuego! ¡que me quemo!
    ¡Que mi cabaña se abrasa!
    Repicad a fuego, amigos,
    Que ya dan mis ojos agua.
    Mi pobre edificio queda
    Hecho otra Troya en las llamas;
    Que después que faltan Troyas,
    Quiere amor quemar cabañas.
    Mas si amor abrasa peñas
    Con gran ira y fuerza extraña,
    Mal podrán de su rigor
    Reservarse humildes pajas
    ¡Fuego, zagales, fuego, agua, agua!
    ¡Amor, clemencia, que se abrasa el alma!
    ¡Ay, choza, vil instrumento
    De mi deshonra y mi infamia!
    ¡Cueva de ladrones fiera,
    Que mis agravios ampara!
    Rayos de ardientes estrellas
    En tus cabelleras caigan,
    Porque abrasadas estén,
    Si del viento mal peinadas.
    ¡Ah, falso huésped, que dejas
    Una mujer deshonrada!
    Nube que del mar salió
    Para anegar mis entrañas.
    ¡Fuego, fuego, zagales, agua, agua!
    ¡Amor, clemencia, que se abrasa el alma!
    Yo soy la que hacía siempre
    De los hombres burla tanta;
    Que siempre las que hacen burla,
    Vienen a quedar burladas.

TISBEA. I'll come and show you.
DON JUAN. You have laid bare heaven's brightness for me.
TISBEA. The very way I give myself should bind you :
  If it does not, then God revenge your crime.
DON JUAN. I'll keep my faith until the end of time.

                                     (*They go out.*)

SCENE XVIII

Tisbea *comes in.*

TISBEA. Fire ! Fire ! my world is overturning,
  My little hut of straw is burning
  Of a flame that never ends !
  Ring all the bells ! help, help, my friends !
  The Fire that once I pleased to flout
  All my tears cannot put out;
  The sudden, climbing flames destroy
  My cottage, like another Troy.
  How could I hope that love's great power
  That beats down citadels, would spare
  My virgin frailty an hour
  Beyond the time he found it fair?
  Help, help, my friends ! the flames roar past control.
  Have mercy, love, you burn my very soul !
  My little cottage built of straw,
  How sweet you were till you became
  A vile, abandoned cave of thieves
  That bound and made me slave to shame !
  Poor, silly girl ! . . . The burning stars
  Of passion shot their streams of fire
  And caught those tresses that you combed
  In vanity and light desire !
  False guest ! you came up from the waves
  And swooped upon me like a cloud
  Heavy with night and falling fire
  And black woes raining in a crowd,—
  To leave, when it had served your mood,
  My frail, dishonoured womanhood !
  Help, help, my friends ! the flames roar past control !
  Have mercy, love, you burn my very soul !
  Alas, I've made a jest of men
  And I am served right fittingly
  If, ravaging my virgin pride,
  A man should make a jest of me.

Engañóme el caballero
Debajo de fe y palabra
De marido, y profanó
Mi honestidad y mi cama.
Gozóme al fin, y yo propia
Le di a su rigor las alas
En dos yeguas que crié,
Con que me burló y se escapa.
Seguilde todos, seguilde.
Mas no importa que se vaya,
Que en la presencia del Rey
Tengo de pedir venganza.
¡Fuego, fuego, zagales! ¡agua, agua!
¡Amor, clemencia, que se abrasa el alma!

(Vase TISBEA.)

PEDRO CALDERÓN DE LA BARCA
[1600–1681]

The writing career of Pedro Calderón de la Barca spanned a period of sixty years. Before he was twenty-five he had gained some fame as an author of plays and poetry; when he died at eighty-one he was well established as the greatest Spanish dramatist of the end of the Golden Age, as well as one of its finest poets.

Calderón left some two hundred dramatic works on all themes. In particular he was the master of the auto, *or short religious play. While his full-length plays are often less spontaneous and lively than Lope de Vega's, they generally have a more universal appeal.*

LA VIDA ES SUEÑO

JORNADA PRIMERA

A un lado monte fragoso, y al otro una torre cuya planta baja sirve de prisión a Segismundo. La puerta que da frente al espectador está entreabierta. La acción principia al anochecer.

ESCENA II

SEGISMUNDO, *en la torre;* ROSAURA, CLARÍN.

SEGIS. (*dentro*). ¡Ay, mísero de mí ! ¡Ay, infelice !
ROSAURA.　　　 ¡ Qué triste voz escucho !
　　　 Con nuevas penas y tormentos lucho.

The gentleman, beneath his word of honour
And his sworn faith, has reaped my flower of honour.
Promising me that he would marry me
He has defiled my honesty and bed,
And I'm deceived, deceived! . . . and worse, alas,
I alone gave his cruelty wings to fly
In my two mares that my own hands have reared—
For he pretended we should fly on them,
But with them he has mocked me and escaped.
Pursue him, every one!
But it does not matter
Which way he goes, for I'll go to the King
And on my naked knees with cries and tears
Implore his sacred Majesty for vengeance!
Help, help, my friends, the flames roar past control!
Have mercy, love! you burn my very soul!

(Tisbea *goes out.*)

HARRY KEMP

Of his works for the theatre, El alcalde de Zalamea, *dealing with the* pundonor *(point of honour) is considered one of the most perfect dramas in the Spanish language; his philosophical drama* La vida es sueño *is probably the most universally known of Spanish plays.* El mágico prodigioso, *the Calderón treatment of the Faust theme, also achieved international acclaim. Excerpts from the latter were translated into English by Percy Bysshe Shelley. (Indeed, the romantic authors of the early nineteenth century especially exalted Calderón.) During the Victorian Age, Edward FitzGerald, of* Rubáiyát *fame, wrote free translations of eight of Calderón's plays.*

LIFE IS A DREAM

ACT THE FIRST

At one side a craggy mountain, at the other a tower, the lower part of which serves as the prison of Sigismund. The door facing the spectators is half open. The action commences at nightfall.

SCENE II

Sigismund, *in the tower.* Rosaura, Clarin.

SIGISMUND (*within*). Alas! Ah, wretched me! Ah, wretched me!
ROSAURA. Oh what a mournful wail!
Again my pains, again my fears prevail.

CLARÍN.   Yo con nuevos temores . . .

ROSAURA.   Clarín . . .

CLARÍN.   Señora . . .

ROSAURA.   Huyamos los rigores
Desta encantada torre.

CLARÍN.   Yo aun no tengo
ánimo para huir, cuando a eso vengo.

ROSAURA.   ¿ No es breve luz aquella
Caduca exhalación pálida estrella,
   Que, en trémulos desmayos,
Pulsando ardores y latiendo rayos,
   Hace más tenebrosa
La obscura habitación con luz dudosa ?
   Sí, pues, a sus reflejos
Puedo determinar, aunque de lejos,
   Una prisión obscura,
Que es de un vivo cadáver sepultura;
   Y porque más me asombre,
En el traje de fiera yace un hombre
   De cadenas cargado,
Y sólo de una luz acompañado.
   Pues que huir no podemos,
Desde aquí sus desdichas escuchemos:
   Sepamos lo que dice.

Abrense las hojas de la puerta, y descúbrese a SEGISMUNDO *con una cadena
y vestido de pieles. Hay luz en la torre.*

SEGISMUNDO. ¡ Ay, mísero de mí ! ¡ Ay, infelice !
   Apurar, cielos, pretendo,
Ya que me tratáis así
¿ qué delito cometí
Contra vosotros, naciendo ?
Aunque si nací, ya entiendo
Qué delito he cometido:
Bastante causa ha tenido
Vuestra justicia y rigor,
Pues el delito mayor
Del hombre, es haber nacido.
   Sólo quisiera saber
Para apurar mis desvelos,
(Dejando a una parte, cielos,
El delito de nacer),

CLARIN. Again with fear I die.

ROSAURA. Clarin !

CLARIN.   My lady !

ROSAURA.   Let us turn and fly
The risks of this enchanted tower.

CLARIN.   For one,
I scarce have strength to stand, much less to run.

ROSAURA. Is not that glimmer there afar—
That dying exhalation—that pale star—
A tiny taper, which, with trembling blaze
Flickering 'twixt struggling flames and dying rays,
With ineffectual spark
Makes the dark dwelling place appear more dark?
Yes, for its distant light,
Reflected dimly, brings before my sight
A dungeon's awful gloom,
Say rather of a living corse, a living tomb;
And to increase my terror and surprise,
Drest in the skins of beasts a man there lies :
A piteous sight,
Chained, and his sole companion this poor light.
Since then we cannot fly,
Let us attentive to his words draw nigh,
Whatever they may be.

(*The doors of the tower open wide, and* Sigismund *is discovered in chains and clad in the skins of beasts. The light in the tower increases.*)

SIGISMUND. Alas ! Ah, wretched me ! Ah, wretched me !
Heaven, here lying all forlorn,
I desire from thee to know,
Since thou thus dost treat me so,
Why have I provoked thy scorn
By the crime of being born?—
Though for being born I feel
Heaven with me must harshly deal,
Since man's greatest crime on earth
Is the fatal fact of birth—
Sin supreme without appeal.
This alone I ponder o'er,
My strange mystery to pierce through;
Leaving wholly out of view
Germs my hapless birthday bore,

¿ qué más os pude ofender
Para castigarme más ?
¿ No nacieron los demás ?
Pues si los demás nacieron:
¿ Qué privilegios tuvieron
Que yo no gocé jamás ?
  Nace el ave y con las galas
Que le dan belleza suma,
Apenas es flor de pluma
O ramillete con alas,
Cuando las etéreas salas
Corta con velocidad,
Negándose a la piedad
Del nido que deja en calma,
¡ Y teniendo yo más alma,
Tengo menos libertad!
  Nace el bruto, y con la piel
Que dibujan manchas bellas
Apenas signo es de estrellas,
(Gracias al docto pincel),
Cuando atrevida y cruel
La humana necesidad
Le enseña a tener crueldad,
Monstruo de su laberinto:
¡ Y yo, con mejor instinto,
Tengo menos libertad !
  Nace el pez, que no respira,
Aborto de ovas y lamas,
Y apenas, bajel de escamas,
Sobre las ondas se mira,
Cuando a todas partes gira,
Midiendo la inmensidad
De tanta capacidad
Como le da el centro frío:
¡ Y yo, con más albedrío,
Tengo menos libertad !
  Nace el arroyo, culebra
Que entre flores se desata,
Y apenas, sierpe de plata,
Entre las flores se quiebra,
Cuando músico celebra
De las flores la piedad,
Que le da la majestad

How have I offended more,
That the more you punish me?
Must not other creatures be
Born? If born, what privilege
Can they over me allege
Of which I should not be free?
Birds are born, the bird that sings,
Richly robed by Nature's dower,
Scarcely floats—a feathered flower
Or a bunch of blooms with wings—
When to heaven's high halls it springs,
Cuts the blue air fast and free,
And no longer bound will be
By the nest's secure control :—
And with so much more of soul,
Must I have less liberty?
Beasts are born, the beast whose skin
Dappled o'er with beauteous spots,
As when the great pencil dots
Heaven with stars, doth scarce begin
From its impulses within—
Nature's stern necessity,
To be schooled in cruelty,—
Monster, waging ruthless war :—
And with instincts better far
Must I have less liberty?
Fish are born, the spawn that breeds
Where the oozy sea-weeds float,
Scarce perceives itself a boat,
Scaled and plated for its needs,
When from wave to wave it speeds,
Measuring all the mighty sea,
Testing its profundity
To its depths so dark and chill :—
And with so much freer will,
Must I have less liberty?
Streams are born, a coiled-up snake
When its path the streamlet finds,
Scarce a silver serpent winds
'Mong the flowers it must forsake,
But a song of praise doth wake,
Mournful though its music be,
To the plain that courteously

Del campo abierto a su huída:
¡ Y teniendo yo más vida
Tengo menos libertad !
En llegando a esta pasión
Un volcán, un Etna hecho,
Quisiera arrancar del pecho
Pedazos del corazón.
¿ Qué ley, justicia o razón,
Negar a los hombres sabe
Privilegio tan süave,
Exención tan principal,
Que Dios ha dado a un cristal,
A un pez, a un bruto y a un ave ?

ROSAURA.   Temor y piedad en mí
Sus razones han causado.

SEGISMUNDO.   ¿ Quién mis voces ha escuchado ?
¿ Es Clotaldo ?

CLARÍN (*aparte a su ama*).   Di que sí.

ROSAURA.   No es sino un triste — ¡ ay de mí ! —
Que en estas bóvedas frías
Oyó tus melancolías.

SEGISMUNDO.   Pues muerte aquí te daré,
Por que no sepas que sé   (*Ásela.*)
Que sabes flaquezas mías.
Sólo porque me has oído,
Entre mis membrudos brazos
Te tengo de hacer pedazos.

CLARÍN.   Yo soy sordo, y no he podido
Escucharte.

ROSAURA.   Si has nacido
Humano, baste el postrarme
A tus pies, para librarme.

SEGISMUNDO.   Tu voz pudo enternecerme,
Tu presencia suspenderme
Y tu respeto turbarme.
¿ Quién eres ? que aunque yo aquí
Tan poco del mundo sé,
Que cuna y sepulcro fué
Esta torre para mí;
Y aunque desde que nací
— si esto es nacer, — sólo advierto
Este rústico desierto

Opes a path through which it flies :—
And with life that never dies,
Must I have less liberty?
And when I think of this I start,
Aetna-like in wild unrest
I would pluck from out my breast
Bit by bit my burning heart :—
For what law can so depart
From all right, as to deny
One lone man that liberty—
That sweet gift which God bestows
On the crystal stream that flows,
Bird and fish that float or fly?
ROSAURA. Fear and deepest sympathy
  Do I feel at every word.
SIGISMUND. Who my sad lament has heard?
  What! Clotaldo!
CLARIN (*aside to his mistress*). Say 'tis he.
ROSAURA. No, 'tis but a wretch (ah, me!)
  Who in these dark caves and cold
  Hears the tale your lips unfold.
SIGISMUND. Then you'll die for listening so,
  That you may not know I know
  That you know the tale I told.
  Yes, you'll die for loitering near :
  In these strong arms gaunt and grim
  I will tear you limb from limb.
CLARIN. I am deaf and couldn't hear :—
  No!
ROSAURA. If human heart you bear,
  'Tis enough that I prostrate me.
  At thy feet, to liberate me!
SIGISMUND. Strange thy voice can so unbend me,
  Strange thy sight can so suspend me,
  And respect so penetrate me!
  Who art thou? for though I see
  Little from this lonely room,
  This, my candle and my tomb,
  Being all the world to me,
  And if birthday it could be,
  Since my birthday I have known
  But this desert wild and lone,

Donde miserable vivo,
Siendo un esqueleto vivo,
Siendo un animado muerto;
   Y aunque nunca vi ni hablé,
Sino a un hombre solamente
Que aquí mis desdichas siente,
Por quien las noticias sé
De cielo y tierra; y aunque
Aquí, por que más te asombres
Y monstruo humano me nombres,
Entre asombros y quimeras,
Soy un hombre de las fieras,
Y una fiera de los hombres.
   Y aunque en desdichas tan graves
La política he estudiado,
De los brutos enseñado,
Advertido de las aves,
Y de los astros süaves
Los círculos he medido:
Tú solo, tú has suspendido
La pasión a mis enojos,
La suspensión a mis ojos,
La admiración a mi oído.
   Con cada vez que te veo
Nueva admiración me das,
Y cuando te miro más,
Aun más mirarte deseo.
Ojos hidrópicos creo
Que mis ojos deben ser;
Pues cuando es muerte el beber
Beben más, y de esta suerte,
Viendo que el ver les da muerte
Se están muriendo por ver.
   Pero, véate yo, y muera;
Que no sé, rendido ya,
Si el verte muerte me da,
El no verte qué me diera.
Fuera más que muerte fiera,
Ira, rabia y dolor fuerte;
Fuera vida; desta suerte
Su rigor he ponderado,
Pues dar vida a un desdichado
Es dar a un dichoso muerte.

Where throughout my life's sad course
I have lived, a breathing corse,
I have moved, a skeleton;
And though I address or see
Never but one man alone,
Who my sorrows all hath known,
And through whom have come to me
Notions of earth, sky, and sea;
And though harrowing thee again,
Since thou'lt call me in this den,
Monster fit for bestial feasts,
I'm a man among wild beasts,
And a wild beast amongst men.
But though round me has been wrought
All this woe, from beasts I've learned
Polity, the same discerned
Heeding what the birds had taught,
And have measured in my thought
The fair orbits of the spheres;
You alone, 'midst doubts and fears,
Wake my wonder and surprise—
Give amazement to my eyes,
Admiration to my ears.
Every time your face I see
You produce a new amaze :
After the most steadfast gaze,
I again would gazer be.
I believe some hydropsy
Must affect my sight, I think
Death must hover on the brink
Of those wells of light, your eyes,
For I look with fresh surprise,
And though death result, I drink.
Let me see and die : forgive me;
For I do not know, in faith,
If to see you gives me death,
What to see you not would give me;
Something worse than death would grieve me,
Anger, rage, corroding care,
Death, but double death it were,
Death with tenfold terrors rife,
Since what gives the wretched life,
Gives the happy death, despair !

Rosaura.   Con asombro de mirarte,
Con admiración de oírte,
Ni sé qué pueda decirte,
Ni qué pueda preguntarte:
Sólo diré que a esta parte
Hoy el cielo me ha guiado
Para haberme consolado,
Si consuelo puede ser
Del que es desdichado, ver
Otro que es más desdichado.
   Cuentan de un sabio, que un día
Tan pobre y mísero estaba,
Que sólo se sustentaba
De unas yerbas que cogía.
¿Habrá otro — entre sí decía —
Más pobre y triste que yo?
Y cuando el rostro volvió,
Halló la respuesta, viendo
Que iba otro sabio cogiendo
Las hojas que él arrojó.
   Quejoso de la fortuna
Yo en este mundo vivía,
Y cuando entre mí decía:
¿Habrá otra persona alguna
De suerte más importuna?;
Piadoso me has respondido;
Pues volviendo en mi sentido
Hallo que las penas mías
Para hacerlas tú alegrías
Las hubieras recogido.
   Y por si acaso, mis penas
Pueden en algo aliviarte,
Óyelas atento, y toma
Las que dellas me sobraren.
Yo soy . . .

ESCENA III

Clotaldo, *Soldados*, Segismundo, Rosaura, Clarín.

Clotaldo (*dentro*).   Guardas desta torre
Que, dormidas o cobardes,
Disteis paso a dos personas
Que han quebrantado la cárcel . . .

Rosaura.   Nueva confusión padezco . . .

ROSAURA. Thee to see wakes such dismay,
Thee to hear I so admire,
That I'm powerless to inquire
That I know not what to say :
Only this, that I today,
Guided by a wiser will,
Have here come to cure my ill,
Here consoled my grief to see,
If a wretch consoled can be
Seeing one more wretched still.
Of a sage, who roamed dejected,
Poor and wretched, it is said,
That one day, his wants being fed
By the herbs which he collected,
'Is there one' (he thus reflected)
'Poorer than I am today?'
Turning round him to survey,
He his answer got, detecting
A still poorer sage collecting
Even the leaves he threw away.
Thus complaining to excess,
Mourning fate, my life I led,
And when thoughtlessly I said
To myself, 'Does earth possess
One more steeped in wretchedness?'
I in thee the answer find.
Since revolving in my mind,
I perceive that all my pains
To become thy joyful gains
Thou hast gathered and entwined.
And if haply some slight solace
By these pains may be imparted,
Hear attentively the story
Of my life's supreme disasters.
I am . . .

SCENE III

Clotaldo, *Soldiers*, Sigismund, Rosaura, Clarin.

CLOTALDO (*within*). Warders of this tower,
Who, or sleeping or faint-hearted,
Give an entrance to two persons
Who herein have burst a passage. . . .
ROSAURA. New confusion now I suffer.

SEGISMUNDO.   Este es Clotaldo, mi alcaide.
¿ Aún no acaban mis desdichas ?
CLOT. (*dentro*). Acudid, y vigilantes,
Sin que puedan defenderse,
O prendedles, o matadles.
VOCES (*den.*)   ¡Traición!
CLARÍN.   Guardas desta torre,
Que entrar aquí nos dejasteis,
Pues que nos dais a escoger.
El prendernos es más fácil.

Salen CLOTALDO, *los Soldados; él con una pistola, y todos con los
rostros cubiertos.*

CLOTALDO (*aparte, a los Soldados al salir*).
Todos os cubrid los rostros;
Que es diligencia importante,
Mientras estemos aquí,
Que no nos conozca nadie.
CLARÍN.   ¿ Enmascaraditos hay ?
CLOTALDO.   Oh, vosotros, que, ignorantes,
De aqueste vedado sitio
Coto y término pasasteis,
Contra el decreto del rey
Que manda que no ose nadie
Examinar el prodigio
Que entre estos peñascos yace:
Rendid las armas y vidas,
O aquesta pistola, áspid
De metal, escupirá
El veneno penetrante
De dos balas, cuyo fuego
Será escándalo del aire.
SEGISMUNDO.   Primero, tirano dueño,
Que los ofendas ni agravies,
Será mi vida despojo
Destos lazos miserables,
Pues en ellos, ¡ vive Dios !
Tengo que despedazarme
Con las manos, con los dientes,
Entre aquestas peñas, antes
Que su desdicha consienta
Y que llore sus ultrajes.

SIGISMUND. 'Tis Clotaldo, who here guards me;
  Are not yet my miseries ended?
CLOTALDO (*within*). Hasten hither, quick! be active!
  And before they can defend them,
  Kill them on the spot or capture!
    (*Voices within*) Treason!
CLARIN.   Watchguards of this tower,
  Who politely let us pass here,
  Since you have the choice of killing
  Or of capturing, choose the latter.

(*Enter* Clotaldo *and Soldiers; he with a pistol, and all with
      faces covered.*)

CLOTALDO (*aside to the Soldiers*). Keep your faces all well covered,
  For it is a vital matter
  That we should be known by no one,
  While I question these two stragglers.
CLARIN. Are there masqueraders here?
CLOTALDO. Ye who in your ignorant rashness
  Have passed through the bounds and limits
  Of this interdicted valley,
  'Gainst the edict of the King,
  Who has publicly commanded
  None should dare descry the wonder
  That among these rocks is guarded,
  Yield at once your arms and lives,
  Or this pistol, this cold aspic
  Formed of steel, the penetrating
  Poison of two balls will scatter,
  The report and fire of which
  Will the air astound and startle.
SIGISMUND. Ere you wound them, ere you hurt them,
  Will my life, O tyrant master,
  Be the miserable victim
  Of these wretched chains that clasp me;
  Since in them, I vow to God,
  I will tear myself to fragments
  With my hands, and with my teeth,
  In these rocks here, in these caverns,
  Ere I yield to their misfortunes,
  Or lament their sad disaster.

CLOTALDO.   Si sabes que tus desdichas,
Segismundo, son tan grandes,
Que antes de nacer moriste
Por ley del cielo; si sabes
Que aquestas prisiones son
De tus furias arrogantes
Un freno que las detenga,
Y una rienda que las pare;
¿ Por qué blasonas La puerta (*A los Soldados.*)
Cerrad de esa estrecha cárcel;
Escondedle en ella.

SEGISMUNDO.   ¡ Ah, cielos !
¡ Qué bien hacéis en quitarme
La libertad !, porque fuera
Contra vosotros gigante
Que, para quebrar al sol,
Esos vidrios y cristales,
Sobre cimientos de piedra
Pusiera montes de jaspe.

CLOTALDO.   Quizá, porque no los pongas
Hoy padeces tantos males.

Llévanse algunos Soldados a SEGISMUNDO, *y enciérranle en su prisión.*

JORNADA SEGUNDA

ESCENA I

BASILIO, CLOTALDO.

CLOTALDO.   Todo, como lo mandaste,
Queda efectuado.

BASILIO.   Cuenta,
Clotaldo, cómo pasó.

CLOTALDO.   Fué, señor, desta manera:
Con la apacible bebida,
Que de confecciones llena
Hacer mandaste, mezclando
La virtud de algunas yerbas
Cuyo tirano poder
Y cuya secreta fuerza
Así el humano discurso
Priva, roba y enajena,
Que deja vivo cadáver

CLOTALDO. If you know that your misfortunes,
  Sigismund, are unexampled,
  Since before being born you died
  By Heaven's mystical enactment;
  If you know these fetters are
  Of your furies oft so rampant
  But the bridle that detains them,
  But the circle that contracts them.
  Why these idle boasts? The door (*To the Soldiers.*)
  Of this narrow prison fasten;
  Leave him there secured.
SIGISMUND.   Ah, heavens,
  It is wise of you to snatch me
  Thus from freedom! since my rage
  'Gainst you had become Titanic,
  Since to break the glass and crystal
  Gold-gates of the sun, my anger
  On the firm-fixed rocks' foundations
  Would have mountains piled of marble.
CLOTALDO. 'Tis that you should not so pile them
  That perhaps these ills have happened.

(*Some of the Soldiers lead* Sigismund *into his prison, the doors
  of which are closed upon him.*)

ACT THE SECOND

SCENE I

A Hall in the Royal Palace.   Basilius *and* Clotaldo.

CLOTALDO. Everything has been effected
  As you ordered.
BASILIUS. How all happened
  Let me know, my good Clotaldo.
CLOTALDO. It was done, sire, in this manner.
  With the tranquillising draught,
  Which was made, as you commanded,
  Of confections duly mixed
  With some herbs, whose juice extracted
  Has a strange tyrannic power,
  Has some secret force imparted,
  Which all human sense and speech
  Robs, deprives, and counteracteth,
  And as 'twere a living corpse

A un hombre a cuya violencia
Adormecido, le quita
Los sentidos y potencias.
No tenemos que argüir,
Que aquesto posible sea,
Pues tantas veces, señor,
Nos ha dicho la experiencia,
Y es cierto, que de secretos
Naturales está llena
La medicina, y no hay
Animal, planta ni piedra
Que no tenga calidad
Determinada; y si llega
A examinar mil venenos
La humana malicia nuestra,
Que den la muerte, ¿ qué mucho
Que, templada su violencia,
Pues hay venenos que matan,
Haya venenos que aduerman ?
Dejando aparte el dudar,
Si es posible que suceda,
Pues que ya queda probado
Con razones y evidencias;
Con la bebida, en efecto,
Que el opio, la adormidera
Y el beleño compusieron,
Bajé·a la cárcel estrecha
De Segismundo; con él
Hablé un rato de las letras
Humanas que le ha enseñado
La muda naturaleza
De los montes y los cielos,
En cuya divina escuela
La retórica aprendió
De las aves y las fieras.
Para levantarle más
El espíritu a la empresa
Que solicitas, tomé
Por asunto la presteza
De un águila caudalosa,
Que despreciando la esfera
Del viento, pasaba a ser,
En las regiones supremas

Leaves the man whose lips have quaffed it
So asleep that all his senses,
All his powers are overmastered. . . .
—No need have we to discuss
That this fact can really happen,
Since, my lord, experience gives us
Many a clear and proved example;
Certain 'tis that Nature's secrets
May by medicine be extracted,
And that not an animal,
Not a stone, or herb that's planted,
But some special quality
Doth possess : for if the malice
Of man's heart, a thousand poisons
That give death, hath power to examine,
Is it then so great a wonder
That, their venom being abstracted,
If, as death by some is given,
Sleep by others is imparted?
Putting, then, aside the doubt
That 'tis possible this should happen,
A thing proved beyond all question
Both by reason and example. . . .
—With the sleeping draught, in fine,
Made of opium superadded
To the poppy and the henbane,
I to Sigismund's apartment—
Cell, in fact—went down, and with him
Spoke awhile upon the grammar
Of the sciences, those first studies
Which mute Nature's gentle masters,
Silent skies and hills, had taught him;
In which school divine and ample,
The bird's song, the wild beast's roar,
Were a lesson and a language.
Then to raise his spirit more
To the high design you planned here,
I discoursed on, as my theme,
The swift flight, the stare undazzled
Of a pride-plumed eagle bold,
Which with back-averted talons,
Scorning the tame fields of air,
Seeks the sphere of fire, and passes

Del fuego, rayo de pluma
O desasido cometa.
Encarecí el vuelo altivo,
Diciendo: 'Al fin eres reina
De las aves, y así, a todas
Es justo que las prefieras.'
Él no hubo menester más;
Que en tocando esta materia
De la majestad, discurre
Con ambición y soberbia;
Porque, en efecto, la sangre
Le incita, mueve y alienta
A cosas grandes, y dijo:
'¡ Que en la república inquieta
De las aves también haya
Quien les jure la obediencia !
En llegando a este discurso,
Mis desdichas me consuelan;
Pues por lo menos si estoy
Sujeto, lo estoy por fuerza;
Porque voluntariamente
A otro hombre no me rindiera.'
Viéndole ya enfurecido
Con esto, que ha sido el tema
De su dolor, le brindé
Con la pócima, y apenas
Pasó desde el vaso al pecho
El licor, cuando las fuerzas
Rindió al suelo, discurriendo
Por los miembros y las venas
Un sudor frío, de modo,
Que a no saber yo que era
Muerte fingida, dudara
De su vida. En esto llegan
Las gentes de quien tú fías
El valor de esta experiencia,
Y poniéndole en un coche
Hasta su cuarto le llevan,
Donde prevenida estaba
La majestad y grandeza
Que es digna de su persona.
Allí en tu cama le acuestan,
Donde al tiempo que el letargo

Through its flame a flash of feathers,
Or a comet's hair untangled.
I extolled its soaring flight,
Saying, 'Thou at last art master
Of thy house, thou'rt king of birds,
It is right thou should'st surpass them.'
He who needed nothing more
Than to touch upon the matter
Of high royalty, with a bearing
As became him, boldly answered;
For in truth his princely blood
Moves, excites, inflames his ardour
To attempt great things : he said,
'In the restless realm of atoms
Given to birds, that even one
Should swear fealty as a vassal!
I, reflecting upon this,
Am consoled by my disasters,
For, at least, if I obey,
I obey through force; untrammelled,
Free to act, I ne'er will own
Any man on earth my master.'—
This, his usual theme of grief,
Having roused him nigh to madness,
I occasion took to proffer
The drugged draught : he drank, but hardly
Had the liquor from the vessel
Passed into his breast, when fastest
Sleep his senses seized, a sweat,
Cold as ice, the life-blood hardened,
In his veins, his limbs grew stiff,
So that, knew I not 'twas acted,
Death was there, feigned death, his life
I could doubt not had departed.
Then those, to whose care you trust
This experiment, in a carriage
Brought him here, where all things fitting
The high majesty and the grandeur
Of his person are provided.
In the bed of your state chamber
They have placed him, where the stupor

Haya perdido la fuerza,
Como a ti mismo, señor,
Le sirvan, que así lo ordenas.
Y si haberte obedecido
Te obliga a que yo merezca
Galardón, sólo te pido
(Perdona mi inadvertencia)
Que me digas ¿ qué es tu intento
Trayendo desta manera
A Segismundo a palacio ?

BASILIO.   Clotaldo, muy justa es esa
Duda que tienes, y quiero
Sólo a ti satisfacerla.
A Segismundo, mi hijo,
El influjo de su estrella
(Bien lo sabes) amenaza
Mil desdichas y tragedias;
Quiero examinar si el cielo
Que no es posible que minenta,
Y más habiéndome dado
De su rigor tantas muestras,
En su crüel condición,
O se mitiga, o se templa
Por lo menos, y vencido,
Con valor y con prudencia
Se desdice; porque el hombre
Predomina en las estrellas.
Esto quiero examinar,
Trayéndole donde sepa
Que es mi hijo, y donde haga
De su talento la prueba.
Si magnánimo la vence,
Reinará; pero si muestra
El ser cruel y tirano,
Le volveré a su cadena.
Ahora preguntarás,
Que para aquesta experiencia,
¿ Qué importó haberle traído
Dormido de esta manera ?
Y quiero satisfacerte
Dándote a todo respuesta.
Si él supiera que es mi hijo
Hoy, y mañana se viera

Having spent its force and vanished,
They, as 'twere yourself, my lord,
Him will serve as you commanded :
And if my obedient service
Seems to merit some slight largess,
I would ask but this alone
(My presumption you will pardon),
That you tell me, with what object
Have you, in this secret manner,
To your palace brought him here?
BASILIUS. Good Clotaldo, what you ask me
Is so just, to you alone
I would give full satisfaction.
Sigismund, my son, the hard
Influence of his hostile planet
(As you know) doth threat a thousand
Dreadful tragedies and disasters;
I desire to test if Heaven
(An impossible thing to happen)
Could have lied—if having given us
Proofs unnumbered, countless samples
Of his evil disposition,
He might prove more mild, more guarded
At the least, and self-subdued
By his prudence and true valour
Change his character; for 'tis man
That alone controls the planets.
This it is I wish to test,
Having brought him to this palace,
Where he'll learn he is my son,
And display his natural talents.
If he nobly hath subdued him,
He will reign; but if his manners
Show him tyrannous and cruel,
Then his chains once more shall clasp him.
But for this experiment,
Now you probably will ask me
Of what moment was't to bring him
Thus asleep and in this manner?
And I wish to satisfy you,
Giving all your doubts an answer.
If today he learns that he
Is my son, and some hours after

Segunda vez reducido
A su prisión y miseria,
Cierto es de su condición
Que desesperara en ella;
Porque sabiendo quién es,
¿ Qué consuelo habrá que tenga?
Y así he querido dejar
Abierta al daño la puerta
Del decir que fué soñado
Cuanto vió esto llegan
A examinarse dos cosas:
Su condición, la primera;
Pues él despierto procede
En cuanto imagina y piensa:
Y el consuelo la segunda;
Pues aunque ahora se vea
Obedecido, y después
A sus prisiones se vuelva,
Podrá entender que soñó,
Y hará bien cuando lo entienda,
Porque en el mundo, Clotaldo,
Todos los que viven sueñan.

CLOTALDO. Razones no me faltaran
Para probar que no aciertas;
Mas ya no tiene remedio;
Y según dicen las señas,
Parece que ha despertado
Y hacia nosotros se acerca.

BASILIO. Yo me quiero retirar:
Tú, como ayo suyo, llega,
Y de tantas confusiones
Como su discurso cercan,
Le saca con la verdad.

CLOTALDO. ¿ En fin, que me das licencia
Para que lo diga ?

BASILIO.   Sí.
Que podrá ser, con saberla,
Que conocido el peligro
Más fácilmente se venza.

Finds himself once more restored
To his misery and his shackles,
Certain 'tis that from his temper
Blank despair may end in madness—
But once knowing who he is,
Can he be consoled thereafter?
Yes, and thus I wish to leave
One door open, one free passage,
By declaring all he saw
Was a dream. With this advantage
We attain two ends. The first
Is to put beyond all cavil
His condition, for on waking
He will show his thoughts, his fancies :
To console him is the second;
Since, although obeyed and flattered,
He beholds himself awhile,
And then back in prison shackled
Finds him, he will think he dreamed.
And he rightly so may fancy,
For, Clotaldo, in this world
All who live but dream they act here.
CLOTALDO. Reasons fail me not to show
That the experiment may not answer;
But there is no remedy now,
For a sign from the apartment
Tells me that he hath awoken
And even hitherward advances.
BASILIUS. It is best that I retire;
But do you, so long his master,
Near him stand; the wild confusions
That his waking sense may darken
Dissipate by simple truth.
CLOTALDO. Then your licence you have granted
That I may declare it?
BASILIUS.   Yes;
For it possibly may happen
That admonished of his danger
He may conquer his worst passions.

ESCENA XVIII

BASILIO, *rebozado*. CLOTALDO, SEGISMUNDO, *adormecido*.

BASILIO.	Clotaldo.
CLOTALDO.	¡ Señor ! ¿ así
	Viene vuestra majestad ?
BASILIO.	La necia curiosidad
	De ver lo que pasa aquí
	A Segismundo (¡ ay de mí !)
	Deste modo me ha traído.
CLOTALDO.	Mírale allí reducido
	A su miserable estado.
BASILIO.	¡ Ay, príncipe desdichado,
	Y en triste punto nacido !
	Llega a despertarle, ya
	Que fuerza y vigor perdió
	Con el opio que bebió.
CLOTALDO.	Inquieto, señor, está,
	Y hablando.
BASILIO.	¿ Qué soñará
	Ahora ? Escuchemos, pues.

SEGISMUNDO (*entre sueños*).
    Piadoso príncipe es
    El que castiga tiranos:
    Clotaldo muera a mis manos.
    Mi padre bese mis pies.

CLOTALDO.	Con la muerte me amenaza.
BASILIO.	A mí con rigor me afrenta.
CLOTALDO.	Quitarme la vida intenta.
BASILIO.	Rendirme a sus plantas trata.

SEGISMUNDO (*entre sueños*).
    Salga a la anchurosa plaza
    Del gran teatro del mundo
    Este valor sin segundo:
    Porque mi venganza cuadre,
    Al príncipe Segismundo
    vean triunfar de su padre (*Despierta.*)
    Mas ¡ ay de mí ! ¿ dónde estoy ?

BASILIO.	Pues a mí no me ha de ver. (*A* CLOTALDO.)
	Ya sabes lo que has de hacer.
	Desde allí a escucharte voy.

SCENE XVIII

Prison of the Prince in the Tower.
Sigismund, *as at the commencement, clothed in skins, chained, and lying on the ground;* Basilius, *disguised, and* Clotaldo.

BASILIUS. Hark, Clotaldo!
CLOTALDO.   My lord here?
  Thus disguised, your majesty?
BASILIUS. Foolish curiosity
  Leads me in this lowly gear
  To find out, ah me! with fear,
  How the sudden change he bore.
CLOTALDO. There behold him as before
  In his miserable state.
BASILIUS.Wretched Prince! unhappy fate!
  Birth by baneful stars watched o'er!—
  Go and wake him cautiously,
  Now that strength and force lie chained
  By the opiate he hath drained.
CLOTALDO. Muttering something restlessly,
  See he lies.
BASILIUS. Let's listen; he
  May some few clear words repeat.
SIGISMUND. (*Speaking in his sleep*)
  Perfect Prince is he whose heat
  Smites the tyrant where he stands,
  Yes, Clotaldo dies by my hands,
  Yes, my sire shall kiss my feet.
CLOTALDO. Death he threatens in his rage.
BASILIUS. Outrage vile he doth intend.
CLOTALDO. He my life has sworn to end.
BASILIUS. He has vowed to insult my age.
SIGISMUND. (*Still sleeping*) On the mighty world's great stage,
  'Mid the admiring nations' cheer,
  Valour mine, that has no peer,
  Enter thou : the slave so shunned
  Now shall reign Prince Sigismund,
  And his sire his wrath shall fear.—(*He awakes.*)
  But, ah me! Where am I? Oh—
BASILIUS. Me I must not let him see. (*To* Clotaldo.)
  Listening I close by will be,
  What you have to do you know.

SEGISMUNDO.   ¿ Soy yo por ventura ? ¿ soy
El que preso y aherrojado
Llego a verme en tal estado ?
¿ No sois mi sepulcro vos
Torre ? Sí. ¡ Válgame Dios,
qué de cosas he soñado !

CLOT. (ap.).   A mí me toca llegar
A hacer la deshecha ahora.—
¿ Es ya de dispertar hora ?

SEGISMUNDO.   Sí, hora es ya de dispertar.

CLOTALDO.   ¿ Todo el día te has de estar
Durmiendo ? ¿ Desde que yo
Al águila que voló
Con tardo vuelo seguí,
Y te quedaste tú aquí,
Nunca has dispertado ?

SEGISMUNDO.   No,
Ni aun agora he dispertado;
Que según, Clotaldo, entiendo,
Todavía estoy durmiendo:
Y no estoy muy engañado;
Porque si ha sido soñado,
Lo que vi palpable y cierto,
Lo que veo será incierto;
Y no es mucho que rendido,
Pues veo estando dormido,
Que sueño estando dispierto.

CLOTALDO.   Lo que soñaste me di.

SEGISMUNDO.   Supuesto que sueño fué,
No diré lo que soñé.
Lo que vi, Clotaldo, sí.
Yo disperté, yo me vi
(¡ qué crueldad tan lisonjera !)
En un lecho que pudiera,
Con matices y colores,
Ser el catre de las flores
Que tejió la Primavera.
Allí mil nobles rendidos
A mis pies nombre me dieron
De su príncipe y sirvieron
Galas, joyas y vestidos.
La calma de mis sentidos
Tú trocaste en alegría,

SIGISMUND. Can it possibly be so?
Is the truth not what it seemed?
Am I chained and unredeemed?
Art not thou my lifelong tomb,
Dark old tower? Yes! What a doom!
God! what wondrous things I've dreamed!
CLOTALDO. Now in this delusive play
Must my special part be taken :—
Is it not full time to waken?
SIGISMUND. Yes, to waken well it may.
CLOTALDO. Wilt thou sleep the livelong day?—
Since we gazing from below
Saw the eagle sailing slow,
Soaring through the azure sphere,
All the time thou waited here,
Didst thou never waken?
SIGISMUND.   No,
Nor even now am I awake,
Since such thoughts my memory fill,
That it seems I'm dreaming still :
Nor is this a great mistake;
Since if dreams could phantoms make
Things of actual substance seen,
I things seen may phantoms deem.
Thus a double harvest reaping,
I can see when I am sleeping,
And when waking I can dream.
CLOTALDO. What you may have dreamed of, say.
SIGISMUND. If I thought it only seemed,
I would tell not what I dreamed,
But what I beheld, I may.
I awoke, and lo! I lay
(Cruel and delusive thing!)
In a bed whose covering,
Bright with blooms from rosy bowers,
Seemed a tapestry of flowers
Woven by the hand of Spring.
Then a crowd of nobles came,
Who addressed me by the name
Of their prince, presenting me
Gems and robes, on bended knee.
Calm soon left me, and my frame
Thrilled with joy to hear thee tell

	Diciendo la dicha mía,
	Que aunque estoy de esta manera,
	Príncipe de Polonia era.
CLOTALDO.	Buenas albricias tendría.
SEGISMUNDO.	No muy buenas: por traidor,
	Con pecho atrevido y fuerte
	Dos veces te daba muerte.
CLOTALDO.	¿ Para mí tanto rigor ?
SEGISMUNDO.	De todos era señor,

Y de todos me vengaba;
Sólo a una mujer amaba . . .
Que fué verdad, creo yo,
En que todo se acabó,
Y esto sólo no se acaba.   *Vase el rey.*

CLOTALDO (*ap.*) (Enternecido se ha ido
El rey de haberlo escuchado.)
Como habíamos hablado,
De aquella águila, dormido,
Tu sueño imperios han sido,
Mas en sueño fuera bien
Honrar entonces a quien
Te crió en tantos empeños,
Segismundo: que aun en sueños,
no se pierde el hacer bien.   *Vase.*

ESCENA XIX

SEGISMUNDO.   Es verdad; pues reprimamos
Esta fiera condición,
esta furia, esta ambición,
Por si alguna vez soñamos.
Y sí haremos, pues estamos
En mundo tan singular,
Que el vivir sólo es soñar;
Y la experiencia me enseña,
Que el hombre que vive, sueña
Lo que es, hasta dispertar.
    Sueña el rey que es rey, y vive
Con este engaño mandando,
disponiendo y gobernando;
Y este aplauso, que recibe
Prestado, en el viento escribe;
Y en cenizas le convierte
La muerte (¡ desdicha fuerte !):

Of the fate that me befell,
For though now in this dark den,
I was Prince of Poland then.
CLOTALDO. Doubtless you repaid me well?
SIGISMUND. No, not well : for, calling thee
Traitor vile, in furious strife
Twice I strove to take thy life.
CLOTALDO. But why all this rage 'gainst me?
SIGISMUND. I was master, and would be
Well revenged on foe and friend.
Love one woman could defend. . . .
That, at least, for truth I deem,
All else ended like a dream,
That alone can never end. (*The King withdraws.*)
CLOTALDO (*aside*). From his place the King hath gone,
Touched by his pathetic words :—   (*Aloud.*)
Speaking of the king of birds
Soaring to ascend his throne,
Thou didst fancy one thine own;
But in dreams, however bright,
Thou shouldst still have kept in sight
How for years I tended thee,
For 'twere well, whoe'er we be,
Even in dreams to do what's right.   (*Exit.*)

SCENE XIX

SIGISMUND. That is true : then let's restrain
This wild rage, this fierce condition
Of the mind, this proud ambition,
Should we ever dream again :
And we'll do so, since 'tis plain,
In this world's uncertain gleam,
That to live is but to dream :
Man dreams what he is, and wakes
Only when upon him breaks
Death's mysterious morning beam.
The king dreams he is a king,
And in this delusive way
Lives and rules with sovereign sway;
All the cheers that round him ring,
Born of air, on air take wing.
And in ashes (mournful fate !)

¿ Que hay quien intente reinar
Viendo que ha de dispertar
En el sueño de la muerte ?
Sueña el rico en su riqueza,
Que más cuidado le ofrece;
Sueña el pobre que padece
Su miseria y su pobreza;
Sueña el que a medrar empieza,
Sueña el que afana y pretende,
Sueña el que agravia y ofende,
Y en el mundo, en conclusión,
Todos sueñan lo que son,
Aunque ninguno lo entiende.
Yo sueño que estoy aquí,
Destas prisiones cargado;
Y soñé que en otro estado
Más lisonjero me vi.
¿ Qué es la vida ? Un frenesí.
¿ Qué es la vida ? Una ilusión,
Una sombra, una ficción,
Y el mayor bien es pequeño:
Que toda la vida es sueño,
Y los sueños sueños son.

JOSE CADALSO
[1741–1782]

José Cadalso, a colonel in the Spanish Army, died at forty-one fighting the British in the siege of Gibraltar. He had already achieved fame as a writer and as a literary mentor who exercised great formative influence particularly upon the poet Juan Meléndez Valdés.

His prose works include Noches lúgubres, *an elegy in imitation of Edward Young's* Night Thoughts; Los eruditos a la violeta, *a literary*

CARTAS MARRUECAS

CARTA XXVI.—DIVERSIDAD DE LAS PROVINCIAS DE ESPAÑA

Por la última tuya veo cuán extraña te ha parecido la diversidad de las provincias que componen esta monarquía. Después de haberlas visitado, hallo ser muy verdadero el informe que me había dado Nuño de esta diversidad.

Death dissolves his pride and state :
Who would wish a crown to take,
Seeing that he must awake
In the dream beyond death's gate?
And the rich man dreams of gold,
Gilding cares it scarce conceals,
And the poor man dreams he feels
Want and misery and cold.
Dreams he too who rank would hold,
Dreams who bears toil's rough-ribbed hands,
Dreams who wrong for wrong demands,
And in fine, throughout the earth,
All men dream, whate'er their birth,
And yet no one understands.
'Tis a dream that I in sadness
Here am bound, the scorn of fate;
'Twas a dream that once a state
I enjoyed of light and gladness.
What is life? 'Tis but a madness.
What is life? A thing that seems,
A mirage that falsely gleams,
Phantom joy, delusive rest,
Since is life a dream at best,
And even dreams themselves are dreams.

DENIS FLORENCE MACCARTHY

satire on pseudo-knowledge; and Cartas marruecas. *The latter, inspired by Montesquieu's* Lettres Persanes, *is a criticism of Spanish society, as seen—supposedly—in the letters of two Moors, one of whom is travelling through the country. Cadalso also published a volume of verse called* Ocios de mi juventud.

MOROCCAN LETTERS

LETTER 26—DIVERSITY OF THE PROVINCES OF SPAIN

By your last letter, I see how strange has seemed to you the dissimilarity of the provinces which compose this monarchy. After having visited them, I consider the information which Nuño had given me, regarding this diversity, to be very accurate.

En efecto, los cántabros, entendiendo por este nombre todos los que hablan el idioma vizcaíno, son unos pueblos sencillos y de notoria probidad. Fueron los primeros marineros de Europa, y han mantenido siempre la fama de excelentes hombres de mar. Su país, aunque sumamente áspero, tiene una población numerosísima, que no parece disminuirse con las continuas colonias que envía a la América. Aunque un vizcaíno se ausente de su patria, siempre se halla en ella como se encuentre un paisano suyo. Tienen entre sí tal unión, que la mayor recomendación que puede uno tener para con otro, es el mero hecho de ser vizcaíno; sin más diferencia entre varios de ellos para alcanzar el favor de un poderoso, que la mayor o menor inmediación de los lugares respectivos. El Señorío de Vizcaya, Guipúzcoa, Alava y el reino de Navarra tienen tal pacto entre sí, que algunos llaman a estos países *las Provincias Unidas* de España.

Los de Asturias y las Montañas hacen sumo aprecio de su genealogía, y de la memoria de haber sido aquel país el que produjo la Reconquista de España con la expulsión de nuestros abuelos. Su población, demasiada para la miseria y estrechez de la tierra, hace que un número considerable de ellos se emplee continuamente en Madrid en la librea, que es la clase inferior de criados; de modo, que si yo fuese natural de este país y me hallara con coche en la Corte, examinaría con mucha madurez los papeles de mis cocheros y lacayos, por no tener algún día la mortificación de ver a un primo mío echar cebada a mis mulas, o a uno de mis tíos limpiarme los zapatos. Sin embargo de todo esto, varias familias respetables de esta provincia se mantienen con el debido lustre, son acreedoras a la mayor consideración y producen continuamente oficiales del más alto mérito en el ejército y marina.

Los gallegos, en medio de la pobreza de su tierra, son robustos. Se esparcen por toda España a emprender los trabajos físicos más duros, para llevar a sus casas algún dinero a costa de tan penosa industria. Sus soldados, aunque carecen de aquel lucido exterior de otras naciones, son excelentes para la infantería por su subordinación, dureza de cuerpo y hábito de sufrir incomodidades de hambre, sed y cansancio.

Los castellanos son, de todos los pueblos del mundo, los que merecen la primacía en línea de lealtad. Cuando el ejército del primer rey de España de la casa de Francia quedó arruinado en la batalla de Zaragoza, la sola provincia de Soria dió a su soberano un

In point of fact, the Cantabrians, understanding by this name all those who speak the Biscayan language, are a simple people, famed for their truthfulness. They were the first mariners of Europe, and they have always maintained their reputation as excellent seamen. Their land, although extremely rugged, has a most numerous population, which does not seem to diminish even with the colonies which it continually sends to America. Even when a Biscayan is away from his fatherland he always feels at home as soon as he meets a fellow-countryman. They have such unity among themselves that the highest qualification which one can have for another is the very fact of being a Biscayan; with no greater difference among several of them, when they seek to attain the favour of a potentate, than the greater or lesser proximity of their respective villages. The seigniory of Biscay, Guipuzcoa, Alava, and the kingdom of Navarre enjoy such solidarity that some call these territories the *United Provinces* of Spain.

The people of Asturias and Montaña place high esteem on their lineage, and on the memory of it having been their country which engendered the Reconquest of Spain with the expulsion of our forefathers. Their population, too great for the poverty and physical limitations of the land, causes a considerable number of them to employ themselves continually in Madrid in liveried positions, which is the inferior class of servants; so that, if I were a native of this territory and were to find myself in the Court, I should examine with much prudence the papers of my coachmen and lackeys, so as not to experience one day the mortification of seeing a cousin of mine throwing barley to my mules, or one of my uncles cleaning my shoes. Regardless of all this, various respectable families of this province maintain themselves with rightful splendour, are meritorious of the highest regard, and continually produce officers of the greatest merit in the army and navy.

The Galicians, notwithstanding the poverty of their land, are vigorous. They scatter themselves throughout all of Spain to undertake the hardest physical occupations, in order to bring a bit of money into their homes at the cost of such laborious industry. Their soldiers, although they lack that outward glitter of other nations, are excellent for the infantry because of their subordination, firmness of body, and their ability to suffer discomforts of hunger, thirst, and fatigue.

The Castilians are, of all the peoples of the world, those who merit first place in the ranks of loyalty. When the army of the first Spanish king from the royal house of France was destroyed in the battle of Zaragoza, the province of Soria alone gave to its

ejército nuevo y numeroso con que salir a campaña, y fué el que ganó las victorias de que resultó la destrucción del ejército y bando austriaco. El ilustre historiador que refiere las revoluciones del principio de este siglo con todo el rigor y verdad que pide la Historia para distinguirse de la fábula, pondera tanto la fidelidad de estos pueblos, que dice será eterna en la memoria de los reyes. Esta provincia aun conserva cierto orgullo, nacido de su antigua grandeza, que hoy no se conserva sino en las ruinas de sus ciudades y en la honradez de sus habitantes. Extremadura produjo los conquistadores del Nuevo Mundo, y ha continuado siendo madre de insignes guerreros. Sus pueblos son poco afectos a las letras, pero los que entre ellos las han cultivado, no han tenido menos sucesos que sus patriotas en las armas.

Los andaluces, nacidos y criados en un país abundante, delicioso y ardiente, tienen fama de ser algo arrogantes. Pero si este defecto es verdadero, debe atribuirse a su clima, siendo tan notorio el influjo de lo físico sobre lo moral. Las ventajas con que naturaleza dotó aquellas provincias, hacen que miren con desprecio la pobreza de Galicia, la aspereza de Vizcaya y la sencillez de Castilla. Pero, como quiera que todo esto sea, entre ellos ha habido hombres insignes que han dado mucho honor a toda España: y en tiempos antiguos, los Trajanos, Sénecas y otros semejantes, que pueden envanecer el país en que nacieron. La viveza, astucia y atractivo de las andaluzas, las hace incomparables: te aseguro que una de ellas sería bastante para llenar de confusión el imperio de Marruecos, de modo que todos nos matásemos unos a otros.

Los murcianos participan del carácter de los andaluces y valencianos. Estos últimos están tenidos por hombres de sobrada ligereza, atribuyéndose este defecto al clima y suelo: pretendiendo algunos que hasta en los mismos alimentos falta aquel jugo que se halla en los de otros países. Mi imparcialidad no me permite someterme a esta preocupación, por general que sea; antes debo observar que los valencianos de este siglo son los españoles que más progresos hacen en las ciencias positivas y lenguas muertas.

Los catalanes son los pueblos más industriosos de España: manufacturas, pescas, navegación, comercio, asientos, son cosas apenas conocidas en otras provincias de la Península respecto de los catalanes. No sólo son útiles en la paz, sino del mayor servicio

sovereign a new and large army with which to take the field, and it was that army which won the victories that resulted in the destruction of the Austrian army and faction. An illustrious historian who relates the revolutions of the beginning of this century—with all the precision and truth which History demands in order to distinguish itself from fiction—extols the faithfulness of these peoples so greatly, that he says it will live eternal in the memory of kings. This province still preserves a certain pride born of its ancient glory, lost today but for the ruins of its cities and the integrity of its inhabitants.

Extremadura produced the conquerors of the New World, and it has continued to be the mother of outstanding warriors. Its people are little inclined to learning, but those among them who have cultivated letters have achieved no less success than their compatriots in the military.

The Andalusians, born and reared in an abundant, delightful, and passionate land, possess the reputation of being somewhat arrogant. But if this defect is real, it should be attributed to their climate, since the influence of the physical over the moral is so well-known. The good things with which nature endowed those provinces make them regard with scorn the poverty of Galicia, the ruggedness of Biscay, and the austerity of Castile. But, be this as it may, among them there have been outstanding men who have bestowed much honour on all Spain, and, in ancient times, the Trajans, Senecas, and others like them, who may well fill with pride the country in which they were born. The gaiety, cunning, and charm of the Andalusian women makes them incomparable : I assure you that just one of them would be enough to throw the Moroccan empire into a tumult, so that we should all kill one another over her.

The Murcians share the character of the Andalusians and Valencians. The latter are considered to be men of excessive slight-ness, this defect being attributed to the climate and soil : some claiming that even in their very foods there is lacking that pith which is found in those of other countries. My impartiality does not permit me to acquiesce to this prejudice, universal though it may be; rather I should observe that the Valencians of this century are the Spaniards who make the greatest advances in the natural sciences and in the dead languages.

The Catalonians are the most industrious people of Spain; manufacturing, fishing, navigation, commerce, contracts, are matters scarcely known in the other provinces of the Peninsula in compari-son with the Catalonians. Not only are they useful in peacetime,

en la guerra: fundición de cañones, fábricas de armas, vestuario y monturas para ejércitos, conducción de artillería, municiones, víveres, formación de tropas ligeras de excelente calidad, todo esto sale de Cataluña. Los campos se cultivan, la población se aumenta, los caudales crecen y, en suma, parece estar aquella nación mil leguas de la gallega, andaluza y castellana. Pero sus genios son poco tratables, únicamente dedicados a su propia ganancia e interés, y así los llaman algunos los holandeses de España. Mi amigo Nuño me dice que esta provincia florecerá mientras no se introduzca en ella el lujo personal y la manía de ennoblecer los artesanos: dos vicios que hasta ahora se oponen al genio que la ha enriquecido.

Los aragoneses son hombres de valor y espíritu, honrados, tenaces en su dictamen, amantes de su provincia y notablemente pre-ocupados a favor de sus paisanos. En otros tiempos cultivaron con suceso las ciencias, y manejaron con mucha gloria las armas contra los franceses en Nápoles y contra nuestros abuelos en España. Su país, como todo lo restante de la Península, fué sumamente poblado en la antigüedad, y tanto que es común tradición entre ellos que en las bodas de uno de sus reyes entraron en Zaragoza diez mil in-fanzones con un criado cada uno, montados los veinte mil en otros tantos caballos de la tierra.

Por causa de los muchos siglos que todos estos pueblos estuvieron divididos, guerrearon unos con otros, hablaron diversos idiomas, se gobernaron por diferentes leyes, llevaron distintos trajes y, en fin, fueron naciones separadas, se mantuvo entre ellos cierto odio, que sin duda ha aminorado y aun llegado a aniquilarse. Pero aun se mantiene cierto desapego entre los de provincias lejanas. Y si éste puede dañar en tiempo de paz, porque es obstáculo considerable para la perfecta unión, puede ser muy ventajoso en tiempo de guerra, por la mutua emulación de unos con otros: un regimiento todo de aragoneses no mirará con frialdad la gloria adquirida por una tropa toda castellana; y un navío tripulado de vizcaínos no se rendirá al enemigo mientras se defienda otro montado por catalanes.

TOMÁS DE IRIARTE
[1750–1791]

For all the dedicated scholarship of this Canary Island-born author, Iriarte's dramatic works and serious poetry are now forgotten. His fame rests on the seventy-six Fábulas literarias, *in which he ridicules, among*

but also they are of the greatest service in war : the casting of cannon, manufacture of arms, equipment for armies, conveyance of artillery, munitions, provisions, the formation of light troops of excellent quality, all this comes from Catalonia. The fields are cultivated, the population grows, wealth increases, and in sum, that nation seems to be a thousand leagues away from the Galician, Andalusian, and Castilian. But they are by temperament rather unsociable, and are dedicated solely to their own profit and interest, and therefore some call them the Hollanders of Spain. My friend Nuño tells me that this province will flourish so long as there are not introduced into it personal luxury and the mania of ennobling artisans : two vices which until now are opposed to the talent which enriched the country.

The Aragonese are men of valour and spirit, honourable, tenacious in judgment, lovers of their province and notably prejudiced in favour of their fellow-countrymen. In other days they cultivated the sciences with success, and they bore arms with much glory against the French in Naples and against our forefathers in Spain. Their land, as all the rest of the Peninsula, was thickly populated in ancient times, and so much so that there is a familiar tradition among them that for the wedding of one of their kings there entered into Zaragoza ten thousand noblemen, each one with a servant, and the twenty thousand mounted on an equal number of native horses.

Because of the many centuries that these peoples were divided, warred with each other, spoke different languages, governed themselves under different laws, wore different costumes, and in sum, were separate nations, there was nourished among them a certain hatred, which without doubt has lessened and even come to disappear. But there still continues a certain coolness among those of distant provinces. And if this can do harm in time of peace, because it is a considerable obstacle to perfect union, it can be most advantageous in time of war, through mutual rivalry : a regiment made up entirely of Aragonese will not view with dispassion the glory acquired by an all-Castilian troop; and a ship manned by Biscayans will not surrender to the enemy so long as another, manned by Catalonians, resists.

JEANNE PASMANTIER

other things, the literary vices of his contemporaries. Iriarte skilfully employs a great variety of metrical forms in these fables, many of which have become extremely popular.

EL OSO, LA MONA Y EL CERDO

Un Oso con que la vida
  Ganaba un piamontés,
La no muy bien aprendida
  Danza ensayaba en dos pies.

Queriendo hacer de persona,
  Dijo a una Mona: '¿Qué tal?'
Era perita la Mona,
  Y respondióle: 'Muy mal.'

Yo creo—replicó el Oso—
  Que me haces poco favor.
¿Pues qué? ¿mi aire no es garboso?
  ¿No hago el paso con primor?

Estaba el Cerdo presente,
  Y dijo:—Bravo, ¡bien va!
Bailarín más excelente
  No se ha visto ni verá.

Echó el Oso, al oír esto,
  Sus cuentas allá entre sí
Y, con ademán modesto,
  Hubo de exclamar así:

Cuando me desaprobaba
  La Mona, llegué a dudar;
Mas ya que el Cerdo me alaba,
  Muy mal debo de bailar.

Guarde para su regalo
  Esta sentencia un autor:
Si el sabio no aprueba, ¡malo!
  Si el necio aplaude, ¡peor!

EL BURRO FLAUTISTA

Esta fabulilla,
  Salga bien o mal,
Me ha ocurrido ahora
  Por casualidad.

THE BEAR, THE MONKEY AND THE HOG

A Bear, with whom a Piedmontese
   A wandering living made,
A dance he had not learn'd with ease,
   On his two feet essay'd :

And, as he highly of it thought,
   He to the Monkey cried,
'How's that?' who, being better taught,
   ' 'Tis very bad,' replied.

'I do believe,' rejoin'd the Bear,
   'You little favour show :
For have I not a graceful air,
   And step with ease to go?'

A Hog, that was beside them set,
   Cried, 'Bravo ! good !' said he;
'A better dancer never yet
   I saw, and ne'er shall see.'

On this the Bear, as if he turn'd
   His thoughts within his mind,
With modest gesture seeming learn'd
   A lesson thence to find.

'When blamed the Monkey, it was cause
   Enough for doubting sad;
But when I have the hog's applause,
   It must be very bad !'

As treasured gift, let authors raise
   This moral from my verse :
'Tis bad, when wise ones do not praise;
   But when fools *do*, 'tis worse.

                         JAMES KENNEDY

THE ASS AND THE FLUTE

This little fable heard,
   It good or ill may be;
But it has just occurr'd
   Thus accidentally.

Cerca de unos prados
Que hay en mi lugar,
Pasaba un Borrico
Por casualidad.

Una flauta en ellos
Halló, que un zagal
Se dejó olvidada
Por casualidad.

Acercóse a olerla
El dicho animal,
Y dió un resoplido
Por casualidad.

En la flauta el aire
Se hubo de colar,
Y sonó la flauta
Por casualidad.

¡Oh! dijo el Borrico:
¡Qué bien sé tocar!
¡Y dirán que es mala
La música asnal!

Sin reglas del arte
Borriquitos hay
Que una vez aciertan
Por casualidad.

FÉLIX MARÍA DE SAMANIEGO
[1745–1801]

*Iriarte's rival as Spain's leading fabulist is Félix María de Samaniego,
author of* Fábulas morales. *While he is less original than Iriarte—*

EL JOVEN FILÓSOFO Y SUS COMPAÑEROS

Un Joven, educado
Con el mayor cuidado
Por un viejo filósofo profundo,
Salió por fin a visitar el mundo.

Passing my abode,
   Some fields adjoining me
A big ass on his road
   Came accidentally.

And laid upon the spot,
   A Flute he chanced to see,
Some shepherd had forgot
   There accidentally.

The animal in front
   To scan it nigh came he,
And snuffing loud as wont,
   Blew accidentally.

The air it chanced around
   The pipe went passing free
And thus the Flute a sound
   Gave accidentally.

'O then,' exclaimed the Ass,
   'I know to play it fine;
And who for bad shall class
   This music asinine?'

Without the rules of art,
   Even asses, we agree,
May once succeed in part,
   Thus accidentally.

JAMES KENNEDY

Samaniego often imitated La Fontaine and Phèdre—he is considered by many critics the better poet of the two.

THE YOUNG PHILOSOPHER AND HIS FRIENDS

A gentleman young and carefully reared
By a venerable scholar of learning,
Abandoned the books which he long revered—
For the taste of the world he was yearning.

Concurrió cierto día
Entre civil y alegre compañía
A una mesa abundante y primorosa.
— ¡Espectáculo horrendo! ¡fiera cosa!
¡ La mesa de cadáveres cubierta
A la vista del hombre! . . . ¡Y éste acierta
A comer los despojos de la muerte!, —
El Joven declamaba de esta suerte.
Al son de filosóficas razones,
Devorando perdices y pichones,
Le responden algunos concurrentes:
— Si usted ha de vivir entre las gentes,
Deberá hacerse a todo.—
Con un gracioso modo,
Alabando el bocado de exquisito,
Le presentan un gordo pajarito.
—Cuando usted ha exclamado, será cierto;
Mas en fin, le decían, ya está muerto.
Pruébelo por su vida . . . Considere
Que otro le comerá, si no le quiere.—
La ocasión, las palabras, el ejemplo,
Y según yo contemplo,
Yo no sé qué olorcillo
Que exhalaba el caliente pajarillo,
Al Joven persuadieron de manera,
Que al fin se lo comió:—¡Quién lo dijera!
¡Haber yo devorado un inocente!—
Así clamaba, pero fríamente.
Lo cierto es que, llevado de aquel cebo,
Con más facilidad cayó de nuevo;
La ocasión se repite
De uno en otro convite,
Y de una codorniz a una becada,
Llegó el Joven al fin de la jornada,
Olvidando sus máximas primeras,
A ser devorador como las fieras.
De esta suerte los vicios se insinúan,
Crecen, se perpetúan
Dentro del corazón de los humanos
Hasta ser sus señores y tiranos.
Pues ¿qué remedio? . . . Incautos jovencitos,
¡Cuenta con los primeros pajaritos!

He found himself soon with light company
In whose manner and charm he delighted.
He joined in their quests for gay revelry
And to dine with them soon was invited.
But when he arrived with his comraderie
To sup at the table's sweet savours,
—Unspeakable horrors! Brute savagery!—
The table was full of cadavers!
'You eat unashamed these spoils of death?'
Declaimed the young man with a sigh.
The guests, looking up without catching breath,
Whilst devouring a bird, did reply :
'If you want to live with us happily,
Our manners and customs you'll follow.'
So saying, they passed to him graciously
A bird they implored him to swallow.
'That may be so, what you have just said;
Remorse your reflections instill.
But after all, it's already dead,
And if you don't eat it, we will.'
Looking on those who partook with delight
Of the food in this sumptuous feast,
And breathing the scent of the bird did excite
In the young man a lust for the beast.
'Who could have said that me too they would find
Eating an innocent creature!'
But still he ate on, not seeming to mind
His own philosophic forfeiture.
Once having fallen, he fell once again;
From his early maxims he did stray.
From quail to woodcock he went without strain,
Like a wild beast devouring his prey.
In this way we may see how bad habits creep in,
And our hearts from good ways they sever.
Enslaved we become and continue to sin,
Their whims we must follow forever.
So rash never be in deed or in word—
Take heed and beware : resist the first bird!

LILLIAN RESNICK

JUAN MELÉNDEZ VALDÉS
[1754–1817]

Juan Meléndez Valdés was the outstanding lyric poet of the eighteenth century. A teacher, magistrate and high government official under Joseph Bonaparte, Meléndez Valdés died in exile after the defeat of the French invaders.

DE MIS NIÑECES

Siendo yo niño tierno,
  Con la niña Dorila
Me andaba por la selva
  Cogiendo florecillas.

De que alegres guirnaldas
  Con gracia peregrina,
Para ambos coronarnos
  Su mano disponía.

Así en niñeces tales
  De juegos y delicias
Pasábamos felices
  Las horas y los días.

Con ellos poco a poco
  La edad corrió de prisa;
Y fué de la inocencia
  Saltando la malicia.

Yo no sé; mas al verme
  Dorila se reía;
Y a mí de sólo hablarla
  También me daba risa.

Luego al darle las flores
  El pecho me latía;
Y al ella coronarme
  Quedábase embebida.

Una tarde tras esto
  Vimos dos tortolitas,

The early compositions of this elegant and graceful poet include traditional eclogues, odes, love poetry and ballads, all distinguished for their technical perfection. He later cultivated the neo-classic school of poetry, and his works of this second period bear a strong philosophic tendency.

JUVENILITIES

When I was yet a child,
   A child Dorila too,
To gather there the flowerets wild,
   We roved the forest through.

And gaily garlands then,
   With passing skill display'd
To crown us both, in childish vein,
   Her little fingers made.

And thus our joys to share,
   In such our thoughts and play,
We pass'd along, a happy pair,
   The hours and days away.

But ev'n in sports like these,
   Soon age came hurrying by!
And of our innocence the ease
   Malicious seem'd to fly.

I knew not how it was,
   To see me she would smile;
And but to speak to her would cause
   Me pleasure strange the while.

Then beat my heart the more,
   When flowers to her I brought;
And she, to wreathe them as before,
   Seem'd silent, lost in thought.

One evening after this
   We saw two turtle-doves,

Que con trémulos picos
Se halagaban amigas.

Y de gozo y deleite,
Cola y alas caídas,
Centellantes sus ojos,
Desmayadas gemían.

Alentónos su ejemplo;
Y entre honestas caricias
Nos contamos turbados
Nuestras dulces fatigas;

Y en un punto cual sombra
Voló de nuestra vista
La niñez; mas en torno
Nos dió el Amor sus dichas.

MARIANO JOSÉ DE LARRA
[1809–1837]

The precocious Mariano José de Larra, journalist, novelist, poet, dramatist, critic and costumbrista, committed suicide at the age of twenty-eight over an unhappy love affair. Had he lived, there is little doubt that he would have become one of the greatest of all Spanish writers. For sharp critical insight and descriptive skill, Larra had no competitors in his own time and few in the entire history of Spanish literature.

EL CASTELLANO VIEJO

Ya en mi edad pocas veces gusto de alterar el orden que en mi manera de vivir tengo hace tiempo establecido, y fundo esta repugnancia en que no he abandonado mis lares ni un solo día para quebrantar mi sistema, sin que haya sucedido el arrepentimiento más sincero al desvanecimiento de mis engañadas esperanzas. Un resto, con todo eso, del antiguo ceremonial que en su trato tenían adoptado nuestros padres, me obliga a aceptar a veces ciertos convites a que parecería el negarse grosería o por lo menos ridícula afectación de delicadeza.

Andábame días pasados por esas calles a buscar materiales para mis artículos. Embebido en mis pensamientos, me sorprendí varias

With trembling throat, who, wrapt in bliss,
    Were wooing in their loves.

In manifest delight,
    With wings and feathers bow'd,
Their eyes fix'd on each other bright,
    They languish'd, moaning loud.

The example made us bold,
    And with a pure caress,
The troubles we had felt we told,
    Our pains and happiness.

And at once from our view
    Then, like a shadow, fled
Our childhood and its joys, but new,
    Love gave us his instead.

JAMES KENNEDY

His romantic drama Macías *and his fine historical novel* El doncel de Don Enrique el Doliente (*both 1834*) *deal with the ill-starred loves of the fourteenth-century troubadour Macías. But it is as a writer of articles satirizing the customs of his day that Larra is most famous. His style is characterized by choice vocabulary, purity of expression, subtle irony and humour. Larra often used the pseudonym* Fígaro, *as he does in* El castellano viejo, *given here.*

THE OLD CASTILIAN

Since I have grown older I very seldom care to change the order of my way of living, which has now been settled a long time, and I base this repugnance upon the fact that I have never for a single day abandoned my Lares to break my system without being over-taken by a most sincere repentance as the aftermath of my deluded hopes. Nevertheless a remnant of the old-fashioned courtesy adopted by our forefathers in their intercourse obliges me at times to accept certain invitations, which to refuse would be rudeness, or at least a ridiculous affectation of delicacy.

Some days ago I was walking through the streets in search of material for my articles. Buried in my thoughts, I surprised myself

veces a mí mismo riendo como un pobre hombre de mis propias ideas y moviendo maquinalmente los labios; algún tropezón me recordaba de cuando en cuando que para andar por el empedrado de Madrid no es la mejor circunstancia la de ser poeta ni filósofo; más de una sonrisa maligna, más de un gesto de admiración de los que a mi lado pasaban, me hacía reflexionar que los soliloquios no se deben hacer en público; y no pocos encontrones que al volver las esquinas di con quien tan distraída y rápidamente como yo las doblaba, me hicieron conocer que los distraídos no entran en el número de los cuerpos elásticos, y mucho menos de los seres gloriosos e impasibles. En semejante situación de espíritu, ¿qué sensación no debería producirme una horrible palmada que una gran mano, pegada (a lo que por entonces entendí) a un grandísimo brazo, vino a descargar sobre uno de mis hombros, que por desgracia no tienen punto alguno de semejanza con los de Atlante?

No queriendo dar a entender que desconocía este enérgico modo de anunciarse, ni desairar el agasajo de quien sin duda había creído hacérmele más que mediano, dejándome torcido para todo el día, traté sólo de volverme por conocer quién fuese tan mi amigo para tratarme tan mal; pero mi castellano viejo es hombre que cuando está de gracias no se ha de dejar ninguna en el tintero. ¿Cómo dirá el lector que siguió dándome pruebas de confianza y cariño? Echóme las manos a los ojos, y sujetándome por detrás:

—¿Quién soy?—gritaba alborozado con el buen éxito de su delicada travesura—. ¿Quién soy?

—Un animal—iba a responderle; pero me acordé de repente de quién podría ser. y substituyendo cantidades iguales: — *Braulio eres*—le dije.

Al oírme, suelta sus manos, ríe, se aprieta los ijares, alborota la calle, y pónenos a entrambos a la escena.

—¡Bien, mi amigo! ¿Pues en qué me has conocido?

—¿Quién pudiera sino tú? . . .

—¿Has venido ya de tu Vizcaya?

—No, Braulio, no he venido.

—Siempre el mismo genio. ¿Qué quieres? es la pregunta del español. ¡Cuánto me alegro de que estés aquí! ¿Sabes que mañana son mis días?

—Te los deseo muy felices.

—Déjate de cumplimientos entre nosotros; ya sabes que yo soy franco y castellano viejo: el pan pan y el vino vino; por consiguiente exijo de ti que no vayas a dármelos; pero estás convidado.

—¿A qué?

—A comer conmigo.

several times, laughing like a poor wretch at my own fancies, and mechanically moving my lips. A stumble or so reminded me now and again that to walk on the pavements of Madrid it is not the best of circumstances to be either poet or philosopher; more than one malicious smile, more than one look of wonder from the passers-by, made me reflect that soliloquies should not be made in public; and when turning corners not a few collisions with those who turned them as heedlessly as I made me recognize that the absent-minded are not among the number of elastic bodies, much less among glorious and insensible beings. Such being my frame of mind, imagine my sensations upon receiving a horrible smack which a huge hand attached (it seemed to me) to a brawny arm administered to one of my shoulders, which unfortunately bear not the slightest resemblance to those of Atlas!

Not wishing to make it understood that I would not recognize this energetic way of announcing oneself, nor to rebuff the good-will, which doubtless wished to show itself to be more than mediocre by leaving me crooked for the rest of the day, I was merely about to turn round to see who was so much my friend as to treat me so badly. But my Old Castilian is a man who, when he is joking, does not stop half-way. What?—my reader will ask—he gave further proofs of his intimacy and affection? He clasped his hands tightly over my eyes from behind, crying out, 'Who am I?' bubbling with delight at the success of his pretty trick. 'Who you are? A brute,' I was about to reply; but I suddenly remembered who it might be, and substituted the words, 'It's Braulio.' Upon hearing me he loosened his hands, held his sides for laughter, disturbing the whole street, and making us both very conspicuous.

'Good, good! How did you recognize me?'

'Who could it be but you? . . .'

'Well, so you've come from your dear Biscay?'

'No, Braulio, I have not come.'

'Always the same merry humour. What does it matter? It's a way we have of talking in Spain. . . . Do you know it's my birthday tomorrow?'

'I wish you many happy returns of the day.'

'Oh, no formalities between us; you know I'm a plain fellow and an Old Castilian, and call a spade a spade; consequently I require no compliments from you, but consider yourself invited——'

'To what?'

'To dine with me.'

—No es posible.

—No hay remedio.

—No puedo—insisto temblando.

—¿No puedes?

—Gracias.

—¿Gracias? Vete a paseo; amigo, como no soy el duque de F..., ni el conde de P...

¿Quién se resiste una sorpresa de esta especie? ¿quién quiere parecer vano?

—No es eso, sino que...

—Pues si no es eso —me interrumpe—, te espero a las dos: en casa se come a la española; temprano. Tengo mucha gente; tendremos al famoso X, que nos improvisará de lo lindo; T. nos cantará de sobremesa una rondeña con su gracia natural; y por la noche J. cantará y tocará alguna cosilla.

Esto me consoló algún tanto, y fué preciso ceder; un día malo, dije para mí, cualquiera lo pasa; en este mundo, para conservar amigos es preciso tener el valor de aguantar sus obsequios.

—No faltarás, si no quieres que riñamos.

—No faltaré—dije con voz exánime y ánimo decaído, como el zorro que se revuelve inútilmente dentro de la trampa donde se ha dejado coger.

—Pues hasta mañana—y me dió un torniscón por despedida.

Vile marchar como el labrador ve alejarse la nube de su sembrado, y quedéme discurriendo cómo podían entenderse estas amistades tan hostiles y tan funestas.

Llegaron las dos, y como yo conocía ya a mi Braulio, no me pareció conveniente acicalarme demasiado para ir a comer; estoy seguro de que se hubiera picado: no quise sin embargo excusar un frac de color y un pañuelo blanco, cosa indispensable en un día de días en semejantes casas; vestíme sobre todo lo más despacio que me fué posible, como se reconcilia al pie del suplicio el infeliz reo, que quisiera tener cien pecados más cometidos que contar para ganar tiempo; era citado a las dos, y entré en la sala a las dos y media.

No quiero hablar de las infinitas visitas ceremoniosas que antes de la hora de comer entraron y salieron en aquella casa, entre los cuales no eran de despreciar todos los empleados de su oficina, con sus señoras y sus niños, y sus capas, y sus paraguas, y sus chanclos, y sus perritos; déjome en blanco los necios cumplimientos que dijeron al señor de los días; no hablo del inmenso

'Impossible.'

'You must.'

'I cannot,' I insist, trembling.

'You can't?'

'Very many thanks——'

'Thanks? Very well, my dear friend; as I'm not the Duke of F., or Count P., of course——'

Who can resist an attack of this kind? Who cares to appear proud? 'It is not that, but——'

'Well, if it's not that,' he breaks in, 'I shall expect you at two. We dine early at my house—Spanish style. I expect a lot of people; there will be the famous improvisor X.; T. will sing after dinner in his usual first-rate style; and in the evening J. will play and sing some trifles.'

This consoled me somewhat, and I had to give way. 'Everybody,' said I to myself, 'has an evil day sometimes. In this world, if one wishes to preserve friends, one must endure their civilities.'

'You won't fail, unless you want to quarrel with me?'

'I shall not fail,' I said in a lifeless voice and low spirits, like a fox vainly revolving in the trap in which it has allowed itself to be caught.

'Then good-bye till tomorrow,' and he gave me a parting slap.

I watched him as the farmer watches the cloud go away from his newly sown field, and remained wondering how one could explain such adverse and fatal friendships.

.   .   .

Two o'clock arrived. As I knew my friend Braulio, I did not think it advisable to make myself too fine for his party; that, I am sure, would have annoyed him; nevertheless I could not dispense with a light frock-coat and a white pocket-handkerchief as essential for such birthday festivities. Above all, I dressed myself as slowly as possible, like the wretched criminal confessing at the foot of the gallows, who would like to have committed a hundred more sins the which to confess in order to gain more time. I was invited for two, and I entered the parlour at half-past two.

I shall not dwell on the ceremonious calls made before dinner-time by an infinite number of visitors, among which were not least all the officials of his department with their spouses and children, their cloaks, umbrellas, galoshes, and house-dogs; I shall be silent as to the foolish compliments paid to the head of the

círculo con que guarnecía la sala el concurso de tantas personas heterogéneas, que hablaron de que el tiempo iba a mudar, y de que en invierno suele hacer más frío que en verano. Vengamos al caso: dieron las cuatro, y nos hallamos solos los convidados. Desgraciadamente para mí, el señor de X., que debía divertirnos tanto, gran conocedor de esta clase de convites, había tenido la habilidad de ponerse malo aquella mañana; el famoso T. se hallaba oportunamente comprometido para otro convite; y la señorita que tan bien había de cantar y tocar estaba ronca en tal disposición que se asombraba ella misma de que se la entendiese una sola palabra, y tenía un panadizo en un dedo. ¡Cuántas esperanzas desvanecidas!

—Supuesto que estamos los que hemos de comer—exclamó don Braulio—, vamos a la mesa, querida mía.

—Espera un momento —le contestó su esposa casi al oído—, con tanta visita yo he faltado algunos momentos de allá dentro y . . .

—Bien, pero mira que son las cuatro . . .

—Al instante comeremos . . .

Las cinco eran cuando nos sentábamos a la mesa.

—Señores —dijo el anfitrión al vernos titubear en nuestras respectivas colocaciones—, exijo la mayor franqueza; en mi casa no se usan cumplimientos. ¡Ah, Fígaro! quiero que estés con toda comodidad; eres poeta, y además estos señores, que saben nuestras íntimas relaciones, no se ofenderán si te prefiero; quítate el frac, no sea que le manches.

—¿Qué tengo de manchar? — le respondí, mordiéndome los labios.

—No importa, te daré una chaqueta mía, siento que no haya para todos.

—No hay necesidad.

—¡Oh!, sí, sí, ¡mi chaqueta! Toma, mírala; un poco ancha te vendrá.

—Pero, Braulio . . .

—No hay remedio, no te andes con etiquetas.

Y en esto me quita él mismo el frac, velis, nolis, y quedo sepultado en una cumplida chaqueta rayada, por la cual sólo asomaba los pies y la cabeza, y cuyas mangas no me permitirían comer probablemente. Dile las gracias: al fin el hombre creía hacerme un obsequio.

Los días en que mi amigo no tiene convidados se contenta con una mesa baja, poco más que banqueta de zapatero, porque él y su mujer, como dice, ¿para qué quieren más? Desde la tal mesita, y como se sube el agua del pozo, hace subir la comida hasta la boca,

family on his birthday, nor describe the monstrous circle which was formed in the parlour by the assembly of so many heterogeneous people, discoursing upon how the weather was about to change, and how the winter is generally colder than the summer. Let us come to the point: four o'clock struck, and we, the invited guests, found ourselves alone. Unluckily for me, Senor X., who was to have entertained us, being a connoisseur of this class of invitation, had had the good idea to fall sick that morning; the celebrated T. found himself opportunely compromised by another invitation, and the young lady who was to sing and play so well was hoarse to such a degree that she was surprised that a single word she said could be understood, and further she had an infection in one of her fingers. Alas, for my beguiled expectations!

'Since all who are to dine are here,' exclaimed Don Braulio, 'let us go to the table, my dear.'

'Wait a bit,' replied his wife in a loud whisper. 'Such a lot of callers prevented my being in the kitchen, and . . .'

'But, look, it's four o'clock . . .'

'Dinner will be ready in a moment . . .'

It was five o'clock when we sat down.

'Ladies and gentlemen,' said our amphitryon, as we staggered into our respective chairs, 'I insist upon your making yourselves quite at home; we don't stand upon ceremony in my house. Oh, Figaro! I want you to be quite comfortable; you are a poet, and besides, these gentlemen who know how intimate we are will not be offended if I make an exception of you; take off your coat; it won't do to stain it.'

'Why should I stain it?' I replied, biting my lips.

'Oh, that's all right; I'll lend you a loose jacket; I'm sorry I haven't one for everybody.'

'I'd sooner not, thank you.'

'Nonsense! My jacket! Here it is; it will be a little large for you!'

'But, Braulio . . .'

'You must have it—bother etiquette!' and he thereupon pulled off my coat himself, *velis nolis*, and buried me in a great striped jacket, through which only my feet and head protruded, and the sleeves of which would probably not permit me to eat. I thanked him; he thought he was doing me a favour.

The days upon which my friend has no visitors he contents himself with a low table, little more than a cobbler's bench, because he and his wife, as he says, what should they want more? From this little table he carries his food, like water drawn up a well, to his

adonde llega goteando después de una larga travesía; porque pensar que estas gentes han de tener una mesa regular, y estar cómodos todos los días del año, es pensar en lo excusado. Ya se concibe, pues, que la instalación de una gran mesa de convite era un acontecimiento en aquella casa; así que, se había creído capaz de contener catorce personas que éramos una mesa donde apenas podrían comer ocho cómodamente. Hubimos de sentarnos de medio lado como quien va a arrimar el hombro a la comida, y entablaron los codos de los convidados íntimas relaciones entre sí con la más fraternal inteligencia del mundo. Colocáronme, por mucha distinción, entre un niño de cinco años, encaramado en unas almohadas que era preciso enderezar a cada momento porque las ladeaba la natural turbulencia de mi joven adlátere, y entre uno de esos hombres que ocupan en el mundo el espacio y sitio de tres, cuya corpulencia por todos lados se salía de madre de la única silla en que se hallaba sentado, digámoslo así, como en la punta de una aguja. Desdobláronse silenciosamente las servilletas, nuevas a la verdad, porque tampoco eran muebles en uso para todos los días, y fueron izadas por todos aquellos buenos señores a los ojales de sus fraques como cuerpos intermedios entre las salsas y las solapas.

—Ustedes harán penitencia, señores—exclamó el anfitrión una vez sentado.

Necia afectación es ésta, si es mentira, dije yo para mí; y si verdad, gran torpeza convidar a los amigos a hacer penitencia.

Desgraciadamente no tardé mucho en conocer que había en aquella expresión más verdad de la que mi buen Braulio se figuraba. Interminables y de mal gusto fueron los cumplimientos con que para dar y recibir cada plato nos aburrimos unos a otros.

—Sírvase usted.

—Hágame usted el favor.

—De ninguna manera.

—No lo recibiré.

—Páselo usted a la señora.

—Está bien ahí.

—Perdone usted.

—Gracias.

—Sin etiqueta, señores—exclamó Braulio, y se echó el primero con su propia cuchara.

Sucedió a la sopa un cocido surtido de todas las sabrosas impertinencias de este engorrosísimo, aunque buen plato; cruza por aquí la carne; por allá la verdura; acá los garbanzos; allá el jamón; la gallina por derecha; por medio el tocino; por izquierda los embuchados de Extremadura: siguióle un plato de ternera mechada,

mouth, where it arrives dripping after its long journey; for to imagine that these people keep a proper table and eat comfortably every day in the year is to expect too much. It is easy, therefore, to conceive that the installation of a large table for a dinner-party was an event in that house, so much so that a table at which scarcely eight people could have eaten comfortably had been considered capable of sitting the whole fourteen of us. We had to sit sideways with one shoulder towards the dinner, and the elbows of the guests entered on intimate relationship with each other in the most confiding fashion possible. They put me as in a place of honour between a child five years old, raised on some cushions, which I had to arrange every minute, as the natural restlessness of my youthful neighbour caused them to slip, and one of those men that occupy in this world the room of three, whose corpulency overflowed on all sides the chair upon which he was seated like, so to speak, upon the point of a needle. The table-napkins which we silently unfolded were new, for they were commodities of little daily use, and were pulled by these good gentlemen through a button-hole of their frock-coats to serve as intermediary bodies between the sauces and their broadcloth.

'You will have to take pot luck, gentlemen,' exclaimed our amphitryon as soon as he had sat down.

'What ridiculous affectation if untrue,' said I to myself; 'and if it is true, what folly to invite one's friends to take pot luck.' Unfortunately it was not long before I knew that there was in that expression more truth than my good Braulio imagined. Interminable and of poor taste were the compliments with which, upon passing and receiving each dish, we wearied one another. 'Pray help yourself.' 'Do me the favour.' 'I couldn't think of it.' 'Pass it on to the lady.' 'Ah, that's right.' 'Pardon me.' 'Thank you.'

'No ceremony, gentlemen,' exclaimed Braulio, and was the first to dip his spoon into his plate.

The soup was followed by an *olla,* an assortment of the most savoury impertinences of that most annoying but excellent dish; here was some meat, there some green stuff; here the dried beans, there the ham; the chicken to the right, the bacon in the middle, and the Estremaduran sausage to the left. Then came some larded

que Dios maldiga, y a éste otro y otros y otros; mitad traídos de la fonda, que esto basta para que excusemos hacer su elogio, mitad hechos en casa por la criada de todos los días, por una vizcaína auxiliar tomada al intento para aquella festividad y por el ama de la casa, que en semejantes ocasiones debe estar en todo, y por consiguiente suele no estar en nada.

—Este plato hay que disimularle—decía ésta de unos pichones—; están un poco quemados.

—Pero, mujer . . .

—Hombre, me aparté un momento, y ya sabes lo que son las criadas.

—¡ Qué lástima que este pavo no haya estado media hora más al fuego! Se puso algo tarde.

—¿No les parece a ustedes que está algo ahumado este estofado?

—¿Qué quieres? Una no puede estar en todo.

—¡Oh, está excelente!—exclamábamos todos dejándonoslo en el plato—; ¡excelente!

—Este pescado está pasado.

—Pues en el despacho de la diligencia del fresco dijeron que acababa de llegar; ¡el criado es tan bruto!

—¿De dónde se ha traído este vino?

—En eso no tienes razón, porque es . . .

—Es malísimo.

Estos diálogos cortos iban exornados con una infinidad de miradas furtivas del marido para advertirle continuamente a su mujer alguna negligencia, queriendo darnos a entender entrambos a dos que estaban muy al corriente de todas las fórmulas que en semejantes casos se reputan en finura, y que todas las torpezas eran hijas de los criados, que nunca han de aprender a servir. Pero estas negligencias se repetían tan a menudo, servían tan poco ya las miradas, que le fué preciso al marido recurrir a los pellizcos y a los pisotones; y ya la señora, que a duras penas había podido hacerse superior hasta entonces a las persecuciones de su esposo, tenía la faz encendida y los ojos llorosos.

—Señora, no se incomode usted por eso—le dijo el que a su lado tenía.

—¡Ah! les aseguro a ustedes que no vuelvo a hacer estas cosas en casa; ustedes no saben lo que es esto: otra vez, Braulio, iremos a la fonda y no tendrás . . .

—Usted, señora mía, hará lo que . . .

—¡Braulio! ¡Braulio!

veal, upon which may the curse of Heaven alight, and after this another dish, and another and another and another, half of which were brought over from a hotel, which will suffice to excuse our praising them, the other half made at home by their own maid and a Biscayan wench, a help hired for this festivity, and the mistress of the house, who on such occasions is supposed to have a hand in everything, and can consequently superintend nothing properly.

'You must be indulgent with this dish,' said the latter of some pigeons, 'they are a little burnt.'

'But, my dear . . .'

'I only left them for a moment, and you know what servants are.'

'What a pity this turkey was not half an hour longer before the fire! It was put in too late. And don't you think that stew is a little smoked?'

'What can you expect? A woman can't be everywhere at once.'

'Oh, they're excellent!' we all exclaimed, leaving the pieces on our plates—'delicious!'

'This fish is bad.'

'Well, they said in the fish market that it had only just arrived; the servant is so stupid!'

'Where does this wine come from?'

'Now there you're wrong, for it's . . .'

'Detestable.'

These short dialogues were accompanied by a number of furtive glances from the husband to acquaint his wife of some negligence, and both tried to give us to understand that they were quite at home in all those formulae which in similar cases are reputed correct, and that all the blunders were the fault of the servants, who can never learn to serve. But these omissions were so numerous, and looks were of such little avail, that the husband had recourse to pinches and kicks, and his wife, who, until the present, had barely succeeded in rising superior to her spouse's persecutions, now became inflamed in the face, and had tears in her eyes.

'Dear madam, do not distress yourself about such trifles,' said her neighbour.

'Ah! I assure you I shall not do this kind of thing in the house again; you don't know what it means; another time, Braulio, we'll dine at the hotel, and then you'll not have . . .'

'You, madam, shall do what I . . .'

'Braulio! Braulio!'

Una tormenta espantosa estaba a punto de estallar; empero todos los convidados a porfía probamos a aplacar aquellas disputas, hijas del deseo de dar a entender la mayor delicadeza, para lo cual no fué poca parte la manía de Braulio y la expresión concluyente que dirigió de nuevo a la concurrencia acerca de la inutilidad de los cumplimientos, que así llama él al estar bien servido y al saber comer. ¿Hay nada más ridículo que estas gentes que quieren pasar por finas en medio de la más crasa ignorancia de los usos sociales; que para obsequiarle le obligan a usted a comer y beber por fuerza, y no le dejan medio de hacer su gusto? ¿Por qué habrá gentes que sólo quieren comer con alguna más limpieza los días de días?

A todo esto, el niño que a mi izquierda tenía, hacía saltar las aceitunas a un plato de magras con tomate, y una vino a parar a uno de mis ojos, que no volvió a ver claro en todo el día; y el señor gordo de mi derecha había tenido la precaución de ir dejando en el mantel, al lado de mi pan, los huesos de las suyas, y los de las aves que había roído; el convidado de enfrente, que se preciaba de trinchador, se había encargado de hacer la autopsia de un capón, o sea gallo, que esto nunca se supo: fuese por la edad avanzada de la víctima, fuese por los ningunos conocimientos anatómicos del victimario, jamás parecieron las coyunturas. 'Este capón no tiene coyunturas', exclamaba el infeliz sudando y forcejeando, más que como quien trincha. ¡Cosa más rara! En una de las embestidas resbaló el tenedor sobre el animal como si tuviera escama, y el capón, violentamente despedido, pareció querer tomar su vuelo como en sus tiempos más felices, y se posó en el mantel tranquilamente como pudiera en un palo de un gallinero.

El susto fué general y la alarma llegó a su colmo cuando un surtidor de caldo, impulsado por el animal furioso, saltó a inundar mi limpísima camisa: levántase rápidamente a este punto el trinchador con ánimo de cazar el ave prófuga, y al precipitarse sobre ella, una botella que tiene a la derecha, con la que tropieza su brazo, abandonando su posición perpendicular, derrama un abundante caño de Valdepeñas sobre el capón y el mantel; corre el vino, auméntase la algazara, llueve la sal sobre el vino para salvar el mantel; para salvar la mesa se ingiere por debajo de él una servilleta, y una eminencia se levanta sobre el teatro de tantas ruinas. Una criada toda azorada retira el capón en el plato de su salsa; al pasar sobre mí hace una pequeña inclinación, y una lluvia maléfica de grasa desciende, como

A terrible storm was about to burst; however, all the guests vied with each other in settling these disputes born of the desire to demonstrate the greatest refinement, and of which not the smallest components were Braulio's mania, and the concluding remark which he again directed to the assembly with regard to the inutility of ceremony, by which he understood being properly served and knowing how to eat. Is there anything more ridiculous than those people who wish to pass for refined in the depths of the crassest ignorance of social usage, and who, to favour you, forcibly oblige you to eat and drink, and will not allow you to do what you like? And why are there people who only care to eat with a little more comfort on birthdays?

To add to all this, the child to my left was making olives jump into a dish of ham and tomatoes, and one of them hit one of my eyes, and prevented me from seeing clearly for the rest of the day; the stout gentleman to my right had taken the precaution to heap up on the tablecloth, by the side of my bread, the crumbs of his own and the bones of the birds which he had gnawed; and the guest opposite me, who piqued himself on his carving, had taken upon himself to make the autopsy of a capon, or cock, for nobody knew which, and whether by reason of the advanced age of the victim, or the lack of anatomical science of the executioner, the joints never appeared.

'This bird has no joints!' exclaimed the poor wretch, the drops of perspiration running down his face from his struggles, looking more like a person digging than carving. And then a wonderful occurrence took place! Upon one of the attacks, the fork slipped upon the animal as if it had scales, and the bird, thus violently dispatched, took flight as in its happier days, and then quietly alighted on the tablecloth, as on a roost in the poultry yard.

The fright was general, and the alarm reached its climax when a sauce-boat, impelled by the bird's wild career, upset, splashing my snow-white shirt. At this point the carver rose hastily, with a mind to chase the fugitive fowl, and as he precipitated himself upon it, a bottle to the right, which he knocked with his arm, abandoning its perpendicular position, poured out an abundant stream of Valdepeñas wine over the capon and the cloth. The wine ran; the uproar increased; salt was abundantly sprinkled over the wine to save the cloth; to save the table a napkin was inserted below the cloth, and an eminence arose on the site of so many ruins. A terrified maid, bearing away the capon now reposing in a dish of gravy, tilted it slightly as she lifted it over me, and an accursed shower of grease descended like the dew upon the.

el rocío sobre los prados, a dejar eternas huellas en mi pantalón color de perla; la angustia y el aturdimiento de la criada no conocen término; retírase atolondrada sin acertar con las excusas; al volverse tropieza con el criado que traía una docena de platos limpios y una salvilla con las copas para los vinos generosos, y toda aquella máquina viene al suelo con el más horroroso estruendo y confusión.

—¡Por San Pedro!—exclama dando una voz Braulio, difundida ya sobre sus facciones una palidez mortal, al paso que brota fuego el rostro de su esposa—. Pero sigamos, señores, no ha sido nada— añade volviendo en sí.

¡Oh honradas casas donde un modesto cocido y un principio final constituyen la felicidad diaria de una familia, huíd del tumulto de un convite de días! Sólo la costumbre de comer y servirse bien diariamente puede evitar semejantes destrozos.

¿Hay más desgracias? ¡Santo cielo! Sí, las hay para mí, ¡infeliz! Doña Juana, la de los dientes negros y amarillos, me alarga de su plato y con su propio tenedor una fineza, que es indispensable aceptar y tragar; el niño se divierte en despedir a los ojos de los concurrentes los huesos disparados de las cerezas; don Leandro me hace probar la manzanilla exquisita, que he rehusado, en su misma copa, que conserva las indelebles señales de sus labios grasientos; mi gordo fuma ya sin cesar y me hace cañón de su chimenea; por fin, ¡oh última de las desgracias! crece el alboroto y la conversación; roncas ya las voces, piden versos y décimas y no hay más poeta que Fígaro.

—Es preciso.

—Tiene usted que decir algo—claman todos.

—Désele pie forzado; que diga una copla a cada uno.

—Yo le daré el pie: *A don Braulio en este día.*

—Señores, ¡por Dios!

—No hay remedio.

—En mi vida he improvisado.

—No se haga usted el chiquito.

—Me marcharé.

—Cerrar la puerta.

—No se sale de aquí sin decir algo.

Y digo versos por fin, y vomito disparates, y los celebran, y crece la bulla y el humo y el infierno.

A Dios gracias, logro escaparme de aquel nuevo *Pandemonio.* Por fin, ya respiro el aire fresco y desembarazado de la calle; ya no hay necios, ya no hay castellanos viejos a mi alrededor.

¡Santo Dios, yo te doy gracias, exclamo respirando, como el ciervo que acaba de escaparse de una docena de perros y que oye

meadows to leave lasting traces on my pearl-grey trousers. The anguish and confusion of the girl were beyond bounds; she withdrew, unsuccessful in her excuses, and, turning round, collided with the waiter, who was carrying a dozen clean plates and a salver for the dessert wines, and the whole business came to the ground with the most horrible clatter and commotion.

'By St. Peter!' roared Braulio, and a mortal pallor diffused itself over his features, while a fire broke out on his wife's face. 'But no matter; let us continue, friends,' said he calming down.

Oh, honest homes where a modest stew and one more course constitute the daily happiness of a family; flee from the tumult of a birthday dinner-party! The custom of eating well and being well served every day can alone avert similar discomfiture.

Are there any more disasters? Alas, there are for my miserable self! Doña Juana, the lady with the black and yellow teeth, holds out to me from her plate and with her own fork a dainty bit, which I am bound to accept and swallow; the child amuses himself by shooting cherry-stones at the eyes of the assembly; Don Leandro makes me taste the delicious orange liqueur, which I had refused, in his own glass, which preserves the indelible traces of his greasy lips; my fat friend is smoking, and makes me the flue of his chimney; finally, oh last of miseries! the clamour and uproar increase, voices already hoarse demand couplets and stanzas, and Figaro is the only poet present.

'You must. It's for you to say something,' they all shout.

'Start him with the first line; let him compose a couplet for each of us.'

'I'll start him : *To Don Braulio on this day* . . .'

'Gentlemen, for Heaven's sake!'

'There's no getting out of it.'

'I've never improvised in my life.'

'Don't play the bashful.'

'I shall leave.'

'Lock the door. He shan't leave here until he recites something.'

And so I repeat some verses at last, and vomit absurdities, which they praise, and the smoke, the hubbub, and the purgatory increase.

Thank Heavens, I succeed in escaping from that new pandemonium. At last I again breathe the pure air of the street; there are now no more lunatics, no more Old Castilians around me.

'Ye gods, I thank you!' I exclaimed, breathing freely like a stag who has just escaped a dozen dogs and can barely hear their

ya apenas sus ladridos; para de aquí en adelante no te pido riquezas, no te pido empleos, no honores; líbrame de los convites caseros y de días de días; líbrame de estas casas en que es un convite un aconteci- miento, en que sólo se pone la mesa decente para los convidados, en que creen hacer obsequios cuando dan mortificaciones, en que se hacen finezas, en que se dicen versos, en que hay niños, en que hay gordos, en que reina, en fin, la brutal franqueza de los castellanos viejos! Quiero que, si caigo de nuevo en tentaciones semejantes, me falte un *roastbeef*, desaparezca del mundo el *beefsteak*, se anonaden los timbales de macarrones, no haya pavos en Perigueux, ni pasteles en Perigord, se sequen los viñedos de Burdeos, y beban, en fin, todos menos yo la deliciosa espuma del Champagne.

JOSÉ DE ESPRONCEDA
[1808–1842]

The stormy life of José de Espronceda, the greatest lyric poet of the romantic period, in itself exemplified the spirit of romanticism. A tortured soul, ever rebelling, he battled his way through exile from Spain for political activity, the Parisian barricade fighting of 1830, Spanish revolutionary struggles in 1835 and 1836, and a host of other freedom-seeking causes. His brief, trouble-streaked years—he died at thirty-four—held one great love: Teresa Mancha, who deserted husband and family for him. Their frequent separations brought bitterness to both; their raptures inspired some of Espronceda's most gripping poetry.

CANCIÓN DEL PIRATA

Con diez cañones por banda,
Viento en popa a toda vela
No corta el mar, sino vuela
Un velero bergantín:
Bajel pirata que llaman
Por su bravura el *Temido*,
En todo mar conocido
Del uno al otro confín.

La luna en el mar ríela,
En la lona gime el viento,
Y alza en blando movimiento
Olas de plata y azul;

distant barks. 'Henceforward I do not pray for riches, office, or honours. But deliver me from invitations to dinner and birthday parties; deliver me from those houses in which a dinner-party is an event, in which a decent table is only laid for visitors, in which they think they are doing you a good turn while they are doing you a bad one, in which they are over-polite, in which they recite verses, in which there are children, in which there are fat men, in which, finally, there reigns the brutal frankness of the Old Castilians! If I fall by similar temptations, may I ever lack roast beef, may beefsteaks vanish from this world, may timbales of macaroni be annihilated, may there be no turkeys in Perigueux, nor pies in Perigord, may the wines of Bordeaux dry up, and finally may everybody but myself drink the delicious foam of champagne!'

SUSETTE M. TAYLOR
(Revised by the editors)

Himself a social outcast by choice and romantic inclination, he often in his short poems describes others beyond the pale of society: the beggar, the criminal, the executioner, the pirate. His two longest works are El estudiante de Salamanca, *on the Don Juan theme, and* El diablo mundo, *an extraordinary attempt to synthesize the struggle of humanity.*

Espronceda's poetry is generally tinged by rebellion, melancholy and despair. But every line sings with innate rhythm. This musical quality is most evident in his famous Canción del pirata.

PIRATE'S SONG

With cannon ten on port and starboard,
Wind just aft and strong,
Flying the sea, not ploughing through,
A brigantine skims along.
    She is called the *Dreaded* by a host
And feared on every side,
From the eastern to the western coast,
Wherever she may ride.

    Across the sea the moonlight shines,
The wind goes wailing through,
Shrill in the canvas, ruffling waves
Of silver and of blue.

Y ve el capitán pirata,
Cantando alegre en la popa,
Asia a un lado, al otro Europa
Y allá a su frente Estambul.

Navega, velero mío,
    Sin temor,
Que ni enemigo navío,
Ni tormenta, ni bonanza
Tu rumbo a torcer alcanza,
Ni a sujetar tu valor.

Veinte presas
Hemos hecho
A despecho
Del inglés,
Y han rendido
Sus pendones
Cien naciones
A mis pies.

Que es mi barco mi tesoro,
Que es mi Dios la libertad,
Mi ley la fuerza y el viento,
Mi única patria la mar.

Allá muevan feroz guerra
    Ciegos reyes
Por un palmo más de tierra:
Que yo tengo aquí por mío
Cuanto abarca el mar bravío,
A quien nadie impuso leyes.

Y no hay playa,
Sea cualquiera,
Ni bandera
De esplendor,
Que no sienta
Mi derecho
Y dé pecho
A mi valor.

Que es mi barco mi tesoro. . . .

There on the poop the captain sings
By whom the band is led,
With Asia left and Europe right
And Istambul ahead.

Sail on, swift bark, at my command,
    So brave and bold,
No warship by your foemen manned,
Nor storm, nor calm, nor any force
Shall turn you from your chosen course
Nor daunt your hardy soul.

> A score of ships
> We've seized aright
> And this despite
> The English fleet.
> And I have forced
> A hundred lords
> To lay their swords
> Beneath my feet.

My only treasure a pirate ship,
My god but liberty,
My law, brute force and a hearty wind,
My land, the open sea.

Kings are plunging into war,
    Unseeing fools,
To fight for land, for a trifle more,
While anything that sails the sea
Belongs by my own laws to me,
Unchecked by others' rules.

> There nowhere lies
> A foreign land
> Or distant strand
> That does not feel,
> Whate'er its flag,
> My crushing might,
> Admit my right,
> And to me yield.

My only treasure a pirate ship . . .

A la voz de ¡barco viene!
  Es de ver
Como vira y se previene
A todo trapo a escapar:
Que yo soy el rey del mar,
Y mi furia es de temer.

        En las presas
        Yo divido
        Lo cogido
        Por igual:
        Sólo quiero
        Por riqueza
        La belleza
        Sin rival.

  Que es mi barco mi tesoro. . . .

¡Sentenciado estoy a muerte!
  Yo me río:
No me abandone la suerte,
Y al mismo que me condena,
Colgaré de alguna entena,
Quizá en su propio navío.

        Y si caigo,
        ¿Qué es la vida?
        Por perdida
        Ya la di,
        Cuando el yugo
        Del esclavo,
        Como un bravo,
        Sacudí.

  Que es mi barco mi tesoro. . . .

Son mi música mejor
  Aquilones;
El estrépito y temblor
De los cables sacudidos,
Del negro mar los bramidos
Y el rugir de mis cañones.

The cry, 'A ship !' is a sudden threat.
    Watch them veer.
See how fast, full canvas set,
In desperate fright they try to flee :
I am king of all the sea,
My wrath inspires their fear.

        The spoils of war
        That raids provide
        I then divide
        With justice fine,
        Unless I claim
        Some damsel rare,
        Surpassing fair,
        And make her mine.

My only treasure a pirate ship . . .

And I have been condemned to die !
    I laugh at that.
Upon good fortune I rely;
And hope to hang him by the neck,
Perhaps from a yardarm on his deck,
Who sentenced me to die.

        If I should fall,
        If life's the cost?
        I'd count well lost
        The life I gave.
        I knew the risk
        Yet with one stroke
        Cast off the yoke
        That held me slave.

My only treasure a pirate ship . . .

Melodies in the winds abound :
    I love to hear
The cables' splashing, scraping sound,
The roar and bark of the loud Black Sea,
The crash of the cannon's battery,
Delightful to my ear.

Y del trueno
Al son violento,
Y del viento
Al rebramar,
Yo me duermo
Sosegado,
Arrullado
Por el mar.

Que es mi barco mi tesoro,
Que es mi Dios la libertad,
Mi ley la fuerza y el viento,
Mi única patria la mar.

JOSÉ ZORRILLA
[1817–1893]

José Zorrilla, Spain's exceedingly popular romantic poet, wrote with an easy and instinctive brilliance; words cascaded from his pen in a stunning melodic flow. His excellent *leyendas, stemming from Spanish traditions and tales, helped earn for him the title 'el poeta nacional'.* Zorrilla *is equally famous for his religious-romantic drama* Don Juan Tenorio (*1844*),

BOABDIL

Dueña de la negra toca,
  La del morado monjil,
Por un beso de tu boca
  Diera a Granada Boabdil.

Diera la lanza mejor
  Del Zenete más bizarro,
Y con su fresco verdor
  Toda una orilla del Darro.

Diera alfombras orientales,
  Y armaduras, y pebetes,
Y diera . . . ¡que tanto vales!,
  Hasta cuarenta jinetes.

Rolls of thunder
Snap and growl
And seawinds howl
Across the deep.
I am calmed
As sounds grow dulled,
And by them lulled
I drift to sleep.

My only treasure a pirate ship,
My god but liberty,
My law, brute force and a hearty wind,
My land, the open sea.

ALICE JANE MᶜVAN

based on Tirso de Molina's often-imitated El burlador de Sevilla (*1630*).
*The success of Zorrilla's play, in which Don Juan attains salvation, has
exceeded that of any other Spanish dramatic work. For more than a century
it has been unfailingly presented during the first week of November in almost
all Spanish theatres.*

BOABDIL

Lady of the dark head-dress,
    And monkish vest of purple hue,
Gladly would Boabdil give
    Granada for a kiss of you.

He would give the best adventure
    Of the bravest horseman tried,
And with all its verdant freshness
    A whole bank of Darro's tide.

He would give rich carpets, perfumes,
    Armours of rare price and force,
And so much he values you,
    A troop, ay, of his favourite horse.

Porque tus ojos son bellos,
Porque la luz de la aurora
Sube al oriente desde ellos,
Y el mundo su lumbre dora.

De tus labios, la sonrisa,
La paz, de tu lengua mana . . .
Leve, aérea como brisa
De purpurina mañana.

¡Oh qué hermosa nazarena
Para un harén oriental,
Suelta la negra melena
Sobre el cuello de cristal,

En lecho de tercipelo,
Entre una nube de aroma,
Y envuelta en el blanco velo
De las hijas de Mahoma!

Ven a Córdoba, cristiana,
Sultana serás allí,
Y el sultán será, ¡oh sultana!,
Un esclavo para ti.

Te dará tanta riqueza,
Tanta gala tunecina,
Que has de juzgar tu belleza
Para pagarle, mezquina.

Dueña de la negra toca,
Por un beso de tu boca
Diera un reino Boabdil;
Y yo, por ello, cristiana,
Te diera de buena gana
Mil cielos, si fueran mil.

'Because thine eyes are beautiful,
   Because the morning's blushing light
From them arises to the East,
   And gilds the whole world bright.

'From thy lips smiles are flowing,
   From thy tongue gentle peace,
Light and aerial as the course
   Of the purple morning's breeze.

'O! lovely Nazarene, how choice!
   For an Eastern harem's pride,
Those dark locks waving freely
   Thy crystal neck beside.

'Upon a couch of velvet,
   In a cloud of perfumed air,
Wrapp'd in the white and flowing veil
   Of Mahomet's daughters fair.

'O, Lady! come to Cordova,
   There Sultana thou shalt be,
And the Sultan there, Sultana,
   Shall be but a slave for thee.

'Such riches he will give thee,
   And such robes of Tunisine,
That thou wilt judge thy beauty,
   To repay him for them, mean.'

O! Lady of the dark head-dress!
That him a kiss of thee might bless,
   Resign a realm Boabdil would!
But I for that, fair Christian, fain
Would give of heavens, and think it gain,
   A thousand if I only could.

                                   JAMES KENNEDY

RAMÓN DE CAMPOAMOR
[1817–1901]

Ramón de Campoamor, an extremely popular poet in his own day, has not been treated kindly by many recent critics. Few dispute, however, the deftness of his wit or the wisdom of his observations. These qualities are

DOLORAS

¡QUIÉN SUPIERA ESCRIBIR!

I

—Escribidme una carta, señor cura.
—Ya sé para quién es.
—¿Sabéis quién es, porque una noche oscura
Nos visteis juntos?—Pues.

—Perdonad; mas . . .—No extraño ese tropiezo.
La noche . . . la ocasión . . .
Dadme pluma y papel. Gracias. Empiezo:
Mi querido Ramón:

—¿Querido? . . . Pero, en fin, ya lo habéis puesto . . .
—Si no queréis . . .—¡Sí, sí!
—*¡Qué triste estoy!* ¿No es eso? —Por supuesto.
—*¡Qué triste estoy sin ti!*

Una congoja, al empezar, me viene . . .
—¿Cómo sabéis mi mal?
—Para un viejo, una niña siempre tiene
el pecho de cristal.

¿Qué es sin ti el mundo? Un valle de amargura.?
¿Y contigo? Un edén.
—Haced la letra clara, señor cura;
Que lo entienda eso bien.

—*El beso aquel que de marchar a punto*
Te di . . .—¿Cómo sabéis? . . .
—Cuando se va y se viene y se está junto
Siempre . . . no os afrentéis.

most evident in the series which he called humoradas *(epigrams in verse)*
and doloras *(poetic vignettes expressing a simple truth or philosophy).*
In the latter group, Quién supiera escribir *is his best-known poem.*

DOLORAS

IF ONLY I COULD WRITE!

I

'I pray you, reverend Sir, this letter write.'
'To whom then? Ah, I know.'
'You know, because that dark and starless night
You saw us meet?' 'E'en so.'

'O Sir, forgive us.' 'Nay, 'twas no great sin,
The hour to love did lend;
Give me a pen and paper, I'll begin :
Raymond, beloved friend!'

'Beloved? Well, 'tis written.' 'You're not vext?
Do you approve it?' 'Yes.'
'*I am so sad alone.* (Should that come next?)
More sad than you can guess.

Such sorrow fills me since we two did part!'
'How do you know my pain?'
'To these old eyes is every young maid's heart
Like crystal, free from stain.

*What without you is life? A vale of woe.
With you? The promised land.*'
'Ah, Señor Cura! Make your writing so
That he may understand.'

'*The kiss I gave you when you left me, sweet—*'
'What! Know you of my kiss?'
'Ever when lovers part, and when they meet—
Oh, take it not amiss.

Y si volver tu afecto no procura
Tanto me harás sufrir . . .
—¿Sufrir y nada más? No, señor cura,
¡Que me voy a morir!

—¿Morir? ¿Sabéis que es ofender al cielo? . . .
—Pues sí, señor, ¡morir!
—Yo no pongo *morir.*—¡Qué hombre de hielo!
¡Quién supiera escribir!

II

¡Señor Rector, señor Rector!, en vano
Me queréis complacer,
Si no encarnan los signos de la mano
Todo el ser de mi ser.

Escribidle, por Dios, que el alma mía
Ya en mí no quiere estar;
Que la pena no me ahoga cada día . . .
Porque puedo llorar.

Que mis labios, las rosas de su aliento,
No se saben abrir;
Que olvidan de la risa el movimiento
A fuerza de sentir.

Que mis ojos, que él tiene por tan bellos,
Cargados con mi afán,
Como no tienen quien se mire en ellos,
Cerrados siempre están.

Que es, de cuantos tormentos he sufrido,
La ausencia el más atroz;
Que es un perpetuo sueño de mi oído
El eco de su voz . . .

Que, siendo por su causa, el alma mía
¡Goza tanto en sufrir! . . .
Dios mío, ¡cuántas cosas le diría
Si supiera escribir! . . .

Oh, if your love should never bring you more,
  How should I grieve and sigh!'
'What grieve, and nothing more? Nay, good Señor,
  Say, I were like to die.'

'To die! My child, such word were blasphemy.'
  'Yet die full well I might.'
'I'll not put "die".' 'Your heart is ice. Ah me!
  If only I could write!'

II

'Ah, Señor Cura, 'tis in vain you seek
  My sorrow thus to still;
Unless, indeed, to make my whole heart speak
  These pen-strokes have the skill.

For God's sake write, my soul would fain be free
  From all its weary grief,
Which day by day would even stifle me,
  But that tears bring relief.

Tell him these rosy lips he loved, that met
  His own dear lips erewhile,
Are now for ever closed, and fast forget
  Even what 'tis to smile.

Tell him, these eyes, that won from him such praise,
  Are drooping and dejected,
Even because therein his well-loved face
  No longer is reflected.

Tell him, of all the torments life can bring,
  Be absence my last choice;
Tell him, that ever in my ears will ring
  The echo of his voice.

Yet say, that since for him so sad I stay,
  I count my sorrow light,
O God, how many are the things I'd say,
  If I could only write!

EPÍLOGO

—Pues señor, ¡bravo amor! Copio y concluyo:
A don Ramón . . . En fin,
Que es inútil saber para esto arguyo
ni el griego ni el latín.—

GUSTAVO ADOLFO BÉCQUER
[1836–1870]

A poverty-stricken orphan, dogged by poor health, unhappily married, Gustavo Adolfo Bécquer spent the few years of his life in a stranglehold of financial and emotional difficulties. But from the depths of his personal grief, Bécquer composed lyric poetry of such breath-taking artistry and bittersweet sentiment that his name is today immortal in Spanish literature. Hardly a Spaniard exists who cannot recite at least one of his seventy-six Rimas, the exquisite poems for which he is most famous.

RIMA II

Saeta que voladora
    Cruza, arrojada al azar,
Y que no se sabe dónde
    Temblando se clavará;

Hoja que del árbol seca
    Arrebata el vendaval,
Y que no hay quien diga el surco
    Donde al polvo volverá;

Gigante ola que el viento
    Riza y empuja en el mar,
Y rueda y pasa y se ignora
    Qué playa buscando va;

Luz que en cercos temblorosos
    Brilla, próxima a expirar,
Y que no se sabe de ellos
    Cuál el último será;

END *

Now Sir, 'tis done. I trace these words for end :
"*To Raymond*", and bestow
Upon it this my mark, the which to send,
Small Latin need I know.'

IDA FARNELL

* A more precise translation of the epilogue would show a change of
speaker and that it is the priest who says the last four lines. The editors
offer the following substitution :
'Well, now, I'll copy what you've said and add
    To Raymond . . . for you speak
More clearly with love's fire than if you had
    All my Latin and my Greek.'

Besides the small collection of Rimas *and other short poems, Bécquer
wrote a brief series of literary letters, and twenty-two* leyendas. *The latter
are dream-like legends of Spain, especially of Toledo, written in prose as
haunting and delicate as his poetry.*

RIMA II

Flitting arrow, speeding onward,
    To the air at random cast,
Ne'er divining where now trembling
    It shall fix itself at last.

Leaf which from the branch now withered
    By the wind is snatched away,
And no one can mark the furrow
    Where at last it falls to stay.

Giant wave urged by a tempest,
    Curling, tumbling o'er the sea,
Rolling, passing, never knowing
    Of what strand its quest must be.

Light in wavering circles gleaming,
    To exhaustion nearing now,
And each circle all unwitting
    Which shall be the last to glow.

Eso soy yo, que al acaso
Cruzo el mundo, sin pensar
De dónde vengo, ni adónde
Mis pasos me llevarán.

RIMA IV

No digáis que agotado su tesoro,
De asuntos falta, enmudeció la lira;
Podrá no haber poetas; pero siempre
Habrá poesía.

Mientras las ondas de la luz al beso
Palpiten encendidas;
Mientras el sol las desgarradas nubes
De fuego y oro vista;

Mientras el aire en su regazo lleve
Perfumes y armonías;
Mientras haya en el mundo primavera
¡Habrá poesía!

Mientras la ciencia a descubrir no alcance
Las fuentes de la vida,
Y en el mar o en el cielo haya un abismo
Que al cálculo resista;

Mientras la humanidad, siempre avanzando,
No sepa a do camina;
Mientras haya un misterio para el hombre,
¡Habrá poesía!

Mientras sintamos que se alegra el alma,
Sin que los labios rían;
Mientras se llore sin que el llanto acuda
A nublar la pupila;

Mientras el corazón y la cabeza
Batallando prosigan;
Mientras haya esperanzas y recuerdos,
¡Habrá poesía!

Mientras haya unos ojos que reflejen
Los ojos que los miran;
Mientras responda el labio suspirando
Al labio que suspira;

This am I, who, aimless roving,
   O'er this earth my way must wend;
Ne'er reflecting whence I came, nor
   To what goal my footsteps tend.

J. D. M. FORD

RIMA IV

Say not that, its treasure exhausted,
   The lyre is mute, lacking a melody :
There may be no poets, but forever
   Poesy will be.

As long as the waves quiver glowingly
   At dawning's caress;
As long as the sun doth, with fire and gold,
   The flying clouds dress;

As long as the breezes are laden with
   Fragrance and harmony;
As long as the springtide comes to the earth,
   Poesy will be !

As long as by science the well of life
   Has not been found,
And in seas or in heavens an abyss remains
   That men cannot sound;

While ignorant whither, but forward yet,
   Goes humanity;
As long as one mystery remains for man,
   Poesy will be !

As long as the soul joys and yet no smile
   Without doth appear;
As long as there's sorrow when from the eye
   There falls no tear;

As long as mankind is still left with hope
   And memory;
As long as the heart and head battle still,
   Poesy will be !

As long as eyes mirror the tender gaze
   Of other eyes;
As long as a sighing mouth still responds
   To a mouth that sighs;

Mientras sentirse puedan en un beso
Dos almas confundidas;
Mientras exista una mujer hermosa,
¡Habrá poesía!

RIMA VII

Del salón en el ángulo oscuro,
De su dueña tal vez olvidada,
Silenciosa y cubierta de polvo
    Veíase el arpa.

¡Cuánta nota dormía en sus cuerdas,
Como el pájaro duerme en las ramas,
Esperando la mano de nieve
    Que sabe arrancarlas!

¡Ay! —pensé—, ¡cuántas veces el genio
Así duerme en el fondo del alma,
Y una voz como Lázaro, espera
    Que diga: '¡Levántate y anda!'

RIMA X

Los invisibles átomos del aire
    En derredor palpitan y se inflaman;
El cielo se deshace en rayos de oro;
    La tierra se estremece alborozada;
Oigo flotando en olas de armonía
    Rumor de besos y batir de alas;
Mis párpados se cierran . . . ¿Qué sucede?
    —¡Es el amor que pasa!

RIMA XI

Yo soy ardiente, yo soy morena,
Yo soy el símbolo de la pasión;
De ansia de goces mi alma está llena.
¿A mí me buscas?—No es a ti; no.

Mi frente es pálida; mis trenzas de oro;
Puedo brindarte dichas sin fin;

As long as two souls in a kiss can feel
    One unity;
As long as one beautiful woman is . . .
    Poesy will be!

YOUNG ALLISON

RIMA VII

In the room, in a corner all darkened,
By its owner perhaps now forgotten,
Mute-voiced and covered over with dust,
    The harp was seen.

What notes lay slumbering in its chord-strings—
As the bird sleeps in the branches—
Awaiting the snow-white fingers
    Which know how to wake them!

Oh! thought I—how often does genius
Thus sleep in the deep of soul's vault,
And, like Lazarus, a voice await, anxious,
That will bid it : 'Arise and walk!'

JEANNE PASMANTIER

RIMA X

The particles invisible of air
    Around me quiver and vehemently glow;
The heavens burst forth in rays of golden light;
    All earth doth tremble in a joyous throe.
Floating in waves of harmony I hear
    A stir of kisses and of wings on high;
Mine eyelids close themselves. . . . What passes now?
    ' 'Tis love goes by!'

YOUNG ALLISON

RIMA XI

I am black and comely; my lips are glowing;
I am passion; my heart is hot;
The rapture of life in my veins is flowing.
For me thou callest?—I call thee not.

Pale is my forehead and gold my tresses;
Endless comforts are locked in me,

Yo de ternura guardo un tesoro.
¿A mí me llamas?—No; no es a ti.

Yo soy un sueño, un imposible,
Vano fantasma de niebla y luz;
Soy incorpórea, soy intangible;
No puedo amarte.—¡Oh, ven; ven tú!

RIMA XXI

¿Qué es poesía?—dices mientras clavas
En mi pupila tu pupila azul;—
¿Que es poesía? ¿Y tú me lo preguntas?
Poesía . . . eres tú.

RIMA XXXVIII

Los suspiros son aire, y van al aire.
   Las lágrimas son agua, y van al mar.
Dime, mujer; cuando el amor se olvida,
   ¿Sabes tú a dónde va?

RIMA LII

Olas gigantes que os rompéis bramando
En las playas desiertas y remotas,
Envuelto entre las sábanas de espuma,
   ¡Llevadme con vosotros!

Ráfagas de huracán, que arrebatáis
Del alto bosque las marchitas hojas,
Arrastrado en el ciego torbellino,
   ¡Llevadme con vosotros!

Nubes de tempestad, que rompe el rayo
Y en fuego encienden las sangrientas orlas,
Arrebatado entre la niebla oscura,
   ¡Llevadme con vosotros!

Llevadme, por piedad, adonde el vértigo
Con la razón me arranque la memoria . . .
¡Por piedad! . . . ¡Tengo miedo de quedarme
   Con mi dolor a solas!

Treasure of hearthside tendernesses.
'Tis I whom thou seekest?—Nay, not thee.

I am a dream, afar, forbidden,
Vague as the mist on the mountain-brow,
A bodiless glory, haunting, hidden;
I cannot love thee.—Oh, come! come thou!

KATHARINE LEE BATES

RIMA XXI

What is poetry, you say,
Holding my eyes with yours of blue,
What is poetry?... *You* ask that?
Poetry... It is you!

INA DUVALL SINGLETON

RIMA XXXVIII

Sighs are air, and go to the air.
   Tears are water, and to the sea flow.
Tell me, woman : when love's forgot,
   Knowest where it doth go?

YOUNG ALLISON

RIMA LII

O waves gigantic that roaring break
And hurl yourselves on a desert strand,
Wrapt in a sheet of the foam you make
   Drag me below with you, bear me on high.

O hurricane, driving with whips of wind
The faded leaves from the forest grand,
Dragged along by the whirlwind blind
   Goad me to go with you, prone as I lie.

O clouds of the tempest, by lightning kiss'd,
Your edges shot with the fire of its love,
Whirled along in the sombre mist
   Bear me away with you, bear me above.

O bear me away with you, bear me away
Where frenzied with vertigo mad I may slay
My reason and memory, for I fear
   To be left all alone with my sorrow here.

MASON CARNES

RIMA LIII

Volverán las oscuras golondrinas
En tu balcón sus nidos a colgar,
Y otra vez con el ala a sus cristales
Jugando llamarán;
Pero aquellas que el vuelo refrenaban
Tu hermosura y mi dicha al contemplar,
Aquellas que aprendieron nuestros nombres,
Ésas . . . ¡no volverán!

Volverán las tupidas madreselvas
De tu jardín las tapias a escalar,
Y otra vez a la tarde, aún más hermosas,
Sus flores se abrirán;
Pero aquellas, cuajadas de rocío,
Cuyas gotas mirábamos temblar
Y caer, como lágrimas del día . . .
Ésas . . . ¡no volverán!

Volverán del amor en tus oídos
Las palabras ardientes a sonar;
Tu corazón de su profundo sueño
Tal vez despertará;

Pero mudo y absorto y de rodillas,
Come se adora a Dios ante su altar,
Como yo te he querido . . . desengáñate,
¡Así no te querrán!

RIMA LXXIII

Cerraron sus ojos,
Que aún tenía abiertos;
Taparon su cara
Con un blanco lienzo;
Y unos sollozando,
Otros en silencio,
De la triste alcoba
Todos se salieron.

La luz, que en un vaso
Ardía en el suelo,

RIMA LIII

The dusky swallows will hang their nests
In your balcony once again,
And with their wings they will lightly tap,
As they flit past your window-pane;
But those who paused in their eager flight
And lingered our names to learn,
That viewed your beauty and my delight. . . .
Ah! these will not return!

Dense honeysuckle will scale the walls
Of your garden, and there once more
Will show its blossoms when evening comes,
Even lovelier than before;
But those, dew-laden, whose drops we watched
Now tremble and fall, alack!
That we saw fall like the tears of day. . . .
Ah! these will not come back!

The burning passionate words of love
Once again in your ears will sound;
And then your heart will perhaps awake,
Will be roused from its sleep profound;
But as one kneels at His altar, mute,
Adoring, with head bent low,
As I have loved you . . . be undeceived,
Ah! they'll not love you so!

MRS. W. S. HENDRIX

RIMA LXXIII

They closed her eyes
That were still open;
They hid her face
With a white linen,
And, some sobbing
Others in silence,
From the sad bedroom
All came away.

The nightlight in a dish
Burned on the floor;

Al muro arrojaba
La sombra del lecho;
Y entre aquella sombra
Veíase a intervalos
Dibujarse rígida
La forma del cuerpo.

Despertaba el día
Y a su albor primero
Con sus mil rüidos
Despertaba el pueblo.
Ante aquel contraste
De vida y misterios,
De luz y tinieblas,
Medité un momento:
¡Dios mío, qué solos
Se quedan los muertos!

De la casa en hombros
Lleváronla al templo
Y en una capilla
Dejaron el féretro.
Allí rodearon
Sus pálidos restos
De amarillas velas
Y de paños negros.

Al dar de las ánimas
El toque postrero
Acabó una vieja
Sus últimos rezos;
Cruzó la ancha nave,
Las puertas gimieron,
Y el ancho recinto
Quedóse desierto.

De un reloj se oía
Compasado el péndulo,
Y de algunos cirios
El chisporroteo.
Tan medroso y triste,
Tan oscuro y yerto
Todo se encontraba . . .

It threw on the wall
The bed's shadow,
And in that shadow
One saw sometime
Drawn in sharp line
The body's shape.

The dawn appeared.
At its first whiteness
With its thousand noises
The town awoke.
Before that contrast
Of light and darkness,
Of life and strangeness
I thought a moment.
My God, how lonely
The dead are!

On the shoulders of men
To church they bore her,
And in a chapel
They left her bier.
There they surrounded
Her pale body
With yellow candles
And black stuffs.

At the last stroke
Of the ringing for the Souls,
An old crone finished
Her last prayers.
She crossed the narrow nave,
The doors moaned,
And the holy place
Remained deserted.

From a clock one heard
The measured ticking,
And from a candle
The guttering.
All things there
Were so dark and mournful,
So cold and rigid,

Que pensé un momento:
¡Dios mío, qué solos
Se quedan los muertos!

De la alta campana
La lengua de hierro,
Le dió, volteando,
Su adiós lastimero.
El luto en las ropas,
Amigos y deudos
Cruzaron en fila,
Formando el cortejo.

Del último asilo,
Oscuro y estrecho,
Abrió la piqueta
El nicho a un extremo.
Allí la acostaron,
Tapiáronle luego,
Y con un saludo
Despidióse el duelo.

La piqueta al hombro,
El sepulturero
Cantando entre dientes
Se perdió a lo lejos.
La noche se entraba,
Reinaba el silencio;
Perdido en las sombras,
Medité un momento:
¡Dios mío, qué solos
Se quedan los muertos!

En las largas noches
Del helado invierno,
Cuando las maderas
Crujir hace el viento
Y azota los vidrios
El fuerte aguacero,
De la pobre niña
A solas me acuerdo.

That I thought a moment :
My God, how lonely
The dead are!

From the high belfry
The tongue of iron
Clanged, giving out
A last farewell.
Crêpe on their clothes,
Her friends and kindred
Passed in a line
In homage to her.

In the last vault
Dark and narrow,
The pickaxe opened
A niche at one end;
They laid her away there.
Soon they bricked the place up,
And with a gesture
Bade grief farewell.

Pickaxe on shoulder
The gravedigger,
Singing between his teeth,
Passed out of sight.
The night came down,
It was all silent.
Alone in the darkness
I thought a moment,—
My God, how lonely
The dead are!

In the dark nights
Of bitter winter,
When the wind makes
The rafter creak,
When the violent rain
Lashes the windows,
Lonely I remember
That poor girl.

Allí cae la lluvia
Con un son eterno;
Allí la combate
El soplo del cierzo.
Del húmedo muro
Tendida en el hueco,
¡Acaso de frío
Se hielan sus huesos! . . .

¿Vuelve el polvo al polvo?
¿Vuela el alma al cielo?·
¿Todo es vil materia,
Podredumbre y cieno?
¡No sé; pero hay algo
Que explicar no puedo,
Que al par nos infunde
Repugnancia y miedo,
Al dejar tan triste,
Tan solos los muertos!

PEDRO ANTONIO DE ALARCÓN
[1833–1891]

An inspired and skilful teller of tales, the Andalusian Pedro Antonio de Alarcón wrote what has been termed the most perfect short story in all Spanish literature—El sombrero de tres picos (*1874*). *Closer to a novelette in length, it is based on the popular legend of the mayor and the miller's wife. The picaresque story is related in graceful, humorous style against a glowing*

EL SOMBRERO DE TRES PICOS

XI

EL BOMBARDEO DE PAMPLONA

—Dios te guarde, Frasquita . . . —dijo el corregidor a media voz, apareciendo bajo el emparrado y andando de puntillas.

—¡Tanto bueno, señor corregidor! —respondió en voz natural, haciéndole mil reverencias—. ¡Usía por aquí a estas horas! ¡Y con el calor que hace! ¡Vaya, siéntese su señoría! . . . Esto está fresquito. ¿Cómo no ha aguardado su señoría a los demás señores? Aquí tienen

There falls the rain
With its noise eternal,
There the northwind
Fights with the rain.
Stretched in the hollow
Of the damp bricks,
Perhaps her bones
Freeze with the cold.

Does the dust return to dust?
Does the soul fly to heaven?
Or is all vile matter,
Rottenness, filthiness?
I know not, but
There is something—something—
Something which gives me
Loathing, terror,—
To leave the dead
So alone, so wretched.

JOHN MASEFIELD

Andalusian background; its characters are so vividly delineated that they seem alive.

Besides the charming Sombrero de tres picos, *Alarcón wrote many excellent short stories and a number of long novels, of which the best is* El escándalo.

THE THREE-CORNERED HAT

CHAPTER XI

THE BOMBARDMENT OF PAMPELUNA

'God save you, Frasquita,' said the Corregidor, in a low tone, appearing under the grapevine and walking on tip-toe.

'Oh, Señor Corregidor, how good of you,' she replied in her usual tone of voice, making a deep curtsy. 'You Honour here at this time of day, and when it is so very warm! Well, well, please sit down here, Your Honour. It is cool here; why did not your Lordship wait for the other gentlemen. I have their seats all ready

ya preparados sus asientos . . . Esta tarde esperamos al señor obispo en persona, que le ha prometido a mi Lucas venir a probar las primeras uvas de la parra. ¿Y cómo lo pasa su señoría? ¿Cómo está la señora?

El corregidor se había turbado. La ansiada soledad en que encontraba a la señá Frasquita le parecía un sueño, o un lazo que le tendía la enemiga suerte para hacerle caer en el abismo de un desengaño. Limitóse, pues, a contestar:

—No es tan temprano como dices . . . Serán las tres y media. El loro dió en aquel momento un chillido.

—Son las dos y cuarto —dijo la navarra, mirando de hito en hito al madrileño.

Este calló, como reo convicto que renuncia a la defensa.

—¿Y Lucas? ¿Duerme? —preguntó al cabo de un rato.

(Debemos advertir aquí que el corregidor, lo mismo que todos los que no tienen dientes, hablaba con una pronunciación floja y silbante, como si se estuviese comiendo sus propios labios.)

—¡De seguro! —contestó la señá Frasquita—. En llegando estas horas se queda dormido donde primero le coge, aunque sea en el borde de un precipicio. . .

—Pues mira . . . ¡déjalo dormir! . . . —exclamó el viejo corregidor, poniéndose más pálido que lo que ya era—. Y tú, mi querida Frasquita, escúchame . . . , oye . . . ven acá . . . ¡Siéntate aquí; a mi lado! . . . Tengo muchas cosas que decirte . . .

—Ya estoy sentada —respondió la molinera, agarrando una silla baja y plantándola delante del corregidor, a cortísima distancia de la suya.

Sentado que se hubo, Frasquita echó una pierna sobre la otra, inclinó el cuerpo hacia delante, apoyó un codo sobre la rodilla cabalgadora, y la fresca y hermosa cara en una de sus manos; y así con la cabeza un poco ladeada, la sonrisa en los labios, los cinco hoyos en actividad, y las serenas pupilas clavadas en el corregidor, aguardó la declaración de su señoría. Hubiera podido comparársela con Pamplona esperando un bombardeo.

El pobre hombre fué a hablar, y se quedó con la boca abierta, embelesado ante aquella grandiosa hermosura, ante aquella esplendidez de gracias, ante aquella formidable mujer, de alabastrino color, de lujosas carnes, de limpia y riente boca, de azules e insondables ojos, que parecía creada por el pincel de Rubens.

for them. We expect the Lord Bishop himself this afternoon, who has promised my Luke to come to taste some of the first grapes off the vine. And how do you do? and how is your lady?'

The Corregidor was confused. He did desire to find Frasquita alone, but it seemed to him now like a dream, or else a snare spread by treacherous fate to decoy him into a yawning gulf of deception. He therefore only answered:

'It is not so early as you imagine it is. It is certainly half-past three.' Just then the parrot squawked the hour.

'It is exactly a quarter-past two!' said the Navarrese, staring at the Corregidor full in the face.

He kept silent like a convicted criminal who renounces his defence.

'And Luke? is he asleep?' he inquired after a short pause.

Now just at this point, we must tell you that the Corregidor, like all who have no teeth, spoke with a drivelling, hissing sound, as though he were chewing his own lips.

'Of course,' replied Señá Frasquita, 'usually at this time he falls asleep, wherever he may be, even if it were on the edge of a precipice.'

'Well, just let him sleep on,' exclaimed the Corregidor, turning even paler than usual. 'And you, my dear Frasquita, listen to me; hark ye, come here. Sit down by my side. I have a great deal to say to you.'

'There now, I'm ready,' replied the miller's wife, bringing a low chair, and putting it in front of the Corregidor at a very short distance from his own.

As soon as she was seated, Frasquita crossed one leg over the other, leaned forward, resting her elbow on her knee, which she kept trotting up and down; and leaning her fresh and lovely face on one of her hands; and so with her head bent a little to one side, a smile on her lips, her bodice provocatively gaping, the five dimples in full play, and her clear eyes fixed on the Corregidor, she waited to hear what he would say. You might have compared her, figuratively, to Pampeluna waiting for the bombardment.

The poor man tried to speak, but remained dumbfounded, with his mouth wide open, before the superb beauty of that formidable woman, with her exuberant charms, her alabaster-like complexion, her magnificent form, her overwhelming bosom, her lovely smiling lips, her deep, unfathomable blue eyes, and looking altogether like one of Rubens' creations.

—¡Frasquita! . . . —murmuró al fin el delegado del rey, con acento desfallecido mientras que su marchito rostro, cubierto de sudor, destacándose sobre su joroba, expresaba una inmensa angustia—. ¡Frasquita! . . .

—¡Me llamo! —contestó la hija de los Pirineos—. ¿Y qué?

—Lo que tú quieras . . . —repuso el viejo con una ternura sin límites.

—Pues lo que yo quiero . . . —dijo la molinera—, ya lo sabe usía. Lo que yo quiero es que usía nombre Secretario del Ayuntamiento de la ciudad a un sobrino mío que tengo en Estella . . . , y que así podrá venirse de aquellas montañas, donde está pasando muchos apuros . . .

—Te he dicho, Frasquita, que eso es imposible. El secretario actual . . .

—¡Es un ladrón, un borracho y un bestia!

—Ya lo sé . . . Pero tiene buenas aldabas entre los regidores perpetuos, y yo no puedo nombrar a otro sin acuerdo del Cabildo. De lo contrario, me expongo . . .

—¡Me expongo! . . . ¡Me expongo! . . . ¿A qué no nos expondríamos por vuestra señoría hasta los gatos de esta casa?

—¿Me querrías a ese precio? —tartamudeó el corregidor.

—No, señor; que lo quiero a usía de balde.

—¡Mujer, no me des tratamiento! Háblame de Vd. o como se te antoje . . . ¿Conque vas a quererme? Di.

—¿No le digo a Vd. que le quiero ya?

—Pero . . .

—No hay pero que valga. ¡Verá Vd. qué guapo y qué hombre de bien es mi sobrino!

—¡Tú sí que eres guapa, Frascuela! . . .

—¿Le gusto a Vd.?

—¡Que si me gustas! . . . ¡No hay mujer como tú!

—Pues mire Vd. . . . Aquí no hay nada postizo . . . —contestó la señá Frasquita, acabando de arrollar la manga de su jubón, y mostrando al corregidor el resto de su brazo, digno de una cariátide y más blanco que una azucena.

—¡Que si me gustas! . . . —prosiguió el corregidor—. ¡De día, de noche, a todas horas, en todas partes, sólo pienso en ti! . . .

—¡Pues qué! ¿No le gusta a Vd. la señora corregidora? —preguntó la señá Frasquita con tan mal fingida compasión, que hubiera hecho reír a un hipocondríaco—. ¡Qué lástima! Mi Lucas me ha dicho que tuvo el gusto de verla y de hablarle cuando fué a componerle a Vd. el reloj de la alcoba, y que es muy guapa, muy buena y de un trato cariñoso.

'Frasquita,' the King's Delegate murmured at last in a faint voice, while his wrinkled face, covered with perspiration rising above his hump, expressed the greatest anguish, 'Frasquita.'

'That's my name,' replied the daughter of the Pyrenees. 'Well, what is it?'

'Whatever you like,' replied the old man most tenderly.

'Well, your Honour already knows what I want. I want you to appoint my nephew in Estella as Secretary of the City Corporation, so that he may get away from those mountains where he is having such a hard time of it.'

'I told you, Frasquita, that it is quite impossible. The Secretary who now holds that office——'

'Is a thief, a drunkard, and a beast!'

'Yes, I know it, but he has a good hold on the Perpetual Alderman, and I cannot appoint a new one without the sanction of the City Corporation. If I did, I would run the risk of——'

'Would run the risk of! Would run the risk of! What wouldn't we risk for your Honour? yes, even to the cats in the house.'

'Would you like me at that price?' stuttered the old Corregidor.

'No, sir, for I love your Lordship gratis.'

'Child, do not treat me with so much formality, say simply—you—do not say your Lordship. Call me what you please. So you will like me? Say now.'

'Have I not already told you that I like you?'

'But.'

'But—there's no but worth a button. You'll see how handsome my nephew is, what an honest fellow he is!'

'You, indeed, are handsome, Frasquita.'

'Do you really like me?'

'Do I like you? There is no woman equal to you.'

'Well, see here, there's nothing false here,' replied Frasquita, rolling up her sleeve of her bodice, and displaying to the Corregidor the rest of her arm whiter than a lily, and a fit model for a sculptor.

'Do I like thee?' continued the Corregidor. 'By day and by night, at all hours, wherever I may be, I am thinking of thee.'

'How's that? Don't you like the Lady Mayoress?' inquired Señá Frasquita, with such poorly feigned compassion that it would have moved even a hypochondriac to mirth. 'What a pity! My Luke says that he had the pleasure of meeting her and talking with her, when he went to regulate the clock in your sleeping chamber, and that she is very beautiful, very good, and has very sweet manners.'

—¡No tanto! ¡No tanto! —murmuró el corregidor con cierta amargura.

—En cambio, otros me han dicho —prosiguió la molinera— que tiene muy mal genio, que es muy celosa, y que Vd. le tiembla más que a una vara verde...

—¡No tanto, mujer!... —repitió don Eugenio de Zúñiga y Ponce de León, poniéndose colorado—. ¡Ni tanto ni tan poco! La señora tiene sus manías, es cierto...; mas de ello a hacerme temblar, hay mucha diferencia. ¡Yo soy el corregidor!...

—Pero, en fin, ¿la quiere Vd., o no la quiere?

—Te diré... Yo la quiero mucho... o, por mejor decir, la quería antes de conocerte. Pero desde que te vi, no sé lo que me pasa, y ella misma conoce que me pasa algo... Bástete saber que hoy... tomarle, por ejemplo, la cara a mi mujer me hace la misma operación que si me la tomara a mí propio... Ya ves, que no puedo quererla más ni sentir menos!... ¡Mientras que por coger esa mano, ese brazo, esa cara, esa cintura, daría lo que no tengo!

Y, hablando así, el corregidor trató de apoderarse del brazo desnudo que la señá Frasquita le estaba refregando materialmente por los ojos; pero ésta, sin descomponerse, extendió la mano, tocó el pecho de Su Señoría con la pacífica violencia e incontrastable rigidez de la trompa de un elefante, y lo tiró de espaldas con silla y todo.

—¡Ave María Purísima! —exclamó entonces la navarra, riéndose a más no poder—. Por lo visto, esa silla estaba rota...

—¿Qué pasa ahí? —exclamó en esto el tío Lucas, asomando su feo rostro entre los pámpanos de la parra.

El corregidor estaba todavía en el suelo boca arriba, y miraba con un terror indecible a aquel hombre que aparecía en los aires boca abajo.

Hubiérase dicho que Su Señoría era el diablo, vencido, no por San Miguel, sino por otro demonio del infierno.

—¿Qué ha de pasar? —se apresuró a responder la señá Frasquita—. ¡Que el señor corregidor puso la silla en vago, fué a mecerse, y se ha caído!...

—¡Jesús, María y José! —exclamó a su vez el molinero—. ¿Y se ha hecho daño Su Señoría? ¿Quiere un poco de agua y vinagre?

—¡No me he hecho nada! —dijo el corregidor, levantándose como pudo.

Y luego añadió por lo bajo, pero de modo que pudiera oírlo la señá Frasquita:

'Not quite, not quite,' murmured the Corregidor, with a certain degree of bitterness.

'On the other hand, some say,' added the miller's wife, 'that she has a bad temper, and is very jealous, and that you fear her more than a green switch.'

'Not quite, my girl,' replied Don Eugene de Zuñiga Ponce de Leon, turning red. 'Not so much, nor so little. My lady has her whims, it's true, but that she makes me quake with fear is a very different matter. I am the Corregidor.'

'But, in short, do you love her or not?'

'I'll tell you the truth. I love her a great deal, or I should say, I did before I knew you. But since I saw you I don't know what is the matter with me, and she herself knows that something ails me. You must know, for instance, to caress my wife's face would not affect me more than if I touched my own. So you see, I cannot like her more, nor feel less, while just to touch your hand, your arm, your waist, I would give what I have not got.'

So saying the Corregidor attempted to seize the bare arm which Frasquita was actually rubbing into his eyes, but she, without losing her self-possession in the least, extended her hand, just touched his Lordship's chest with the pacific force and incomparable rigidity of an elephant's trunk, and threw him sprawling on the ground, chair and all.

'*Ave Maria Purisima!*' exclaimed the Navarrese, laughing until she could laugh no longer. 'It seems that chair must have been broken.'

'What's going on down there?' just at this moment exclaimed Uncle Luke, with his homely face looming out among the leaves and the tendrils of the grapevine. The Corregidor was still lying on his back on the ground, and looked up with unutterable fear at the man who now appeared suspended in the air face downward. One might say that his Honour was the devil conquered not by St. Michael, but by some fiend from the infernal regions.

'What's going on?' answered Frasquita briskly. 'Why, the Señor Corregidor went to balance his chair on nothing, went to rock on it, and over he fell!'

'Jesus, Mary and Joseph!' piously exclaimed the miller. 'And has his Honour hurt himself? Do you want some vinegar and water?'

'Oh, no, I have not hurt myself,' said the Corregidor, getting up as well as he could, while he added in a low tone, but so that Frasquita could hear him:

—¡Me la pagaréis!

—Pues, en cambio, Su Señoría me ha salvado a mí la vida —repuso el tío Lucas sin moverse de lo alto de la parra—. Figúrate, mujer, que estaba yo aquí sentado contemplando las uvas, cuando me quedé dormido sobre una red de sarmientos y palos que dejaban claros suficientes para que pasase mi cuerpo . . . Por consiguiente, si la caída de Su Señoría no me hubiese despertado tan a tiempo, esta tarde me habría yo roto la cabeza contra esas piedras.

—Conque sí . . . ¿eh? . . . replicó el corregidor—. Pues, ¡vaya, hombre! me alegro . . . ¡Te digo que me alegro mucho de haberme caído!

—¡Me la pagarás —agregó en seguida, dirigiéndose a la molinera.

Y pronunció estas palabras con tal expresión de reconcentrada furia, que la señá Frasquita se puso triste.

Veía claramente que el corregidor se asustó al principio, creyendo que el molinero lo había oído todo; pero que, persuadido ya de que no había oído nada (pues la calma y el disimulo del tío Lucas hubieran engañado al más lince), empezaba a abandonarse a toda su iracundia y a concebir planes de venganza.

—¡Vamos! ¡Bájate ya de ahí, y ayúdame a limpiar a Su Señoría, que se ha puesto perdido de polvo! —exclamó entonces la molinera.

Y, mientras el tío Lucas bajaba, díjole ella al corregidor, dándole golpes con el delantal en la chupa y alguno que otro en las orejas:

—El pobre no ha oído nada . . . Estaba dormido como un tronco . . .

Más que estas frases, la circunstancia de haber sido dichas en voz baja, afectando complicidad y secreto, produjo un efecto maravilloso.

—¡Pícara! ¡Proterva! —balbuceó don Eugenio de Zúñiga con la boca hecha un agua, pero gruñendo todavía. . .

—¿Me guardará usía rencor? —replicó la navarra zalameramente.

Viendo el corregidor que la severidad le daba buenos resultados, intentó mirar a la señá Frasquita con mucha rabia; pero se encontró con su tentadora risa y sus divinos ojos, en los cuales brillaba la caricia de una súplica, y, derritiéndosele la gacha en el acto, le dijo con un acento baboso y silbante, en que se descubría más que nunca la ausencia total de dientes y muelas.

—¡De ti depende, amor mío!

En aquel momento se descolgó de la parra el tío Lucas.

'You'll pay for this.'

'But, then, on the other hand, his Honour saved my life,' added the miller, without moving from his perch, 'Just imagine, wife, I was seated up here, gazing at the grapes, when I fell asleep on a network of twigs and stalks, which left an opening big enough for my body to fall through. So if you had not awakened me by your fall, just as you did, I might have broken my head against those stones.'

'Is that so? Eh,' replied the Corregidor; 'well, I am glad of it, I assure you. I am really glad that I fell down.'

'I'll pay you up for this,' he added immediately after, addressing the miller's wife.

He pronounced these words with such an expression of concentrated rage that Frasquita immediately became serious. She perceived that the Corregidor had got frightened at first, thinking that the miller had overheard all, but since he was convinced now that he had not, for Uncle Luke's dissimulation would have disarmed the most suspicious being, he began to give way to his passion and try to devise some means of revenging himself.

'Come now, get down from there and help me brush his Honour, for he is covered with dust,' exclaimed Frasquita.

While Uncle Luke was getting down from the trellis, she remarked to the Corregidor, brushing his coat with her apron and, in her zeal, occasionally giving him some hard cuffs over the ears :

'The poor fellow did not hear anything. He was as sound asleep as a log.' The very fact that she uttered these words in a low tone, more than the words themselves, pretending to have a secret understanding with him, produced a most marvellous effect.

'You rogue, you sly kitten,' stammered Don Eugene de Zuñiga, with his mouth watering, but still grunting.

'Do you still feel angry with me?' asked Frasquita coaxingly.

As the Corregidor noticed that his severity produced a good effect, he tried to look at her with anger; but when he met her bewitching smile, her heavenly eyes gazing at him so imploringly, his ire melted at once, and he said with a drivelling and hissing accent, displaying more than ever his total lack of teeth :

'It all depends on you, my darling—' Now at this particular moment, down dropped Uncle Luke from the grapevine trellis.

MARY J. SERRANO

JUAN VALERA
[1824–1905]

Juan Valera combined a distinguished diplomatic career with that of a dedicated littérateur. *An exponent of 'art for art's sake', he excelled in the field of literary criticism. But he is most famous for his penetrating psychological novel,* Pepita Jiménez (*1874*).

PEPITA JIMÉNEZ

19 de mayo.

Gracias a Dios y a usted por las nuevas cartas y nuevos consejos que me envía. Hoy los necesito más que nunca.

Razón tiene la mística doctora Santa Teresa cuando pondera los grandes trabajos de las almas tímidas que se dejan turbar por la tentación; pero es mil veces más trabajoso el desengaño para quienes han sido, como yo, confiados y soberbios.

Templos del Espíritu Santo son nuestros cuerpos, mas si se arrima fuego a sus paredes, aunque no ardan, se tiznan.

La primera sugestión es la cabeza de la serpiente. Si no la hollamos con planta valerosa y segura, el ponzoñoso repitil sube a esconderse en nuestro seno.

El licor de los deleites mundanos, por inocentes que sean, suele ser dulce al paladar, y luego se trueca en hiel de dragones y veneno de áspides.

Es cierto; ya no puedo negárselo a usted. Yo no debí poner los ojos con tanta complacencia en esta mujer peligrosísima.

No me juzgo perdido, pero me siento conturbado.

Como el corzo sediento desea y busca el manantial de las aguas, así mi alma busca a Dios todavía. A Dios se vuelve para que le dé reposo, y anhela beber en el torrente de sus delicias, cuyo ímpetu alegra el Paraíso, y cuyas ondas claras ponen más blanco que la nieve; pero un abismo llama a otro abismo, y mis pies se han clavado en el cieno que está en el fondo.

Sin embargo, aun me quedan voz y aliento para clamar con el Salmista: ¡Levántate, gloria mía! Si te pones de mi lado, ¿quién prevalecerá contra mí?

The first part of the novel consists of letters from a young seminary student, Don Luis, to his uncle. The youth's character reveals itself in the course of these letters, and Valera masterfully depicts his hero's panic as he becomes aware of his perilous situation. Valera's prose is faultless; his style, almost classic in feeling.

PEPITA JIMÉNEZ

LETTERS FROM DON LUIS TO HIS UNCLE

May 19th.

I return thanks to Heaven and to you for the letters and the counsels you have lately sent me. Today I need them more than ever.

The mystical and learned St. Theresa is right in dwelling upon the suffering of timid souls that allow themselves to be disturbed by temptation; but a thousand times worse than that suffering is the awakening from error of those who, like me, have permitted themselves to indulge in arrogance and self-confidence.

Our bodies are the temples of the Holy Spirit; but when fire is set to the walls of the temple, though they do not burn, yet they are blackened.

The first evil thought is the head of the serpent; if we do not crush it with firm and courageous foot, then will the venomous reptile climb up and hide himself in our bosom.

The nectar of earthly joys, however innocent they be, is sweet to the taste; but afterward it is converted into gall, and into the venom of the serpent.

It is true—I can no longer deny it to you—I ought not to have allowed my eyes to rest with so much complacency on this dangerous woman.

I do not deem myself lost; but I feel my soul troubled.

Even as the thirsty hart desires and seeks the water-brooks, so does my soul still seek God. To God does it turn that He may give it rest; it longs to drink at the torrent of His delights, whose gushing waters rejoice Paradise, and whose clear waves can wash us whiter than snow; but deep calleth unto deep, and my feet have stuck fast in the mire that is hidden in their abysses.

Yet have I still breath and voice to cry out with the psalmist: 'Arise, my joy! If thou art on my side, who shall prevail against me?'

Yo digo a mi alma pecadora, llena de quiméricas imaginaciones y de vagos deseos, que son sus hijos bastardos: ¡Oh, hija miserable de Babilonia, bienaventurado el que te dará tu galardón; bienaventurado el que deshará contra las piedras a tus pequeñuelos! Las mortificaciones, el ayuno, la oración y la penitencia serán las armas de que me revista para combatir y vencer con el auxilio divino.

No era sueño, no era locura; era realidad. Ella me mira a veces con la ardiente mirada de que ya he hablado a usted. Sus ojos están dotados de una atracción magnética inexplicable. Me atrae, me seduce, y se fijan en ella los míos. Mis ojos deben arder entonces, como los suyos, con una llama funesta; como los de Amón cuando se fijaban en Tamar; como los del príncipe de Siquén cuando se fijaban en Dina.

Al mirarnos así, hasta de Dios me olvido. La imagen de ella se levanta en el fondo de mi espíritu, vencedora de todo. Su hermosura resplandece sobre toda hermosura; los deleites del cielo me parecen inferiores a su cariño; una eternidad de penas creo que no paga la bienaventuranza infinita que vierte sobre mí en un momento con una de estas miradas, que pasan cual relámpago.

Cuando vuelvo a casa, cuando me quedo solo en mi cuarto, en el silencio de la noche, reconozco todo el horror de mi situación y formo buenos propósitos, que luego se quebrantan.

Me prometo a mí mismo fingirme enfermo, buscar cualquier otro pretexto para no ir a la noche siguiente a casa de Pepita, y sin embargo voy.

Mi padre, confiado hasta lo sumo, sin sospechar lo que pasa en mi alma, me dice cuando llega la hora:

—Vete a la tertulia. Yo iré más tarde, luego que despache al aperador.

Yo no atino con la excusa, no hallo el pretexto y en vez de contestar: —No puedo ir—, tomo el sombrero y voy a la tertulia.

Al entrar, Pepita y yo nos damos la mano, y al dárnosla me hechiza. Todo mi ser se muda. Penetra hasta mi corazón un fuego devorante, y ya no pienso más que en ella. Tal vez soy yo mismo quien provoca las miradas si tardan en llegar. La miro con insano ahinco, por un estímulo irresistible, y a cada instante creo descubrir en ella nuevas perfecciones. Ya los hoyuelos de sus mejillas cuando sonríe, ya la blancura sonrosada de la tez, ya la forma recta de la nariz, ya la pequeñez de la oreja, ya la suavidad de contornos y admirable modelado de la garganta.

I say unto my sinful soul, full of the chimerical imaginings and sinful desires engendered by unlawful thoughts : 'Oh, miserable daughter of Babylon! happy shall he be who shall give thee thy reward! Happy shall he be that dasheth thy little ones against the stones!'

Works of penance, fasting, prayer, and penitence, are the weapons wherewith I shall arm myself to the combat, and, with the Divine help, to vanquish.

It was not a dream, it was not madness; it was the truth. She lets her eyes rest upon me at times with the ardent glance of which I have told you. There is in her glance an inexplicable magnetic attraction. It draws me on, it seduces me, and I cannot withdraw my gaze from her. On such occasions my eyes must burn, like hers, with a fatal flame, as did those of Ammon when he turned them upon Tamar, as did those of the prince of Shechem when they were fixed upon Dinah.

When our glances thus meet, I forget even God. Her image rises up within my soul, the conqueror of everything. Her beauty outshines all other beauty; the joys of heaven seem to me less desirable than her affection. An eternity of suffering would be little in exchange for a moment of the infinite bliss with which one of those glances which pass like lightning inundates my soul.

When I return home, when I am alone in my room, in the silence of the night, I realize all the horror of my position, and I form good resolutions, only to break them again.

I resolve to feign sickness, to make use of any pretext so as not to go to Pepita's on the following night, and yet I go.

My father, confiding to the last degree, says to me when the hour arrives, without any suspicion of what is passing in my soul :

'Go to Pepita's; I will go later, when I have finished with the overseer.'

No excuse occurs to me; I can find no pretext for not going, and instead of answering, 'I cannot go,' I take my hat and depart.

On entering the room I shake hands with Pepita, and as our hands touch she casts a spell over me; my whole being is changed; a devouring fire penetrates my heart, and I think only of her. Moved by an irresistible impulse, I gaze at her with insane ardour, and at every instant I think I discover in her new perfections. Now it is the dimples in her cheeks when she smiles, now the roseate whiteness of her skin, now the straight outline of her nose, now the smallness of her ear, now the softness of contour and the admirable modelling of her throat.

Entro en su casa, a pesar mío, como evocado por un conjuro; y, no bien entro en su casa, caigo bajo el poder de su encanto; veo claramente que estoy dominado por una maga cuya fascinación es ineluctable.

No es ella grata a mis ojos solamente, sino que sus palabras suenan en mis oídos como la música de las esferas, revelándome toda la armonía del universo, y hasta imagino percibir una sutilísima fragancia que su limpio cuerpo despide, y que supera al olor de los mastranzos que crecen a orillas de los arroyos y al aroma silvestre del tomillo que en los montes se cría.

Excitado de esta suerte, no sé cómo juego al tresillo, ni hablo, ni discurro con juicio, porque estoy todo en ella.

Cada vez que se encuentran nuestras miradas se lanzan en ellas nuestras almas, y en los rayos que se cruzan se me figura que se unen y compenetran. Allí se descubren mil inefables misterios de amor, allí se comunican sentimientos que por otro medio no llegarían a saberse, y se citan poesías que no caben en lengua humana, y se cantan canciones que no hay voz que exprese ni acordada cítara que module.

Desde el día en que vi a Pepita en el Pozo de la Solana, no he vuelto a verla a solas. Nada le he dicho ni me ha dicho, y, sin embargo, nos lo hemos dicho todo.

Cuando me sustraigo a la fascinación cuando estoy solo por la noche en mi aposento, quiero mirar con frialdad el estado en que me hallo, y veo abierto a mis pies el precipicio en que voy a sumirme, y siento que me resbalo y que me hundo.

Me recomienda usted que piense en la muerte; no en la de esta mujer, sino en la mía. Me recomienda usted que piense en lo instable, en lo inseguro de nuestra existencia y en lo que hay más allá. Pero esta consideración y esta meditación ni me atemorizan ni me arredran. ¿Cómo he de temer la muerte cuando deseo morir? El amor y la muerte son hermanos. Un sentimiento de abnegación se alza de las profundidades de mi ser, y me llama a sí, y me dice que todo mi ser debe darse y perderse por el objeto amado. Ansío confundirme en una de sus miradas; diluir y evaporar toda mi esencia en el rayo de luz que sale de sus ojos, quedarme muerto mirándola, aunque me condene.

Lo que es aún eficaz en mí contra el amor, no es temor, sino el amor mismo. Sobre este amor determinado, que ya veo con evidencia que Pepita me inspira, se levanta en mi espíritu el amor divino en consurrección poderosa. Entonces todo se cambia en mí, y aun me prometo la victoria. El objeto de mi amor superior se ofrece a

I enter her house against my will, as though summoned there by a conjurer, and no sooner am I there than I fall under the spell of her enchantment. I see clearly that I am in the power of an enchantress whose fascination is irresistible.

Not only is she pleasing to my sight, but her words sound in my ears like the music of the spheres, revealing to my soul the harmony of the universe; and I even fancy that a subtle fragrance emanates from her, sweeter than the perfume of the mint that grows by the brookside, or the woodlike odour of the thyme that is found among the hills.

I know not how, in this state of exaltation, I am able to play *ombre*, or to converse rationally, or even to speak, so completely am I absorbed in her.

When our eyes meet, our souls rush forth in them and seem to join and interpenetrate each other. In that meeting a thousand feelings are communicated that in no other way could be made known; poems are recited that could be uttered in no human tongue, and songs are sung that no human voice could sing, and no guitar accompany.

Since the day I met Pepita by the Pozo de la Solana I have not seen her alone. Not a word has passed between us, yet we have told each other everything.

When I withdraw myself from this fascination, when I am again alone at night in my chamber, I set myself to examine coolly the situation in which I am placed; I see the abyss that is about to engulf me yawning before me; I feel my feet slip from under me, and that I am sinking into it.

You counsel me to reflect upon death—not on the death of this woman, but on my own. You counsel me to reflect on the instability, on the insecurity of our existence, and on what there is beyond it. But these considerations, these reflections neither terrify nor daunt me. Why should I, who desire to die, fear death? Love and death are brothers. A sentiment of self-abnegation springs to life within me, and tells me that my whole being should be consecrated to and annihilated in the beloved object. I long to merge myself in one of her glances; to diffuse and exhale my whole being in the ray of light shot forth from her eyes; to die while gazing on her, even though I should be eternally lost.

What is still to some extent efficacious with me against this love is not fear, but love itself. Superior to this deep-rooted love with which I now have evidence that Pepita inspires me, Divine love exalts itself in my spirit in mighty uprising. Then everything is changed within me, and I feel that I may yet obtain the victory.

los ojos de mi mente como el sol que todo lo enciende y alumbra, llenando de luz los espacios; y el objeto de mi amor, más bajo, como átomo de polvo que vaga en el ambiente y que el sol dora. Toda su beldad, todo su resplandor y todo su atractivo no es más que el reflejo de ese sol increado, no es más que la chispa brillante, transitoria, inconsistente de aquella infinita y perenne hoguera.

Mi alma, abrasada de amor, pugna por criar alas, y tender el vuelo, y subir a esa hoguera, y consumir allí cuanto hay en ella de impuro.

Mi vida, desde hace algunos días, es una lucha constante. No sé cómo el mal que padezco no me sale a la cara. Apenas me alimento; apenas duermo. Si el sueño cierra mis párpados, suelo despertar azorado, como si me hallase peleando en una batalla de ángeles rebeldes y de ángeles buenos. En esta batalla de la luz contra las tinieblas, yo combato por la luz; pero tal vez imagino que me paso al enemigo, que soy un desertor infame; y oigo la voz del águila de Patmos que dice: 'Y los hombres prefirieron las tinieblas a la luz'; y entonces me lleno de terror y me juzgo perdido.

No me queda más recurso que huir. Si en lo que falta para terminar el mes mi padre no me da su venia y no viene conmigo, me escapo como un ladrón; me fugo sin decir nada.

23 *de mayo.*

Soy un vil gusano, y no un hombre; soy el oprobio y la abyección de la humanidad; soy un hipócrita.

Me han circundado dolores de muerte, y torrentes de iniquidad me han conturbado.

Vergüenza tengo de escribir a usted, y no obstante le escribo. Quiero confesárselo todo.

No logro enmendarme. Lejos de dejar de ir a casa de Pepita, voy más temprano todas las noches. Se diría que los demonios me agarran de los pies y me llevan allá sin que yo quiera.

Por dicha, no hallo sola nunca a Pepita. No quisiera hallarla sola. Casi siempre se me adelanta el excelente padre Vicario, que atribuye nuestra amistad a la semejanza de gustos piadosos, y la funda en la devoción, como la amistad inocentísima que él le profesa.

El progreso de mi mal es rápido. Como piedra que se desprende de lo alto del templo y va aumentando su velocidad en la caída, así mi espíritu ahora.

The object of my higher love presents itself to my mental vision, as the sun that kindles and illuminates all things, and fills all space with light; and the object of my inferior love appears but as an atom of dust floating in the sunbeam. All her beauty, all her splendour, all her attractions are nothing but the reflection of this uncreated sun, the brilliant, transitory, fleeting spark that is cast off from that infinite and inexhaustible fire.

My soul, burning with love, would fain take itself wings and rise to that flame, in order that all that is impure within it might be consumed therein.

My life, for some days past, is a constant struggle. I know not how it is that the malady which I suffer does not betray itself in my countenance. I scarcely eat, I scarcely sleep; and if by chance sleep closes my eyelids, I awake in terror, as from a dream in which rebel angels are arrayed against good angels, and in which I am one of the combatants. In this conflict of light against darkness I do battle for the right, but I sometimes imagine that I have gone over to the enemy, that I am a vile deserter; and I hear a voice from Patmos saying, 'And men loved darkness rather than light'; and then I am filled with terror, and I look upon myself as lost.

No recourse is left me but flight. If, before the end of the month, my father does not go with me, or consent to my going alone, I shall steal away like a thief, without a word to any one.

May 23rd.

I am a vile worm, not a man; I am the opprobrium and disgrace of humanity. I am a hypocrite.

I have been encompassed by the pangs of death, and the waters of iniquity have passed over me.

I am ashamed to write to you, and yet I write. I desire to confess everything to you.

I can not turn away from evil. Far from abstaining from going to Pepita's, I go there each night earlier than the last. It would seem as if devils took me by the feet and carried me there against my will!

Happily, I never find Pepita alone; I do not desire to find her alone. I almost always find the excellent vicar there before me, who attributes our friendship to similarity of feeling in religious matters, and bases it on piety, like the pure and innocent friendship he himself entertains for her.

The progress of my malady is rapid. Like the stone that is loosened from the mountain-top and gathers force as it falls, so is it with my spirit.

Cuando Pepita y yo nos damos la mano, no es ya como al principio. Ambos hacemos un esfuerzo de voluntad y nos transmitimos, por nuestras diestras enlazadas, todas las palpitaciones del corazón. Se diría que, por arte diabólico, obramos una transfusión y mezcla de lo más sutil de nuestra sangre. Ella debe de sentir circular mi vida por sus venas, como yo siento en las mías la suya.

Si estoy cerca de ella, la amo; si estoy lejos, la odio. A su vista, en su presencia, me enamora, me atrae, me rinde con suavidad, me pone un yugo dulcísimo.

Su recuerdo me mata. Soñando con ella, sueño que me divide la garganta, como Judit al capitán de los asirios, o que me atraviesa las sienes con un clavo, como Jael a Sisara; pero a su lado, me parece la esposa del *Cantar de los Cantares*, y la llamo con voz interior, y la bendigo, y la juzgo fuente sellada, huerto cerrado, flor del valle, lirio de los campos, paloma mía y hermana.

Quiero libertarme de esta mujer y no puedo. La aborrezco y casi la adoro. Su espíritu se infunde en mí al punto que la veo, y me posee, y me domina, y me humilla.

Todas las noches salgo de su casa diciendo: 'Esta será la última noche que vuelvo aquí', y vuelvo a la noche siguiente.

Cuando habla, y estoy a su lado, mi alma queda como colgada de su boca; cuando sonríe, se me antoja que un rayo de luz inmaterial se me entra en el corazón y le alegra.

A veces, jugando al tresillo, se han tocado por acaso nuestras rodillas, y he sentido un indescriptible sacudimiento.

Sáqueme usted de aquí. Escriba usted a mi padre que me dé licencia para irme. Si es menester, dígaselo todo. ¡Socórrame usted! ¡Sea usted mi amparo!

BENITO PÉREZ GALDÓS
[1843-1920]

The great master of the modern Spanish novel is Benito Pérez Galdós, born in the Canary Islands. He delved into painting and law as a young man, but soon dedicated himself entirely to writing, publishing his first novel at the age of twenty-seven. Until his death in 1920 he wrote unceasingly and prodigiously, despite blindness in his later years.

The universal appeal of his works combined with their brilliant execution has given Pérez Galdós a place unique in contemporary Spanish literature.

When Pepita and I shake hands, it is not now as at first. Each one of us, by an effort of the will, transmits to the other, through the handclasp, every throb of the heart. It is as if, by some diabolical art, we had effected a transfusion and a blending together of the most subtle elements of our blood. She must feel my life circulate through her veins, as I feel hers in mine.

When I am near her, I love her; when I am away from her, I hate her. When I am in her presence she inspires me with love; she draws me to her; she subjugates me with gentleness; she lays upon me a very easy yoke.

But the recollection of her undoes me. When I dream of her, I dream that she is severing my head from my body, as Judith slew the captain of the Assyrians; or that she is driving a nail into my temple, as Jael did to Sisera. But when I am near her, she appears to me the Spouse of the Song of Songs, and a voice within me calls to her and I bless her, and I regard her as a sealed fountain, as an enclosed garden, as the flower of the valley, as the lily of the fields, my dove and my sister.

I desire to free myself from her, and I cannot. I abhor, yet I almost worship her. Her spirit enters into me and takes possession of me as soon as I behold her; it subjugates me, it abases me.

I leave her house each night, saying, 'This is the last night I shall return here'; and I return there on the following night!

When she speaks, and I am near, my soul hangs, as it were, upon her words. When she smiles, I imagine that a ray of spiritual light enters into my heart and rejoices it.

It has happened, when playing *ombre*, that our knees have touched by chance, and then I have felt a thrill run through me impossible to describe.

Get me away from this place. Write to my father and ask him to let me return to you. If it be necessary, tell him everything. Help me! Be my refuge!

MARY J. SERRANO

No other modern novelist has been so widely read by all classes of people and at the same time been so admired by critics. His voluminous production includes thirty novels, forty-six episodios nacionales (*semi-historical novels which range in period from the battle of Trafalgar, 1805, to the end of the nineteenth century), twenty-two dramas and numerous short stories.*

A crusading reformer, Galdós consistently defends the liberal side of social problems. One of his best novels, Doña Perfecta, *depicts the evils of religious fanaticism, personified by the character of a strong and ruthless woman.*

DOÑA PERFECTA

IX

La Desavenencia Sigue Creciendo y Amenaza Convertirse en Discordia

.... Doña Perfecta y el señor don Cayetano aparecieron frente a los cuatro.

—¡Qué hermosa está la tarde! —dijo la señora—. ¿Qué tal, sobrino, te aburres mucho? ...

—Nada de eso, —repuso el joven.

—No me lo niegues. De eso veníamos hablando Cayetano y yo. Tú estás aburrido, y te empeñas en disimularlo. No todos los jóvenes de estos tiempos tienen la abnegación de pasar su juventud, como Jacinto, en un pueblo donde no hay teatro Real, ni bufos, ni bailarinas, ni filósofos, ni Ateneos, ni papeluchos, ni Congresos, ni otras diversiones y pasatiempos.

—Yo estoy aquí muy bien —replicó Pepe—. Ahora le estaba diciendo a Rosario que esta ciudad y esta casa me son tan agradables, que me gustaría vivir y morir aquí.

Rosario se puso muy encendida, y los demás callaron. Sentáronse todos en una glorieta, apresurándose Jacinto a ocupar el lugar a la izquierda de la señorita.

—Mira, sobrino, tengo que advertirte una cosa —dijo doña Perfecta, con aquella risueña expresión de bondad que emanaba de su alma, como de la flor el aroma—. Pero no vayas a creer que te reprendo, ni que te doy lecciones: tú no eres niño, y fácilmente comprenderás mis ideas.

—Ríñame usted, querida tía, que sin duda lo mereceré, —replicó Pepe, que ya empezaba a acostumbrarse a las bondades de la hermana de su padre.

—No, no es más que una advertencia. Estos señores verán cómo tengo razón.

Rosarito oía con toda su alma.

—Pues no es más —añadió la señora—, sino que cuando vuelvas a visitar nuestra hermosa catedral, procures estar en ella con un poco más de recogimiento.

—Pero ¿qué he hecho yo?

—No extraño que tú mismo no conozcas tu falta —indicó la señora con aparente jovialidad—. Es natural: acostumbrado a entrar con la mayor desenvoltura en los ateneos, clubs, academias

DOÑA PERFECTA

The Disagreement Continued to Increase and Threatened to Become Discord

...Doña Perfecta and Señor Don Cayetano at this moment made their appearance.

'What a beautiful evening!' said the former. 'Well, nephew, are you getting terribly bored?'

'I am not bored in the least,' responded the young man.

'Don't try to deny it. Cayetano and I were speaking of that as we came along. You are bored, and you are trying to hide it. It is not every young man of the present day who would have the self-denial to spend his youth, like Jacinto, in a town where there are neither theatres, nor opera bouffe, nor dancers, nor philosophers, nor athenaeums, nor magazines, nor congresses, nor any other kind of diversions or entertainments.'

'I am quite contented here,' responded Pepe. 'I was just now saying to Rosario that I find this city and this house so pleasant that I would like to live and die here.'

Rosario turned very red and the others were silent. They all sat down in a summer-house, Jacinto hastening to take the seat on the left of the young girl.

'See here, nephew, I have a piece of advice to give you,' said Doña Perfecta, smiling with that expression of kindness that seemed to emanate from her soul, like the aroma from the flower. 'But don't imagine that I am either reproving you or giving you a lesson —you are not a child, and you will easily understand what I mean.'

'Scold me, dear aunt, for no doubt I deserve it,' replied Pepe, who was beginning to accustom himself to the kindnesses of his father's sister.

'No, it is only a piece of advice. These gentlemen, I am sure, will agree that I am in the right.'

Rosario was listening with her whole soul.

'It is only this,' continued Doña Perfecta, 'that when you visit our beautiful cathedral again, you will endeavour to behave with a little more decorum while you are in it.'

'Why, what have I done?'

'It does not surprise me that you are not yourself aware of your fault,' said his aunt, with apparent good humour. 'It is only natural; accustomed as you are to enter athenaeums and clubs,

y congresos, crees que de la misma manera se puede entrar en un templo donde está la Divina Majestad.

—Pero, señora, dispénseme usted —dijo Pepe con gravedad—. Yo he entrado en la catedral con la mayor compostura.

—Si no te riño, hombre, si no te riño. No lo tomes así, porque tendré que callarme. Señores, disculpen ustedes a mi sobrino. No es de extrañar un descuidillo, una distracción . . . ¿Cuántos años hace que no pones los pies en lugar sagrado?

—Señora, yo juro a usted . . . Pero en fin, mis ideas religiosas podrán ser lo que quiera; pero acostumbro guardar compostura dentro de la iglesia.

—Lo que yo aseguro . . . vamos, si te has de ofender no sigo . . . lo que aseguro es que muchas personas lo advirtieron esta mañana. Notáronlo los señores de González, doña Robustiana, Serafinita, en fin . . . con decirte que llamaste la atención del señor Obispo . . . Su Ilustrísima me dió las quejas esta tarde en casa de mis primas. Díjome que no te mandó plantar en la calle porque le dijeron que eras sobrino mío.

Rosario contemplaba con angustia el rostro de su primo, procurando adivinar sus contestaciones antes que las diera. ·

—Sin duda me han tomado por otro.

—No . . . no . . . Fuiste tú . . . Pero no vayas a ofenderte, que aquí estamos entre amigos y personas de confianza. Fuiste tú, yo misma te vi.

—¡Usted!

—Justamente. ¿Negarás que te pusiste a examinar las pinturas, pasando por un grupo de fieles que estaban oyendo misa . . . ? Te juro que me distraje de tal modo con tus idas y venidas, que . . . Vamos . . . es preciso que no vuelvas a hacerlo. Luego entraste en la capilla de San Gregorio; alzaron en el altar mayor, y ni siquiera te volviste para hacer una demostración de religiosidad. Después atravesaste de largo a largo la iglesia, te acercaste al sepulcro del Adelantado, pusiste las manos sobre el altar, pasaste en seguida otra vez por entre el grupo de los fieles, llamando la atención. Todas las muchachas te miraban, y tú parecías satisfecho de perturbar tan lindamente la devoción y ejemplaridad de aquella buena gente.

—¡Dios mío! ¡Cuántas abominaciones! . . . —exclamó Pepe, entre enojado y risueño—. Soy un monstruo, y ni siquiera lo sospechaba.

—No, bien sé que eres un buen muchacho —dijo doña Perfecta,

and academies and congresses without any ceremony, you think that you can enter a temple in which the Divine Majesty is in the same manner.'

'But excuse me, señora,' said Pepe gravely, 'I entered the cathedral with the greatest decorum.'

'But I am not scolding you, man; I am not scolding you. If you take it in that way I shall have to remain silent. Excuse my nephew, gentlemen. A little carelessness, a little heedlessness on his part is not to be wondered at. How many years is it since you set foot in a sacred place before?

'What I assure you is—— There, if you are going to be offended I won't go on. What I assure you is that a great many people noticed it this morning. The Señores de González, Doña Robustiana, Serafinita—in short, when I tell you that you attracted the attention of the bishop—— His lordship complained to me about it this afternoon when I was at my cousin's. He told me that he did not order you to be put out of the church only because you were my nephew.'

Rosario looked anxiously at her cousin, trying to read in his countenance, before he uttered it, the answer he would make to these charges.

'No doubt they mistook me for some one else.'

'No, no! it was you. But there, don't get angry! We are talking here among friends and in confidence. It was you. I saw you myself.'

'You saw me!'

'Just so. Will you deny that you went to look at the pictures, passing among a group of worshippers who were hearing mass? I assure you that my attention was so distracted by your comings and goings that—well, you must not do it again. Then you went into the chapel of San Gregorio. At the elevation of the Host at the high altar you did not even turn around to make a gesture of reverence. Afterward you traversed the whole length of the church, you went up to the tomb of the Adelantado, you touched the altar with your hands, then you passed a second time among the group of worshippers, attracting the notice of every one. All the girls looked at you, and you seemed pleased at disturbing so finely the devotions of those good people.'

'Good Heavens! How many things I have done!' exclaimed Pepe, half angry, half amused. 'I am a monster, it seems, without ever having suspected it.'

'No, I am very well aware that you are a good boy,' said Doña

observando el semblante afectadamente serio e inmutable del canónigo, que parecía tener por cara una máscara de cartón—. Pero, hijo, de pensar las cosas a manifestarlas así con cierto desparpajo, hay una distancia que el hombre prudente y comedido no debe salvar nunca. Bien sé que tus ideas son ... no te enfades; si te enfadas me callo ... digo que una cosa es tener ideas religiosas y otra manifestarlas ... Me guardaré muy bien de vituperarte porque creas que no nos crió Dios a su imagen y semejanza, sino que descendemos de los micos; ni porque niegues la existencia del alma, asegurando que ésta es una droga como los papelillos de magnesia o de ruibarbo que se venden en la botica ...

—¡Señora, por Dios ...! —exclamó Pepe con disgusto—. Veo que tengo muy mala reputación en Orbajosa.

Los demás seguían guardando silencio.

—Pues decía que no te vituperaré por esas ideas ... Además de que no tengo derecho a ello; si me pusiera a disputar contigo, tú, con tu talentazo descomunal, me confundirías mil veces ... no, nada de eso. Lo que digo es que estos pobres y menguados habitantes de Orbajosa son piadosos y buenos cristianos, si bien ninguno de ellos sabe filosofía alemana; por lo tanto, no debes despreciar públicamente sus creencias.

—Querida tía —dijo el ingeniero con gravedad—. Ni yo he despreciado las creencias de nadie, ni tengo las ideas que usted me atribuye. Quizás haya estado un poco irrespetuoso en la iglesia: soy algo distraído. Mi entendimiento y mi atención estaban fijos en la obra arquitectónica, y francamente, no advertí ... Pero no era esto motivo para que el señor Obispo intentase echarme a la calle, ni para que usted me supusiera capaz de atribuir a un papelillo de la botica las funciones del alma. Puedo tolerar eso como broma, nada más que como broma.

Pepe Rey sentía en su espíritu excitación tan viva, que a pesar de su mucha prudencia y mesura no pudo disimularla.

—Vamos, veo que te has enfadado —dijo doña Perfecta, bajando los ojos y cruzando las manos—. ¡Todo sea por Dios! Si hubiera sabido que lo tomabas así, no te habría dicho nada. Pepe, te ruego que me perdones.

Al oír esto y ver la actitud sumisa de su bondadosa tía, Pepe se sintió avergonzado de la dureza de sus anteriores palabras, y pro-

Perfecta, observing the canon's expression of unalterable gravity, which gave his face the appearance of a pasteboard mask. 'But, my dear boy, between thinking things and showing them in that irreverent manner, there is a distance which a man of good sense and good breeding should never cross. I am well aware that your ideas are—— Now, don't get angry! If you get angry, I will be silent. I say that it is one thing to have certain ideas about religion and another thing to express them. I will take good care not to reproach you because you believe that God did not create us in his image and likeness, but that we are descended from the monkeys; nor because you deny the existence of the soul, asserting that it is a drug, like the little papers of rhubarb and magnesia that are sold at the apothecary's——'

'Señora, for Heaven's sake!' exclaimed Pepe, with annoyance. 'I see that I have a very bad reputation in Orbajosa.'

The others still remained silent.

'As I said, I will not reproach you for entertaining those ideas. And, besides, I have not the right to do so. If I should undertake to argue with you, you, with your wonderful talents, would confute me a thousand times over. No, I will not attempt any thing of that kind. What I say is that these poor and humble inhabitants of Orbajosa are pious and good Christians, although they know nothing about German philosophy, and that, therefore, you ought not publicly to manifest your contempt for their beliefs.'

'My dear aunt,' said the engineer gravely, 'I have shown no contempt for any one, nor do I entertain the ideas which you attribute to me. Perhaps I may have been a little wanting in reverence in the church, I am somewhat absent-minded. My thoughts and my attention were engaged with the architecture of the building and, frankly speaking, I did not observe—— But this was no reason for the bishop to think of putting me out of the church, nor for you to suppose me capable of attributing to a paper from the apothecary's the functions of the soul. I may tolerate that as a jest, but only as a jest.'

The agitation of Pepe Rey's mind was so great that, notwithstanding his natural prudence and moderation, he was unable to conceal it.

'There! I see that you are angry,' said Doña Perfecta, casting down her eyes and clasping her hands. 'I am very sorry. If I had known that you would have taken it in that way, I should not have spoken to you. Pepe, I ask your pardon.'

Hearing these words and seeing his kind aunt's deprecating attitude Pepe felt ashamed of the sternness of his last words, and

curó serenarse. Sacóle de su embarazosa situación el venerable penitenciario, que, sonriendo con su habitual benevolencia, habló de
este modo:

—Señora doña Perfecta, es preciso tener tolerancia con los artis-
tas... ¡oh! yo he conocido muchos. Estos señores, como vean
delante de sí una estatua, una armadura mohosa, un cuadro podri-
do, o una pared vieja, se olvidan de todo. El señor don José es
artista, y ha visitado nuestra catedral como la visitan los ingleses, los
cuales de buena gana se llevarían a sus museos hasta la última
·baldosa de ella... Que estaban los fieles rezando; que el sacerdote
alzó la Sagrada Hostia; que llegó el instante de la mayor piedad y
recogimiento: pues bien... ¿qué le importa nada de esto a un
artista? Es verdad que yo no sé lo que vale el arte, cuando se le
disgrega de los sentimientos que expresa... pero, en fin, hoy es
costumbre adorar la forma, no la idea... Líbreme Dios de meterme
a discutir este tema con el señor don José, que sabe tanto, y argu-
mentando con la primorosa sutileza de los modernos, confundiría al
punto mi espíritu, en el cual no hay más que fe.

—El empeño de ustedes de considerarme como el hombre más
sabio de la tierra me mortifica bastante —dijo Pepe, recobrando la
dureza de su acento—. Ténganme por tonto, que prefiero la fama
de necio a poseer esa ciencia de Satanás que aquí me atribuyen.

Rosarito se echó a reír, y Jacinto creyó llegado el momento más
oportuno para hacer ostentación de su erudita personalidad.

—El panteísmo o panenteísmo están condenados por la Iglesia,
así como las doctrinas de Schopenhauer y del moderno Hartmann.

—Señores y señoras —manifestó gravemente el canónigo—: los
hombres que consagran culto tan fervoroso al arte, aunque sólo sea
atendiendo a la forma, merecen el mayor respeto. Más vale ser
artista y deleitarse ante la belleza, aunque sólo esté representada en
las ninfas desnudas, que ser indiferente y descreído en todo. En
espíritu que se consagra a la contemplación de la belleza no entrará
completamente el mal. *Est Deus in nobis ... Deus*, entiéndase bien.
Siga, pues, el señor don José admirando los prodigios de nuestra
iglesia, que por mi parte le perdonaré de buen grado las irreveren-
cias, salva la opinión del señor prelado.

—Gracias, señor don Inocencio —dijo Pepe, sintiendo en sí pun-
zante y revoltoso el sentimiento de hostilidad hacia el astuto
canónigo, y no pudiendo dominar el deseo de mortificarle—. Por lo

he made an effort to recover his serenity. The venerable Penitentiary extricated him from his embarrassing position, saying with his accustomed benevolent smile :

'Señora Doña Perfecta, we must be tolerant with artists. Oh, I have known a great many of them! Those gentlemen, when they have before them a statue, a piece of rusty armour, a mouldy painting, or an old wall, forget everything else. Señor Don José is an artist, and he has visited our cathedral as the English visit it, who would willingly carry it away with them to their museums, to its last tile, if they could. That the worshippers were praying, that the priest was elevating the Sacred Host, that the moment of supreme piety and devotion had come—what of that? What does all that matter to an artist? It is true that I do not know what art is worth, apart from the sentiments which it expresses, but, in fine, at the present day, it is the custom to adore the form, not the idea. God preserve me from undertaking to discuss this question with Señor Don José, who knows so much, and who, reasoning with the admirable subtlety of the moderns, would instantly confound my mind, in which there is only faith.'

'The determination which you all have to regard me as the most learned man on earth annoys me exceedingly,' said Pepe, speaking in his former hard tone. 'Hold me for a fool; for I would rather be regarded as a fool than as the possessor of that Satanic knowledge which is here attributed to me.'

Rosarito laughed, and Jacinto thought that a highly opportune moment had now arrived to make a display of his own erudition.

'Pantheism or panentheism,' he said, 'is condemned by the Church, as well as by the teachings of Schopenhauer and of the modern Hartmann.'

'Ladies and gentlemen,' said the canon gravely, 'men who pay so fervent a worship to art, though it be only to its form, deserve the greatest respect. It is better to be an artist, and delight in the contemplation of beauty, though this be only represented by nude nymphs, than to be indifferent and incredulous in every thing. The mind that consecrates itself to the contemplation of beauty, evil will not take complete possession of. *Est Deus in nobis. Deus*, be it well understood. Let Señor Don José, then, continue to admire the marvels of our church; I, for one, will willingly forgive him his acts of irreverence, with all due respect for the opinions of the bishop.'

'Thanks, Señor Don Inocencio,' said Pepe, feeling a bitter and rebellious sentiment of hostility springing up within him toward the canon, and unable to conquer his desire to mortify him. 'But

demás, no crean ustedes que absorbían mi atención las bellezas artísticas de que suponen lleno el templo. Esas bellezas, fuera de la imponente arquitectura de una parte del edificio y de los tres sepulcros que hay en las capillas del ábside y de algunas tallas del coro, yo no las veo en ninguna parte. Lo que ocupaba mi entendimiento era el considerar la deplorable decadencia de las artes religiosas, y no me causaban asombro, sino cólera, las innumerables monstruosidades artísticas de que está llena la catedral.

El estupor de los circunstantes fué extraordinario.

—No puedo resistir —añadió Pepe—, aquellas imágenes charoladas y bermellonadas, tan semejantes, perdóneme Dios la comparación, a las muñecas con que juegan las niñas grandecitas. ¿Qué puedo decir de los vestidos de teatro con que las cubren? Vi un San José con manto, cuya facha no quiero calificar por respeto al Santo Patriarca y a la Iglesia que le adora. En los altares se acumulan las imágenes del más deplorable gusto artístico, y la multitud de coronas, ramos, estrellas, lunas y demás adornos de metal o papel dorado forman un aspecto de quincallería que ofende el sentimiento religioso y hace desmayar nuestro espíritu. Lejos de elevarse a la contemplación religiosa, se abate, y la idea de lo cómico le perturba. Las grandes obras del arte, dando formas sensibles a las ideas, a los dogmas, a la fe, a la exaltación mística, realizan misión muy noble. Los mamarrachos y las aberraciones del gusto, las obras grotescas con que una piedad mal entendida llena las iglesias, también cumplen su objeto; pero éste es bastante triste: fomentan la superstición, enfrían el entusiasmo, obligan a los ojos del creyente a apartarse de los altares, y con los ojos se apartan las almas que no tienen fe muy profunda ni muy segura.

—La doctrina de los iconoclastas —dijo Jacintito—, también parece que está muy extendida en Alemania.

—Yo no soy iconoclasta, aunque prefiero la destrucción de todas las imágenes a estas chocarrerías de que me ocupo —continuó el joven—. Al ver esto, es lícito defender que el culto debe recobrar la sencillez augusta de los antiguos tiempos; pero no: no se renuncie al auxilio admirable que las artes todas, empezando por la poesía y acabando por la música, prestan a las relaciones entre el hombre y Dios. Vivan las artes, despliéguese la mayor pompa en los ritos religiosos. Yo soy partidario de la pompa . . .

—¡Artista, artista y nada más que artista! —exclamó el canónigo, moviendo la cabeza con expresión de lástima—. Buenas pinturas, buenas estatuas, bonita música . . . Gala de los sentidos; y el alma que se la lleve el demonio.

let none of you imagine, either, that it was the beauties of art, of which you suppose the temple to be full, that engaged my attention. Those beauties, with the exception of the imposing architecture of a portion of the edifice and of the three tombs that are in the chapel of the apse, I do not see. What occupied my mind was the consideration of the deplorable decadence of the religious arts; and the innumerable monstrosities of which the cathedral is full, caused me not astonishment, but disgust.'

The amazement of all present was profound.

'I cannot endure,' continued Pepe, 'those glazed and painted images that resemble so much—God forgive me for the comparison —the dolls that little girls play with. And what am I to say of the theatrical robes that cover them? I saw a St. Joseph with a mantle whose appearance I will not describe, out of respect for the holy patriarch and for the church of which he is the patron. On the altar are crowded together images in the worst possible taste; and the innumerable crowns, branches, stars, moons, and other ornaments of metal or gilt paper have an air of an ironmongery that offends the religious sentiment and depresses the soul. Far from lifting itself up to religious contemplation, the soul sinks, and the idea of the ludicrous distracts it. The great works of art which give sensible form to ideas, to dogmas, to religious faith, to mystic exaltation, fulfil a noble mission. The caricatures, the aberrations of taste, the grotesque works with which a mistaken piety fills the churches, also fulfil their object; but this is a sad one enough : They encourage superstition, cool enthusiasm, oblige the eyes of the believer to turn away from the altar, and, with the eyes, the souls that have not a very profound and a very firm faith turn away also.'

'The doctrine of the iconoclasts, too,' said Jacinto, 'has, it seems, spread widely in Germany.'

'I am not an iconoclast, although I would prefer the destruction of all the images to the exhibition of buffooneries of which I speak,' continued the young man. 'Seeing it, one may justly advocate a return of religious worship to the august simplicity of olden times. But no; let us not renounce the admirable aid which all the arts, beginning with poetry and ending with music, lend to the relations between man and God. Let the arts live; let the utmost pomp be displayed in religious ceremonies. I am a partisan of pomp.'

'An artist, an artist, and nothing more than an artist !' exclaimed the canon, shaking his head with a sorrowful air. 'Fine pictures, fine statues, beautiful music; pleasure for the senses, and let the devil take the soul !'

—Y a propósito de música —dijo Pepe Rey sin advertir el deplorable efecto que sus palabras producían en la madre y la hija—: figúrense ustedes que dispuesto estaría mi espíritu a la contemplación religiosa al visitar la catedral, cuando de buenas a primeras, y al llegar al ofertorio en la misa mayor, el señor organista tocó un pasaje de *La Traviata.*

—En eso tiene razón el señor de Rey —dijo el abogadillo enfáticamente—. El señor organista tocó el otro día el brindis y el vals de la misma ópera, y después un rondó de *La gran duquesa.*

—Pero cuando se me cayeron las alas del corazón —continuó el ingeniero implacablemente—, fué cuando vi una imagen de la Virgen, que parece estar en gran veneración, según la mucha gente que ante ella había y la multitud de velas que la alumbraban. La han vestido con ahuecado ropón de terciopelo bordado de oro, de tan extraña forma, que supera a las modas más extravagantes del día. Desaparece su cara entre un follaje espeso, compuesto de mil suertes de encajes, rizados con tenacillas; y la corona de media vara de alto, rodeada de rayos de oro, es un disforme catafalco que le han armado sobre la cabeza. De la misma tela y con los mismos bordados son los pantalones del Niño Jesús . . . No quiero seguir, porque la descripción de cómo están la Madre y el Hijo me llevaría quizás a cometer alguna irreverencia. No diré más, sino que me fué imposible tener la risa, y que por breve rato contemplé la profanada imagen, exclamando: '¡Madre y Señora mía, cómo te han puesto!'

Concluídas estas palabras, Pepe observó a sus oyentes, y aunque la sombra crepuscular no permitía distinguir bien los semblantes, creyó ver en alguno de ellos señales de amarga consternación.

—Pues, señor don José —exclamó vivamente el canónigo, riendo y con expresión de triunfo—, esa imagen que a la filosofía y panteísmo de usted parece tan ridícula, es Nuestra Señora del Socorro, patrona y abogada de Orbajosa, cuyos habitantes la veneran de tal modo, que serían capaces de arrastrar por las calles al que hablase mal de ella. Las crónicas y la historia, señor mío, están llenas de los milagros que ha hecho, y aun hoy día vemos constantemente pruebas irrecusables de su protección. Ha de saber usted también que su señora tía doña Perfecta es camarera de la Santísima Virgen del Socorro, y que ese vestido que a usted le parece tan grotesco . . . pues . . . digo que ese vestido tan grotesco a los impíos ojos de usted,

'Apropos of music,' said Pepe Rey, without observing the deplorable effect which his words produced on both mother and daughter, 'imagine how disposed my mind would be to religious contemplation on entering the cathedral, when just at that moment, and precisely at the offertory at high mass, the organist played a passage from "Traviata".'

'Señor de Rey is right in that,' said the little lawyer emphatically. 'The organist played the other day the whole of the drinking song and the waltz from the same opera, and afterward a rondeau from the "Grande Duchesse".'

'But when I felt my heart sink,' continued the engineer implacably, 'was when I saw an image of the Virgin, which seems to be held in great veneration, judging from the crowd before it and the multitude of tapers which lighted it. They have dressed her in a puffed-out garment of velvet, embroidered with gold, of a shape so extraordinary that it surpasses the most extravagant of the fashions of the day. Her face is almost hidden under a voluminous frill, made of innumerable rows of lace, crimped with a crimping-iron, and her crown, half a yard in height, surrounded by golden rays, looks like a hideous catafalque erected over her head. Of the same material, and embroidered in the same manner, are the trousers of the Infant Jesus. I will not go on, for to describe the Mother and the Child might perhaps lead me to commit some irreverence. I will only say that it was impossible for me to keep from smiling, and for a short time I contemplated the profaned image, saying to myself : "Mother and Lady mine, what a sight they have made of you!" '

As he ended Pepe looked at his hearers, and although, owing to the gathering darkness, he could not see their countenances distinctly, he fancied that in some of them he perceived signs of angry consternation.

'Well, Señor Don José !' exclaimed the canon quickly, smiling with a triumphant expression, 'that image, which to your philosophy and pantheism appears so ridiculous, is Our Lady of Help, patroness and advocate of Orbajosa, whose inhabitants regard her with so much veneration that they would be quite capable of dragging any one through the streets who should speak ill of her. The chronicles and history, Señor Don José, are full of the miracles which she has wrought, and even at the present day we receive constantly incontrovertible proofs of her protection. You must know also that your aunt, Doña Perfecta, is chief lady in waiting to the Most Holy Virgin of Help, and that the dress that to you appears so grotesque—well, the dress, I repeat, which, to your impious eyes,

salió de esta casa, y que los pantalones del Niño, obra son juntamente de la maravillosa aguja y de la acendrada piedad de su prima
de usted, Rosarito, que nos está oyendo.

Pepe Rey se quedó bastante desconcertado. En el mismo instante
levantóse bruscamente doña Perfecta, y sin decir una palabra se
dirigió hacia la casa, seguida por el señor Penitenciario. Levan-
táronse también los restantes. Disponíase el aturdido joven a pedir
perdón a su prima por la irreverencia, cuando observó que Rosarito
lloraba. Clavando en su prima una mirada de amistosa y dulce
reprensión, exalamó:

—¡Pero qué cosas tienes! . . .

Oyóse la voz de doña Perfecta, que con alterado acento gritaba:

—¡Rosario, Rosario!

Esta corrió hacia la casa.

JOSÉ ECHEGARAY
[1832–1916]

*A remarkable man who had been a brilliant mathematician, engineer and
politician before turning to the theatre, José Echegaray wrote his first
drama after the age of forty. During the next thirty years he poured out more
than sixty plays.*

*They are for the most part exaggerated, moralizing melodramas. But
Echegaray was Spain's most popular dramatist during the last quarter of the*

EL GRAN GALEOTO

DIÁLOGO

ESCENA I

*La escena representa un gabinete de estudio. A la izquierda, un balcón.
A la derecha una puerta; casi en el centro una mesa con papeles, libros y un
quinqué encendido; hacia la derecha un sofá. Es de noche.* ERNESTO, *sentado
a la mesa y como preparándose a escribir.*

ERN. ¡Nada! . . . ¡Imposible! . . . Esto es luchar con lo imposible.
La idea está aquí; ¡bajo mi ardorosa frente se agita! Yo la siento. A
veces luz interna la ilumina, y la veo. La veo con su forma flotante,
con sus vagos contornos, y de repente, suenan en sus ocultos senos
voces que la animan, gritos de dolor, amorosos suspiros, carcajadas
sardónicas . . . ¡todo un mundo de pasiones que viven y luchan! ¡Y

appears so grotesque—went out from this house, and that the trousers of the Infant are the work of the skilful needle and the ardent piety combined of your cousin Rosarito, who is now listening to us.'

Pepe Rey was greatly disconcerted. At the same instant Doña Perfecta rose abruptly from her seat, and, without saying a word, walked toward the house, followed by the Penitentiary. The others rose also. Recovering from his stupefaction, the young man was about to get his cousin's pardon for his irreverence, when he observed that Rosarito was weeping. Fixing on her cousin a look of friendly and gentle reproof, she said :

'What ideas you have !'

The voice of Doña Perfecta was heard crying in an altered accent :

'Rosario ! Rosario !'

The latter ran toward the house.

MARY J. SERRANO

nineteenth century, and in 1904 he was awarded the Nobel Prize for literature, thus becoming the first Spaniard to be so honoured.

His masterpiece, El gran Galeoto (1881), is a powerful drama whose theme is the destruction of a happy home by the consuming force of slander. It is written in verse, with a prose prologue.

THE GREAT GALEOTO

PROLOGUE

Ernesto's study. To the left, a french window; to the right, a door.—Nearly in the centre, a table on which are books, papers, and a lighted lamp.—To the right is a sofa. It is evening. Ernesto is seated at the table, as though about to write.

ERN. There's no use. I can't do it. It is impossible. I am simply contending with the impossible. The idea is here; it is stirring in my brain; I can feel it. Sometimes a light from within illumines it and I see it with its shifting form and vague contours, and suddenly there sound in the hidden depths voices that give it life; cries of grief, sighs of love, sardonic, mocking laughter—a whole world of living, struggling passions. They break from me, and

fuera de mí se lanzan, y a mi alrededor se extienden, y los aires llenan! Entonces, entonces me digo a mí mismo: 'Éste es el instante,' y tomo la pluma, y con la mirada fija en el espacio, con el oído atento, conteniendo los latidos del corazón, sobre el papel me inclino . . . Pero, ¡ah sarcasmo de la impotencia! . . . ¡Los contornos se borran, la visión se desvanece, gritos y suspiros se extinguen . . . y la nada, la nada me rodea! . . . ¡La monotonía del espacio vacío, del pensamiento inerte, del cansancio soñoliento! Más que todo eso: la monotonía de una pluma inmóvil y de un papel sin vida, sin la vida de la idea. ¡Ah! . . . ¡Cuántas formas tiene la nada, y cómo se burla, negra y silenciosa, de creadores de mi estofa! Muchas, muchas formas; lienzos sin colores, pedazos de mármol sin contornos, ruidos confusos de caóticas vibraciones; pero ninguna más irritante, más insolente, más ruin que esta pluma miserable (*Tirándola.*) y que esta hoja en blanco. ¡Ah! . . . ¡No puedo llenarte, pero puedo destruírte, cómplice vil de mis ambiciones y de mi eterna humillación! Así . . . así . . . más pequeños . . . aun más pequeños . . . (*Rompiendo el papel. Pausa.*) ¿Y qué? . . . La fortuna es que nadie me ha visto; que, por lo demás, estos furores son ridículos y son injustos. No . . . pues yo no cedo. Pensaré más, más . . . hasta vencer o hasta estrellarme. No; yo nunca me doy por vencido. A ver . . . a ver si de este modo . . ,

ESCENA II

ERNESTO, DON JULIÁN

Éste por la derecha, de frac y con el abrigo al brazo.

JUL. (*Asomándose a la puerta, pero sin entrar.*) Hola, Ernesto.
ERN. ¡Don Julián!
JUL. ¿Trabajando aún? . . . ¿Estorbo?
ERN. (*Levantándose.*) ¡Estorbar! ¡Por Dios, don Julián! . . . Entre usted, entre usted. ¿Y Teodora? (*D. Julián entra.*)
JUL. Del Teatro Real venimos. Subió ella con mis hermanos aí tercero, a ver no sé qué compras de Mercedes, y yo me encaminaba hacia mi cuarto, cuando vi luz en el tuyo, y me asomé a darte las buenas noches.
ERN. ¿Mucha gente?
JUL. Mucha, como siempre; y todos los amigos me preguntaron por ti. Extrañaban que no hubieses ido.
ERN. ¡Oh! . . . ¡Qué interés!
JUL. El que tú te mereces, y aún es poco. Y tú, ¿has aprovechado estas tres horas de soledad y de inspiración?

spread out, and fill the air all about me! Then, then, I say to myself, the moment has come, and I take up my pen, and with eyes gazing into space, with straining ears, with fast-beating heart, I bend over my paper.—But oh, the irony of impotence! The contours become blurred, the vision disappears, the shouts and sighs die away, and nothingness, nothingness surrounds me! The desolation of empty space, of meaningless thought, of deadly weariness! More than all that, the desolation of an idle pen and a barren page—a page bereft of all life-giving thought. Ah, how many forms has nothingness, and how it mocks, dark and silent, at creatures of my sort! Many, many forms :—the colourless canvas, the shapeless piece of marble, the discordant sound, but none more irritating, more mocking, more blighting, than this worthless pen and this blank paper. Ah, I cannot cover you, but I can destroy you, vile accomplice in my wrecked ambitions and my everlasting humiliation!—So, so,—smaller, still smaller. (*Tearing the paper— then, a pause.*) Well, it's fortunate that no one saw me, for at best such ranting is foolish, and it's all wrong. No—I will not give in; I will think harder, harder, until I conquer or blow up in a thousand pieces. No, I will never admit I am beaten. Come, let's see whether now——

(*Enter* Don Julian, *right, wearing a frock coat and carrying his overcoat on his arm. He looks in at the door but doesn't come in.*)

JUL. Hello, Ernesto!

ERN. Don Julian!

JUL. Still working? Am I disturbing you?

ERN. Disturbing me? Indeed, no. Come in, come in, Don Julian. Where's Teodora?

JUL. We've just come from the opera. She went up to the third floor with my brother and his wife to see some purchases of Mercedes, and I was on my way to my own room, when I saw a light in yours and looked in to say good night.

ERN. Were there many people there?

JUL. A good many—as usual. All my friends were asking for you. They were surprised at your not going.

ERN. How kind of them!

JUL. Not so very, considering all that you deserve. But how about you? Have you made good use of these three hours of solitude and inspiration?

ERN. De soledad, sí; de inspiración, no. No vino a mí, aunque rendido y enamorado la llamaba.

JUL. ¿Faltó a la cita?

ERN. Y no por vez primera. Pero si nada hice de provecho, hice, en cambio, un provechoso descubrimiento.

JUL. ¿Cuál?

ERN. Éste: que soy un pobre diablo.

JUL. ¡Diablo! Pues me parece descubrimiento famoso.

ERN. Ni más, ni menos.

JUL. ¿Y por qué tal enojo contigo mismo? ¿No sale acaso el drama que me anunciaste el otro día.

ERN. ¡Qué ha de salir! Quien sale de quicio soy yo.

JUL. ¿Y en qué consiste ese desaire que juntos hacen la inspiración y el drama a mi buen Ernesto?

ERN. Consiste en que, al imaginarlo, yo creí que la idea del drama era fecunda, y al darle forma, y al vestirla con el ropaje propio de la escena, resulta una cosa extraña, difícil, antidramática, imposible.

JUL. Pero ¿en dónde consiste lo imposible del caso? Vamos, dime algo, que ya voy entrando en curiosidad. (*Sentándose en el sofá.*)

ERN. Figúrese usted que el principal personaje, el que crea el drama, el que lo desarrolla, el que lo anima, el que provoca la catástrofe, el que la devora y la goza, no puede salir a escena.

JUL. ¿Tan feo es? ¿Tan repugnante o tan malo?

ERN. No es eso. Feo, como cualquiera: como usted o como yo. Malo, tampoco: ni malo ni bueno. Repugnante, no en verdad: no soy tan escéptico, ni tan misántropo, ni tan desengañado de la vida estoy, que tal cosa afirme o que tamaña injusticia cometa.

JUL. Pues, entonces, ¿cuál es la causa?

ERN. Don Julián: la causa es que el personaje de que se trata no cabría materialmente en el escenario.

JUL. ¡Virgen Santísima, y qué cosas dices! ¿Es drama mitológico por ventura y aparecen los titanes?

ERN. Titanes son, pero a la moderna.

JUL. ¿En suma? . . .

ERN. En suma: ese personaje es . . . ¡'Todo el mundo', que es una buena suma!

JUL. '¡Todo el mundo!' Pues tienes razón: todo el mundo no cabe en el teatro; he ahí una verdad indiscutible y muchas veces demostrada.

ERN. Pues ya ve usted cómo yo estaba en lo cierto.

ERN. Solitude, yes; inspiration, no. That would not come to me, though I called upon it desperately and with passion.

JUL. It wouldn't obey the summons?

ERN. No, and this was not the first time. But I did make a profitable discovery, though I accomplished nothing.

JUL. What?

ERN. Simply this—that I am a poor good-for-nothing.

JUL. Good-for-nothing! Well, that's a profitable discovery, indeed.

ERN. Precisely.

JUL. And why so disgusted with yourself? Isn't the play you told about the other day going well?

ERN. I'm the one who is going—out of my mind!

JUL. And what is all this trouble that inspiration and the play together are making for my Ernesto?

ERN. The trouble is this : when I conceived it I thought the idea a good one; but when I give it form and dress it out in the proper stage trappings the result is extraordinary; contrary to all laws of the drama; utterly impossible.

JUL. But why impossible? Come, tell me about it. I am curious.

ERN. Imagine, then, that the principal character, the one who creates the drama, who develops, who animates it, who brings about the catastrophe, and who thrives upon that catastrophe and revels in it—that person cannot appear on the stage.

JUL. Is he so ugly? Or so repulsive? Or so wicked?

ERN. It's not that. He is no uglier than any one else—than you or I. Nor is he bad. Neither bad nor good. Repulsive? No indeed. I am not such a sceptic, nor such a misanthrope, nor so at odds with the world that I would say such a thing or commit such an injustice.

JUL. Well, then, what is the reason?

ERN. Don Julian, the reason is that there probably wouldn't be room on the stage for the character in question.

JUL. Good heavens, listen to the man! Is this a mythological play, then, and do Titans appear on the stage?

ERN. They are Titans; but a modern variety.

JUL. In short?

ERN. In short this character is—*Everybody*.

JUL. *Everybody!* Well, you are right! There's not room in the theatre for everybody. That is an indisputable fact that has often been demonstrated.

ERN. Now you see how right I was.

JUL. No completamente. 'Todo el mundo' puede condensarse en unos cuantos tipos o caracteres. Yo no entiendo de esas materias; pero tengo oído que esto han hecho los maestros más de una vez.

ERN. Sí; pero en mi caso, es decir, en mi drama, no puede hacerse.

JUL. ¿Por qué?

ERN. Por muchas razones que fuera largo de explicar, y, sobre todo, a estas horas.

JUL. No importa: vengan algunas de ellas.

ERN. Mire usted: cada individuo de esa masa total, cada cabeza de ese monstruo de cien mil cabezas de ese titán del siglo que yo llamo 'todo el mundo', toma parte en mi drama un instante brevísimo, pronuncia una palabra no más, dirige una sola mirada, quizá toda su acción en la fábula es una sonrisa; aparece un punto y luego se aleja: obra sin pasión, sin saña, sin maldad, indiferente y distraído; por distracción muchas veces.

JUL. ¿Y qué?

ERN. Que de esas palabras sueltas, de esas miradas fugaces, de esas sonrisas indiferentes, de todas esas pequeñas murmuraciones y de todas esas pequeñísimas maldades; de todos esos que pudiéramos llamar rayos insignificantes de luz dramática, condensados en un foco o en una familia, resulta el incendio y la explosión, la lucha y las víctimas. Si yo represento la totalidad de las gentes por unos cuantos tipos o personajes simbólicos, tengo que poner en cada uno lo que realmente está disperso en muchos, y resulta falseado el pensamiento; unos cuantos tipos en escena, repulsivos y malvados, inverosímiles porque su maldad no tiene objeto; y resulta, además, el peligro de que se crea que yo trato de pintar una sociedad infame, corrompida y cruel, cuando yo sólo pretendo demostrar que ni aun las acciones más insignificantes son insignificantes ni perdidas para el bien o para el mal, porque sumadas por misteriosas influencias de la vida moderna pueden llegar a producir inmensos efectos.

JUL. Mira: no sigas, no sigas; todo eso es muy metafísico. Algo vislumbro, pero al través de muchas nubes. En fin, tú entiendes de estas cosas más que yo: si se tratase de giros, cambios, letras, y descuentos, otra cosa sería.

ERN. ¡Oh, no: usted tiene buen sentido, que es lo principal!

JUL. Gracias, Ernesto, eres muy amable.

ERN. Pero ¿está usted convencido?

JUL. No lo estoy. Debe de haber manera de salvar ese inconveniente.

JUL. Not altogether. *Everybody* can be condensed into a certain number of types, or characters. I don't understand these things myself, but I have heard that authors have done it more than once.

ERN. Yes, but in my case, that is, in my play, it can't be done.

JUL. Why not?

ERN. For many reasons that it would take too long to explain; especially at this time of night.

JUL. Never mind, let's have some of them.

ERN. Well then, each part of this vast whole, each head of this thousand-headed monster, of this Titan of today whom I call *Everybody*, takes part in my play only for the briefest instant, speaks one word and no more, gives one glance; perhaps his entire action consists in the suggestion of one smile; he appears for a moment and goes away again; he works without passion, without guile, without malice, indifferently, and absently—often *by* his very abstraction.

JUL. And what then?

ERN. From those words, from those fleeting glances, from those indifferent smiles, from all those little whispers, from all those peccadilloes; from all these things that we might call insignificant rays of dramatic light, when brought to a focus in one family, result the spark and the explosion, the struggle and the victims. If I represent the whole of mankind by a given number of types or symbolic characters, I have to ascribe to each one that which is really distributed among many, with the result that a certain number of characters must appear who are made repulsive by vices that lack verisimilitude, whose crimes have no object. And, as an additional result, there is the danger that people will believe I am trying to paint society as evil, corrupt, and cruel, when I only want to show that not even the most insignificant acts are really insignificant or impotent for good or evil; for, gathered together by the mysterious agencies of modern life, they may succeed in producing tremendous results.

JUL. Come, stop, stop! That is all dreadfully metaphysical. I get a glimmering, but the clouds are pretty thick. In fact, you understand more than I do about these things. Now, if it were a question of drafts, of notes, of letters of credit, of discount, it would be another matter.

ERN. Oh, no, you have common sense, which is the main thing.

JUL. Thanks, Ernesto, you are very kind.

ERN. But are you convinced?

JUL. No, I'm not. There must be some way of getting round the difficulty.

ERN. ¡Si fuera eso sólo!

JUL. ¿Hay más?

ERN. Yo lo creo. Dígame usted, ¿cuál es el resorte dramático por excelencia?

JUL. Hombre, yo no sé a punto fijo qué es eso que tú llamas 'resorte dramático'; pero yo lo que te digo es que no me divierto en los dramas en que no hay amores, sobre todo amores desgraciados, que para amores felices tengo bastante con el de mi casa y con mi Teodora.

ERN. Bueno, magnífico; pues en mi drama casi, casi no puede haber amores.

JUL. Malo, pésimo, digo yo. Oye: no sé lo que es tu drama, pero sospecho que no va a interesar a nadie.

ERN. Ya se lo dije yo a usted. Sin embargo, amores pueden ponerse, y hasta celos.

JUL. Pues por eso, con una intriga interesante y bien desarrollada, con alguna situación de efecto . . .

ERN. No, señor; eso sí que no; todo ha de ser sencillo, corriente, casi vulgar . . . Como que el drama no puede brotar a lo exterior. El drama va por dentro de los personajes; avanza lentamente; se apodera hoy de un pensamiento, mañana de un latido del corazón; mina la voluntad poco a poco.

JUL. Pero todo eso, ¿en qué se conoce? Esos estragos interiores, ¿qué manifestación tienen? ¿Quién se los cuenta al espectador? ¿Dónde los ve? ¿Hemos de estar toda la noche a caza de una mirada, de un suspiro, de un gesto, de una frase suelta? Pero, hijo, ¡eso no es divertirse! ¡Para meterse en tales profundidades se estudia filosofía!

ERN. Nada: repite usted como un eco todo lo que yo estoy pensando.

JUL. No; yo tampoco quiero desanimarte. Tú sabrás lo que haces. Y . . . ¡vaya! . . . aunque el drama sea un poco pálido, parezca pesado y no interese . . . con tal que luego venga la catástrofe con bríos . . . y con la explosión . . . ¿eh?

ERN. ¡Catástrofe . . . explosión! . . . Casi, casi, cuando cae el telón.

JUL. Es decir, ¿que el drama empieza cuando el drama acaba?

ERN. Estoy por decir que sí, aunque ya procuraré ponerle un poquito de calor.

JUL. Mira: lo que has de hacer es escribir 'ese segundo drama', ese que empieza cuando acaba el primero; porque el primero, según tus noticias, no vale la pena y ha de darte muchas.

ERN. De eso estaba yo convencido.

ERN. If only there were!

JUL. Is there something more?

ERN. I should say so! Tell me, what is the moving force of the drama?

JUL. I don't know exactly what you mean by the moving force of the drama, but I will say that I don't find any pleasure in plays in which there are no love-affairs; preferably unhappy love-affairs, for I have plenty of happy love-making in my own house with my Teodora.

ERN. Good. Splendid! Well, in my play there is hardly any love-making at all.

JUL. Bad, very bad indeed, I say. Listen, I don't know what your play is about, but I am afraid that it won't interest anybody.

ERN. That's just what I told you. Still, love-making might be put in, and even a little jealousy.

JUL. Well, with that, with an interesting and well-developed intrigue, with some really striking situation . . .

ERN. No, señor, certainly not that. Everything must be quite commonplace, almost vulgar. This drama can have no outward manifestation. It goes on in the hearts and minds of the characters; it progresses slowly; today it is a question of a thought; tomorrow of a heartbeat; gradually the will is undermined . . .

JUL. But how is all this shown? How are these inner struggles expressed? Who tells the audience about them? Where are they seen? Are we to spend the whole evening in pursuit of a glance, a sigh, a gesture, a word? My dear boy, that is no sort of amusement. When a man wants to meddle with such abstractions he studies philosophy.

ERN. That's it, exactly. You repeat my thoughts like an echo.

JUL. I don't want to discourage you, however. You probably know what you are doing. And, even though the play may be a little colourless, even though it may seem a bit heavy and uninteresting, so long as it has a fine climax and the catastrophe . . . eh?

ERN. Catastrophe—climax! They have hardly come when the curtain falls.

JUL. You mean that the play begins when the play ends?

ERN. I'm afraid so—though, of course, I shall try to put a little warmth into it.

JUL. Come now, what you ought to do is write the second play, the one that begins when the first ends; for the first, judging by what you say, isn't worth the trouble—and plenty of trouble it's bound to give you.

ERN. I was convinced of that.

JUL. Y ahora lo estamos los dos; tal maña te has dado y tal es la fuerza de tu lógica. ¿Y qué título tiene?

ERN. ¡Título!... ¡Pues ésa es otra!... Que no puede tener título.

JUL. ¿Qué?... ¿Qué dices?... ¡Tampoco!...

ERN. No, señor; a no ser que lo pusiéramos en griego para mayor claridad, como dice don Hermógenes.

JUL. Vamos, Ernesto; tú estabas durmiendo cuando llegué; soñabas desatinos y me cuentas tus sueños.

ERN. ¿Soñando?... Sí. ¿Desatinos?... Tal vez. Y sueños y desatinos cuento. Usted tiene buen sentido y en todo acierta.

JUL. Es que para acertar en este caso no se necesita de gran penetración. Un drama en que el principal personaje no sale, en que no sucede nada que no suceda todos los días, que empieza al caer el telón en el último acto y que no tiene título, yo no sé cómo puede escribirse, ni cómo puede representarse, ni cómo ha de haber quien lo oiga, ni cómo es drama.

ERN. ¡Ah!... Pues drama es. Todo consiste en darle forma y en que yo no sé dársela.

JUL. ¿Quieres seguir mi consejo?

ERN. ¿Su consejo de usted?... ¿De usted, mi amigo, mi protector, mi segundo padre? ¡Ah!... ¡Don Julián!

JUL. Vamos, vamos, Ernesto; no hagamos aquí un drama sentimental a falta del tuyo que hemos declarado imposible. Te preguntaba si quieres seguir mi consejo.

ERN. Y yo decía que sí.

JUL. Pues déjate de dramas; acuéstate, descansa, vente a cazar conmigo mañana, mata unas cuantas perdices, con lo cual te excusas de matar un par de personajes de tu obra, y quizá de que el público haga contigo otro tanto, y a fin de cuentas tú me darás las gracias.

ERN. Eso sí que no. El drama lo escribiré.

JUL. Pero desdichado, tú lo concebiste en pecado mortal.

ERN. No sé cómo, pero lo concebí. Lo siento en mi cerebro; en él se agita; pide vida en el mundo exterior, y he de de dársela.

JUL. Pero ¿no puedes buscar otro argumento?

ERN. Pero ¿y esta idea?

JUL. Mándala al diablo.

ERN. ¡Ah, don Julián! ¿Usted cree que una idea que se ha aferrado aquí dentro se deja anular y destruir porque así nos plazca? Yo

JUL. And now we both are—thanks to your cleverness and the force of your logic. What is the title?

ERN. Title! Why, that's another thing. It has no title.

JUL. What! What did you say? No title, either?

ERN. No, señor.

JUL. Well, Ernesto, you must have been asleep when I came in— you were having a nightmare and now you are telling me your dreams.

ERN. Dreaming? Yes. A nightmare? Perhaps. And I am telling you my dreams, good and bad. You have common sense, and you always guess right in everything.

JUL. It didn't take much penetration to guess right in this case. A play in which the principal character doesn't appear, in which there is almost no love-making, in which nothing happens that doesn't happen every day, which begins as the curtain falls on the last act, and which has no title.—Well, I don't see how it can be written, how it can be acted, or how any one can be found to listen to it,—or, indeed, how it is a play at all.

ERN. Ah, but it is a play. The only trouble is that I must give it form, and *that* I don't know how to do.

JUL. Do you want my advice?

ERN. Your advice? The advice of my friend, my benefactor, my second father! Oh, Don Julian!

JUL. Come, come, Ernesto, let us not have a little sentimental play of our own here in place of yours which we have pronounced impossible. I only asked you whether you wanted to know my advice.

ERN. And I said, Yes.

JUL. Well, forget all about plays—go to bed—go to sleep—go shooting with me tomorrow, kill any number of partridges instead of killing two characters, and perhaps having the audience kill you —and when all is said and done, you'll be thankful to me.

ERN. That can't be : I must write the play.

JUL. But, my dear fellow, you must have thought of it by way of penance for your sins.

ERN. I don't know why it happened, but think of it I did. I feel it stirring in my mind, it begs for life in the outer world, and I am bound to give it that.

JUL. Can't you find some other plot?

ERN. But what about this idea?

JUL. Let the devil take care of it.

ERN. Ah, Don Julian, do you think that when an idea has been hammered out in our minds, we can destroy it and bring it to

quisiera pensar en otro drama; pero éste, este maldito de la cuestión no le dejará sitio hasta que no brote al mundo.

JUL. Pues nada . . . que Dios te dé feliz alumbramiento.

ERN. Ahí está el problema, como dice Hamlet.

JUL. ¿Y no podrías echarlo a la inclusa literaria de las obras anónimas? (*En voz baja y con misterio cómico.*)

ERN. ¡Ah, don Julián! Yo soy hombre de conciencia. Mis hijos, buenos o malos, son legítimos: llevarán mi nombre.

JUL. (*Preparándose a salir.*) No digo más. Lo que ha de ser está escrito.

ERN. Eso quisiera yo. No está escrito, por desgracia, pero no importa; si yo no lo escribo, otro lo escribirá.

JUL. Pues a la obra; y buena suerte, y que nadie te tome la delantera.

ESCENA III

ERNESTO, DON JULIÁN, TEODORA

TEO. (*Desde fuera.*) ¡Julián! . . . ¡Julián!

JUL. Es Teodora.

TEO. ¿Estás aquí, Julián?

JUL. (*Asomámdose a la puerta.*) Sí, aquí estoy; entra.

TEO. (*Entrando.*) Buenas noches, Ernesto.

ERN. Buenas noches, Teodora. ¿Cantaron bien?

TEO. Como siempre. Y usted, ¿ha trabajado mucho?

ERN. Como siempre: nada.

TEO. Pues para eso, mejor le hubiera sido acompañarnos. Todas mis amigas me han preguntado por usted.

ERN. Está visto que 'todo el mundo' se interesa por mí.

JUL. ¡Ya lo creo! . . . Como que de 'todo el mundo' vas a hacer el principal personaje de tu drama. Figúrate si les interesará tenerte por amigo.

TEO. (*Con curiosidad.*) ¿Un drama?

JUL. ¡Silencio! . . . Es un misterio . . . No preguntes nada. Ni título, ni personajes, ni acción, ni catástrofe . . . ¡lo sublime! Buenas noches, Ernesto: Vamos, Teodora.

ERN. ¡Adiós, don Julián!

TEO. Hasta mañana.

ERN. Buenas noches.

TEO. (*A don Julián.*) ¡Qué preocupada estaba Mercedes!

JUL. Y Severo hecho una furia.

TEO. ¿Por qué sería?

JUL. ¡Qué sé yo! En cambio, Pepito, alegre por ambos.

naught whenever we choose? I should like to think of another play, but this accursed one won't let me until it has been born into the world.

JUL. There's no use talking, then. I only hope you get some light on the subject.

ERN. That is the question, as Hamlet says.

JUL. (*In a low voice, with mock mystery.*) Couldn't you put it in the literary orphanage for anonymous works?

ERN. Don Julian, I am a man of conscience. My children, good or bad, are legitimate, and shall bear my name.

JUL. I'll say no more. It must be—it is written.

ERN. I only wish it were. Unfortunately it is not written, but no matter, if I don't write it, someone else will.

JUL. Well, to work! Good luck, and don't let any one get ahead of you.

TEO. (*Without.*) Julian! Julian!

JUL. There's Teodora!

TEO. Are you here, Julian?

JUL. Yes, here I am. Come in !

(*Enter* Teodora.)

TEO. Good evening, Ernesto.

ERN. Good evening, Teodora. Did they sing well?

TEO. As usual. Have you done a lot of work?

ERN. As usual; nothing.

TEO. Why, you might better have gone with us. All my friends were asking for you.

ERN. It seems that everybody is taking an interest in me.

JUL. I should say so; since you are going to make *Everybody* the principal character in your play, naturally it is to his interest to have you for his friend.

TEO. A play?

JUL. Hush, it's a great mystery; you mustn't ask anything about it. It has no title, no actors, no action, no catastrophe! Oh, how sublime! Good night, Ernesto.—Come, Teodora.

ERN. Good-bye, Julian.

TEO. Until tomorrow.

ERN. Good night.

TEO. (*To* Julian.) How preoccupied Mercedes seemed !

JUL. And Severo was in a rage.

TEO. I wonder why.

JUL. I'm sure I don't know. Pepito, on the other hand, was lively enough for both.

TEO. Ése siempre. Y hablando mal de todos.

JUL. Personaje para el drama de Ernesto.

(*Salen Teodora y don Julián por la derecha.*)

ERN. Diga lo que quiera don Julián, yo no abandono mi empresa. Fuera insigne cobardía. No, no retrocedo . . . ; adelante. (*Se levanta y se pasea agitadamente. Después se acerca al balcón.*) Noche, protégeme, que en tu negrura, mejor que en el manto azul del día, se dibujan los contornos luminosos de la inspiración. Alzad vuestros techos, casas mil de la heroica villa, que, por un poeta en necesidad suma, no habéis de hacer menos que por aquel diablillo cojuelo que traviesamente os descaperuzó. Vea yo entrar en vuestras salas y gabinetes damas y caballeros buscando, tras las agitadas horas de públicos placeres, el nocturno descanso. Lleguen a mis aguzados oídos las mil palabras sueltas de todos esos que a Julián y a Teodora preguntaron por mí. Y como de rayos dispersos de luz por diáfano cristal recogidos se hacen grandes focos, y como de líneas cruzadas de sombra se forjan las tinieblas, y de granos de tierra los montes, y de gotas de agua los mares, así yo, de vuestras frases perdidas, de vuestras vagas sonrisas, de vuestras miradas curiosas, de esas mil trivialidades que en cafés, teatros, reuniones y espectáculos dejáis dispersas, y que ahora flotan en el aire, forje también mi drama, y sea el modesto cristal de mi inteligencia lente que traiga al foco luces y sombras, para que en él broten el incendio dramático y la trágica explosión de la catástrofe. Brote mi drama, que hasta título tiene, porque allá, bajo la luz del quinqué, veo la obra inmortal del inmortal poeta florentino, y dióme en italiano lo que en buen español fuera buena imprudencia y mala osadía escribir en un libro y pronunciar en la escena. Francesca y Paolo, ¡válganme vuestros amores! (*Sentándose a la mesa y preparándose a escribir.*) ¡Al drama! . . . ¡El drama empieza! Primera hoja: ya no está en blanco . . . ya tiene título. (*Escribiendo.*) EL GRAN GALEOTO. (*Escribe febrilmente.*)

TEO. He always is—and speaking ill of every one.
JUL. A character for Ernesto's play.

(Teodora *and* Julian *go out, right.*)

ERN. Let Julian say what he likes, I am not going to give up my undertaking. It would be rank cowardice. No, I will not retreat. Forward! (*He rises and walks up and down in agitation. Then he goes over to the french window.*) Night, lend me your protection, for against your blackness the luminous outlines of my inspiration are defined more clearly than against the blue cloak of day. Lift up your roofs, ye thousands of houses in this mighty city; for surely you should do as much for a poet in distress as for that crooked devil who mischievously lifted your tops off. Let me see the men and women coming back to your rooms to rest after the busy hours of pleasure-seeking. As my ears become more sensitive, let them distinguish the many words of those who were asking Julian and Teodora about me; and as a great light is made from scattered rays when they are gathered into a crystal lens, as the mountains are formed from grains of sand and the sea from drops of water, so from your chance words, your stray smiles, your idle glances, from a thousand trivial thoughts which you have left scattered in cafés, in theatres, in ball-rooms, and which are now floating in the air, I shall shape my drama, and the crystal of my mind shall be the lens that brings to a focus the lights and shadows, so that from them shall result the dramatic spark and the tragic explosion. My drama is taking shape. Now it has a title, for there in the lamp-light I see the work of the immortal Florentine poet, and in Italian it has given me the name which it would be madness or folly to write or speak in plain Spanish. Paolo and Francesca, may your love help me! (*Sitting down at the table and beginning to write.*) The play! the play begins! The first page is no longer blank. (*Writing.*) Now it has a title. (*Writes madly.*) The Great Galeoto!

(*Curtain.*)

ELEANOR BONTECOU

VICENTE BLASCO IBÁÑEZ
[1867-1928]

Vicente Blasco Ibáñez began his prolific writing career as a regionalist, vividly portraying scenes from his native Valencia. To this early period belong his best novels: La barraca *(1898) and* Cañas y barro *('Reeds and Mud') (1902). There followed a number of novels on social themes in which Blasco Ibáñez projects his own attitudes. The best known are the anti-clerical* La catedral *(1903), set in Toledo, and* Sangre y arena

LA BARRACA

... Eran más de las doce, y las siete acequias comenzaban a mostrarse cansadas de tanto derramar pródigamente el caudal de su justicia, cuando el alguacil llamó a gritos a Bautista Borrull, denunciado por infracción y desobediencia en el riego.

Atravesaron la verja Pimentó y Batiste, y la gente se apretó más contra los hierros.

Veíanse allí muchos de los que vivían en las inmediaciones de las antiguas tierras de Barret.

Aquel juicio era interesante. El odiado novato había sido denunciado por Pimentó, que era el atandador, el que representaba la autoridad de la acequia en su partida.

El valentón, mezclándose en elecciones y galleando en toda la contornada, había conquistado este cargo, que le daba cierto aire de autoridad y consolidaba su prestigio entre los convecinos, los cuales le mimaban y convidaban en los días de riego.

Batiste estaba asombrado con la injusta denuncia. Su palidéz era de indignación. Miraba con ojos de rabia todas las caras conocidas y burlonas que se agolpaban en la verja, y a su enemigo Pimentó, que se contoneaba con altivez, como hombre acostumbrado a comparecer ante el tribunal y a quien correspondía una pequeña parte de su indiscutible autoridad.

—*Parle vosté*—dijo avanzando un pie la acequia más vieja, pues por secular vicio, el tribunal, en vez de usar de las manos, señalaba con la blanca alpargata al que debía de hablar.

Pimentó soltó su acusación. Aquel hombre que estaba junto a él, tal vez por ser nuevo en la Huerta, creía que el reparto del agua era cosa de broma y que podía hacer su santísima voluntad.

(*'Blood and Sand'*), *depicting the brutality of bullfighting, set in Seville. Blasco Ibáñez finally undertook novels of international scope, and one of them,* Los cuatro jinetes del Apocalipsis (*'The Four Horsemen of the Apocalypse'*) (*1916*), *a war novel favouring the Allies, brought him great fame and fortune. His style is vigorous and he is a master of realistic description. Blasco Ibáñez was extremely popular in his own country, and he is no doubt one of the most translated of all Spanish authors.*

THE CABIN

BATISTE'S TRIAL

. . . .

It was after twelve, and the seven judges were beginning to show signs of being weary of such prodigious outpouring of the stream of justice, when the bailiff called out loudly to Bautista Borrull, denouncing him for infraction and disobedience of irrigation-rights.

Pimentó and Batiste passed the railing, and the people pressed up even closer against the bar.

Here were many of those who lived near the ancient land of Barret.

This trial was interesting. The hated newcomer had been denounced by Pimentó, who was the '*atandador*'* of that district.

The bully, by mixing up in elections, and strutting about like a fighting cock all over the neighbourhood, had won this office which gave him a certain air of authority and strengthened his prestige among the neighbours, who made much of him and treated him on irrigation days.

Batiste was amazed at this unjust denunciation. His pallor was that of indignation. He gazed with eyes full of fury at all the familiar mocking faces, which were pressing against the rail, and at his enemy Pimentó, who was strutting about proudly, like a man accustomed to appearing before the tribunal, and to whom a small part of its unquestionable authority belonged.

'Speak,' said the eldest of the judges, putting one foot forward, for according to a century-old custom, the tribunal, instead of using the hands, signalled with the white sandal to him who should speak.

Pimentó poured forth his accusation. This man who was beside him, perhaps because he was new in the *huerta*, seemed to think

* One in charge of the *tanda*, or turn in irrigating.

Él, Pimentó, el atandador, le había dado a Batiste la hora para regar su trigo: las dos de la mañana. Pero sin duda el señor, no queriendo levantarse a tal hora, había dejado perder su turno, y a las cinco, cuando el agua era ya de otros, había alzado la compuerta sin permiso de nadie (primer delito), había robado el riego a los demás vecinos (segundo delito) e intentado regar sus campos, queriendo oponerse a viva fuerza a las órdenes del atandador, lo que constituía el tercero y último delito.

El triple delincuente, volviéndose de mil colores e indignado por las palabras de Pimentó, no pudo contenerse:

—¡Mentira y recontramentira!

El tribunal se indignó ante la energía y la falta de respeto con que protestaba aquel hombre.

Si no guardaba silencio, se le impondría una multa. Pero ¡gran cosa eran las multas para su reconcentrada cólera de hombre pacífico! Siguió protestando contra la injusticia de los hombres, contra el tribunal, que tenía por servidores a pillos embusteros como Pimentó.

Alteróse el tribunal; las siete acequias se encresparon.

—¡Cuatre sòus de multa!

Batiste, dándose cuenta de su situación, calló de repente, asustado por haber incurrido en multa, mientras en el público sonaban las risas y los aullidos de alegría de sus enemigos.

Quedó inmóvil, con la cabeza baja y los ojos empañados por lágrimas de rabia, mientras su brutal enemigo acababa de formular la denuncia.

—Parle vosté—le dijo el tribunal.

Pero en la mirada de los jueces se notaba poca simpatía por aquel alborotador que venía a turbar con sus protestas la solemnidad de las deliberaciones.

Batiste, trémulo por la ira, balbuceó, no sabiendo cómo empezar su defensa, por lo mismo que la creía justísima.

Había sido engañado; Pimentó era un embustero y además su enemigo declarado.

Le había dicho que su hora de riego era a las cinco, se acordaba muy bien, y ahora afirmaba que a las dos; todo por hacerle incurrir en multa, para matar unos trigos en los que estaba la vida de su familia ... ¿Valía para el tribunal la palabra de un hombre honra-

that the apportionment of the water was a trifling matter, and that he could suit his own blessed will.

He, Pimentó, the *atandador,* who represented the authority of the canals in his district, had set for Batiste the hour for watering his wheat. It was two o'clock in the morning. But doubtless the señor, not wishing to arise at that hour, had let his turn go, and at five, when the water was intended for others, he had raised the flood-gate without permission from anybody (the *first* offence), and attempted to water his fields, resolving to oppose, by main force, the orders of the *atandador,* which constituted the *third* and last offence.

The thrice-guilty delinquent, turning all the colours of the rainbow, and indignant at the words of Pimentó, was not able to restrain himself.

'You lie, and lie doubly!'

The tribunal became indignant at the heat and the lack of respect with which this man was protesting.

If he did not keep silent he would be fined.

But what was a fine for the concentrated wrath of a peaceful man! He kept on protesting against the injustice of men, against the tribunal which had, as its servants, such rogues and liars as Pimentó.

The tribunal was stirred up; the seven judges became excited.

Four *sous* for a fine!

Batiste, realizing his situation, suddenly grew silent, terrified at having incurred a fine, while laughter came from the crowd and howls of joy from his enemies.

He remained motionless, with bowed head, and his eyes dimmed with tears of rage, while his brutal enemy finished formulating his denunciation.

'Speak,' the tribunal said to him. But little sympathy was noted in the looks of the judges for this disturber, who had to trouble the solemnity of their deliberations with his protests.

Batiste, trembling with rage, stammered, not knowing how to begin his defence because of the very fact that it seemed to him perfectly just.

The court had been misled; Pimentó was a liar and furthermore his declared enemy. He had told him that his time for irrigation came at five, he remembered it very well, and was now affirming that it was two; just to make him incur a fine, to destroy the wheat upon which the life of his family depended. . . . Did the tribunal value the word of an honest man? Then this was the truth,

do? Pues ésta era la verdad, aunque no podía presentar testigos. ¡Parecía imposible que los señores síndicos, todos buenas personas, se fiasen de un pillo como Pimentó!

La blanca alpargata del presidente golpeó la baldosa de la acera, conjurando el chaparrón de protestas y faltas de respeto que veía en lontananza.

—*Calle vosté.*

Y Batiste calló, mientras el monstruo de las siete cabezas, replegándose en el sofá de damasco, cuchicheaba preparando la sentencia.

—*El tribunal sentènsia* . . . —dijo la acequia más vieja, y se hizo un silencio absoluto.

Toda la gente de la verja mostraba en sus ojos cierta ansiedad, como si ellos fueran los sentenciados. Estaban pendientes de los labios del viejo síndico.

—*Pagará el Batiste Borrull dos lliures de pena y cuatre sòus de multa.*

Esparcióse un murmullo de satisfacción y hasta una vieja comenzó a palmotear gritando: '¡vítor! ¡vítor!' entre las risotadas de la gente.

Batiste salió ciego del tribunal, con la cabeza baja, como si fuera a embestir, y Pimentó permaneció prudentemente a sus espaldas.

Si la gente no se aparta abriéndole paso, es seguro que hubiera disparado sus puños de hombre forzudo, aporreando allí mismo a la canalla hostil.

RAMÓN DEL VALLE-INCLÁN
[1869–1936]

The most polished stylist of the modernist novelists is probably Ramón María del Valle-Inclán. Endowed with a fantastic imagination and exquisite sensitivity, he creates a moody, exotic atmosphere for the many novels set in his native Galicia. His style is musical and poetic (he was a poet and dramatist, as well as a novelist) and is flavoured by numerous literary, archaic and popular expressions.

Valle-Inclán's most famous novels are the four Sonatas *(1902–1905), one for each season of the year, symbolizing the four phases of man's amatory*

although he was not able to present witnesses. It seemed impossible that the honourable syndics, all good people, should trust a rascal like Pimentó!

The white sandal of the president struck the square tile of the sidewalk, as if to avert the storm of protests and the lack of respect which he saw from afar.

'Be silent.'

And Batiste was silent, while the seven-headed monster, folding itself up again on the sofa of damask, was whispering, preparing the sentence.

'The tribunal decrees . . .' said the eldest judge, and there was absolute silence.

All the people around the roped space showed a certain anxiety in their eyes, as if they were the sentenced. They were hanging on the lips of the eldest judge.

'Batiste Borrull shall pay two pounds for penalty, and four *sous* for a fine.'

A murmur of satisfaction arose and spread, and one old woman even began to clap her hands, shouting 'Hurrah! hurrah!' amid the loud laughter of the people.

Batiste went out blindly from the tribunal, with his head lowered as though he were about to fight, and Pimentó prudently stayed behind.

If the people had not parted, opening the way for him, it is certain that he would have struck out with his powerful fists, and given the hostile rabble a beating on the spot. . . .

FRANCIS HAFFKINE SNOW
and BEATRICE M. MEKOTA

life as seen in the memoirs of a sentimental Don Juan, the Marquis de Bradomín. Some of Valle-Inclán's novels deal with the Carlist wars, and in his later writings he developed a satirical, grotesque style—the esperpento—reminiscent of Quevedo.

SONATA DE PRIMAVERA

XVI

Aquella noche las hijas de la Princesa habíanse refugiado en la
terraza, bajo la luna, como las hadas de los cuentos: Rodeaban a
una amiga joven y muy bella, que de tiempo en tiempo me miraba
llena de curiosidad. En el salón, las señoras ancianas conversaban
discretamente, y sonreían al oír las voces juveniles que llegaban en
ráfagas perfumadas con el perfume de las lilas que se abrían al pie
de la terraza. Desde el salón distinguíase el jardín, inmóvil bajo la
luna, que envolvía en pálida claridad la cima mustia de los cipreses
y el balconaje de la terraza, donde otras veces el pavo real abría su
abanico de quimera y de cuento.

Yo quise varias veces acercarme a María Rosario. Todo fué inútil:
Ella adivinaba mis intenciones y alejábase cautelosa, sin ruido, con
la vista baja y las manos cruzadas sobre el escapulario del hábito
monjil que conservaba puesto. Viéndola a tal extremo temerosa, yo
sentía halagado mi orgullo donjuanesco, y algunas veces sólo por
turbarla, cruzaba de un lado al otro. La pobre niña al instante se
prevenía para huir. Yo pasaba aparentando no advertirlo. Tenía la
petulancia de los veinte años. Otros momentos entraba en el salón
y deteníame al lado de las viejas damas, que recibían mis homenajes
con timidez de doncellas. Recuerdo que me hallaba hablando con
aquella devota Marquesa de Téscara, cuando, movido por un oscuro
presentimiento, volví la cabeza y busqué con los ojos la blanca figura
de María Rosario: La Santa ya no estaba.

Una nube de tristeza cubrió mi alma. Dejé a la vieja linajuda
y salí a la terraza. Mucho tiempo permanecí reclinado sobre el
florido balconaje de piedra, contemplando el jardín. En el silencio
perfumado cantaba un ruiseñor, y parecía acordar su voz con la voz
de las fuentes. El reflejo de la luna iluminaba aquel sendero de los
rosales que yo había recorrido otra noche. El aire suave y gentil, un
aire a propósito para llevar suspiros, pasaba murmurando, y a lo
lejos, entre mirtos inmóviles, ondulaba el agua de un estanque. Yo
evocaba en la memoria el rostro de María Rosario y no cesaba de
pensar:

—¿Qué siente ella . . . ? ¿Qué siente ella por mí . . . ?

Ligeras nubes blancas erraban en torno de la luna y la seguían
en su curso fantástico y vagabundo: Empujadas por un soplo invisible, la cubrieron y quedó sumido en sombras el jardín. El
estanque dejó de brillar entre los mirtos inmóviles: sólo la cima de
los cipreses permaneció iluminada. Como para armonizar con la

SONATA OF SPRING

CHAPTER XVI

That night the daughters of the Princess gathered in the moonlight on the terrace; they were like sprites in the fairytales as they surrounded a beautiful young friend who from time to time gazed on me in curiosity. In the salon the older ladies were carrying on a discreet conversation, smiling at the sound of the young voices that came in eddies with the perfume of lilies from the openings on the terrace. The garden stretched out motionless in the moonlight which wove magic over the pallid tops of the cypresses and the balconies, where a peacock was spreading his fantastic fan of feathers.

I tried at various times to approach Maria Rosario. It was useless; she divined my intentions and cautiously and noiselessly defeated them with her eyes lowered and her hands crossed on the conventual scapular, she was already wearing. The sight of her timidity so aroused, flattered my pride as a Don Juan, and sometimes merely to torment her I would pass from one side to another. The poor child prepared for flight on the instant. I would pass apparently without seeing her. I had all the impetuosity of my twenty years. Again I would enter the salon and approach the old ladies who received my intentions with the timidity of damsels. I remember I was once talking with the devout old Marquise de Téscara when intuitively I turned my head toward the white form of Maria Rosario, and suddenly found my saint had gone.

A cloud of gloom came over me; I left the elderly lady and hurried to the terrace. I remained a long time leaning on the marble baluster, gazing on the garden. A nightingale was singing amid the silent perfume and its voice seemed to harmonize with the fountains. The moon shone down the path of roses I had followed the night before; the breeze was light and soft as though it carried sighs and would murmur them far among the myrtle groves and over the stirring waters of the pool. With Maria Rosario's face in my memory I incessantly asked myself: 'What does she think? What does she think of me?'

Light clouds gathered about the moon and followed her on her fantastic journey; suddenly in a heap they blinded her and left the garden in darkness. The pool lost its gleam among the still myrtles; only the tops of the cypresses held the light. As if to harmonize with the darkness a breeze arose and swept in a great gust across the scene, bringing the scent of scattered roses. I

sombra, se levantó una brisa que pasó despertando largo susurro en todo el recinto y trajo hasta mí el aroma de las rosas deshojadas. Lentamente volví hasta el Palacio: Mis ojos se detuvieron en una ventana iluminada, y no sé qué oscuro presentimiento hizo palpitar mi corazón. Aquella ventana alzábase apenas sobre la terraza, permanecía abierta, y el aire ondulaba la cortina. Me pareció que por el fondo de la estancia cruzaba una sombra blanca. Quise acercarme, pero el rumor de unas pisadas bajo la avenida de los cipreses me detuvo: El viejo mayordomo paseaba a la luz de la luna sus ensueños de artista. Yo quedé inmóvil en el fondo del jardín. Y contemplando aquella luz, el corazón latía:

—¿Qué siente ella . . . ? ¿Qué siente ella por mí . . . ?

¡Pobre María Rosario! Yo la creía enamorada, y sin embargo, mi corazón presentía no sé qué quimérica y confusa desventura. Quise volver a sumergirme en mi amoroso ensueño, pero el canto de un sapo repetido monótonamente bajo la arcada de los cipreses, distraía y turbaba mi pensamiento. Recuerdo que de niño he leído muchas veces en un libro de devociones donde rezaba mi abuela, que el Diablo solía tomar ese aspecto para turbar la oración de un santo monje. Era natural que a mí me ocurriese lo mismo. Yo, calumniado y mal comprendido, nunca fuí otra cosa que un místico galante, como San Juan de la Cruz. En lo más florido de mis años, hubiera dado gustoso todas las glorias mundanas por poder escribir en mis tarjetas: El Marqués de Bradomín, Confesor de Princesas.

XXIV

Qué triste es para mí el recuerdo de aquel día. María Rosario estaba en el fondo de un salón llenando de rosas los floreros de la capilla. Cuando yo entré, quedóse un momento indecisa: Sus ojos miraron medrosos hacia la puerta, y luego se volvieron a mí con un ruego tímido y ardiente. Llenaba en aquel momento el último

returned to the Palace; one of the windows was lighted up and a strange presentiment caused my heart to palpitate. The window was raised only a little above the terrace and the wind was waving its curtains. It seemed to me that a pale shadow crossed the room. I wished to draw closer but the sound of steps on the avenue of the cypresses held me back; it was the old major-domo walking in his dreams of art. I stood still in the depths of the garden. Gazing on her lighted window, my heart repeated : 'What does she think? What does she think of me?'

Poor Maria Rosario! I believe she was in love and yet her heart forewarned her of some strange confused adventure. I wished to lose myself in my amorous dreams but the croak of a frog, monotonously sounding under the arching cypresses, distracted and disturbed my thoughts. I remember that as a child I had read many times in my grandmother's prayerbook that the devil used to take the form of a frog to interrupt the devotions of a holy monk. It seemed natural that the same thing should occur to me. I, the calumniated and misunderstood, was just such another mystical gallant as Saint John of the Cross! In the flower of my youth I would gladly have given up all other early glories to be able to inscribe on my cards : 'The Marquis de Bradomín, Confessor of Princesses.'

Chapter XXIV

What a sad memory that day has become to me! Maria Rosario was filling the flower-jars of the chapel at the end of the salon; when I entered she stood undecided for a moment. With a timid, ardent light her eyes looked in fear on the door and back again

florero, y sobre sus manos deshojóse una rosa. Yo entonces le dije, sonriendo:

—¡Hasta las rosas se mueren por besar vuestras manos!

Ella también sonrió contemplando las hojas que había entre sus dedos, y después con leve soplo las hizo volar. Quedamos silenciosos: Era la caída de la tarde y el sol doraba una ventana con sus últimos reflejos. Los cipreses del jardín levantaban sus cimas pensativas en el azul del crepúsculo, al pie de la vidriera iluminada. Dentro, apenas si se distinguía la forma de las rosas, y en el recogimiento del salón las rosas esparcían un perfume tenue y las palabras morían lentamente igual que la tarde. Mis ojos buscaban los ojos de María Rosario con el empeño de aprisionarlos en la sombra. Ella suspiró angustiada como si el aire le faltase, y apartándose el cabello de la frente con ambas manos, huyó hacia la ventana. Yo, temeroso de asustarla, no intenté seguirla y sólo le dije después de un largo silencio:

—¿No me daréis una rosa?

Volvióse lentamente y repuso con voz tenue:

—Si la queréis . . .

Dudó un instante, y de nuevo se acercó. Procuraba mostrarse serena, pero yo veía temblar sus manos sobre los floreros, al elegir la rosa. Con una sonrisa llena de angustia me dijo:

—Os daré la mejor.

Ella seguía buscando en los floreros. Yo suspiré romántico:

—La mejor está en vuestros labios.

Me miró apartándose pálida y angustiada:

—No sois bueno . . . ¿Por qué me decís esas cosas?

—Por veros enojada.

—¿Y eso os agrada? ¡Algunas veces me parecéis el Demonio! . . .

—El Demonio no sabe querer.

Quedóse silenciosa. Apenas podía distinguirse su rostro en la tenue claridad del salón, y sólo supe que lloraba cuando estallaron sus sollozos. Me acerqué queriendo consolarla:

—¡Oh! . . . Perdonadme.

Y mi voz fué tierna, apasionada y sumisa. Yo mismo, al oírla, sentí su extraño poder de seducción. Era llegado el momento supremo, y presintiéndolo, mi corazón se estremecía con el ansia de la espera cuando está próxima una gran aventura. María Rosario cerraba los ojos con espanto, como al borde de un abismo. Su boca descolorida parecía sentir una voluptuosidad angustiosa. Yo cogí sus manos que estaban yertas: Ella me las abandonó sollozando, con un frenesí doloroso:

at me. As she was filling the last jar, a rose broke over her hand. I smiled and said to her : 'Even the roses die in kissing your hands.'

She also smiled, seeing the petals between her fingers, and gave a slight sigh as they drifted away. We remained silent. It was nightfall, and the sun shone in its last golden glow upon the window. The cypresses lifted their pensive points in the twilight azure below. Within, one could hardly make out the arrangement of things; throughout the salon the roses scattered a perfume as light as the light words that died away with the sun. My eyes sought the eyes of Maria Rosario with the hope of imprisoning them in the shadows. She sighed heavily as though for want of air, and drawing back her locks with both hands from her forehead she took refuge by a window. I was afraid to assist her, and without following her merely said after a long silence : 'Are you not going to give me a rose?'

She turned and answered softly : 'Would you like one?'

I hesitated a moment and then drew nearer. I managed to appear calm, but I could see her hands trembling over the jars as she selected the flower. With a sorrowful smile she said : 'I shall give you the most beautiful one.'

She continued to search among the roses. I sighed romantically : 'The loveliest would be your lips.'

She drew back and looked at me in pain : 'You are not kind. Why do you say such things to me?'

'To see your anger.'

'And that delights you? Sometimes I think you are the devil.'

'The devil does not know what love is.'

Silence fell again. I could hardly make out her face in the dying light, and I only knew from her soft sobs that she wept. I came closer to console her : 'Oh! forgive my faults.'

My voice was tender and passionate. I myself as I heard it felt its strange seductive power. The supreme moment had arrived; my heart was seized with anxiety over the great adventure that faced me. Maria Rosario closed her eyes in dread, as though she were on the brink of an abyss. Her colourless lips expressed a painful voluptuousness. I seized her hands, which were lying inert. She abandoned them to me, sobbing in her grief : 'Why do you

—¿Por qué os gozáis en hacerme sufrir? . . . ¡Si sabéis que todo es imposible!

—¡Imposible! . . . Yo nunca esperé conseguir vuestro amor . . . ¡Ya sé que no lo merezco! . . . Solamente quiero pediros perdón y oír de vuestros labios que rezaréis por mí cuando esté lejos.

—¡Callad! . . . ¡Callad! . . .

—Os contemplo tan alta, tan lejos de mí, tan ideal, que juzgo vuestras oraciones como las de una santa.

—¡Callad! . . . ¡Callad! . . .

—Mi corazón agoniza sin esperanza. Acaso podré olvidaros, pero este amor habrá sido para mí como un fuego purificador.

—¡Callad! . . . ¡Callad! . . .

Yo tenía lágrimas en los ojos, y sabía que cuando se llora, las manos pueden arriesgarse a ser audaces. ¡Pobre María Rosario, quedóse pálida como una muerta, y pensé que iba a desmayarse en mis brazos! Aquella niña era una santa, y viéndome a tal extremo desgraciado, no tenía valor para mostrarse más cruel conmigo. Cerraba los ojos, y gemía agobiada:

—¡Dejadme! . . . ¡Dejadme! . . .

Yo murmuré:

—¿Por qué me aborrecéis tanto?

—¡Porque sois el Demonio!

Me miró despavorida, como si al sonido de mi voz se despertase, y arrancándose de mis brazos huyó hacia la ventana que doraban todavía los últimos rayos del sol. Apoyó la frente en los cristales y comenzó a sollozar. En el jardín se levantaba el canto de un ruiseñor, que evocaba en la sombra azul de la tarde un recuerdo ingenuo de santidad.

PÍO BAROJA
[1872–1956]

The Basque Pío Baroja was a doctor and baker before he turned to writing as his exclusive occupation. He is one of the most original and unorthodox of modern authors. His numerous novels cover a wide variety of themes, but he has a penchant, in particular, for writing about the lower classes of society, and reflects in his novels a sceptical and pessimistic view of our civilization. His style is careless and abrupt, perhaps deliberately so, and his plots are, by design, often incomplete.

take pleasure in making me suffer? You know that everything is impossible!'

'Impossible! I know I shall never obtain your love! I know I do not deserve it! Only I want you to pardon me and to know that you will pray for me when I am far away.'

'Silence! Silence!'

'I regard you as so high, so far above me, so ideal, that I want your prayers as I should want those of a saint.'

'Silence! Silence!'

'My heart suffers, without a single hope. Perhaps I may learn to forget you, but your love will always be a purifying fire.'

'Silence! Silence!'

There were tears in my eyes and I knew that with tears the hands may show some boldness. Poor Maria Rosario seemed pale as death and I thought she was about to faint in my arms. This maiden was really a saint; seeing the extremity of my grief she did not wish to show me any more cruelty. She closed her eyes and murmured in agony: 'Leave me! Leave me!'

I whispered to her: 'Why do you abhor me so?'

'Because you are the devil!'

She gazed at me in terror, and as if the sound of my voice were awakening her she broke from my arms and fled toward the window, which was golden with the sunset. She leaned her forehead against the glass and sobbed. From the garden came the song of the nightingale, stirring in the twilight some innocent memory of holiness.

MAY HEYWOOD BROUN
and THOMAS WALSH

A number of Baroja's novels deal with the Carlist wars. The swift-moving Zalacaín el aventurero (1909) *belongs in this category, as well as some of the twenty-two novels of the series* Memorias de un hombre de acción. *Among the works in which Baroja best reveals his iconoclastic ideas are* Camino de perfección (1902), Paradox Rey (1906) *and* El árbol de la ciencia (1911). *Baroja has termed the latter 'probably my most finished and complete book'.*

EL ÁRBOL DE LA CIENCIA

LA CRUELDAD UNIVERSAL

Tenía Andrés un gran deseo de comentar filosóficamente las vidas de los vecinos de la casa de Lulú. A sus amigos no les interesaban estos comentarios y filosofías, y decidió, una mañana de un día de fiesta, ir a ver a su tío Iturrioz.

Al principio de conocerle—Andrés no le trató a su tío hasta los catorce o quince años—, Iturrioz le pareció un hombre seco y egoísta, que lo tomaba todo con indiferencia; luego, sin saber a punto fijo hasta dónde llegaba su egoísmo y su sequedad, encontró que era una de las pocas personas con quienes podía conversar acerca de puntos trascendentales.

Iturrioz vivía en un quinto piso del barrio de Argüelles, en una casa con una hermosa azotea.

Le asistía un criado, antiguo soldado de la época en que Iturrioz fué médico militar.

Entre amo y criado habían arreglado la azotea, pintado las tejas con alquitrán, sin duda para hacerlas impermeables, y puesto unas graderías donde estaban escalonados las cajas de madera y los cubos llenos de tierra, donde tenían sus plantas.

Aquella mañana en que se presentó Andrés en casa de Iturrioz, su tío se estaba bañando y el criado le llevó a la azotea.

Se veía desde allí el Guadarrama entre dos casas altas; hacia el oeste, el tejado del cuartel de la Montaña ocultaba los cerros de la Casa de Campo, y a un lado del cuartel se destacaba la torre de Móstoles y la carretera de Extremadura, con unos molinos de viento en sus inmediaciones. Más al sur brillaban, al sol de una mañana de abril, las manchas verdes de los cementerios de San Isidro y San Justo, las dos torres de Getafe y la ermita del Cerrillo de los Ángeles.

Poco después salió Iturrioz a la azotea.

—¿Qué, te pasa algo?—le dijo a su sobrino al verle.

—Nada; venía a charlar un rato con usted.

—Muy bien, siéntate; yo voy a regar mis tiestos.

Iturrioz abrió la fuente que tenía en un ángulo de la terraza, llenó una cuba y comenzó con un cacharro a echar agua en las plantas.

Andrés habló de la gente de la vecindad de Lulú, de las escenas del hospital, como casos extraños, dignos de un comentario; de Manolo el Chafandín, del tío Miserias, de don Cleto, de doña Virginia . . .

THE TREE OF KNOWLEDGE

UNIVERSAL CRUELTY

Andrés felt a great desire to comment philosophically on the lives of these lodgers in Lulu's house; but his friends were not interested in these comments or philosophies, and one morning, a holiday, he resolved to pay a visit to his Uncle Iturrioz.

When he first knew him—he had not met him till he was about fifteen—Iturrioz seemed to him a dry and selfish man who looked on everything with indifference; later, without exactly knowing how far his dryness and egoism went, he found he was one of the few persons with whom one could discuss transcendental subjects.

Iturrioz lived on the fifth floor of a house in the Argüelles quarter, a house with a fine flat roof.

He was attended by a servant who had been a soldier when Iturrioz was an army doctor.

Between them they had set the house-top in order, painted the tiles with pitch to make them waterproof, and set up steps for the wooden boxes and tubs full of earth in which they kept their plants.

The morning on which Andrés paid him a visit, Iturrioz was having his bath, and the servant took Andrés up to the roof.

Between two tall houses one had a view of the Guadarrama Mountains; to the west the roof of the Montaña barracks concealed the hills of the Casa del Campo; and on one side of the barracks appeared the Torre de Móstoles and the highroad to Extremadura with some windmills near it. Farther to the south shone in the April sun the green patches of the cemeteries of San Justo and San Isidro, the two towers of Getafe, and the hermitage of the Cerrillo de los Angeles.

After a little Iturrioz came out on to the house-top.

'Well, is anything the matter?' he asked, when he saw his nephew.

'Nothing; I came to have a talk with you.'

'Very good. Sit down; I am going to water my flower-pots.'

Iturrioz opened a tap at a corner of the terrace and filled a tub with water, and then with a piece of pot began to throw water on to the plants.

Andrés spoke of Lulu's neighbours and of the scenes at the hospital as strange things requiring a commentary, of Manolo the Buffoon, Old Skinflint, Don Cleto, and Doña Virginia.

—¿Qué consecuencias puede sacarse de todas estas vidas?—preguntó Andrés al final.

—Para mí la consecuencia es fácil—contestó Iturrioz con el bote de agua en la mano.—Que la vida es una lucha constante, una cacería cruel en que nos vamos devorando los unos a los otros. Plantas, microbios, animales.

—Si yo también he pensado en eso—repuso Andrés;—pero voy abandonando la idea. Primeramente el concepto de la lucha por la vida llevada así a los animales, a las plantas y hasta a los minerales, como se hace muchas veces, no es más que un concepto antropomórfico; después, ¿qué lucha por la vida es la de ese hombre don Cleto, que se abstiene de combatir, o la de ese hermano Juan, que da su dinero a los enfermos?

—Te contestaré por partes—repuso Iturrioz dejando el bote para regar, porque estas discusiones le apasionaban.—Tú me dices, este concepto de lucha es un concepto antropomórfico. Claro, llamamos a todos los conflictos lucha, porque es la idea humana que más se aproxima a esa relación que para nosotros produce un vencedor y un vencido. Si no tuviéramos este concepto en el fondo, no hablaríamos de lucha. La hiena que monda los huesos de un cadáver, la araña que sorbe una mosca, no hace más ni menos que el árbol bondadoso llevándose de la tierra el agua y las sales necesarias para su vida. El espectador indiferente, como yo, ve a la hiena, a la araña y al árbol, y se los explica. El hombre justiciero le pega un tiro a la hiena, aplasta con la bota a la araña y se sienta a la sombra del árbol, y cree que hace bien.

—Entonces, ¿para usted no hay lucha, ni hay justicia?

—En un sentido absoluto, no; en un sentido relativo, sí. Todo lo que vive tiene un proceso para apoderarse primero del espacio, ocupar un lugar; luego para crecer y multiplicarse; este proceso de la energía de un vivo contra los obstáculos del medio, es lo que llamamos lucha. Respecto de la justicia, yo creo que lo justo en el fondo es lo que nos conviene. Supón, en el ejemplo de antes, que la hiena, en vez de ser muerta por el hombre, mata al hombre, que el árbol cae sobre él y le aplasta, que la araña le hace una picadura venenosa; pues nada de eso nos parece justo, porque no nos conviene. A pesar de que en el fondo no haya más que esto, un interés utilitario, ¿quién duda que la idea de justicia y de equidad es una tendencia que existe en nosotros? ¿Pero cómo la vamos a realizar?

—Eso es lo que yo me pregunto, ¿cómo realizarla?

—¿ Hay que indignarse porque una araña mate a una mosca? —siguió diciendo Iturrioz.—Bueno. Indignémonos. ¿Qué vamos a hacer? ¿Matarla? Matémosla. Eso no impedirá que sigan las arañas

'What inference can one draw from all these lives?' he asked.

'For me the inference is easy,' answered Iturrioz, waterpot in hand: 'that life is a constant struggle, a cruel carnage in which we devour one another. Plants, microbes, animals.'

'Yes,' answered Andrés, 'the same idea occurred to me, but I do not think it will hold water. In the first place the conception of life as a struggle among animals, plants and even minerals is an anthropomorphic idea; and then what kind of a struggle for life is that of Don Cleto, who refuses to fight, or of Brother Juan, who gives his money to the poor?'

'I will answer the two questions separately,' said Iturrioz, setting down his watering-pot, for such questions were his delight. 'You say the idea of a struggle is an anthropomorphic idea. Well, of course, we give to all the various conflicts the name of a struggle because it is the human idea best fitted to express the relations which with us produce a victor and a vanquished. If that were not, essentially, what we meant we would not speak of a struggle. The hyena picking clean the bones of a carcass, the spider sucking the life out of a fly, is acting precisely in the same way as the kindly tree which takes from the earth the moisture and salts necessary to its life. An indifferent spectator like myself watches the hyena, the spider, and the tree and understands them; a man with a sense of justice shoots the hyena, crushes the spider under his foot, and sits down under the shade of the tree, imagining that he has done a good deed.'

'Then you consider there is no struggle and no justice?'

'In an absolute sense there is none; in a relative sense there is. Every living thing has first to gain possession of space, of a place to exist, and then of the means to grow and multiply; this process carried on by the energy of the living against the obstacles which surround it is what we call a struggle. As to justice I think that, essentially, it is what happens to suit us. Suppose, for instance, that the hyena, instead of being killed, kills the man, or that the tree falls upon him and kills him, or that the spider gives him a poisonous bite; nothing in all that seems to us just, because it does not suit us. Yet, although essentially it is no more than a question of utilitarian interest, who can doubt that the idea of justice and equity is a tendency which exists in us? But how are we to put it into practice?'

'That's what I ask myself, how put it into practice?'

'Are we to grow indignant because a spider kills a fly?' went on Iturrioz. 'What are we to do—kill the spider? If we kill it, that will not prevent spiders from devouring flies. Are we to cure man-

comiéndose a las moscas. ¿Vamos a quitarle al hombre esos instintos fieros que te repugnan? ¿Vamos a borrar esa sentencia del poeta latino: *Homo homini lupus*, el hombre es un lobo para el hombre? Está bien. En cuatro o cinco mil años lo podremos conseguir. El hombre ha hecho de un carnívoro como el chacal, un omnívoro como el perro; pero se necesitan muchos siglos para eso. No sé si habrás leído que Spallanzani había acostumbrado a una paloma a comer carne y a un águila a comer y digerir el pan. Ahí tienes el caso de esos grandes apóstoles religiosos y laicos; son águilas que se alimentan de pan en vez de alimentarse de carnes palpitantes; son lobos vegetarianos. Ahí tienes el caso del hermano Juan . . .

—Ese no creo que sea un águila, ni un lobo.

—Será un mochuelo o una garduña; pero de instintos perturbados.

—Sí, es muy posible—respuso Andrés;—pero creo que nos hemos desviado de la cuestión; no veo la consecuencia.

—La consecuencia, a la que yo iba, era ésta: que ante la vida no hay más que dos soluciones prácticas para el hombre sereno, o la abstención y la contemplación indiferente de todo, o la acción limitándose a un círculo pequeño. Es decir, que se puede tener el quijotismo contra una anomalía; pero tenerlo contra una regla general, es absurdo.

—De manera que, según usted, el que quiera hacer algo tiene que restringir su acción justiciera a un medio pequeño.

—Claro, a un medio pequeño; tú puedes abarcar en tu contemplación la casa, el pueblo, el país, la sociedad, el mundo, todo lo vivo y todo lo muerto; pero si intentas realizar una acción, y una acción justiciera, tendrás que restringirte hasta el punto de que todo te vendrá ancho, quizá hasta la misma conciencia.

—Es lo que tiene de bueno la filosofía—dijo Andrés con amargura;—le convence a uno de que lo mejor es no hacer nada.

Iturrioz dió unas cuantas vueltas por la azotea y luego dijo:

—Es la única objeción que me puedes hacer; pero no es mía la culpa . . .

—Sí, sí, no siga usted más; la vida es una cacería horrible.

—La naturaleza es la que tiene la culpa; cuando trata de reventar a uno, lo revienta a conciencia. La justicia es una ilusión humana; en el fondo todo es destruir, todo es crear. Cazar, guerrear, digerir, respirar, son formas de creación y de destrucción al mismo tiempo.

—Y entonces, ¿qué hacer?—murmuró Andrés.—¿Ir a la inconsciencia? ¿Digerir, guerrear, cazar, con la serenidad de un salvaje?

—¿Crees tú en la serenidad del salvaje?—preguntó Iturrioz.— ¡Qué ilusión! Eso también es una invención nuestra. El salvaje nunca ha sido sereno.

kind of these ferocious instincts to which you object? Are we to
erase the Latin writer's verdict that man is a wolf to man : *homo
homini lupus?* Very well; in four or five thousand years we shall
be able to do so. Man has converted a carnivorous animal like the
jackal into an omnivorous animal like the dog; but it requires
centuries to effect this. You may have read that Spallanzini taught
a dove to eat meat, and an eagle to eat and digest bread. That is
the case of these great religious and lay apostles : they are eagles
eating bread instead of raw meat; they are wolves turned vege-
tarians. Brother Juan for instance.'

'I don't think he's an eagle, nor a wolf.'

'He may be an owl or a martin, a perverted one.'

'Possibly,' answered Andrés, 'but I think we have wandered
from the point; I don't see what inference is to be drawn.'

'The inference that I wished to draw is this : that a man of
clear mind confronted with life has but two practical courses open,
either to abstain from action and contemplate everything with
indifference, or to limit his action to a small area; in other words
one may be quixotic in an anomalous case but to be so as a general
rule is absurd.'

'Then you think that a man of action must limit his love of
justice within narrow bounds?'

'Of course he must; you may include in your view your house,
your town, your region, society, the world, every dead and living
thing; but if you attempt to act, and to act in a spirit of justice,
you must restrict yourself more and more, even perhaps within
your own conscience.'

'That is the beauty of philosophy,' said Andrés bitterly. 'It
convinces one that it is best to do nothing.'

Iturrioz walked up and down the house-top and then said :
'That is the only objection you can bring against me, and it's not
my fault.' . . .

'Yes, yes, you need say no more : life is a horrible carnage.'

'It is characteristic of Nature that when it intends to ruin you, it
does so thoroughly. Justice is a human illusion : essentially everything is destruction and creation. Hunting, war, digestion,
breathing are instances of simultaneous creation and destruction.'

'But what must one do?' murmured Andrés. 'Become indifferent?
Digest, fight, and hunt with the serenity of a savage?'

'You believe in the serenity of the savage? What an illusion!
That is another of our inventions. The savage has never been
serene.'

—¿Es que no habrá plan ninguno para vivir con cierto decoro?—
preguntó Andrés.

—El que lo tiene es porque ha inventado uno para su uso. Yo hoy
creo que todo lo natural, que todo lo espontáneo es malo; que sólo
lo artificial, lo creado por el hombre, es bueno. Si pudiera, viviría
en un club de Londres; no iría nunca al campo, sino a un parque;
bebería agua filtrada y respiraría aire esterilizado . . .

Andrés ya no quiso atender a Iturrioz, que comenzaba a fanta-
sear por entretenimiento. Se levantó y se apoyó en el barandado de
la azotea.

Sobre los tejados de la vecindad revoloteaban unas palomas; en
un canalón grande corrían y jugueteaban unos gatos.

Separados por una tapia alta había dos jardines: uno era de un
colegio de niñas; el otro, de un convento de frailes.

El jardin del convento se hallaba rodeado por árboles frondosos;
el del colegio no tenía más que algunos macizos con hierbas y flores,
y era una cosa extraña que daba cierta impresión de algo alegórico,
ver al mismo tiempo jugar a las niñas corriendo y gritando, y a los
frailes que pasaban silenciosos en filas de cinco o seis dando la vuelta
al patio.

—Vida es lo uno y vida es lo otro—dijo Iturrioz filosóficamente
comenzando a regar sus plantas.

Andrés se fué a la calle.

—¿Qué hacer? ¿Qué dirección dar a la vida?—se preguntó con
angustia. Y, la gente, las cosas, el sol, le parecían sin realidad ante
el problema planteado en su cerebro.

MIGUEL DE UNAMUNO
[1864–1936]

*In the opinion of many scholars Miguel de Unamuno was the outstanding
Spaniard of the twentieth century. Professor, philosopher, essayist, poet and
novelist, he exerted an important influence upon Spanish intellectuals.*

His most famous work, Del sentimiento trágico de la vida *(1913),
develops one of the author's main themes, the struggle between faith and*

NIEBLA

XXXI

Aquella tempestad del alma de Augusto terminó, como en terrible
calma, en decisión de suicidarse. Quería acabar consigo mismo, que
era la fuente de sus desdichas propias. Mas antes de llevar a cabo su

'Is there no possible plan to live with a certain decency?' asked Andrés.

'Only if one invents one for one's own use. And, today, I believe that whatever is spontaneous and natural is bad, that only the artificial, man's creation, is good. If I could I would live in a London club; I would never go into the country except to a park; the water I drank would be filtered, the air sterilized——'

But Andrés was no longer listening to Iturrioz, who had begun to follow the bent of his fancy. He got up and leant upon the balustrade running around the roof.

Some doves were flying above the neighbouring roofs; on a large gutter cats were running and playing.

In front, separated by a high wall, were two gardens; one belonged to a girls' college, the other to a monastery.

The convent garden was surrounded by shady trees; that of the college had nothing but plots of grass and flowers; and it was a strange thing, not without a certain impression of allegory, to see at one and the same time the girls running and shouting and the friars walking silently round their court, in rows of five or six.

'Both the one and the other are life,' said Iturrioz philosophically, and began to water his plants.

Andrés went out into the street.

What should he do? How order his life? he asked himself searchingly. And with this problem in his mind the people he met, the things he saw, the sun itself seemed to lack reality.

AUBREY F. G. BELL

reason. Since his novels do not conform to conventional novelistic requirements, Unamuno invented the term 'nivolas'. One of his most popular 'nivolas' is Niebla (1914), from which our excerpt comes. It is of unusual interest for it presents a lively argument between the author and one of his characters.

MIST

AUGUSTO HAS AN INTERVIEW WITH THE AUTHOR

The storm in the soul of Augusto ended in a terrible calm : he had resolved to kill himself. He wanted to put an end to that self which had been the cause of all his misery. But before carrying

propósito, como el náufrago que se agarra a una débil tabla, ocurriósele consultarlo conmigo, con el autor de todo este relato. Por entonces había leído Augusto un ensayo mío en que, aunque de pasada, hablaba del suicidio, y tal impresión pareció hacerle, así como otras cosas que de mí había leído, que no quiso dejar este mundo sin haberme conocido y platicado un rato conmigo. Emprendió, pues, un viaje acá, a Salamanca, donde hace más de veinte años vivo, para visitarme.

Cuando me anunciaron su visita sonreí enigmáticamente y le mandé pasar a mi despacho-librería. Entró en él como un fantasma, miró a un retrato mío al óleo que allí preside a los libros de mi librería, y a una seña mía se sentó, frente a mí.

Empezó hablándome de mis trabajos literarios y más o menos filosóficos, demostrando conocerlos bastante bien, lo que no dejó, ¡claro está!, de halagarme, y en seguida empezó a contarme su vida y sus desdichas. Le atajé diciéndole que se ahorrase aquel trabajo, pues de las vicisitudes de su vida sabía yo tanto como él, y se lo demostré citándole los más íntimos pormenores y los que él creía más secretos. Me miró con ojos de verdadero terror y como quien mira a un ser increíble; creí notar que se le alteraba el color y traza del semblante y que hasta temblaba. Le tenía yo fascinado.

—¡Parece mentira! —repetía—, ¡parece mentira! A no verlo no lo creería . . . No sé si estoy despierto o soñando . . .

—Ni despierto ni soñando —le contesté.

—No me lo explico . . . no me lo explico —añadió—; mas puesto que usted parece saber sobre mí tanto como sé yo mismo, acaso adivine mi propósito . . .

—Sí —le dije—, tú —y recalqué este *tú* con un tono autoritario—, tú, abrumado por tus desgracias, has concebido la diabólica idea de suicidarte, y antes de hacerlo, movido por algo que has leído en uno de mis últimos ensayos, vienes a consultármelo.

El pobre hombre temblaba como un azogado, mirándome como un poseído miraría. Intentó levantarse, acaso para huir de mí; no podía. No disponía de sus fuerzas.

—¡No, no te muevas! —le ordené.

—Es que . . . es que . . . —balbuceó.

—Es que tú no puedes suicidarte, aunque lo quieras.

out his plan it occurred to him, like a drowning sailor who grasps at a straw, to come and talk it over with me, the author of this whole story. Augusto had read an essay of mine in which I made a passing reference to suicide and this, together with some other things of mine that he had read, had evidently made such an impression upon him that he did not wish to leave this world without having met me and talked with me for a while. Accordingly, he came here to Salamanca, where I have been living for twenty years past, to pay me a visit.

When his call was announced I smiled enigmatically, and I had him come into my study. He entered like a ghost. He looked at a portrait of me in oil which presides over the books of my library, and then at a sign from me he took a seat opposite me.

He began by speaking of my literary works, in particular of those that were more or less philosophical, showing that he knew them very well; which, of course, did not fail to please me. Then he began to tell me of his life and of his misfortunes. I interrupted him by telling him to spare himself the trouble; I was as familiar with the vicissitudes of his life as he himself; and this I demonstrated to him by citing some of the most intimate details, and in particular some things that he thought to be utterly hidden. He looked at me with genuine terror in his eyes, as one looks at some incredible being. I seemed to see a change in the colour and in the lines of his face, and I saw that he even trembled. I had him fascinated.

'It hardly seems true,' he kept repeating, 'it hardly seems true. I shouldn't believe it if I had not seen it. I don't know whether I am awake or dreaming——'

'Neither awake nor dreaming,' I replied.

'I can't explain it—I can't explain it,' he went on. 'But since you seem to know as much about me as I know myself, perhaps you guess my purpose in coming.'

'Yes,' I said. 'You'—and I gave to this 'you' the emphasis of authority—'you, oppressed by the weight of your misfortunes, have conceived the diabolical idea of killing yourself; and before doing it, impelled by something you have read in one of my last essays, you have come to consult me about it.'

The poor man shook like a drop of mercury and looked at me with the stare of one possessed. He tried to rise, perhaps with the idea of flight, but he could not. He could not summon the strength.

'No, don't move,' I commanded him.

'Do you mean—do you mean——' he stammered.

'I mean that you cannot commit suicide even if you wish to do so.'

—¿Cómo? —exclamó al verse de tal modo negado y contradicho.

—Sí. Para que uno se pueda matar a sí mismo, ¿qué es menester? —le pregunté.

—Que tenga valor para hacerlo —me contestó.

—No —le dije—, ¡que esté vivo!

—¡Desde luego!

—¡Y tú no estás vivo!

—¿Cómo que no estoy vivo? ¿es que he muerto? —y empezó, sin darse clara cuenta de lo que hacía, a palparse a sí mismo.

—¡No, hombre, no! —le repliqué—. Te dije antes que no estabas ni despierto ni dormido, y ahora te digo que no estás ni muerto ni vivo.

—¡Acabe usted de explicarse de una vez, por Dios! ¡acabe de explicarse! —me suplicó consternado—, porque son tales las cosas que estoy viendo y oyendo esta tarde, que temo volverme loco.

—Pues bien; la verdad es, querido Augusto —le dije con la más dulce de mis voces—, que no puedes matarte porque no estás vivo, y que no estás vivo, ni tampoco muerto, porque no existes . . .

—¿Cómo que no existo? —exclamó.

—No, no existes más que como ente de ficción; no eres, pobre Augusto, más que un producto de mi fantasía y de las de aquellos de mis lectores que lean el relato que de tus fingidas venturas y malandanzas he escrito yo; tú no eres más que un personaje de novela, o de *nivola*, o como quieras llamarle. Ya sabes, pues, tu secreto.

Al oír esto quedóse el pobre hombre mirándome un rato con una de esas miradas perforadoras que parecen atravesar la mira e ir más allá, miró luego un momento a mi retrato al óleo que preside a mis libros, le volvió el color y aliento, fué recobrándose, se hizo dueño de sí, apoyó los codos en mi camilla, a que estaba arrimado frente a mí, y, la cara en las palmas de las manos y mirándome con una sonrisa en los ojos, me dijo lentamente:

—Mire usted bien, don Miguel . . . no sea que esté usted equivocado y que ocurra precisamente todo lo contrario de lo que usted se cree y me dice.

'What!' he cried, finding himself so flatly opposed and contradicted.

'Yes, if a man is going to kill himself what is the first thing that is necessary?' I asked him.

'That he should have the courage to do it,' he replied.

'No,' I said, 'that he should be alive.'

'Of course!'

'And you are not alive.'

'Not alive! What do you mean? Do you mean that I have died?' And without clearly knowing what he was doing he began to pass his hands over his body.

'No, my man, no!' I replied. 'I told you before that you were neither waking nor sleeping; now I tell you that you are neither alive nor dead.'

'Tell me all of it at once; God, tell me all,' he begged me in terror. 'With what I am seeing and hearing this afternoon I am afraid of going mad.'

'Very well, then. The truth is, my dear Augusto,' I spoke to him the softest of tones, 'you can't kill yourself because you are not alive; and you are not alive—or dead either—because you do not exist.'

'I don't exist! What do you mean by that?'

'No, you do not exist except as a fictitious entity, a character of fiction. My poor Augusto, you are only a product of my imagination and of the imagination of those of my readers who read this story which I have written of your fictitious adventures and misfortunes. You are nothing more than a personage in a novel, or a *nivola*, or whatever you choose to call it. Now, then, you know your secret.'

Upon hearing this the poor man continued to look at me for a while with one of those perforating looks that seem to pierce your own gaze and go beyond; presently he glanced for a moment at the portrait in oil which presides over my books, then his colour returned and his breathing became easier, and gradually recovering, he was again master of himself. He rested his elbows on the arm of the sofa opposite me, against which he was leaning; and then with his face in the palms of his hands he looked at me with a smile and he said slowly :

'Listen to me, Don Miguel—it can't be that you are mistaken, and that what is happening is precisely the contrary of what you think and of what you have told me?'

—Y ¿qué es lo contrario? —le pregunté alarmado de verle recobrar vida propia.

—No sea, mi querido don Miguel —añadió—, que sea usted y no yo el ente de ficción, el que no existe en realidad, ni vivo, ni muerto . . . No sea que usted no pase de ser un pretexto para que mi historia llegue al mundo . . .

—¡Eso más faltaba! —exclamé algo molesto.

—No se exalte usted así, señor de Unamuno —me replicó—, tenga calma. Usted ha manifestado dudas sobre mi existencia . . .

—Dudas no —le interrumpí—; certeza absoluta de que tú no existes fuera de mi producción novelesca.

—Bueno, pues no se incomode tanto si yo a mi vez dudo de la existencia de usted y no de la mía propia. Vamos a cuentas: ¿no ha sido usted el que no una sino varias veces ha dicho que Don Quijote y Sancho son no ya tan reales, sino más reales que Cervantes?

—No puedo negarlo, pero mi sentido al decir eso era . . .

—Bueno, dejémonos de esos sentires y vamos a otra cosa. Cuando un hombre dormido e inerte en la cama sueña algo, ¿qué es lo que más existe, él como conciencia que sueña, o su sueño?

—¿Y si sueña que existe él mismo, el soñador? —le repliqué a mi vez.

—En ese caso, amigo don Miguel, le pregunto yo a mi vez, ¿de qué manera existe él, como soñador que sueña, o como soñado por sí mismo? Y fíjese, además, en que al admitir esta discusión conmigo me reconoce ya existencia independiente de sí.

—¡No, eso no! ¡eso no! —le dije vivamente—. Yo necesito discutir, sin discusión no vivo y sin contradicción, y cuando no hay fuera de mí quien me discuta y contradiga, invento dentro de mí quien lo haga. Mis monólogos son diálogos.

—Y acaso los diálogos que usted forje no sean más que monólogos . . .

—Puede ser. Pero te digo y repito que tú no existes fuera de mí . . .

—Y yo vuelvo a insinuarle a usted la idea de que es usted el que no existe fuera de mí y de los demás personajes a quienes usted cree haber inventado. Seguro estoy de que serían de mi opinión don Avito Carrascal y el gran don Fulgencio . . .

—No mientes a ese . . .

'And what do you mean by the contrary?' I asked, rather alarmed to see him regaining his self-possession.

'May it not be, my dear Don Miguel,' he continued, 'that it is you and not I who are the fictitious entity, the one that does not really exist, who is neither living nor dead? May it not be that you are nothing more than a pretext for bringing my history into the world?'

'Really this is too much!' I cried, now becoming irritated.

'Please don't get so excited, Señor de Unamuno,' he replied. 'Keep calm. You have expressed doubts about my existence——'

'Doubts? No!' I interrupted. 'Absolute certainty that you do not exist outside of the novel that I have created.'

'Very well; then please don't be disturbed if I in turn doubt your existence rather than my own. Let us come to the point. Are you not the person who has said, not once but several times, that Don Quixote and Sancho are not only real persons but more real than Cervantes himself?'

'I can't deny it, but the sense in which I said it was——'

'Very well, never mind in what sense. Let us come to another point. When a man who is lying asleep in his bed dreams of something, which is it that more truly exists, he as the consciousness that dreams or the dreams themselves?'

'And what if the dreamer dreams that he himself exists?'—I turned the question on him.

'In that case, friend Don Miguel, my own question would be, in what fashion does he exist? As the dreamer who dreams of himself or as something dreamed by himself? And note this, moreover: in entering this discussion with me you are already recognizing me as an existence independent of yourself.'

'Not at all. Not at all,' I said quickly. 'In entering this discussion I am merely satisfying a private need of my own. Apart from discussion and contradiction I am never alive; and when there is no one outside of me to question and contradict me I invent some one to do it within me. My monologues are dialogues.'

'And perhaps the dialogues that you fabricate are nothing more than monologues.'

'It may be. But in any case I tell you, and I wish to repeat it, that you do not exist outside of me——'

'And I will again suggest this to you, namely, that you do not exist outside of me and of the other characters that you think you have invented. I am certain that Don Avito Carrascal would be of my opinion and the great Don Fulgencio——'

'You needn't mention them——'

—Bueno, basta, no le moteje usted. Y vamos a ver, ¿qué opina usted de mi suicidio?

—Pues opino que como tú no existes más que en mi fantasía, te lo repito, y como no debes ni puedes hacer sino lo que a mí me dé la gana, y como no me da la real gana de que te suicides, no te suicidarás. ¡Lo dicho!

—Eso de no me da la real gana, señor de Unamuno, es muy español, pero muy feo. Y además, aun suponiendo su peregrina teoría de que yo no existo de veras y usted sí, de que no soy más que un ente de ficción, producto de la fantasía novelesca o *nivolesca* de usted, aun en ese caso yo no debo estar sometido a lo que llama usted su real gana, a su capricho. Hasta los llamados entes de ficción tienen su lógica interna . . .

—Sí, conozco esa cantata.

—En efecto; un novelista, un dramaturgo, no pueden hacer en absoluto lo que se les antoje de un personaje que creen; un ente de ficción novelesca no puede hacer, en buena ley de arte, lo que ningún lector esperaría que hiciese . . .

—Un ser novelesco tal vez . . .

—¿Entonces?

—Pero un ser *nivolesco* . . .

—Dejemos esas bufonadas que me ofenden y me hieren en lo más vivo. Yo, sea por mí mismo, según creo, sea porque usted me lo ha dado, según supone usted, tengo mi carácter, mi modo de ser, mi lógica interior, y esta lógica me pide que me suicide . . .

—¡Eso te creerás tú, pero te equivocas!

—A ver, ¿por qué me equivoco?, ¿en qué me equivoco? Muéstreme usted en qué está mi equivocación. Como la ciencia más difícil que hay es la de conocerse uno a sí mismo, fácil es que esté yo equivocado y que no sea el suicidio la solución más lógica de mis desventuras, pero demuéstremelo usted. Porque si es difícil, amigo don Miguel, ese conocimiento propio de sí mismo, hay otro conocimiento que me parece no menos difícil que él . . .

—¿Cuál es? —le pregunté.

Me miró con una enigmática y socarrona sonrisa y lentamente me dijo:

—Pues más difícil aún que el que uno se conozca a sí mismo es el que un novelista o un autor dramático conozca bien a los personajes que finge o cree fingir . . .

'Very well, then, I won't; but you shouldn't make fun of them. And now let us see; what do you really think about my suicide?'

'I think, then, that since you do not exist except in my imagination—as I tell you again—and since you neither ought nor are you able to do anything but just what I please, and since it does not really suit me that you should kill yourself—well, you are not going to kill yourself. And that settles it.'

'Your saying that "it does not really suit me" is very Spanish, Señor de Unamuno, but it is far from edifying. Moreover, even granting your strange theory that I do not really exist and that you do, that I am nothing but a character of fiction, the product of your imagination as a novelist—or as a "nivolist"—even so there is no reason why I should submit to "what really suits you", that is, to your caprice. For even those whom we call characters of fiction have their own inwrought logic——'

'Yes, I know that song.'

'But, really, it is a fact that neither a novelist nor a playwright is at all able to do anything that happens to occur to him, to a character that he creates. That a fictitious character in a novel should do that which no reader would ever expect him to do, is forbidden by all of the established principles of art——'

'Doubtless a character in a novel——'

'Well, then?'

'But a character in a *nivola*—a "nivolistic" character——'

'Let us drop these buffooneries. They are offensive, and they wound me where I am most sensitive. Whether of myself, as I think, or because you have given it to me, as you suppose, I have my own character, my own manner of being, my own inwrought logic, and this logic demands that I kill myself——'

'You may think so, but you are wrong.'

'Let us see. Why am I wrong? And where am I wrong? Show me where my mistake lies. Since the most difficult knowledge that there is, is knowing yourself, I may easily be mistaken and it may be that suicide is not the logical solution of my problem. But prove it to me. For though this self-knowledge be difficult, Don Miguel, there is another kind of knowledge that seems no less difficult——'

'And that is?——' I asked.

He looked at me with a smile that was shrewd and enigmatic and then he said slowly :

'Well, that which is more difficult than self-knowledge is this : that a novelist or a playwright should know the characters that he creates or thinks he creates.'

Empezaba yo a estar inquieto con estas salidas de Augusto, y a perder mi paciencia.

—E insisto —añadió— en que aun concedido que usted me haya dado el ser y un ser ficticio, no puede usted, así como así y porque sí, porque le dé la real gana, como dice, impedirme que me suicide.

—¡Bueno, basta! ¡basta! —exclamé dando un puñetazo en la camilla—, ¡cállate!, ¡no quiero oír más impertinencias! . . . ¡Y de una criatura mía! Y como ya me tienes harto y además no sé ya qué hacer de ti, decido ahora mismo no ya que no te suicides, sino matarte yo. ¡Vas a morir, pues, pero pronto! ¡Muy pronto!

—¿Cómo? —exclamó Augusto sobresaltado—, ¿que me va usted a dejar morir, a hacerme morir, a matarme?

—Sí, voy a hacer que mueras!

—¡Ah, eso nunca! ¡nunca! ¡nunca! —gritó.

—¡Ah! —le dije mirándole con lástima y rabia—. ¿Conque estabas dispuesto a matarte y no quieres que yo te mate? ¿Conque ibas a quitarte la vida y te resistes a que te la quite yo?

—Sí, no es lo mismo . . .

—En efecto, he oído contar casos análogos. He oído de uno que salió una noche armado de un revólver y dispuesto a quitarse la vida; salieron unos ladrones a robarle, le atacaron, se defendió, mató a uno de ellos, huyeron los demás y al ver que había comprado su vida por la de otro renunció a su propósito.

—Se comprende —observó Augusto—; la cosa era quitar a alguien la vida, matar un hombre, y ya que mató a otro, ¿a qué había de matarse? Los más de los suicidas son homicidas frustrados; se matan a sí mismos por falta de valor para matar a otros . . .

—¡Ah, ya te entiendo, Augusto, te entiendo! Tú quieres decir que si tuvieses valor para matar a Eugenia o a Mauricio o a los dos no pensarías en matarte a ti mismo, ¿eh?

—¡Mire usted, precisamente a esos . . . no!

—¿A quién, pues?

These sallies of Augusto were beginning to make me uneasy and I was losing my patience.

'And I insist,' he added, 'that even granting you have given me my being—a fictitious being, if you please—even so, and because it is so, you cannot prevent me from killing myself just because, as you say, it does not really suit you.'

'Very well, that will do—enough!' I cried, bringing my fist down on the sofa. 'Hold your tongue! I don't wish to hear any more impertinence! And from a creature of mine, too! And since I have had enough of you and I don't know, moreover, what more to do with you, I have now decided, not that you may not now kill yourself, but that I shall kill you. You are to die, then, but soon! Very soon!'

Augusto was horror-struck. 'What!' he cried. 'Do you mean that you are going to let me die, make me die—you are going to kill me?'

'Yes, I am going to cause you to die.'

'Oh, never! never! never!' he shrieked.

'Ah!' I said, looking at him with mingled pity and rage. 'And so you were ready to kill yourself, but you don't want me to kill you? And you were about to take your own life, but you object to my taking it?'

'Yes, it is not the same thing——'

'To be sure, it is not. I have heard of cases of that kind. I heard of a man who went out one night armed with a revolver, intending to take his own life, when some thieves undertook to rob him. They attacked him, he defended himself, killed one of them and the others fled. And then, seeing that he had bought his life at the cost of another's, he renounced his intention.'

'One can understand that,' observed Augusto. 'It was a matter of taking the life of somebody, of killing a man; and after he had killed another, what was the use of killing himself? Most suicides are frustrated homicides; men kill themselves because they have not the courage to kill others——'

'Ah! now I understand you, Augusto, I understand. You mean that if you had had the courage to kill Eugenia* or Mauricio, or both, you would not be thinking of killing yourself, isn't that so?'

'Let me tell you, it is not precisely of them that I am thinking—no!'

'Of whom, then?'

---

* Augusto's fiancée, who ran off with Mauricio just before the wedding day.

—¡A usted! —y me miró a los ojos.

—¿Cómo? —exclamé poniéndome en pie—, ¿cómo? Pero, ¿se te ha pasado por la imaginación matarme?, ¿tú?, ¿y a mí?

—Siéntese y tenga calma. ¿O es que cree usted, amigo don Miguel, que sería el primer caso en que un ente de ficción, como usted me llama, matara a aquel a quien creyó darle ser . . . ficticio?

—¡Esto ya es demasiado —decía yo paseándome por mi despacho—, esto pasa de la raya! Esto no sucede más que . . .

—Más que en las *nivolas* —concluyó él con sorna.

—¡Bueno, basta! ¡basta! ¡basta! ¡Esto no se puede tolerar! ¡Vienes a consultarme a mí, y tú! Empiezas por discutirme mi propia existencia, después el derecho que tengo a hacer de ti lo que me dé la real gana, sí, así como suena, lo que me dé la real gana, lo que me salga de . . .

—No sea usted tan español, don Miguel . . .

—¡Y eso más, mentecato! ¡Pues sí, soy español, español de nacimiento, de educación, de cuerpo, de espíritu, de lengua y hasta de profesión y oficio; español sobre todo y ante todo y el españolismo es mi religión, y el cielo en que quiero creer es una España celestial y eterna y mi Dios un Dios español, el de Nuestro Señor Don Quijote, un Dios que piensa en español y en español dijo: ¡sea la luz!, y su verbo fué verbo español . . .

—Bien, ¿y qué? —me interrumpió, volviéndome a la realidad.

—Y luego has insinuado la idea de matarme. ¿Matarme? ¿a mí? ¿tú? ¡Morir yo a manos de una de mis criaturas! No tolero más. Y para castigar tu osadía y esas doctrinas disolventes, extravagantes, anárquicas, con que te me has venido, resuelvo y fallo que te mueras. En cuanto llegues a tu casa te morirás. ¡Te morirás, te lo digo, te morirás!

—¡Pero, por Dios! . . . —exclamó Augusto, ya suplicante y de miedo tembloroso y pálido.

—No hay Dios que valga. ¡Te morirás!

—Es que yo quiero vivir, don Miguel, quiero vivir, quiero vivir . . .

—¿No pensabas matarte?

—¡Oh, si es por eso, yo le juro, señor de Unamuno, que no me mataré, que no me quitaré esta vida que Dios o usted me han dado;

'Of you'—and he looked me straight in the eye.

'What!' I cried, rising to my feet. 'What! Have you conceived the idea of killing me? You? And of killing me?'

'Sit down and keep cool. Do you think, Don Miguel, that it would the first case in which a fictitious entity, as you call me, had killed him whom he believed to have given him his being—his fictitious being, of course?'

'This is really too much,' I said, walking up and down my study. 'This passes all limits. This couldn't happen except——'

'Except in *nivolas*,' Augusto completed with a drawl.

'Very well, enough! enough! enough! This is more than I can stand. You came here to consult me—me, you understand—and you? You begin by disputing my own existence, forgetting that I have the right to do with you anything that suits me—yes, just what I say, anything that may happen to occur to——'

'Don't be so Spanish, Don Miguel——'

'And now this too, you idiot! Well, yes, I am indeed a Spaniard, Spanish by birth, by education, by profession and occupation; Spanish above everything and before everything. Spanishism is my religion, the heaven in which I wish to believe is a celestial and eternal Spain, and my God is a Spanish God, the God of our Lord Don Quixote, a God who thinks in Spanish and who said in Spanish, Let there be light! *Sea luz!*—His word was a Spanish word——'

'Well, and what of it?' he interrupted, recalling me to reality.

'And now you have conceived the idea of killing me. Of killing me—*me*? And you? Am I to die at the hands of one of my creatures? I'll stand no more of it. And so to punish you for your insolence, and to put an end to these disintegrating, extravagant, and anarchistic ideas with which you have come to me, I hereby render judgment and pass the sentence that you are to die. As soon as you reach home you shall die. You shall die, I tell you, you shall die.'

'But—for God's sake!' cried Augusto, now in a tone of supplication, pale and trembling with fear.

'There is no God that can help you. You shall die.'

'Yes, but I want to live, Don Miguel, I want to live—I want to live——'

'Weren't you just now thinking of killing yourself?'

'Oh! if that is why, Don Miguel, then I swear to you that I will not kill myself, I will not take away this life which God, or yourself,

se lo juro . . . Ahora que usted quiere matarme quiero yo vivir, vivir, vivir . . .

—¡Vaya una vida! —exclamé.

—Sí, la que sea. Quiero vivir, aunque vuelva a ser burlado, aunque otra Eugenia y otro Mauricio me desgarren el corazón. Quiero vivir, vivir, vivir . . .

—No puede ser ya . . . no puede ser . . .

—Quiero vivir, vivir . . . y ser yo, yo, yo . . .

—Pero si tú no eres sino lo que yo quiera . . .

—¡Quiero ser yo, ser yo! ¡quiero vivir! —y le lloraba la voz.

—No puede ser . . . no puede ser . . .

—Mire usted, don Miguel, por sus hijos, por su mujer, por lo que más quiera . . . Mire que usted no será usted . . . que se morirá . . .

Cayó a mis pies de hinojos, suplicante y exclamando:

—¡Don Miguel, por Dios, quiero vivir, quiero ser yo!

—¡No puede ser, pobre Augusto —le dije cogiéndole una mano y levantándole—, no puede ser! Lo tengo ya escrito y es irrevocable; no puedes vivir más. No sé qué hacer ya de ti. Dios, cuando no sabe qué hacer de nosotros, nos mata. Y no se me olvida que pasó por tu mente la idea de matarme . . .

—Pero si yo, don Miguel . . .

—No importa; sé lo que me digo. Y me temo que, en efecto, si no te mato pronto acabes por matarme tú.

—Pero, ¿no quedamos en que . . . ?

—No puede ser, Augusto, no puede ser. Ha llegado tu hora. Está ya escrito y no puedo volverme atrás. Te morirás. Para lo que ha de valerte ya la vida . . .

—Pero . . . por Dios . . .

—No hay pero ni Dios que valga. ¡Vete!

—¿Conque no, eh? —me dijo—, ¿conque no? No quiere usted dejarme ser yo, salir de la niebla, vivir, vivir, vivir, verme, oírme, tocarme, sentirme, dolerme, serme: ¿conque no lo quiere? ¿conque he de morir ente de ficción? Pues bien, mi señor creador don Miguel, también usted se morirá, también usted, y se volverá a la nada de que salió . . . ¡Dios dejará de soñarle! Se morirá usted, sí, se morirá, aunque no lo quiera; se morirá usted y se morirán todos los que lean mi historia, todos, todos, todos sin quedar uno! ¡Entes de ficción

has given me; I swear it to you—now that you wish to kill me I myself want to live—to live—to live——'

'What a life!' I exclaimed.

'Yes, whatever it may be. I want to live even though I am again to be mocked at, even though another Eugenia and another Mauricio tear my heart out. I wish to live—live—live——'

'Now it cannot be—it cannot be——'

'I want to live—live—I want to be myself, myself, myself.'

'But what if that self is only what I wish to be——?'

'I wish to be myself—to be myself! I wish to live!' and his voice was choked with sobs.

'It cannot be—cannot be——'

'Listen, Don Miguel, for the sake of your children, of your wife, of whatever is dearest to you! Remember that you will then cease to be yourself—that *you* will die——'

He fell on his knees at my feet, begging and imploring me : 'Don Miguel, for God's sake! I want to live. I want to be myself.'

'It cannot be, my poor Augusto,' I said, taking him by the hand and lifting him up. 'It cannot be. I have now decreed it—it is written—and irrevocably; you can live no longer. I no longer know what to do with you. God, when he does not know what to do with us, kills us. And I do not forget that there passed through your mind the idea of killing me——'

'But, Don Miguel, if I——'

'It makes no difference. I know where I stand. And really I am afraid that if I do not kill you soon, you will end by killing me.'

'But are we not agreed that——?'

'It cannot be, Augusto, it cannot be. Your hour has come. It is now written, and I cannot now recall it. And for all that your life can now be worth to you——'

'But——good God!'

'There is neither "but" nor "God" that can avail you. Go!'

'And so you won't?' he said. 'You refuse? You are unwilling to let me be myself, come out of the mist and live, live, live; to see myself, hear myself, touch myself, feel myself, feel my own pain, be myself—you are unwilling, then? And so I am to die as a fictitious character? Very well, then, my lord creator Don Miguel, you too are to die, you too! And you will return to that nothing from which you came! God will cease to dream you! You are to die, yes, you are to die, even though you do not wish to; and die shall all of those who read my story, all of them, all, all, without a

como yo; lo mismo que yo! Se morirán todos, todos, todos. Os lo digo yo, Augusto Pérez, ente ficticio como vosotros, *nivolesco*, lo mismo que vosotros. Porque usted, mi creador, mi don Miguel, no es usted más que otro ente *nivolesco*, y entes *nivolescos* sus lectores, lo mismo que yo, que Augusto Pérez, que su víctima . . .

—¿Víctima? —exclamé.

—¡Víctima, sí! ¡Crearme para dejarme morir! Usted también se morirá! El que crea se crea y el que se crea se muere. ¡Morirá usted, don Miguel, morirá usted, y morirán todos los que me piensen! ¡A morir, pues!

Este supremo esfuerzo de pasión de vida, de ansia de inmortalidad, le dejó extenuado al pobre Augusto.

Y le empujé a la puerta, por la que salió cabizbajo. Luego se tanteó como si dudase ya de su propia existencia. Yo me enjugué una lágrima furtiva.

JACINTO BENAVENTE
[1866–1954]

When Jacinto Benavente began to write, towards the end of the nineteenth century, the exaggerated melodramas of José Echegaray dominated the Spanish stage. Benavente's art was a radical and refreshing change. Most of his plays fall into the category of social satire and deal mainly with the upper classes of his native Madrid. The dialogue, in prose, is calm and sophisticated, with frequent ironic and sceptical overtones.

Benavente's masterpiece, Los intereses creados (1907), takes its stock characters from the old Italian commedia dell'arte. Two of Benavente's

LOS INTERESES CREADOS

CUADRO I

Plaza de una ciudad. A la derecha, en primer término, fachada de una hostería con puerta practicable y en ella un aldabón. Encima de la puerta un letrero que diga: 'Hostería.'

ESCENA I

LEANDRO *y* CRISPÍN, *que salen por la segunda izquierda.*

LEANDRO. Gran ciudad ha de ser ésta, Crispín; en todo se advierte su señoría y riqueza.

single exception. Fictitious entities like myself—just like myself!
All of them are to die; all, all. And it is I who tell you this—I,
Augusto Pérez, a fictitious entity, a "nivolistic" entity, and your
readers are "nivolistic" entities, just like me, just the same as
Augusto Pérez, your victim——'
'Victim!' I cried.
'Victim, yes! To create me only to let me die! Well, you
too are to die! He who creates creates himself, and he who creates
himself dies. You will die, Don Miguel, you will die, and all those
who think me, they are to die too! To death, then!'
This supreme effort of the passion for life—of the thirst for
immortality—left poor Augusto utterly weak.
I pushed him towards the door. He walked out with his eyes
fixed upon the ground, passing his hands wonderingly over himself
as if he were uncertain of his own existence. I wiped away a furtive
tear.

WARNER FITE

powerful dramas have a rural setting: Señora ama (*1908*) *and* La
malquerida (*1913*). *The latter, translated for the American stage as*
The Passion Flower, *is the gripping story of a stepfather's illicit love for
his beautiful stepdaughter.*

*One of the most prolific of modern dramatists, Benavente received the
Nobel Prize in 1922. Many of his plays have been translated into English by
John Garrett Underhill.*

THE BONDS OF INTEREST

Act I

SCENE I

*A plaza in a city. The façade of an Inn is at the right, having
a practicable door, with a knocker upon it. Above the door is
a sign which reads* Inn.

(Leander *and* Crispin *enter from the left.*)

LEANDER. This must be a very great city, Crispin. Its riches and its
power appear in everything.

CRISPÍN. Dos ciudades hay. ¡Quiera el Cielo que en la mejor hayamos dado!

LEANDRO. ¿Dos ciudades dices, Crispín? Ya entiendo, antigua y nueva, una de cada parte del río.

CRISPÍN. ¿Qué importa el río ni la vejez ni la novedad? Digo dos ciudades como en toda ciudad del mundo: una para el que llega con dinero, y otra para el que llega como nosotros.

LEANDRO. ¡Harto es haber llegado sin tropezar con la Justicia! Y bien quisiera detenerme aquí algún tiempo, que ya me cansa tanto correr tierras.

CRISPÍN. A mí no, que es condición de los naturales, como yo, del libre reino de Picardía no hacer asiento en parte alguna, si no es forzado y en galeras, que es duro asiento. Pero ya que sobre esta ciudad caímos y es plaza fuerte a lo que se descubre, tracemos como prudentes capitanes nuestro plan de batalla si hemos de conquistarla con provecho.

LEANDRO. ¡Mal pertrechado ejército venimos!

CRISPÍN. Hombres somos, y con hombres hemos de vernos.

LEANDRO. Por todo caudal, nuestra persona. No quisiste que nos desprendiéramos de estos vestidos, que, malvendiéndolos, hubiéramos podido juntar algún dinero.

CRISPÍN. ¡Antes me desprendiera yo de la piel que de un buen vestido! Que nada importa tanto como parecer, según va el mundo, y el vestido es lo que antes parece.

LEANDRO. ¿Qué hemos de hacer, Crispín? Que el hambre y el cansancio me tienen abatido, y mal discurro.

CRISPÍN. Aquí no hay sino valerse del ingenio y de la desvergüenza, que sin ella nada vale el ingenio. Lo que he pensado es que tú has de hablar poco y desabrido, para darte aires de persona de calidad; de vez en cuando te permito que descargues algún golpe sobre mis costillas; a cuantos te pregunten, responde misterioso; y cuando hables por tu cuenta, sea con gravedad; como si sentenciaras. Eres joven, de buena presencia; hasta ahora sólo supiste malgastar tus cualidades; ya es hora de aprovecharse de ellas. Ponte en mis manos, que nada conviene tanto a un hombre como llevar a su lado quien haga notar sus méritos, que en uno mismo la modestia es necedad y

CRISPIN. Yes, there are two cities. Pray God that we have chanced upon the better one!

LEANDER. Two cities do you say, Crispin? Ah! Now I understand —an old city and a new city, one on either side of the river.

CRISPIN. What has the river to do with it, or newness or age? I say two cities just as there are in every city in the world; one for people who arrive with money and the other for persons who arrive like us.

LEANDER. We are lucky to have arrived at all without falling into the hands of Justice. I should be heartily glad to stop here awhile and rest myself, for I am tired of this running about the world so continually.

CRISPIN. Not I! No, it is the natural condition of the freeborn subjects of the Kingdom of Roguery, of whom am I, not to remain seated long in any one place, unless it be through compulsion, as to say in the galleys, where, believe me, they are very hard seats. But now since we have happened upon this city, and to all appearances it is a well-fortified and provisioned one, let us like prudent captains map out our plan of battle beforehand, if we are to conquer it with any advantage to ourselves.

LEANDER. A pretty army we shall make to besiege it.

CRISPIN. We are men and we have to do with men.

LEANDER. All our wealth is on our backs. You were not willing to take off these clothes and sell them, when by doing so we could easily have obtained money.

CRISPIN. I would sooner take off my skin than my good clothes. As the world goes nothing is so important as appearances, and the clothes, as you must admit, are the first things to appear.

LEANDER. What are we going to do, Crispin? Hunger and fatigue have been too much for me. I am overcome; I cannot talk.

CRISPIN. There is nothing for us to do but to take advantage of our talents and our effrontery, for without effrontery talents are of no use. The best thing, as it seems to me will be for you to talk as little as possible, but be very impressive when you do, and put on the airs of a gentleman of quality. From time to time then I will permit you to strike me across the back. When anybody asks you a question, reply mysteriously, and if you open your mouth upon your own account, be sure that it is with dignity, as if you were pronouncing sentence. You are young; you have a fine presence. Until now you have known only how to dissipate your resources; this is the time for you to begin to profit by them. Put yourself in my hands. There is nothing so useful to a man as to have some one always at his heels to point out his merits, for modesty in one's

la propia alabanza locura, y con las dos se pierde para ·el mundo.
Somos los hombres como mercancía, que valemos más o menos
según la habilidad del mercader que nos presenta. Yo te aseguro que
así fueras vidrio, a mi cargo corre que pases por diamante. Y ahora
llamemos a esta hostería, que lo primero es acampar a vista de la
plaza.

LEANDRO. ¿A la hostería dices? ¿Y cómo pagaremos?

CRISPÍN. Si por tan poco te acobardas, busquemos un hospital o casa
de misericordia, o pidamos limosna, si a lo piadoso nos acogemos; y
si a lo bravo, volvamos al camino y salteemos al primer viandante;
si a la verdad de nuestros recursos nos atenemos, no son otros
nuestros recursos.

LEANDRO. Yo traigo cartas de introducción para personas de vali-
miento en esta ciudad, que podrán socorrernos.

CRISPÍN. ¡Rompe luego esas cartas, y no pienses en tal bajeza! ¡Pre-
sentarnos a nadie como necesitados! ¡Buenas cartas de crédito son
ésas! Hoy te recibirán con grandes cortesías, te dirán que su casa y
su persona son tuyas, y a la segunda vez que llames a su puerta, ya
te dirá el criado que su señor no está en casa ni para en ella; y a otra
visita, ni te abrirán la puerta. Mundo es éste de toma y daca; lonja
de contratación, casa de cambio, y antes de pedir, ha de ofrecerse.

LEANDRO. ¿Y qué podré yo ofrecer si nada tengo?

CRISPÍN. ¡En qué poco te estimas! Pues qué, un hombre por sí, ¿nada
vale? Un hombre puede ser soldado, y con su valor decidir una
victoria; puede ser galán o marido, y con dulce medicina curar a
alguna dama de calidad o doncella de buen linaje que se sienta
morir de melancolía; puede ser criado de algún señor poderoso que
se aficione de él y le eleve hasta su privanza, y tantas cosas más que
no he de enumerarte. Para subir, cualquier escalón es bueno.

LEANDRO. ¿Y si aun ese escalón me falta?

CRISPÍN. Yo te ofrezco mis espaldas para encumbrarte. Tú te verás
en alto.

LEANDRO. ¿Y si los dos damos en tierra?

CRISPÍN. Que ella nos sea leve . . .

self is imbecility, while self-praise is madness, and so between the two we come into disfavour with the world. Men are like merchandise; they are worth more or less according to the skill of the salesman who markets them. I tell you, though you were but muddy glass, I will so contrive that in my hands you shall pass for pure diamond. And now let us knock at the door of this inn, for surely it is the proper thing to have lodgings on the main square.

LEANDER. You say at this inn? But how are we going to pay?

CRISPIN. If we are to be stopped by a little thing like that, then we had better search out an asylum or an almshouse or else beg on the streets, if so be that you incline to virtue. Or if to force, then back to the highway and cut the throat of the first passer-by. If we are to live upon our means, strictly speaking, we have no other means to live.

LEANDER. I have letters of introduction to persons of importance in this city, who will be able to lend us aid.

CRISPIN. Then tear those letters up; never think of such baseness again. Introduce yourself to no man when you are in need. Those would be pretty letters of credit indeed! Today you will be received with the greatest courtesy; they will tell you that their houses and their persons are to be considered as yours. The next time you call, the servant will tell you that his master is not at home. No, he is not expected soon . . . and at the next visit nobody will trouble so much as to open the door. This is a world of giving and taking, a shop, a mart, a place of exchange, and before you ask you have to offer.

LEANDER. But what can I offer when I have nothing?

CRISPIN. How low an opinion you must have of yourself! Is a man in himself, then, worth nothing? A man may be a soldier, and by his valour win great victories. He may be a husband or a lover, and with love's sweet, oblivious medicine, restore some noble dame to health, or some damsel of high degree, who has been pining away through melancholy. He may be the servant of some mighty and powerful lord, who becomes attached to him and raises him up through his favour, and he may be so many other things besides that I have not the breath even to begin to run them over. When one wants to climb, why, any stair will do.

LEANDER. But if I have not even that stair?

CRISPIN. Then accept my shoulders, and I will lift you up. I offer you the top.

LEANDER. And if we both fall down upon the ground?

CRISPIN. God grant that it may be soft! . . .

Cuadro II

ESCENA IX

Leandro *y* Crispín, *que salen por la segunda derecha.*

Crispín. ¿Qué tristeza, qué abatimiento es ése? ¡Con mayor alegría pensé hallarte!

Leandro. Hasta ahora no me ví perdido; hasta ahora no me importó menos perderme. Huyamos, Crispín; huyamos de esta ciudad antes de que nadie pueda descubrirnos y vengan a saber lo que somos.

Crispín. Si huyéramos, es cuando todos lo sabrían y cuando muchos corrieran hasta detenernos y hacernos volver a nuestro pesar, que no parece bien ausentarnos con tanta descortesía, sin despedirnos de gente tan atenta.

Leandro. No te burles, Crispín, que estoy desesperado.

Crispín. ¡Así eres! Cuando nuestras esperanzas llevan mejor camino.

Leandro. ¿Qué puedo esperar? Quisiste que fingiera un amor, y mal sabré fingirlo.

Crispín. ¿Por qué?

Leandro. Porque amo, amo con toda verdad y con toda mi alma.

Crispín. ¿A Silvia? ¿Y de eso te lamentas?

Leandro. ¡Nunca pensé que pudiera amarse de este modo! ¡Nunca pensé que yo pudiera amar! En mi vida errante por todos los caminos, no fuí siquiera el que siempre pasa, sino el que siempre huye, enemiga la tierra, enemigos los hombres, enemiga la luz del sol. La fruta del camino, hurtada, no ofrecida, dejó acaso en mis labios algún sabor de amores, y alguna vez, después de muchos días azarosos, en el descanso de una noche, la serenidad del cielo me hizo soñar con algo que fuera en mi vida como aquel cielo de la noche que traía a mi alma el reposo de su serenidad. Y así esta noche en el encanto de la fiesta . . . me pareció que era un descanso en mi vida . . . y soñaba . . . ¡He soñado! Pero mañana será otra vez la huida azarosa, será la Justicia que nos persigue . . . y no quiero que me halle aquí, donde está ella, donde ella pueda avergonzarse de haberme visto.

Crispín. Yo creí ver que eras acogido con agrado . . . Y no fuí yo solo en advertirlo. Doña Sirena y nuestros buenos amigos el Capitán y el Poeta le hicieron de ti los mayores elogios. A su excelente madre,

ACT II

SCENE IX

(Leander *and* Crispin *enter.*)

CRISPIN. What is this sadness, this dejection? I expected to find you in better spirits.

LEANDER. I was never unfortunate till now; at least it never mattered to me whether or not I was unfortunate. Let us fly, Crispin, let us fly from this city before any one can discover us and find out who we are.

CRISPIN. If we fly it will be after every one has discovered us and they are running after us to detain us and bring us back in spite of ourselves. It would be most discourteous to depart with such scant ceremony without bidding our attentive friends good-bye.

LEANDER. Do not jest, Crispin; I am in despair.

CRISPIN. So you are. And just when our hopes are under fullest sail.

LEANDER. What could you expect? You wanted me to pretend to be in love, but I have not been able to pretend it.

CRISPIN. Why not?

LEANDER. Because I love—I love in spirit and in truth!

CRISPIN. Silvia? Is that what you are complaining about?

LEANDER. I never believed it possible a man could love like this. I never believed that I could ever love. Through all my wandering life along the dusty roads, I was not only the one who passed, I was the one who fled, the enemy of the harvest and the field, the enemy of man, enemy of sunshine and the day. Sometimes the fruit of the wayside tree, stolen, not given, left some savour of joy on my parched lips, and sometimes, after many a bitter day, resting at night beneath the stars, the calm repose of heaven would invite and soothe me to a dream of something that might be in my life like that calm night sky, brooding infinite over my soul— serene! And so tonight, in the enchantment of this fête, it seemed to me as if there had come a calm, a peace into my life—and I was dreaming! Ah! How I did dream! But tomorrow it will be again the bitter flight with justice at our heels, and I cannot bear that they should take me here where she is, and where she may ever have cause to be ashamed at having known me.

CRISPIN. Why, I thought that you had been received with favour! And I was not the only one who noticed it. Doña Sirena and our good friends, the Captain and the poet, have been most eloquent in your praises. To that rare excellent mother, the Wife of

la señora Polichinela, que sólo sueña emparentar con un noble, le pareciste el yerno de sus ilusiones. En cuanto al señor Polichinela . . .
LEANDRO. Sospecha de nosotros . . . , nos conoce . . .
CRISPÍN. Sí; al señor Polichinela no es fácil engañarle como a un hombre vulgar. A un zorro viejo como él hay que engañarle con lealtad. Por eso me pareció el mejor medio prevenirle de todo.
LEANDRO. ¿Cómo?
CRISPÍN. Sí; él me conoce de antiguo . . . Al decirle que tú eres mi amo supuso, con razón, que el amo sería digno del criado. Y yo, por corresponder a su confianza, le advertí que de ningún modo consintiera que hablaras con su hija.
LEANDRO. ¿Eso hiciste? ¿Y qué puedo esperar?
CRISPÍN. ¡Necio eres! Que el señor Polichinela ponga todo su empeño en que no vuelvas a ver a su hija.
LEANDRO. ¡No lo entiendo!
CRISPÍN. Y que de este modo sea nuestro mejor aliado, porque bastará que él se oponga, para que su mujer le lleve la contraria y su hija se enamore de ti más locamente. Tú no sabes lo que es una joven, hija de un padre rico, criada en el mayor regalo, cuando ve por primera vez en su vida que algo se opone a su voluntad. Estoy seguro de que esta misma noche, antes de terminar la fiesta, consigue burlar la vigilancia de su padre para hablar todavía contigo.
LEANDRO. ¿Pero no ves que nada me importa del señor Polichinela ni del mundo entero? Que es a ella, sólo a ella, a quien yo no quiero parecer indigno y despreciable . . . , a quien yo no quiero mentir.
CRISPÍN. ¡Bah! ¡Deja locuras! No es posible retroceder. Piensa en la suerte que nos espera si vacilamos en seguir adelante. ¿Que te has enamorado? Ese amor verdadero nos servirá mejor que si fuera fingido. Tal vez de otro modo hubieras querido ir demasiado de prisa; y si la osadía y la insolencia convienen para todo, sólo en amor sienta bien a los hombres algo de timidez. La timidez del hombre hace ser más atrevidas a las mujeres. Y si lo dudas, aquí tienes a la inocente Silvia, que llega con el mayor sigilo y sólo espera para acercarse a ti que yo me retire o me esconda.
LEANDRO. ¿Silvia dices?

Polichinelle, who thinks of nothing but how she can relate herself by marriage to some nobleman, you have seemed the son-in-law of her dreams. As for Signor Polichinelle . . .

LEANDER. He knows . . . he suspects. . . .

CRISPIN. Naturally. It is not so easy to deceive Signor Polichinelle as it is an ordinary man. An old fox like him has to be cheated truthfully. I decided that the best thing for us to do was to tell him everything.

LEANDER. How so?

CRISPIN. Obviously. He knows me of old. When I told him that you were my master, he rightly supposed that the master must be worthy of the man. And upon my part, in appreciation of his confidence, I warned him not to permit you under any circumstances to come near to or speak with his daughter.

LEANDER. You did? Then what have I to hope?

CRISPIN. You are a fool! Why, that Signor Polichinelle will exert all his authority to prevent you from meeting her.

LEANDER. I do not understand.

CRISPIN. In that way he will become our most powerful ally, for if he opposes it, that will be enough to make his wife take the opposite side, and the daughter will fall in love with you madly. You have no idea what a young and beautiful daughter of a rich father, who has been brought up to the gratification of her every whim, can do when she finds out for the first time in her life that somebody is opposing her wishes. I am certain that this very night, before the fête is over, she will find some way of eluding the vigilance of her father at whatever cost, and return to speak with you.

LEANDER. But can't you see that Signor Polichinelle is nothing to me, no, nor the wide world either? It is she, only she! It is to her that I am unwilling to appear unworthy or mean, it is to her—to her that I cannot lie.

CRISPIN. Bah! Enough of this nonsense! Don't tell me that. It is too late to draw back. Think what will happen if we vacillate now and hesitate in going on. You say that you have fallen in love? Well, this real love will serve us better than if it were put on. Otherwise you would have wanted to get through with it too quickly. If insolence and effrontery are the only qualities which are of use elsewhere, in love a faint suggestion of timidity is of advantage to a man. Timidity in a man always makes the woman bolder. If you don't believe it, here is the innocent Silvia now, skulking in the shadows and only waiting for a chance to come near until I retire or am concealed.

LEANDER. Silvia, do you say?

CRISPÍN. ¡Chito! ¡Que pudiera espantarse! Y cuando esté a tu lado, mucha discreción . . ., pocas palabras, pocas . . . Adora, contempla, admira, y deja que hable por ti el encanto de esta noche azul, propicia a los amores, y esa música que apaga sus sones entre la arboleda y llega como triste de la alegría de la fiesta.

LEANDRO. No te burles, Crispín; no te burles de este amor que será mi muerte.

CRISPÍN. ¿Por qué he de burlarme? Yo sé bien que no conviene siempre rastrear. Alguna vez hay que volar por el cielo para mejor dominar la tierra. Vuela tú ahora; yo sigo arrastrándome. ¡El mundo será nuestro! (*Vase por la segunda izquierda.*)

ANTONIO MACHADO
[1875–1939]

Antonio Machado, though born in Seville, is intimately associated with Castile, where he spent most of his life. His verse, small in quantity, is serious, intense and restrained. His most characteristic work is contained in Campos

CAMPOS DE SORIA

III

Es el campo undulado, y los caminos
Ya ocultan los viajeros que cabalgan
En pardos borriquillos,
Ya al fondo de la tarde arrebolada
Elevan las plebeyas figurillas,
Que el lienzo de oro del ocaso manchan.
Mas si trepáis a un cerro y veis el campo
Desde los picos donde habita el águila,
Son tornasoles de carmín y acero,
Llanos plomizos, lomas plateadas,
Circuídos por montes de violeta,
Con las cumbres de nieve sonrosada.

IV

¡Las figuras del campo sobre el cielo!
Dos lentos bueyes aran
En un alcor, cuando el otoño empieza,

CRISPIN. Hush! You may frighten her. When she is with you, remember, discretion—only a few words, very few. Adore her, admire her, contemplate her, and let the enchantment of this night of pallid blue speak for you, propitious as it is to love, and whisper to her in the music whose soft notes die away amid the foliage and fall upon our ears like sad overtones of this festival of joy.

LEANDER. Do not trifle, Crispin! Do not trifle with my love! It will be my death.

CRISPIN. Why should I trifle with it? I know, too, it is not always well to grovel on the ground. Sometimes we must soar and mount up into the sky better to dominate the earth. Mount now and soar —and I will grovel still. The world lies in our hands!

(*He goes out to the right.*)

JOHN GARRETT UNDERHILL

de Castilla (*1912*), *in which he exalts the austere beauty of the plains of Castile. Some critics believe him to be Spain's greatest poet of the twentieth century.*

FIELDS OF SORIA

III

An undulating country, where the roads
Do now conceal the travellers, astride
Their dusky-coated asses,
Now, in the crimson light of dying day,
Uplift in full relief their rustic forms,
Darkening the golden canvas of the West.
Climb now yon mount, and from those jagged peaks
Where dwells the eagle, gaze upon the scene;
And see the leaden plains and silvery slopes
All bathed in carmine, shot with steely grey,
Circled by mountains of deep violet,
With snowy summits blushing like the rose.

IV

Lo, these are they that move 'twixt land and sky;
Two oxen, slowly ploughing
Upon a hillside, touched by Autumn's breath,

Y entre las negras testas doblegadas
Bajo el pesado yugo,
Pende un cesto de juncos y retama,
Que es la cuna de un niño;
Y tras la yunta marcha
Un hombre que se inclina hacia la tierra,
Y una mujer que en las abiertas zanjas
Arroja la semilla.
Bajo una nube de carmín y llama,
En el oro flúido y verdinoso
Del poniente, las sombras se agigantan.

CONSEJOS

Sabe esperar, aguarda que la marea fluya
    —Así en la costa un barco—sin que al partir te inquiete.
Todo 'el que aguarda sabe que la victoria es suya;
    Porque la vida es larga y el arte es un juguete.
Y si la vida es corta
    Y no llega la mar a tu galera,
    Aguarda sin partir y siempre espera,
Que el arte es largo y, además, no importa.

JUAN RAMÓN JIMÉNEZ
[1881–1958]

*At first a follower of the modernist innovations of Rubén Darío, the
Andalusian Juan Ramón Jiménez soon developed a highly personal and
original style. His numerous poems, contained in more than twenty volumes,
are notable for their imagery, delicate romanticism and musicality. His
earlier poems were inspired by Nature and beauty; more recently Jiménez*

LA VERDECILLA

Verde es la niña. Tiene
verdes ojos, pelo verde.

Su rosilla silvestre
no es rosa ni blanca. Es verde.

¡En el verde aire viene!
(La tierra se pone verde).

The while between their sturdy heads, low bent
Beneath the heavy yoke,
A basket hangs woven of reeds and broom—
An infant's rustic cradle;
And, following the team,
A man, who bows him down towards the earth,
Likewise a woman, who in the gaping furrows
Scatters the precious seed.
Beneath a cloud of crimson and of flame
See in the West, all liquid gold and green,
Their shadows slowly lengthen as they pass.

IDA FARNELL

COUNSELS

Learn how to hope, to wait the proper tide—
    As on the coast a bark—then part without a care;
He who knows how to wait wins victory for bride;
    For life is long and art a plaything there.
But should your life prove short
    And never come a tide,
    Wait still, unsailing, hope is on your side,
Art may be long or, else, of no import.

THOMAS WALSH

sought to achieve 'pure poetry'. He is also the author of a number of prose works, among them the delightful tale about a child and his pet donkey, Platero y yo (1914). Juan Ramón Jiménez has exerted a tremendous influence on the younger poets of Spain and Spanish America. He was awarded the Nobel Prize for Literature in 1956. •

GREEN

Green was the maiden, green, green!
Green her eyes were, green her hair.

The wild rose in her green wood
was neither red nor white, but green.

Through the green air she came.
(The whole earth turned green for her.)

Su espumilla fuljente
no es blanca ni azul. Es verde.

¡En el mar verde viene!
(El cielo se pone verde).

Mi vida le abre siempre
una puertecita verde.

NOCTURNO SOÑADO

La tierra lleva por la tierra;
Mas tú, mar,
Llevas por el cielo.
¡Con qué seguridad de luz de plata y oro,
Nos marcan las estrellas
La ruta!—Se diría
Que es la tierra el camino
Del cuerpo,
Que el mar es el camino
Del alma—.
Sí, parece
Que es el alma la sola viajera
Del mar, que el cuerpo, solo,
Se quedó allá en las·playas,
Sin ella, despidiéndola,
Pesado, frío, igual que muerto.
¡Qué semejante
El viaje del mar al de la muerte,
Al de la eterna vida!

QUISIERA QUE MI LIBRO . . .

Quisiera que mi libro
fuese, como es el cielo por la noche,
todo verdad presente, sin historia.

Que, como él, se diera en cada instante,
todo, con todas sus estrellas; sin
que niñez, juventud, vejez quitaran
ni pusieran encanto a su hermosura inmensa.

The shining gauze of her garment
was neither blue nor white, but green.

Over the green sea she came.
(And even the sky turned green then.)

My life will always leave unlatched
a small green gate to let her in.

J. B. TREND

DREAM NOCTURNE

The earth leads by the earth.
But, sea,
You lead by the heavens.
With what security of gold and silver light
Do the stars mark the road for us !
One would think
That the earth was the road
Of the body,
That the sea was the road
Of the soul.
Yes. It seems
That the soul is the only traveller
Of the sea; that the body, alone,
Remains behind, on the beach,
Without her, saying goodbye,
Heavy, cold, as though dead.
How like
Is a journey by sea
To death,
To eternal life !

THOMAS McGREEVY

I WOULD THAT ALL MY VERSES

I would that all my verses
could be such as the sky is in the night-time :
truth of the moment—now—without history.

That, like the sky, they would yield at every instant
all things, with all their streaming stars, and
neither childhood, nor youth, nor age could rob them,
nor cast a spell on the immensity of their beauty.

¡Temblor, relumbre, música
presentes y totales!
¡Temblor, relumbre, música en la frente
—cielo del corazón —del libro puro!

BIBLIOGRAPHY

I. HISTORIES OF SPANISH LITERATURE

Nicholson B. Adams and John E. Keller, *Spanish Literature; A Brief Survey*, Paterson, N. J. 1960.

Aubrey F. G. Bell, *Castilian Literature,* Oxford, 1938.

——, *Contemporary Spanish Literature*, New York, 1938.

Gerald Brenan, *The Literature of the Spanish People*, Cambridge, 1952.

Richard E. Chandler and Kessel Schwartz, *A New History of Spanish Literature*, Baton Rouge, 1961.

James Fitzmaurice-Kelly, *Chapters on Spanish Literature*, London, 1908.

——, *A History of Spanish Literature*, New York, 1898.

J. D. M. Ford, *Main Currents of Spanish Literature*, New York, 1919.

Ernest Mérimée and S. Griswold Morley, *A History of Spanish Literature*, New York, 1930.

Maxim Newmark, *Dictionary of Spanish Literature*, New York, 1956.

George Tyler Northup, *An Introduction to Spanish Literature*, Chicago, 1936.

George Ticknor, *History of Spanish Literature*, 3 vols., New York, 1849.

II. SPANISH LITERATURE IN ENGLISH TRANSLATION

Eric Bentley, *The Classic Theater: Six Spanish Plays*, Garden City, 1959.

John Bowring, *Ancient Poetry and Romances of Spain*, London, 1824.

Barrett H. Clark, *Masterpieces of Modern Spanish Drama*, New York, 1917.

J. M. Cohen, *The Penguin Book of Spanish Verse*, Penguin Books, 1956.

Harriet de Onís, *Spanish Stories and Tales*, New York, 1954.

Ida Farnell, *Spanish Prose and Poetry*, Oxford, 1920.

Angel Flores, *An Anthology of Spanish Poetry from Garcilaso to García Lorca*, Garden City, 1961.

——, *Great Spanish Stories*, New York, 1956.

——, *Masterpieces of the Spanish Golden Age*, New York, 1957.

——, *Spanish Literature in English Translation: a bibliographical syllabus*, New York, 1926.

——, *Spanish Stories: Cuentos Españoles*, New York, 1960.

Mildred E. Johnson, *Spanish Poems of Love*, New York, 1955.

Willis Knapp Jones, *Spanish One Act Plays in English*, Dallas, 1934.

James Kennedy, *Modern Poets and Poetry of Spain*, London, 1852.

John Gibson Lockhart, *Ancient Spanish Ballads*, London, 1841.

Henry Wadsworth Longfellow, *The Poets and Poetry of Europe*, Philadelphia, 1845.

Charles B. McMichael, *Short Stories from the Spanish*, New York, 1920.

Paul T. Manchester, *Joyas Poéticas: Spanish and Spanish-American Poetry*, New York, 1951.

Remigio U. Pane, *English Translations from the Spanish, 1484–1943: a bibliography*, New Brunswick, 1944.

Samuel Putnam, *The European Caravan*, New York, 1931.

Thomas Roscoe, *The Spanish Novelists*, London, 1832.

Tales from the Italian and Spanish, New York, 1920.

Susette M. Taylor, *The Humour of Spain*, London, 1894.

Translations from Hispanic Poets, New York, 1938.

J. B. Trend, *Spanish Short Stories of the 16th Century in Contemporary Translation*, London, 1928.

Eleanor L. Turnbull, *Contemporary Spanish Poetry*, Baltimore, 1945.

——, *Ten Centuries of Spanish Poetry*, Baltimore, 1955.

J. F. Vingut, *Selections from the Best Spanish Poets*, New York, 1856.

Thomas Walsh, *Hispanic Anthology: Poems Translated from the Spanish by English and North American Poets*, New York, 1920.

Warre B. Wells, *Great Spanish Short Stories*, New York, 1932. (Published in England as *The Spanish Omnibus*, London, 1932.)

III. A Brief English Bibliography of Spanish-American Literature

Germán Arciniegas, *The Green Continent*, New York, 1944.

Alice Stone Blackwell, *Some Spanish-American Poets*, Philadelphia, 1937.

Alfred Coester, *The Literary History of Spanish America*, New York, 1928.

G. Dundas Craig, *The Modernist Trend in Spanish-American Poetry*, Berkeley, 1934.

Harriet de Onís, *The Golden Land*, New York, 1948.

Dudley Fitts, *Anthology of Contemporary Latin-American Poetry*, Norfolk (Conn.), 1942.

Isaac Goldberg, *Studies in Spanish-American Literature*, New York, 1920.

Pedro Henríquez-Ureña, *Literary Currents in Hispanic America*, Cambridge (Mass.), 1945.

E. Herman Hespelt and others, *An Outline History of Spanish-American Literature*, New York, 1942.

Jefferson Rea Spell, *Contemporary Spanish-American Fiction*, Chapel Hill, 1944.

Arturo Torres-Ríoseco, *New World Literature*, Berkeley and Los Angeles, 1949.

INDEX

AUTHORS AND MAJOR ANONYMOUS WORKS

A CATALOG OF SELECTED
DOVER BOOKS
IN ALL FIELDS OF INTEREST

STICKLEY CRAFTSMAN FURNITURE CATALOGS, Gustav Stickley and L. & J. G. Stickley. Beautiful, functional furniture in two authentic catalogs from 1910. 594 illustrations, including 277 photos, show settles, rockers, armchairs, reclining chairs, bookcases, desks, tables. 183pp. 6½ x 9¼. 0-486-23838-5

AMERICAN LOCOMOTIVES IN HISTORIC PHOTOGRAPHS: 1858 to 1949, Ron Ziel (ed.). A rare collection of 126 meticulously detailed official photographs, called "builder portraits," of American locomotives that majestically chronicle the rise of steam locomotive power in America. Introduction. Detailed captions. xi+ 129pp. 9 x 12. 0-486-27393-8

AMERICA'S LIGHTHOUSES: An Illustrated History, Francis Ross Holland, Jr. Delightfully written, profusely illustrated fact-filled survey of over 200 American lighthouses since 1716. History, anecdotes, technological advances, more. 240pp. 8 x 10¾. 0-486-25576-X

TOWARDS A NEW ARCHITECTURE, Le Corbusier. Pioneering manifesto by founder of "International School." Technical and aesthetic theories, views of industry, economics, relation of form to function, "mass-production split" and much more. Profusely illustrated. 320pp. 6⅛ x 9¼. (Available in U.S. only.) 0-486-25023-7

HOW THE OTHER HALF LIVES, Jacob Riis. Famous journalistic record, exposing poverty and degradation of New York slums around 1900, by major social reformer. 100 striking and influential photographs. 233pp. 10 x 7⅞. 0-486-22012-5

FRUIT KEY AND TWIG KEY TO TREES AND SHRUBS, William M. Harlow. One of the handiest and most widely used identification aids. Fruit key covers 120 deciduous and evergreen species; twig key 160 deciduous species. Easily used. Over 300 photographs. 126pp. 5⅜ x 8½. 0-486-20511-8

COMMON BIRD SONGS, Dr. Donald J. Borror. Songs of 60 most common U.S. birds: robins, sparrows, cardinals, bluejays, finches, more–arranged in order of increasing complexity. Up to 9 variations of songs of each species.
Cassette and manual 0-486-99911-4

ORCHIDS AS HOUSE PLANTS, Rebecca Tyson Northen. Grow cattleyas and many other kinds of orchids–in a window, in a case, or under artificial light. 63 illustrations. 148pp. 5⅜ x 8½. 0-486-23261-1

MONSTER MAZES, Dave Phillips. Masterful mazes at four levels of difficulty. Avoid deadly perils and evil creatures to find magical treasures. Solutions for all 32 exciting illustrated puzzles. 48pp. 8¼ x 11. 0-486-26005-4

MOZART'S DON GIOVANNI (DOVER OPERA LIBRETTO SERIES), Wolfgang Amadeus Mozart. Introduced and translated by Ellen H. Bleiler. Standard Italian libretto, with complete English translation. Convenient and thoroughly portable–an ideal companion for reading along with a recording or the performance itself. Introduction. List of characters. Plot summary. 121pp. 5¼ x 8½. 0-486-24944-1

FRANK LLOYD WRIGHT'S DANA HOUSE, Donald Hoffmann. Pictorial essay of residential masterpiece with over 160 interior and exterior photos, plans, elevations, sketches and studies. 128pp. 9¼ x 10¾. 0-486-29120-0

THE CLARINET AND CLARINET PLAYING, David Pino. Lively, comprehensive work features suggestions about technique, musicianship, and musical interpretation, as well as guidelines for teaching, making your own reeds, and preparing for public performance. Includes an intriguing look at clarinet history. "A godsend," *The Clarinet,* Journal of the International Clarinet Society. Appendixes. 7 illus. 320pp. 5⅜ x 8½. 0-486-40270-3

HOLLYWOOD GLAMOR PORTRAITS, John Kobal (ed.). 145 photos from 1926-49. Harlow, Gable, Bogart, Bacall; 94 stars in all. Full background on photographers, technical aspects. 160pp. 8⅜ x 11¼. 0-486-23352-9

THE RAVEN AND OTHER FAVORITE POEMS, Edgar Allan Poe. Over 40 of the author's most memorable poems: "The Bells," "Ulalume," "Israfel," "To Helen," "The Conqueror Worm," "Eldorado," "Annabel Lee," many more. Alphabetic lists of titles and first lines. 64pp. 5$\frac{3}{16}$ x 8¼. 0-486-26685-0

PERSONAL MEMOIRS OF U. S. GRANT, Ulysses Simpson Grant. Intelligent, deeply moving firsthand account of Civil War campaigns, considered by many the finest military memoirs ever written. Includes letters, historic photographs, maps and more. 528pp. 6⅛ x 9¼. 0-486-28587-1

ANCIENT EGYPTIAN MATERIALS AND INDUSTRIES, A. Lucas and J. Harris. Fascinating, comprehensive, thoroughly documented text describes this ancient civilization's vast resources and the processes that incorporated them in daily life, including the use of animal products, building materials, cosmetics, perfumes and incense, fibers, glazed ware, glass and its manufacture, materials used in the mummification process, and much more. 544pp. 6⅛ x 9¼. (Available in U.S. only.) 0-486-40446-3

RUSSIAN STORIES/RUSSKIE RASSKAZY: A Dual-Language Book, edited by Gleb Struve. Twelve tales by such masters as Chekhov, Tolstoy, Dostoevsky, Pushkin, others. Excellent word-for-word English translations on facing pages, plus teaching and study aids, Russian/English vocabulary, biographical/critical introductions, more. 416pp. 5⅜ x 8½. 0-486-26244-8

PHILADELPHIA THEN AND NOW: 60 Sites Photographed in the Past and Present, Kenneth Finkel and Susan Oyama. Rare photographs of City Hall, Logan Square, Independence Hall, Betsy Ross House, other landmarks juxtaposed with contemporary views. Captures changing face of historic city. Introduction. Captions. 128pp. 8¼ x 11. 0-486-25790-8

NORTH AMERICAN INDIAN LIFE: Customs and Traditions of 23 Tribes, Elsie Clews Parsons (ed.). 27 fictionalized essays by noted anthropologists examine religion, customs, government, additional facets of life among the Winnebago, Crow, Zuni, Eskimo, other tribes. 480pp. 6⅛ x 9¼. 0-486-27377-6

TECHNICAL MANUAL AND DICTIONARY OF CLASSICAL BALLET, Gail Grant. Defines, explains, comments on steps, movements, poses and concepts. 15-page pictorial section. Basic book for student, viewer. 127pp. 5⅜ x 8½. 0-486-21843-0

THE MALE AND FEMALE FIGURE IN MOTION: 60 Classic Photographic Sequences, Eadweard Muybridge. 60 true-action photographs of men and women walking, running, climbing, bending, turning, etc., reproduced from rare 19th-century masterpiece. vi + 121pp. 9 x 12. 0-486-24745-7

FRENCH STORIES/CONTES FRANÇAIS: A Dual-Language Book, Wallace Fowlie. Ten stories by French masters, Voltaire to Camus: "Micromegas" by Voltaire; "The Atheist's Mass" by Balzac; "Minuet" by de Maupassant; "The Guest" by Camus, six more. Excellent English translations on facing pages. Also French-English vocabulary list, exercises, more. 352pp. 5⅜ x 8½. 0-486-26443-2

CHICAGO AT THE TURN OF THE CENTURY IN PHOTOGRAPHS: 122 Historic Views from the Collections of the Chicago Historical Society, Larry A. Viskochil. Rare large-format prints offer detailed views of City Hall, State Street, the Loop, Hull House, Union Station, many other landmarks, circa 1904-1913. Introduction. Captions. Maps. 144pp. 9⅜ x 12¼. 0-486-24656-6

OLD BROOKLYN IN EARLY PHOTOGRAPHS, 1865-1929, William Lee Younger. Luna Park, Gravesend race track, construction of Grand Army Plaza, moving of Hotel Brighton, etc. 157 previously unpublished photographs. 165pp. 8⅞ x 11¾. 0-486-23587-4

THE MYTHS OF THE NORTH AMERICAN INDIANS, Lewis Spence. Rich anthology of the myths and legends of the Algonquins, Iroquois, Pawnees and Sioux, prefaced by an extensive historical and ethnological commentary. 36 illustrations. 480pp. 5⅜ x 8½. 0-486-25967-6

AN ENCYCLOPEDIA OF BATTLES: Accounts of Over 1,560 Battles from 1479 B.C. to the Present, David Eggenberger. Essential details of every major battle in recorded history from the first battle of Megiddo in 1479 B.C. to Grenada in 1984. List of Battle Maps. New Appendix covering the years 1967-1984. Index. 99 illustrations. 544pp. 6½ x 9¼. 0-486-24913-1

SAILING ALONE AROUND THE WORLD, Captain Joshua Slocum. First man to sail around the world, alone, in small boat. One of great feats of seamanship told in delightful manner. 67 illustrations. 294pp. 5⅜ x 8½. 0-486-20326-3

ANARCHISM AND OTHER ESSAYS, Emma Goldman. Powerful, penetrating, prophetic essays on direct action, role of minorities, prison reform, puritan hypocrisy, violence, etc. 271pp. 5⅜ x 8½. 0-486-22484-8

MYTHS OF THE HINDUS AND BUDDHISTS, Ananda K. Coomaraswamy and Sister Nivedita. Great stories of the epics; deeds of Krishna, Shiva, taken from puranas, Vedas, folk tales; etc. 32 illustrations. 400pp. 5⅜ x 8½. 0-486-21759-0

MY BONDAGE AND MY FREEDOM, Frederick Douglass. Born a slave, Douglass became outspoken force in antislavery movement. The best of Douglass' autobiographies. Graphic description of slave life. 464pp. 5⅜ x 8½. 0-486-22457-0

FOLLOWING THE EQUATOR: A Journey Around the World, Mark Twain. Fascinating humorous account of 1897 voyage to Hawaii, Australia, India, New Zealand, etc. Ironic, bemused reports on peoples, customs, climate, flora and fauna, politics, much more. 197 illustrations. 720pp. 5⅜ x 8½. 0-486-26113-1

THE PEOPLE CALLED SHAKERS, Edward D. Andrews. Definitive study of Shakers: origins, beliefs, practices, dances, social organization, furniture and crafts, etc. 33 illustrations. 351pp. 5⅜ x 8½. 0-486-21081-2

THE MYTHS OF GREECE AND ROME, H. A. Guerber. A classic of mythology, generously illustrated, long prized for its simple, graphic, accurate retelling of the principal myths of Greece and Rome, and for its commentary on their origins and significance. With 64 illustrations by Michelangelo, Raphael, Titian, Rubens, Canova, Bernini and others. 480pp. 5⅜ x 8½. 0-486-27584-1

MAKING FURNITURE MASTERPIECES: 30 Projects with Measured Drawings, Franklin H. Gottshall. Step-by-step instructions, illustrations for constructing handsome, useful pieces, among them a Sheraton desk, Chippendale chair, Spanish desk, Queen Anne table and a William and Mary dressing mirror. 224pp. 8⅛ x 11¼. 0-486-29338-6

NORTH AMERICAN INDIAN DESIGNS FOR ARTISTS AND CRAFTSPEOPLE, Eva Wilson. Over 360 authentic copyright-free designs adapted from Navajo blankets, Hopi pottery, Sioux buffalo hides, more. Geometrics, symbolic figures, plant and animal motifs, etc. 128pp. 8⅜ x 11. (Not for sale in the United Kingdom.) 0-486-25341-4

THE FOSSIL BOOK: A Record of Prehistoric Life, Patricia V. Rich et al. Profusely illustrated definitive guide covers everything from single-celled organisms and dinosaurs to birds and mammals and the interplay between climate and man. Over 1,500 illustrations. 760pp. 7½ x 10⅛. 0-486-29371-8

VICTORIAN ARCHITECTURAL DETAILS: Designs for Over 700 Stairs, Mantels, Doors, Windows, Cornices, Porches, and Other Decorative Elements, A. J. Bicknell & Company. Everything from dormer windows and piazzas to balconies and gable ornaments. Also includes elevations and floor plans for handsome, private residences and commercial structures. 80pp. 9⅜ x 12¼. 0-486-44015-X

WESTERN ISLAMIC ARCHITECTURE: A Concise Introduction, John D. Hoag. Profusely illustrated critical appraisal compares and contrasts Islamic mosques and palaces–from Spain and Egypt to other areas in the Middle East. 139 illustrations. 128pp. 6 x 9. 0-486-43760-4

CHINESE ARCHITECTURE: A Pictorial History, Liang Ssu-ch'eng. More than 240 rare photographs and drawings depict temples, pagodas, tombs, bridges, and imperial palaces comprising much of China's architectural heritage. 152 halftones, 94 diagrams. 232pp. 10¾ x 9⅞. 0-486-43999-2

THE RENAISSANCE: Studies in Art and Poetry, Walter Pater. One of the most talked-about books of the 19th century, *The Renaissance* combines scholarship and philosophy in an innovative work of cultural criticism that examines the achievements of Botticelli, Leonardo, Michelangelo, and other artists. "The holy writ of beauty."–Oscar Wilde. 160pp. 5⅜ x 8½. 0-486-44025-7

A TREATISE ON PAINTING, Leonardo da Vinci. The great Renaissance artist's practical advice on drawing and painting techniques covers anatomy, perspective, composition, light and shadow, and color. A classic of art instruction, it features 48 drawings by Nicholas Poussin and Leon Battista Alberti. 192pp. 5⅜ x 8½. 0-486-44155-5

THE MIND OF LEONARDO DA VINCI, Edward McCurdy. More than just a biography, this classic study by a distinguished historian draws upon Leonardo's extensive writings to offer numerous demonstrations of the Renaissance master's achievements, not only in sculpture and painting, but also in music, engineering, and even experimental aviation. 384pp. 5⅜ x 8½. 0-486-44142-3

WASHINGTON IRVING'S RIP VAN WINKLE, Illustrated by Arthur Rackham. Lovely prints that established artist as a leading illustrator of the time and forever etched into the popular imagination a classic of Catskill lore. 51 full-color plates. 80pp. 8⅜ x 11. 0-486-44242-X

HENSCHE ON PAINTING, John W. Robichaux. Basic painting philosophy and methodology of a great teacher, as expounded in his famous classes and workshops on Cape Cod. 7 illustrations in color on covers. 80pp. 5⅜ x 8½. 0-486-43728-0

CATALOG OF DOVER BOOKS

LIGHT AND SHADE: A Classic Approach to Three-Dimensional Drawing, Mrs. Mary P. Merrifield. Handy reference clearly demonstrates principles of light and shade by revealing effects of common daylight, sunshine, and candle or artificial light on geometrical solids. 13 plates. 64pp. 5⅜ x 8½. 0-486-44143-1

ASTROLOGY AND ASTRONOMY: A Pictorial Archive of Signs and Symbols, Ernst and Johanna Lehner. Treasure trove of stories, lore, and myth, accompanied by more than 300 rare illustrations of planets, the Milky Way, signs of the zodiac, comets, meteors, and other astronomical phenomena. 192pp. 8⅜ x 11. 0-486-43981-X

JEWELRY MAKING: Techniques for Metal, Tim McCreight. Easy-to-follow instructions and carefully executed illustrations describe tools and techniques, use of gems and enamels, wire inlay, casting, and other topics. 72 line illustrations and diagrams. 176pp. 8¼ x 10⅞. 0-486-44043-5

MAKING BIRDHOUSES: Easy and Advanced Projects, Gladstone Califf. Easy-to-follow instructions include diagrams for everything from a one-room house for bluebirds to a forty-two-room structure for purple martins. 56 plates; 4 figures. 80pp. 8¾ x 6⅜. 0-486-44183-0

LITTLE BOOK OF LOG CABINS: How to Build and Furnish Them, William S. Wicks. Handy how-to manual, with instructions and illustrations for building cabins in the Adirondack style, fireplaces, stairways, furniture, beamed ceilings, and more. 102 line drawings. 96pp. 8¾ x 6⅜. 0-486-44259-4

THE SEASONS OF AMERICA PAST, Eric Sloane. From "sugaring time" and strawberry picking to Indian summer and fall harvest, a whole year's activities described in charming prose and enhanced with 79 of the author's own illustrations. 160pp. 8¼ x 11. 0-486-44220-9

THE METROPOLIS OF TOMORROW, Hugh Ferriss. Generous, prophetic vision of the metropolis of the future, as perceived in 1929. Powerful illustrations of towering structures, wide avenues, and rooftop parks–all features in many of today's modern cities. 59 illustrations. 144pp. 8¼ x 11. 0-486-43727-2

THE PATH TO ROME, Hilaire Belloc. This 1902 memoir abounds in lively vignettes from a vanished time, recounting a pilgrimage on foot across the Alps and Apennines in order to "see all Europe which the Christian Faith has saved." 77 of the author's original line drawings complement his sparkling prose. 272pp. 5⅜ x 8½. 0-486-44001-X

THE HISTORY OF RASSELAS: Prince of Abissinia, Samuel Johnson. Distinguished English writer attacks eighteenth-century optimism and man's unrealistic estimates of what life has to offer. 112pp. 5⅜ x 8½. 0-486-44094-X

A VOYAGE TO ARCTURUS, David Lindsay. A brilliant flight of pure fancy, where wild creatures crowd the fantastic landscape and demented torturers dominate victims with their bizarre mental powers. 272pp. 5⅜ x 8½. 0-486-44198-9

Paperbound unless otherwise indicated. Available at your book dealer, online at **www.doverpublications.com**, or by writing to Dept. GI, Dover Publications, Inc., 31 East 2nd Street, Mineola, NY 11501. For current price information or for free catalogs (please indicate field of interest), write to Dover Publications or log on to **www.doverpublications.com** and see every Dover book in print. Dover publishes more than 500 books each year on science, elementary and advanced mathematics, biology, music, art, literary history, social sciences, and other areas.